Cold War Jet Combat: Air-to-Air Jet Fighter Operations 1950-1972

Martin W. Bowman

Pen & Sword
AVIATION

First published in Great Britain in 2016 by
Pen and Sword Aviation

An imprint of
Pen & Sword Books Ltd
47 Church Street
Barnsley
South Yorkshire
S70 2AS

ISBN 9781473837737

A CIP catalogue record for this book is
available from the British Library

Printed and bound by CPI Group (UK) Ltd, Croydon, CR0 4YY

Pen & Sword Books Ltd incorporates the Imprints of Pen & Sword Aviation,
Pen & Sword Family History, Pen & Sword Maritime, Pen & Sword Military,
Pen & Sword Discovery, Wharncliffe Local History, Wharncliffe True Crime,
Wharncliffe Transport, Pen & Sword Select, Pen & Sword Military Classics,
Leo Cooper, The Praetorian Press, Remember When, Seaforth Publishing and
Frontline Publishing

For a complete list of Pen & Sword titles please contact
PEN & SWORD BOOKS LIMITED
47 Church Street, Barnsley, South Yorkshire, S70 2AS, England
E-mail: enquiries@pen-and-sword.co.uk
Website: www.pen-and-sword.co.uk

Contents

Acknowledgements

My thanks also go to the late Roland H. Baker for images aboard the USS *Philippine Sea* during the Korean War; Larry Davis for Sabre images during the Korean War; the late Group Captain R. J. F. 'Dickie' Dickinson AFC; Mohammed Shaukat-ul-Islam; Reg Adams.

Thanks also go to my fellow author, friend and colleague, Graham Simons, for getting the book to press ready standard and for his detailed work on the photographs; to Pen & Sword and in particular, Laura Hirst; and Jon Wilkinson, for his unique jacket design once again.

Previous page: F-105 Thunderchiefs passing Mount Fuji.

This page: AD-4B Skyraider of VA-115 taking off from the deck of the USS *Philippine Sea* (CV-47) crowded with F9F-2 Panther Jets during the Korean War. Before sailing from San Diego, California on 5 July 150, the carrier embarked Air Group 11 (CVG-1); two F9F-2B squadrons (VF-111 and VF-112); two F4U-4 fighter-bomber squadrons and the AD-4 Skyraider squadron. The F9F-2 remained the US Navy's first-line jet fighter throughout the first year of the Korean War. Demobilization following the Second World War had severely reduced the fighting capability of the US forces and no fewer than twenty-eight Navy and Marine Reserve squadrons were called to active duty from July to September 1950. In all eighteen Reserve squadrons made twenty-nine deployments on board carriers during the Korean War. (Roland H. Baker).

Chapter One

The First Jet War;
Task Force 77: Korea

The hand of the aggressor is stayed by strength - and strength alone.
Dwight D. Eisenhower, a speech at an English Speaking Union Dinner (3 July 1951).
When North Korean forces invaded South Korea on 25 June 1950 the USAF was actually
at the lowest point in its strength since 1941. 'Ike' became the 34th president of the US in
1953.

Six small silver jet fighters bearing red stars on their stubby fuselages and swept-back wings took off from the safety of their air base at Antung in Manchuria, climbed rapidly to 30,000 feet and crossed the Yalu River into North Korea. It was 1 November 1950. Five years earlier, on 2 September - VJ Day[1] - the official surrender ceremony took place aboard the *Missouri* in Tokyo Bay. World War Two was finally at an end. The Japanese surrender to the Allies on 2 September 1945 created a vacuum in South East Asia and in China the Communist and Nationalist forces took up opposing stances. The US tried to mediate between the two sides and USMC squadrons were used in sporadic operations in northern China as tensions boiled over; a number of US personnel were killed. In January 1949 the Nationalist Chinese set up a government in exile on the island of Formosa (Taiwan) and in May the last of the US units left China. Tension in the area remained and it was to spread to other parts of South-East Asia. In 1945 the Soviet Union took the surrender of Japanese forces in Korea north of the 38th parallel, while the United States handled the enemy surrender south of the dividing line. Early on Sunday morning, 25 June 1950, in an attack reminiscent of Sunday 7 December 1941, peace in the land of the morning calm was shattered.

The formation of F-51 Mustangs and F-80 Shooting Stars flying on the North Korean side of the river was surprised at the devastating closing speed of the Communist jets, whose pilots only failed to destroy the American aircraft through their own inexperience. It was one of a series of setbacks UN forces had suffered since 25 June 1950 when the North Korean Army, using the false pretext that the South had invaded the North, crossed the 38th parallel, completely wrong-footing the Republic of Korea (ROK) Army and its American advisers. From the outset the North Koreans enjoyed total air superiority, although on paper the NKAF had no chance against the UN forces but the USAF aircraft available for war in Korea were ill-suited to operate in a close air support and interdiction campaign. They needed paved runways 6,000 feet long and these only existed in Japan, which meant that air operations over Korea were restricted to no more than a few minutes. Up until that fateful November day US commanders had no reason to fear the Communist air threat because only piston-engined aircraft had confronted them but intervention by China and the appearance of the Soviet-built jets in North Korean airspace dramatically changed the balance of air power at a stroke.

Fortunately, the North Koreans lacked the capability to strike back at the UN fleet off its coasts.[2] The USN was in a state of transition, with the first jet fighters joining the more numerous piston-engined aircraft aboard its carriers. While Navy jets were about 100mph faster than the Corsair fighter-bomber or Skyraider attack aircraft, the early jets could not haul as great a war load over a long distance. And they were also slow to respond from the point when the throttle was advanced, to when the engine 'spooled up' sufficiently to accelerate the aircraft. This delay could prove fatal if a jet had to he waved off a landing at the last moment. American air superiority during 1950 meant that Korea was an ideal hunting ground for both the slower Corsair and the Skyraider in which to operate in the ground attack and interdiction roles. Flying from flat-tops, Navy and Marine units could operate in the Sea of Japan and be sent off at a point about seventy miles from the coast of Korea (the shallow sea bed off the east coast of Korea prevented them from getting any nearer).

But of the fifteen US Navy carriers[3] in service around the world on the day of the invasion, only *Valley Forge* (CV-45), which had sailed from Subic Bay in the Philippines with CVG-5 (Air Group Five)[4] embarked, was deployed to the Far East. *Valley Forge* and the Royal Navy's light fleet carrier HMS *Triumph,* which with other vessels constituted Task Force (TF) 77 arrived on station in the Yellow Sea off Korea on 3 July. At 0545 hours the first strike by TF 77 went ahead when sixteen of VF-53 and VF-54's F4U-4s and twelve AD Skyraiders of VA-55 took off to hit North Korean lines of communications, railway bridges, rail yards, airfields and roads near the North Korean capital, Pyongyang. Thirty F9F-3 Panthers of VF-51 'Screaming Eagles' provided top cover for the Corsairs and Skyraiders and thus became the first jet fighters in the US Navy to go into action.

Two F9F-3 pilots, Lieutenant (junior grade) Leonard 'Len' H. Plog who flew the SB2C Helldiver in WWII and Ensign Eldon W. Brown, each destroyed a NKAF Yak-9 fighter in addition to destroying two more on the ground. Carrier Air Group Commander (CAG) Commander Harvey Lanham led the Panthers. Brown recalled: 'We were a mix of older and younger Navy pilots. The Navy did not yet have a combat aircraft with swept wings, nor did it have a lead-computing gunsight. The F9F-3 was armed with four 20 mm cannon but was not yet fitted with pylons to carry ordnance. Plog recalled: 'You could certainly accuse me of bridging the gap between props and jets. I was on another jet pilot's wing as our Panthers approached Pyongyang at 16,000 feet. In contrast to the brightness of the day, Pyongyang was cloaked in industrial smoke, soot and haze. There were no obvious muzzle flashes or tracers, but our pilots believed they were fired upon once we were within a few

F9F Pantherjets on the snow covered deck of the USS *Essex* in January 1952.

miles of the city. When we arrived over the North Korean airfield well ahead of the Corsairs and Skyraiders, CAG Lanham went down on the deck and strafed a transport plane on the edge of the airfield. I watched Lanham's cannon shells stir up the area around the transport, which may have been a Tachikawa Ki-54 Army Type 1 'Hickory,' inherited by the North Koreans from Japanese forces during WWII. Lanham's hits punctured the transport and kicked up dust but started no fire. I doubt that plane ever flew again. We made a strafing run. Lanham led the Panthers in circling the airfield and returning for a second strafing run. Some of the WWII veterans in the air that day thought this was risky.

'It was a big airport but we initially saw no aircraft. We began flying up one of the runways when my attention was drawn to a hangar to my right. An airplane taxied out of that hangar and took off from a taxiway. That's when I thought, 'Something is happening here …' 'I watched the North Korean aircraft climb and saw Eldon Brown turn to get into position behind him. I looked back and did a double take. A second Yak-9 taxied out of the hangar and took off from the taxiway. The second Yak got 300 to 400 feet into the air and tucked in his wheels. I fired. My 20 mm cannon rounds blew the Yak's wing off. It spun wildly out of control and went down.'

Brown saw a Yak-9 coming at him from his right. 'This was the first Yak seen by Plog but became the second that we engaged. 'I saw him at three o'clock, coming in. He passed over me and fired bursts at Plog, who by then had turned for home. I made a 360-degree turn and went after him. I rolled out on his tail, had the throttle all the way up, and closed on him pretty fast. 'I had time only for a short burst. It blew his tail off. The aft section

Right: Lieutenant (jg) Leonard 'Len' H. Plog of VF-51. The first carrier air strike of the Korean War was launched from *Valley Forge*'s flight deck (below) on 3 July 1950. Successive waves of A-1 Skyraiders and F-4U Corsairs struck the North Korean airfield at Pyongyang bombing hangars, fuel storages, parked aircraft and railroad marshalling yards while F9F Panthers, flying top cover, downed two Yak-9s and damaged another.

A F9F-2 of VF-112 about to take off from the deck of the USS *Philippine Sea.*

came off and the main fuselage went into a steep dive. He was on fire. The tail came flying back at me. I flew between his tail and main fuselage, and then headed for home. I landed on *Valley Forge* with just 300lbs of fuel. They fussed at me for coming in with a low fuel load.'

The carriers mounted further air strikes that day and on 4 July three hangars and some NKAF aircraft were destroyed on the ground at Pyongyang while rolling stock, buildings and various installations were bombed and strafed. Four Skyraiders were slightly damaged by flak and one, unable to lower its flaps, bounced over *Valley Forge's* crash-barriers and landed among the aircraft ranged forward on deck. A Skyraider and two Corsairs were destroyed and three more Skyraiders, two Panthers and a Corsair were badly damaged. The carriers withdrew from the combat area for replenishment at sea on 5 July.

Aircraft from *Valley Forge* continued their strikes on North Korean targets on 18 July with strikes on Pyongyang and Onjong-ni. On the 19th they attacked Yonpo airfield. These two strikes resulted in the loss of 32 NKAF aircraft destroyed on the ground and another thirteen damaged. *Valley Forge* left Korean waters at the end of July and sailed to Okinawa, Japan for rest and replenishment. Its place in TF 77 was taken on 31 July by the fast attack Essex-class carrier *Philippine Sea* (CV-47) with Air Group 11 (CVG-11) embarked.[5] *Philippine Sea* arrived in Buckner Bay, Okinawa on 1 August [6] to begin work-ups for combat with *Valley Forge* in attacks on Korea from both the Yellow Sea and the Sea of Japan. On 2 August the carrier *Sicily* (CVE-118) arrived off Korea and began operations with ASW squadrons.[7] CVG-11 launched its first attacks on 3 August when Lieutenant Commander William T. Amen led VF-111 in attacks on airfields at Mokpo, Kwangju and Kusan. Eight F9F Panthers of VF-112 and twelve Corsairs of VF-114 hit rail and road bridges in the Mokpo-Kwangju area. The F4Us destroyed a bridge and damaged two dams south of Iri before strafing warehouses, sampans and junks on the way home. The F4U-4s of VMF-214 flying off the *Sicily* bombed Chinju and Sinhan-ni; VMF-323 from the *Badoeng Strait* (CVE-116) flew close air support (CAS) missions for 8th Army units, attacking vehicles, supply dumps, bridges and railway lines. VMF-214 and VMF-323 flew on average forty-five ground-attack sorties a day during the fierce UN counter-offensive around Pusan.[8]

Between 7 and 13 August *Philippine Sea* supported the UN counter-offensive in the Masan Sector as the North Koreans attempted to break through the Pusan Perimeter. VF-113 lost two F4Us, which collided during a strafing run while providing close air support and interdiction of enemy supply lines. Ensign J. F. Krail was killed, while Ensign G. T. Farnsworth nursed his damaged Corsair out to sea where he ditched. Farnsworth was picked up that same afternoon. On 9 August Commander Raymond W. 'Sully' Vogel (CAG 11) flew with VF-114, leading a strike against the Riken Metal Company in Seoul, Korea; using 500lb bombs and rockets, Vogel's flight hit the target 'very effectively.' Later that day,

VF-114 and VA-115 teamed up to blast the marshalling yards and the Standard Oil Company warehouses in Seoul, leaving the latter burning and knocked out several boxcars and a locomotive. That same day VF-113 Corsairs bombed, strafed and rocketed a factory at Inchon, setting it afire. CAG Vogel led another VF-114 strike on 13 August; this time against targets near Pyongyang. After replenishing at Sasebo, Japan on 14-15 August, *Philippine Sea* returned to the east coast of Korea, commencing CAS (Close Air Support) for hard-pressed United Nations Forces and bombing key bridges near Seoul on the 16th. Next day, VF-113 caught a twenty-truck convoy with a cargo of artillery on the road south of Songjin and obliterated it. On 16 August, after replenishing in Japan, *Philippine Sea* sent its aircraft over Korea again.

At 1531 on the 19th escorted by Panthers, 37 F4Us and Skyraiders from *Philippine Sea* and *Valley Forge* scored eight direct hits on a large steel railway bridge west of Seoul.[9] Commander 'Sully' Vogel leading eight F4Us of VF-114 carried out a strike near Seoul. While the four-plane CAP (Combat Air Patrol) element encountered no enemy aircraft, the four strike aircraft hit a bridge span with one 500 pounder on the first pass. 'Sully' Vogel came around again for a second pass, but enemy anti-aircraft fire hit his Corsair and set it afire. Vogel bailed out of the burning Corsair and pilots saw his chute stream, but it did not open and his body hurtled to the ground. Vogel was a little under a month shy of his 36th

F2H-2P Banshee of VC-61 of CVG-101 on the USS *Kearsarge* (CVA-33) off Korea in 1952.

Right: F9F-2 Panthers of VF-71 and a F9F-5P Photo Panther of VC-61 (PP) of CVG-101 on the flight deck of the USS *Bon Homme Richard* in 1952.

birthday; a veteran of aerial combat in the Pacific in World War II. He left a widow and five children. Although CVG-11 destroyed the Han River Bridge near Seoul that day, little solace lay in the feat. The next day, Ensign C. L. Smith of VF-112 died when his Panther crashed and burned near Sariwon. *Philippine Sea* cleared Korean waters on 20 August and Commander Ralph Weymouth, skipper of VF-112 temporarily became CAG-11. The next day, as the ship lay anchored at Sasebo, a memorial service was held for Commander Vogel and Ensign Smith. CV-47 finished her replenishment at Sasebo on 25 August and returned to the east coast of Korea. On the 27th CVG-11 hit shipping in Wonsan Harbour - damaging what pilots claimed as a 'destroyer escort', with rockets and cannon fire and two 'gunboats' by strafing. Between 26 August and 4 September CVG-11 claimed destruction of a 'fleet type minelayer' and four patrol craft at Wonsan. They conducted emergency CAS in defence of the Pusan perimeter and destroyed key bridges along the North Korean lines of communication. *Philippine Sea's* aviators also discovered the enemy's major staging base at Kangge and photographed Inchon prior to the amphibious landing there.[10]

On 1 September the North Koreans made an all-out attempt to pierce the Pusan perimeter and the USN fighters and the Far East Air Force fighters and bombers were used to repel the attacks. At night the F4U-SNs of VMF(N)-513 and USAF B-26s flew numerous night interdiction missions, while at sea, squadrons from Task Force 77 added their striking power to the counter-offensive operation. All this activity attracted the attention of the Soviets, who had a naval air base at Port Arthur on the tip of the Liaotung peninsular. On 4 September 1950 a VP-53 Corsair from *Valley Forge* on CAP shot down a twin-engined Soviet aircraft that approached the task force. Next day the North Korean People's Army (NKPA) offensive had petered out and on 11 September the breakout from Pusan began. Two days later the pre-invasion sea bombardment began and then on 15 September General Douglas MacArthur launched Operation 'Chromite' using amphibious landings behind the enemy lines at Inchon with the majority of the air cover provided by F4Us and Skyraiders from *Valley Forge*, *Philippine Sea* and *Boxer* (recently arrived from the USA) and Seafires and Fireflies from HMS *Triumph*. During 12-14 September F4Us and Skyraiders provided the majority of the 'deep support' from *Valley Forge*, *Philippine Sea* and *Boxer*, which had recently

Bombing and strafing attack on a rail target south of Wonsan.

F9F-2B 123713 of VF-721, a Glenview, Illinois reserve unit embarked aboard USS *Boxer* in August 1951. Flying with VMF-311 of MAG-33 on 3 January 1952 123713 was shot down by AAA near Seoul. The pilot, Major George Major, was killed. (Grumman)

arrived on station with CVG-2. US Navy and USMC fighter-bombers strafed and bombed positions along the Inchon waterfront prior to the main landing.

The UN forces enjoyed total air superiority and by midnight on the 15th the 1st Marine Division had secured the port of Inchon and, with the Army's 7th Infantry Division, moved on Seoul and Kimpo airfield, severing Communist supply routes to the south. The North Koreans fell back in the face of the offensive and the Navy pilots went in search of interdiction targets behind the 'main line of resistance' (MLR) and over North Korea. CVG-5 from the *Valley Forge* discovered a North Korean convoy of trucks in open terrain at Taejong six miles east of Inchon and destroyed no fewer than eighty-seven of these. During this period Lieutenant Carl C. Dace made the first combat ejection from a jet fighter when he banged out after his Panther was hit by AA fire during a ground attack run over North Korea. On 27 September Seoul was recaptured. When the American amphibious landing went ahead at Wonsan on the east coast of Korea on 10 October the Marines were supported by aircraft from *Boxer*, the fast carrier *Leyte* (CV-32), *Philippine Sea* and *Valley Forge*. By 28 September the Communists were in full retreat. But the North Koreans rejected a surrender ultimatum and General MacArthur had no choice but to continue the war north of the 38th Parallel and march on the North Korean capital, Pyongyang. By the end of October the North Korean capital of Pyongyang had fallen and the war seemed to be won. The carriers of TF-77 were relieved and retired to Sasebo, Japan, while the USMC squadrons moved up to Yonpo airfield to carry on CAS missions for the ground troops pursuing the remnants of the NKPA to the Yalu River that bordered Communist China.

On 14 October MacArthur's intelligence staff had reported thirty-eight Chinese divisions in Manchuria but it was believed that none had entered North Korea. In fact six Chinese armies began storming across the border at night and by the end of October almost 300,000 Communist 'Chinese People's Volunteers' were deployed for battle with the UN forces. Only small groups of Chinese troops were identified and the majority remained virtually undetected. On 17 October aircraft from *Philippine Sea* and *Leyte* dropped both bridges across the Yalu and Hyosanjin but by using pontoons the Chinese were able to cross the river. On 1 November American aircraft were confronted by Red Chinese MiG-15s for the first time. An area 100 miles deep between Sinuiju on the Yalu and Sinanju on the Chongchon River soon became known as 'MiG Alley'.

A pair of F9F-2B Panthers of VF-721 and a F9F-5P Photo Panther of VC-61 (PP) of CVG-101 circle for landing back aboard the USS *Boxer* (CVA-21) off Korea in 1951.

For three consecutive days beginning on 9 November, F4Us and AD-4s from *Valley Forge*, *Leyte* and *Philippine Sea* protected by F9Fs flying top cover hit bridges on the Yalu and supply concentrations in Hungnam, Songjin and Chongjin. Because of political considerations the Navy pilots were only permitted to bomb the southern end of the bridges. Skyraiders flying in formations of eight, supported by eight to sixteen Corsairs on flak suppression duty, destroyed a road bridge at Sinuiju and two more, 200 miles upstream at Hvesanjin. Up above, as many as sixteen Panther jets kept an eye on proceedings, flying top cover for the bombers. The MiG outclassed the Grumman Panther but the superior experience of the Navy pilots gave them the edge. On 10 November a Panther from *Philippine Sea* was the first US Navy jet to down another jet aircraft when Lieutenant Commander William T. Amen, CO of VF-111 flying a VF-112 Panther, destroyed a MiG-15 near Sinuiju. The Panther pilots lost no time as they aggressively streaked in to protect the bombers and the battle swirled from just above ground level up to 18,000 feet. Turning inside of a tight loop on the tail of a poorly flown MiG-15, Amen closed the gap and shot down his opponent with a quick burst. 'I was coming head on at one of them and he didn't even try to get in a shot,' Amen recalled. 'When I got on his tail he tried to evade but he wasn't very sharp.' Along with many of the pilots, Amen had already chalked-up quite a record during WWII and added Gold Stars in lieu of four Air Medals. Amen further received the Distinguished Flying Cross following no less than 35 missions over Korea. This first tangle with the MiGs nonetheless produced a macabre comedy. Admiring Panther pilots surrounded Commander Albert D. Pollack, the skipper of VF-51'Screaming Eagles', when he returned to the ready room on board *Valley Forge*. 'Were you nervous about those MiGs Dave?' they asked. 'No, I was just keeping an eye on them', wearily replied Pollack. 'Then why did you report 20,000 MiGs coming in at five feet?' his men quipped.

For the next nine days the Corsairs and Skyraiders continued their attacks on the bridges across the Yalu. When in late November the Yalu froze over the Chinese were able to cross almost at will. This build-up of its forces led to the first real confrontation on 28 November when heavy fighting broke out between Chinese forces in the Hagaru-nian and Yudam-ni areas and the 1st Marine Division. The 5th and 7th Marines became cut off from the rest of the division and they were forced to withdraw to the rugged terrain around the Chosin Reservoir. All available land-based and carrier-borne aircraft were thrown into the battle and also the evacuation from Hungnam. *Valley Forge* had departed the area for a much-needed overhaul[11] and the light carriers were involved in ferrying replacement aircraft to the USMC squadrons in the battle zone. Leading the way were USN and USMC close air support Corsairs and Skyraiders protected by USAF F-86 Sabres flying top cover. On 1 December the USMC breakout of Chosin began, but by this time *Leyte* and *Philippine Sea* were on station and they were soon supported by the light carrier *Bataan* (CVL-29) and *Badoeng Strait*. The successful completion of the Chosin breakout was achieved mainly due to the total Navy and Marine air support.

On 5 December the task force was strengthened still further by the arrival of the *Princeton* (CV-37), with CVG-19 consisting of two F4U-4 Corsair squadrons, one F9F-2 squadron and one AD-4 squadron. On 7 December the *Sicily* arrived on station and on the 16th the *Bataan* arrived and next day they covered the Hungnan evacuation. On 23 December the *Valley Forge* again took up station in the Sea of Japan after its much-needed overhaul. The Marines who were holed up in the Chosin Reservoir were given around-the-clock protection by fighters and fighter-bombers that often ended up flying in and around the treacherous

F-2H-2 Banshee 124974 of VF-172 'Night Owls', CVG-5 being brought up to the flight deck on the forward elevator aboard the USS *Essex* off Korea on 25 August 1951. Unlike the F9F Panther the wingtip tanks were detachable.

mountainous passes in appalling weather conditions. The weather in this region is one of extremes. While the summers are hot - so hot that many pilots in fact considered these conditions to be worse than those endured in winter, Korean winters are freezing, with sub-zero temperatures being the norm. The ten-mile long Funchilin Pass was particularly dangerous, while some of the others were around 4,000 feet and experienced temperatures that dropped to 32° below zero.

Philippine Sea and *Leyte* completed their operations in the Chosin Reservoir area on Christmas Day 1950 having been on the line for fifty-two consecutive days and they departed for rest and replenishment in Japan, arriving at Sasebo and Yokosuka on 26 and 28 December respectively. But their departure was followed by a Chinese New Year offensive on 31 December. On 5 January 1951 the Chinese recaptured Seoul and the UN forces were soon in headlong retreat. On 8 January the *Philippine Sea*, *Leyte* and the *Valley Forge*, were on station again, helping to repel the Chinese New Year offensive. After days of concerted and unremitting attacks, the Chinese advance was finally stopped on 15 January. An incident of the most remarkable character also occurred on this date: Ensign Edward J. Hofstra, Jr., of VF-64 aboard *Valley Forge* was strafing coastal roads when his F4U-4 struck the ground flat on its belly, shearing off its belly tank, napalm bomb and wing bombs. The

engine was also stopped when the propeller made contact with the ground. But following impact, the Corsair bounced back into the air and the remaining inertia carried it about 1,000 yards further forwards and 500 yards out to sea where Hofstra was able to ditch it and get into his life raft. He was rescued by a Sunderland flying boat about three hours later.

Aircraft from the *Philippine Sea* attacked enemy positions until 1

Left: A naval airman fuses and secures the arming wire on a bomb mounted below the wing of a VF-172 'Banjo' destined for Communist forces ashore. (USN)

Right: In August 1951 USS *Essex* (CV-9) arrived on station joining TF-77 and its McDonnell F2H-2 Banshees made their combat debut on 23 August with VF-172, flying an escort mission for the B-29s. A naval airman rides the starboard wing tank of a Banshee while fuelling the aircraft for one of its first combat missions in Korea. (USN)

Photographed from a F9F-5P photo Panther of VC-61 piloted by Lieutenant (jg) George Elmies, two F9F-2 Panthers dump fuel as they fly past USS *Princeton* (CV-37) in May 1951

February, when the carrier replenished again in Japan and from 12 February to 13 March. Four days later *Philippine Sea* and *Valley Forge* returned to Yokosaka and an exchange of air groups began. CVG-11 disembarked and three Corsair squadrons and VA-65, equipped with the Skyraider and the usual Composite Squadron detachments were embarked from Air Group Two aboard Valley Forge. On 15 March Seoul was back in UN hands but the continued presence of Chinese troops in South Korea meant that reinforcements were needed and the wholesale reactivation of naval reservists began. By 27 March, Air Group 101 embarked on *Boxer* was composed entirely of recalled reserve squadrons. On 2 April Panthers relinquished their escort role and carried out their first ground attack mission in Korea when two F9F-2Bs of VF-191 from *Princeton*, each carrying four 250lb and two 100lb GP bombs, bombed a rail bridge near Songjin. *Philippine Sea* rejoined TF-77 on 4 April and her Corsairs and Skyraiders resumed operations in the Sea of Japan until the 8th when CV-47 and her screen sailed for Formosa to counter Red Chinese threats against the island. After a show of force off the Chinese coast and over the northern part of Formosa between 11 and 13 April, CV-47 returned north, giving support to UN ground forces between 16 April and 3 May and returning to Yokosuka on 6 May. The North Korean spring offensive, however, soon pulled the *Philippine Sea* back to the line and during the period 17-30 May 1951 she furnished close air support for the hard-pressed UN forces.[12] Attack and counter-attack continued for weeks until on 31 May Operation 'Strangle', an air interdiction campaign using Far East Air Forces, notably the 5th Air Force, 1st Marine Air Wing and TF 77, was mounted against road and rail routes and bridges in northeast Korea. 'Strangle', which was named for the Sicilian operation of 1943, was meant to achieve the same success claimed in 'Husky' but success was not forthcoming in Korea because no attacks were permitted on the Chinese Communist bases in Manchuria and the relative simplicity of the enemy supply system.[13]

On 18 August aircraft from TF 77 attacked twenty-seven bridges and rail lines running to the east coast. Samdong-ni to Kowon was soon christened 'Death Valley' by Navy aviators, who grew to respect the enemy AA fire in the area. *Essex* arrived on station joining TF 77 and on 23 August its McDonnell F2H-2 Banshees made their combat debut for VF-172 with an escort for the B-29s.[14] During 1951 the aircraft aboard TF-77 flew 29,000 interdiction missions over Korea: their contribution to the war effort was immense.

Throughout the winter of 1951-52, the war in Korea reached stalemate on the ground. At sea, the Navy and USMC squadrons continued their interdiction and close air support

F9F-2 Panther (BuNo 123469) *Papa San* of VF-71, CVG-7 on the USS *Bon Homme Richard* (CVA-31) over Task Force 77 on 1 August 1952. This was the personal aircraft of Lieutenant Commander J. M. Hill commanding VF-71. (Grumman)

strikes against North Korean targets. Eight carriers took their turn in the Sea of Japan and normally four US carriers were on station at any one time.[15]

Armistice talks faltered in October 1952. Despite attempts by new president Dwight D. Eisenhower to finish the war, the conflict was destined to spill over into 1953 with no end in sight. Another major concern was that the Soviet Union and Communist China had to be kept out of any direct involvement in the war. On 24 October ATG-2 joined *Bon Homme Richard* - the 'Bonnie Dick' - aircraft in strikes against mining and railway facilities at Hyesanjin very close to Manchuria. The mission was the latest in a series into previous communist sanctuaries in north-eastern Korea. Air Force B-29s were denied operations in the area owing to concern about high-level bombing so near to the Soviet and Chinese borders but there was not the same risk when using carrier aircraft, which could deliver ordnance more accurately.

November followed much the same pattern as before. After two days of refresher operations on the 14th and 15th *Essex* rejoined TF 77 and launched eighty aircraft on the 16th. Next morning joint strikes were made against Chongjin by aircraft from *Essex* and *Oriskany*. One of the few Essex-class aircraft carriers completed only after WWII for the USN, nicknamed 'Mighty O' and occasionally referred to as the 'O-boat', the ship was named for the Revolutionary War Battle of Oriskany. That afternoon 96 aircraft of ATG-2 bombed warehouses and supplies at Kyongsang. On the 18th ATG-2 from *Essex* and aircraft from the *Kearsarge* (CVA-33) hit bridges and rail targets at the border city of Hoeryong. At this time *Essex* was having trouble with the port catapult and on the 20th it put an F2H-2P in the water. The pilot was recovered without serious injury but next day the same thing happened again and this time VF-23's Lieutenant Commander Leo Thomas Freitas was not as fortunate. He went down with his F9F only 250 yards off the port bow and drowned. In all, *Essex* lost three pilots killed and four aircraft in four days. On the 22nd VF-23's Lieutenant Commander Daniel Lorenz Musetti was lost without trace over North Korea. Next day Lieutenant Commander John William Healy of VA-55 was among those looking

A fuel or ammunition train burns near Kumchon, North Korea after being hit by rocket and cannon fire from USS *Valley Forge's* Air Group 5 on the morning of 22 July 1950.

F9F-2 Panthers of VF-91 over Task
Force 77 off Korea in 1951.

Colonel John Herschel Glenn, Jr. USMC, born 18 July 1921, aviator, engineer, astronaut and US senator. In WWII he was assigned to VMJ-353, flying R4D transports. He transferred to VMF-155 as an F4U Corsair pilot and flew 59 combat missions in the South Pacific. In Korea he was assigned to VMF-311, flying the F9F Panther jet on 63 combat missions, gaining the nickname 'magnet ass' from his alleged ability to attract enemy flak. On two occasions, he returned to his base with over 250 holes in his aircraft.

F9F-2 of VF-64 'Freelancers' piloted by Lieutenant Paul R. Lovrien making an arrested landing on USS *Yorktown* (CVA-10).

for Musetti when his Skyraider's tail was shot off. Healy's wingman followed the AD all the way down and saw it explode on impact. Healy was declared KIA.)[16]

After a brief sojourn in Yokosuka in early December, *Essex* began its fourth and final period on the line. Combat operations were resumed on 8 December and next day it was back to 'working on the railroad' when strikes were carried out by 108 ATG-2 aircraft in co-ordination with other air groups on Hunyuing's rail facilities in the morning and a follow-up strike on Rashin's coastal rail facilities. Aircraft from the *Oriskany* hit rail targets at Hyesanjin and planes from the *Bon Homme Richard* attacked the Musan iron works. A Skyraider from

Memorial Service aboard the USS *Boxer* off Korea in 1953.

Essex, which took hits that punctured an oil line, was safely ditched offshore. On 22 December there was a change in targets when aircraft from the *Essex*, *Kearsarge* and *Oriskany* attacked the Kwangsuwon airfield complex. A 37mm battery hit VF-23's Lieutenant Commander Gordon Farmer's Panther, inflicting lacerations and contusions but he recovered safely to the *Essex*. A few days later, on 27 December, aircraft of CVG-101 from *Kearsarge* and ATG-2 aboard *Essex* blasted transport lines. Two planes from VA-55 and VF-23 were damaged and the next day VF-23 lost a F9F to flameout but the pilot safely ditched and was rescued.[17]

On 30 December aircraft from *Kearsarge* and *Essex* returned to Rashin to bomb the northern railroad again. Next day the first of a series of irksome but important close air support (CAS) sorties were begun with attacks on enemy frontline positions, troops and supplies. Bad weather on New Year's Day brought a temporary halt to CAS operations but they were continued well into January 1953.[18] Bitter fighting took place during late March around a series of USMC outposts known collectively as the 'Nevada Cities' complex. It was only strong air support by Panther jets, Tigercats, Skyraiders and Corsair fighter-bombers that retrieved the situation, albeit temporarily. Finally, the ground forces were forced to abandon the Marine outposts and the decision was made not to retake them. To have done so would have cost too many lives. Bitter fighting broke out along the MLR in May-June 1953 and carrier-borne aircraft from *Boxer*, *Philippine Sea*,[19] *Princeton* and *Lake Champlain* flew round-the-clock CAS and interdiction missions for seven days in support of the I and II ROK Corps' attacks to regain 'Anchor Hill' as the Communist forces tried to land a final knockout blow. It proved to be the Navy's last great all-out offensive of the war. Peace talks that had resumed on 26 April after being recessed for 199 days were by now progressing, albeit slowly.

But there was no let-up as the Communists tried to regain lost ground prior to a negotiated cease-fire agreement. Even with the signing of the armistice just days away, the Communists continued their ground action right to the wire. On 27 July, the last day of the war, four of TF-77's carriers - *Lake Champlain, Boxer, Philippine Sea* and *Princeton* - were operating off the east coast, while off the west coast the *Barioko* with Corsairs of VMA-312 and VMA-332 was on station. Altogether, 649 sorties were flown this day and the USMC squadrons, too, were active over Korea.

Endnotes for Chapter 1

1 There were seven carriers in the area of Japan and 3 more carriers were en route: Intrepid (CV-11) with CVG (Air Group)-10; *Boxer* (CV-21) with Air Group 93 and *Antietam* (CV-36), with Air Group 89.

2 On 27 June Martin Mariners at Iwakuni in Japan began patrols off the Korean coast and a squadron of Lockheed P2V Neptunes were ordered to Korea but the peninsular is 600 miles long, 135 miles wide, with an area of 86,000 square miles. On 28 June the first US ground troops were ordered to Korea although they were not flown in until 2 July. North Korean Air Force (NKAF) Yak 9P fighters and Il'yushin 1l-10 Shturmovik attack aircraft bombed and strafed airfields near the capital Seoul and Kimpo and quickly established air superiority over the whole country. The NKAF entered the offensive with only about 162 aircraft; all of Soviet manufacture and all of them piston-engined. Mostly the fighter and ground-attack regiments consisted of Yak-3 and Yak-9 fighters and Il-10s.

3   Four CVs (Attack carriers, re-designated CVAs in October 1952), 3 CVBs (large or 'battle' carriers), 4 CVLs (small or 'light' carriers) and 4 CVEs (escort carriers). Throughout the Korean War, 11 CVAs, five CVEs and one CVL made a total of 38 combat deployments. They operated 13 air groups, six ASW and five Marine Corps squadrons from both the Pacific and Atlantic commands. Eighteen Reserve squadrons logged a total of 29 deployments, including five Reserve air group cruises. By November 1951 nearly three-quarters of all Navy strikes in Korea were flown by Reservists, including those in Regular fleet squadrons. Barrett Tillman (*The Hook: Journal of Carrier Aviation*. Summer1989).

4   In January 1950 a carrier's air group (CVG) composition had been changed from three fighter and two attack squadrons, to four fighter squadrons (VF) - namely two F4U-4 Corsair and two Grumman F9F-3 Panther jets and one attack (VA) squadron (AD-4 Skyraiders). Each group comprised 90 aircraft, or 18 in each squadron. CVG-5 consisted of VF-51 'Screaming Eagles' and VF-52 flying F9F-2 Panther jets, VF-53 and VF-54 flying F4U-4Bs, VA-55 flying AD-2 Skyraiders and VC-61 with F4U-5Ps. CVG-5 was the most experienced jet air group in the Navy. F9F-3s had replaced VF-51's FJ-1 Fury's in May 1949 and the Screaming Eagles became the first Grumman F9F Panther squadron and the first to operate jets from a carrier when VF-51 began operations from *Boxer* in September.

5   CAG was Commander W. 'Sully' Vogel Jr. VF-111 and VF-112 were equipped with the F9F-2, VF-113 and VF-114 with F4U-4s and VA-115 with AD-4B Skyraiders. Detachments from Composite Squadron 3 (CV-3) were equipped with F4U-5N night-fighters/-5P photo- reconnaissance models and AD-4Bs. VC-11 with AD-4Bs, VC-61 with F4U-4s and VC-35 with the AD-4N were also embarked. A single HO3 S-1 from HU-1 were for plane-guard and utility duties.

6   After WWII the USN had been consistently pruned and many carriers were either mothballed or undermanned. It was for the latter reason that the *Philippine Sea*, commissioned in May 1946 had to remain at Quonset Point in a reduced-commission state. On 24 May 1950 she sailed from Norfolk, Virginia for San Diego, California arriving on 10 June. On 5 July, 15 days after the North Koreans crossed the 38th Parallel *Philippine Sea* was ordered to Hawaii and ultimately Korea with Air Group 11 (CVG-11).

7   *Sicily* was joined on 6 August by the Badoeng Strait. The newly re-commissioned *Bataan* (CVL-29) left Philadelphia for the US west coast and arrived in Korea in December 1950. In 1951 these were joined by the escort carriers *Bairoko* (CVE 115) and *Rendova* (CVE-116). *Badoeng Strait* (CVE-116) was en route to Pearl Harbor with a Marine fighter squadron onboard.

8   During the war 46% of all Navy-Marine sorties were close air support. Also, it was time to send for the 'Flying Leathernecks'. In July Marine Air Group 33 (MAG-33) and USMC ground troop reinforcements left for Korea. MAG-33 arrived at Kohe, Japan on 31 July and proceeded to Itami for maintenance and testing.

22

On 2 August 1950 the carrier *Sicily* (CVE-118) arrived in Tsushima Strait with F4U-4Bs of VMF-214 'Black Sheep' and began rocket and incendiary attacks on Chinju neat the south coast. *Sicily* was joined on 6 August by the *Badoeng Strait* (CVE-116) with F4U-4Bs of VMF-323 'Death Rattlers' embarked.

9   The bridge had withstood days of heavy bombing by B-29s of the 19th Bomb Group, including one strike which saw 54 tons of bombs explode around it. General George E. Stratemeyer, CIC, FEAF (Far East Air Force), had promised a case of Scotch whisky to the first crew to destroy the bridge. The spans fell into the Han River that night before B-29s of the 19th Bomb Group could drop their special 2,000 and 4,000lb bombs the following morning. Honours were declared even, with the 19th Bomb Group and CAG-11 both receiving cases of whisky!

10   *The Hook.*

11   *Valley Forge* returned to San Diego on 1 December but the Chinese Communist intervention required her immediate return to WestPac, so CVG-5 were unloaded and on 6 December, with CVG-2 embarked, she was westbound again. In all *Happy Valley* made three combat cruises, as did *Princeton* (CVA-37) and *Philippine Sea*. *Boxer* (CVA-21) made four deployments.

12   Finally, on 2 June 1951 she detached from TF-77 and departed for California for a complete overhaul). The only use of aerial torpedoes during the Korean War occurred on 1 May when eight Skyraiders and twelve Corsair escorts from *Princeton* attacked the Hwachon dam. The ADs breached the dam, releasing a flood of water into the Pulchan River, which prevented the Communist forces from making an easy crossing.

13   Even TF 77's 'Cherokee' strikes which divided North Korea into what a later generation would call route packages failed to achieve desired results. Barrett Tillman. (*The Hook*: *Journal of Carrier Aviation*. Summer 1989).

14   Late in 1951 two future astronauts made the headlines. On 23 October Lieutenant Walter M. Schirra USN shot down a MiG while on an exchange with the 136th Fighter-Bomber Wing. On a later mission, Ensign Neil A. Armstrong from *Essex* bailed out and was rescued after his Panther was hit during a strafing run near Wonsan. Armstrong joined the NASA Astronaut Corps in 1962. He made his first space flight, as command pilot of Gemini 8, in 1966, becoming NASA's first civilian astronaut to fly in space. On this mission, he performed the first docking of two spacecraft, with pilot David Scott. Armstrong's second and last spaceflight was as mission commander of the Apollo 11 moon landing, in July 1969. On this mission, Armstrong and Buzz Aldrin descended to the lunar surface and spent two and a half hours exploring, while Michael Collins remained in lunar orbit in the Command Module. Armstrong died on 25 August 2012 at the age of 82 after complications from coronary artery bypass surgery. Upon the outbreak of the Korean War, Schirra was dispatched to South Korea as an exchange pilot on loan to the USAF. He served as a flight leader with the 136th Fighter Bomber Wing and then as operations officer with the 154th Fighter-Bomber Squadron. He flew 90 combat missions between 1951 and 1952, mostly in F-84s. Schirra was credited with downing one MiG-15 and damaging two others. Schirra received the Distinguished Flying Cross and the Air Medal with an oak leaf cluster for his service in Korea. He died at the age of 84 on 3 May 2007

15   After an overhaul, *Philippine Sea* rejoined TF-77 on 3 February with CVG-11. *Essex, Antietam, Boxer, Princeton* (with CVG-19), *Bataan, Valley Forge* (with ATG-1, the Navy's first Air Task Group) and *Barioko* (CVE- 115) were the other carriers.

16   See *Air Task Group Two: Ready When Needed* by Barrett Tillman. (*The Hook*: *Journal of Carrier Aviation*. Summer 1989).

17   During *Kearsarge's* 1952-53 deployment three CVG-101 squadron CO's were KIA. (*The Hook*: *Journal of Carrier Aviation*. Summer 1989).

18   *Essex* closed out her final line period on 9 January with 49 sorties and replenished the 10th. En route to Yokosuka ATG-2 transferred 45 aircraft to Atsugi, K-3 (Pohang) and *Valley Forge*, newly arrived with CVG-5. From 18 July 1952 to 11 January 1953 ATG-2 had launched just over 7,600 sorties and had expended 31,000 bombs and rockets amounting to 5,522 tons of ordnance for the loss of five pilots and 15 aircraft. *Air Task Group Two: Ready When Needed* by Barrett Tillman. (*The Hook*: *Journal of Carrier Aviation*. Summer 1989).

19   Now returned from a sojourn to California and re-designated an attack aircraft carrier (CVA-47) with Air Group 9 (VF-91, 93 and 94, VA-95, detachments from VC-3, 11, 35 and 61 and a unit of HU-1) embarked. The '*Phil Sea*' had relieved sister ship *Essex*, CVG-9 launching its first strikes from CVA-47's deck on 31 January 1953. She performed interdiction and CAS duties into the spring. *The Fighting Phil Sea* by Robert Cressman. (Fall 1988 edition of *The Hook: Journal of Carrier Aviation*).

Chapter Two

The MiG Killers:
Sabres in the Korean War 1950-53

'It's the teamwork out here that counts. The lone wolf stuff is out. Your life always depends on your wingman and his life on you. I may get credit for a MiG, but it's the team that does it, not myself alone.'
Joseph C. McConnell, reflecting on his air victories.

When in early November 1950 5th Air Force F-80 Shooting Stars first encountered the Soviet-built MiG-15 jets of the Chinese Communist Air Force over NW Korea, it was the first time since early WWII that US forces lacked air superiority in a theatre of war. The UN had no combat aircraft in the theatre capable of meeting the MiG-15 on equal terms. The appearance of the Soviet-built swept-wing jet fighter sent shockwaves through the US military. It was 75 mph faster than any aircraft in the USAF inventory. (The Soviet design also benefited from Britain's world lead in jet propulsion development when in 1946 twenty-five Rolls Royce Nene turbojets were sold to the Soviets as part of the Anglo-Soviet Trade Agreement!) A month later the USAF had regained the initiative thanks largely to the F-86A Sabre, which proved to be the equal of the MiG-15 but the lighter enemy jet proved to have the edge over the F-86A in climb and altitude performance and was more manoeuvrable.

On 26 November, eighteen Chinese divisions entered the battle and soon the UN Forces were in headlong retreat. On 8 November General Hoyt S. Vandenberg, USAF Chief of Staff, had offered to release the 4th FIW and its F-86A-5 Sabres and the 27th Fighter-Escort Wing (FEW) and its Republic F-84E Thunderjets for operations in Korea. General Earle E. Partridge commanding US Far East Air Forces (FEAF) and General George E. Stratemeyer, commanding 5th Air Force Force immediately accepted the offer. The 4th FIW, commanded

F-86 Sabres with their 51st Fighter Interceptor Wing 'Checkertails' are readied for combat at Suwon Air Base, South Korea.

36th Fighter Bomber Squadron F-86 Sabres lined up. On 26 February 1953 the 36th FBS stopped combat operations with their F-80s and began the transition to the F-86F Sabre.

by Colonel John C. 'Whips' Meyer, a WWII fighter pilot with 24 victories, was at New Castle County Airport, Wilmington, Delaware, where it was assigned to the Eastern Air Defense Force. On 11 November the Sabres were flown to San Diego, California, where on 29 November the aircraft of the 334th and 335th FIS were deck-loaded aboard the escort carrier Cape Esperance and the 336th FIS on board a fast tanker for Yokosuka, Japan. Advance personnel were sent to Japan by air and the main contingents followed by rail and then by naval transport. The Sabres arrived on 13 December and an advance detachment flew to Kimpo (K-IA) a few miles south of the 38th Parallel and to the north of Seoul, the South Korean capital. They were soon in action. Four F-86A-5s of the 336th FIS engaged in combat with the MiG-15 for the first time on 17 December 1950. Lieutenant Colonel Bruce H. Hinton, CO, 336th Squadron shot down the first MiG and the other three, too fast for the pursuing F-86s, made for the border. Hinton's was the first of 792 MiGs to be destroyed in the Korean War. On 22 December Colonel John Meyer destroyed a MiG-15 near Sinuiju.

Sabres and MiGs clashed again on the morning of 19 December when Lieutenant Colonel Glenn T. 'Eagle' Eagleston damaged one of the enemy jets. He also claimed a probable two days later when eight of the Sabres tried to intercept two MiGs flying at 34,000 feet. On the morning of 22 December, the first Sabre was shot down in combat with a MiG but the F-86 pilots gained revenge later that day when the 4th Wing destroyed six MiGs in one combat. On New Year's Day 1951 the Chinese launched a new invasion of South Korea, which succeeded in removing the UN Forces from Seoul. Next day, the 4th FIW had to evacuate to Johnson AFB in Japan. In desperation a detachment of Sabres arrived at Taegu on 14 January to begin ground attack sorties over the enemy lines. However, they were of limited success - only two five-inch rockets could be carried in addition to the Sabre's machine-guns because of the need to carry drop tanks - and the extreme operating range meant that pilots only had a short time to locate and hit targets. By 31 January, though, the F-86s had completed 150 valuable close-support sorties.

UN Forces launched a counter-offensive which recaptured Seoul and the airbases at Suwon and Kimpo but they were so badly damaged the USAF would have to wait until engineering battalions made them habitable again. On 22 February the 334th Squadron, 4th FIW flew into Taegu (K-5) in the south of the country but it was too far for the Sabres to hunt MiG-15s over MiG Alley. The furthest the Sabres could fly was to Pyongyang. Finally, on 10 March, the single concrete runway at Suwon (K-l3) was able to take jets again and the 334th Squadron occupied the battered airfield. Meanwhile, the 336th Squadron, which flew in from Japan, occupied Taegu.

Despite their experience Sabre pilots found it increasingly difficult to maintain air superiority over the Communist air force. Senior Lieutenant Kum Sok No, North Korean Air Force recalled:

'My assignment to go into combat on the Korean side of the Yalu came as a surprise. Until then, all our air bases had been confined to Manchuria because of the constant B-29 raids on North Korea. In November 1951, Uiju, where I reported after finishing MiG training, was the only operational communist airfield in North Korea. The others were abandoned, bombed-out concrete strips. Kim Il Sung and Air Force General Young Wang were banking on the propaganda value of the first North Korean jet division 'defending' our country from Korean soil. Before that, the Russian and Chinese MiG pilots based in Manchuria had been the only jets fighting the UN. But the experiment was doomed from the start. One morning soon after I arrived, I saw eight MiGs on the apron, pilots ready in the cockpit. General Wang and our Russian adviser were talking in front of headquarters. Suddenly, seemingly from nowhere, I saw two American Sabres - more than 200 miles from their home base - swoop low over the field. I hit the ground just as a trail of .50-calibre bullets started tearing up the dirt. From the corner of my eye, I could see General Wang and the Russian do the same. But the pilots were trapped in their MiGs. When the Sabres left, we counted our casualties: Senior Lieutenant Yontae Chong killed in his cockpit, one MiG destroyed in flames and two pilots wounded.

'On 15 November 1951 I faced the Americans in the air for the first time. I took off early from Uiju in a formation of eight MiGs headed south. I had no desire to fight the Americans, but I had no choice. The squadron commander kept up a spirited series of orders and words of encouragement over the intercom, but I scarcely heard what he said. I kept remembering the words of our political officer: 'The cowardly Americans will flee and desert their comrades to certain death.' With my survival at stake, I guess I hoped the Reds were telling the truth for once.

'My old-style MiG-15A was, I believe, a better fighting instrument than the F-80 or the F-84, but no better than the old Sabre which most UN pilots were flying. Fortunately, the ferocious new Sabre, the F-86F, had not yet appeared in Korea. We met the Americans near Pyongyang. They, too, were flying a close formation, feeling us out. Suddenly they broke for the attack and quickly split our inexperienced group. The fighting was over almost before it began and we turned and raced northward for Uiju. There were no casualties, but the battle taught me another lesson about Red propaganda. The Americans were not cowards. The Sabres attacked with more courage than my fellow MiG pilots and they

Colonel John Glenn Jr flew a second Korean combat tour in an interservice exchange programme with the 51st Fighter Wing, flying F-86F *MiG Mad Marine*. He logged 27 missions and in July 1953 shot down three MiG-15s in the final days before the ceasefire. His total service was 149 combat missions in two wars. On 20 February 1962 Glenn flew the *Friendship 7* mission and became the first American to orbit the Earth and the fifth person in space.

understood co-operation. When one of our MiGs got on the tail of a Sabre, three of the Americans risked their lives to shake him off. In all the time I flew for North Korea, I never once saw a Red pilot try to save another's life. The fighter scrambles at Uiju were inconclusive. During the next six weeks we lost three of our thirty MiGs and shot down one South Korean propeller P-51 and an American F-80 jet.

'The American bombing of Uiju took a greater toll. I slept with my clothes on every night; at least half a dozen times after dark, B-29s droned overhead and plastered our field. Whenever I heard the alert, I raced for the mountains a mile away. My MiG wasn't equipped for night fighting; the Russians had refused to give us or the Chinese their radar-equipped night fighters. They didn't even want us to see them. A suspicious Russian mechanic once shooed me away from a parked radar MiG. Occasionally, the Russians sent night fighters from Manchuria to meet the B-29s over Uiju, but they usually failed to make contact in the darkness. The Russians kept a monopoly on their radar fighters. I can safely say that every B-29 shot down in night raids during the Korean War was the handiwork of Russian pilots.

'After six weeks we had reached the limit of our endurance. Our runway, gutted with twenty-foot bomb craters, kept our MiGs virtually grounded. On 15 December 1951 the decision was made to abandon Uiju. Immediately 5,000 civilians, including women and children, were put to work repairing the runway with basketfuls of stones and earth. When it was done, The other MiG pilots and myself happily took off across the Yalu for the sanctuary of Antung, Manchuria, not to return until after the truce. Almost immediately the complexion of the air was changed. Antung, headquarters for 210 MiGs of three communist air divisions - one Russian (Kozhedub had gone there from Anshan), one Chinese and our North Korean - became the focus of that war.

William B. 'Brad' Hoelscher was credited with 2.5 aerial victories in WWII and he went on to fight in two more wars. On 11 October 1952 he shot down a MiG-15 near the Yalu River and was later credited with a half share in a victory. A seasoned veteran of two wars now, Hoelscher had not yet flown 'his most difficult or dangerous missions' that came in Việtnam when Hoelscher was stationed in Thailand and flew the A-1E Skyraider on low-level close air support missions.

Colonel Harrison Reed Thyng. Deployed to Kimpo AB in October 1951 and while still on unassigned duty recorded his first MiG 15 kill on 24 October, leading a flight of 4th FIW F-86s, when he attacked a formation of 11 MiGs and hit the leader, causing him to eject. Thyng was made CO on 1 November 1951 and commanded the 4th FIW until 2 October 1952, flying 114 missions. Credited with the destruction of five MiGs, Thyng flew a number of aircraft during his Korean tour, but his personal aircraft was F-86E 50-0623 which carried the nickname *Pretty Mary and the J's* after his family, on the lower portion of the nose.

Pilots in the 36th Fighter Bomber Squadron.

'In January 1952 the United States Air Force switched to a new Sabre. Until then the jet fighting had been almost a draw. The new Sabre was at least a ton heavier than the MiG and had a faster rate of descent. It could break the sound barrier in a dive. Our latest MiG-15B could not exceed Mach .98 - that is, 98 per cent of the speed of sound at a given altitude - in a dive and Mach .95 in level flight. One Russian pilot once tried to push his MiG through the sonic barrier, but his wings collapsed and he crashed to his death. The new Sabre, although heavier and better armoured, was more manoeuvrable than our MiG. We were so hopelessly outclassed by the new Sabre and the better-trained American pilots that it became virtual suicide even for the new MiG-15B to take one on single-handed. We were told to maintain large, tight formations, never to get below a Sabre in a fight and to attack only in much greater strength. The Russian pilots were jaunty at first. At mess, which we shared with them, one of them boasted to me 'The Americans are all right, but we are better. No one can out fly our new MiG.

'Kozhedub's division had received a host of commendations from Stalin himself for shooting down propeller P-51s, B-29s on daylight raids, F-80 Shooting Star jets and British-built Meteor Mk.8 jets. With only a few months left to their Korean combat tour, they were impatiently waiting to return to Moscow in honour. Then the new Sabres appeared over the Yalu. Every clear flying day from January 1952 until the truce in July 1953, the alert sounded in my barracks at four am. By five o'clock the regimental bus would have brought us to Antung field. At the second alert we'd run to our planes and wait for the signal to take off. Approximately thirty Sabres, forming a loose circle composed of little clusters of two and four planes, would come and we'd send up a hundred or more MiGs to meet them. On average we lost four to five MiGs a day, many of them piloted by Russians. Some days we lost as many as ten planes. I saw one disabled MiG after another splash into the Yalu or crash-land on the runway, engulfed in flames. Sabre losses, on the other hand, were very light.

'I had my first close brush with the Sabre on the morning of 25 January 1952. Sixteen of us took off early and crossed the Yalu into North Korea, flying at 8000 metres. Ahead of me I saw the inevitable groups of two and four Sabres coming toward Antung. In my earphones

F-86F-35-NA 52-5233 of the 72nd Fighter Bomber Squadron.

I heard orders to climb above the Sabres and wait to attack. The MiG's only advantage is that it can climb higher and faster than the Sabre. I started to climb with the formation when suddenly I heard the staccato of machine-gun bullets. We had wandered into the middle of the scattered Sabre groups by mistake and overlooked two Americans in a deadly position, above and behind us. The Sabres - two against sixteen - made their pass in a near-sonic dive, guns blazing, then dived out of range. The fight was over in an instant. I nervously assessed the damage. My plane seemed all right, but I could see three flaming MiGs hurtling toward the ground. Only one parachute opened. The formation was badly scattered, so I turned and raced thankfully the forty miles toward home.

'The total Red air strength was a little over 900 MiGs: 400 Russians, 400 Chinese and our two North Korean divisions of 125 MiGs. There were divisions stationed at Antung, Anshan, Tat'ungho, Ta Hua Shan, Taepo, North Mukden, West Mukden, East Mukden, Liaoyuan, Kwantien, Tientsin and Chingtao. In addition, the North Korean Air Force had 100 operational propeller planes in Manchuria and forty Il-28 jet bombers training at Kungchuling that never saw combat. Before the war was finally over the Reds had lost more than 800 MiGs and pilots - 400 Russians, 300 Chinese and 100 North Korean - almost a 100 per cent turnover. My division of seventy MiGs lost thirty, none of which were replaced. I personally survived sixty missions unscathed and without any Sabres to my credit.

'By May 1952, when Kozhedub's pilots were ready to go home, their cockiness was gone. My old instructor, Captain Nichenko, had been killed by a Sabre. The few months of warfare with the new Sabre had cut their ranks in half. The night before they left, I heard them singing Russian folk songs and carousing drunkenly in their barracks. The next morning one of them told me it had been no victory celebration, but one of thanksgiving by those who had come through alive. Their replacements were not so fortunate. Two new Russian divisions, one to replace Kozhedub's and another to go to Tat'ungho, arrived from Europe heady with home-front propaganda tales of Red air victories. But within two months both Soviet divisions were almost entirely wiped out by the new Sabre jets. The Russian commander of the replacement division at Antung was sent back to Moscow in disgrace.

'Their propaganda still boasted about the MiG's superiority, but we pilots knew the truth. After dinner, the hundred grams of wine we drank to make sleep easier loosened the stubbornness of Red tongues. 'I had a hundred Sabres after me today,' one worried Russian pilot exaggerated. Another, a World War II ace, confessed that he was mortally afraid of the Americans, who really were 'air murderers,' as the party claimed. But our political officers would admit only that 'the American mercenaries have more flying hours.' (I had gone into combat with only fifty jet hours.) They rationalized their defeats: 'We are not fighting for money and women, but for our country, communism and our people.'

'Our air defeats were demoralizing in themselves. In addition, we were subjected to political harassment at our own bases. A pilot in my outfit, Lieutenant Yun Chul Sin, was discharged in disgrace when the security officer learned that his brother had fled to South Korea. Other pilots were executed for little more. Colonel Tal Hion Kim, the popular commander of the 11th Division, which consisted of propeller-driven Yak-9s and Il-10s, stationed at Feng Cheng, Manchuria, was accused of defecting to the West. He was executed without a trial. I had ignored politics in my first year in the air force, but during MiG training in 1951, I realized that the most suspicious thing about my career to date was not joining the Communist Party. I was afraid my aloofness would invite a fatal investigation of my background.'[20]

Communist tactics in April 1952 showed a marked reluctance to continue with large formations of fifty-plus MiGs. They were replaced by more flexible formations of sixteen fighters in four flights of four, so the USAF dispatched small patrols of twelve F-86As backed up by supporting flights, which could be called upon when the first group had flushed the MiGs. On 22 April four enemy jets were shot down and four more damaged. One of the victories went to Captain James 'Jabby' Jabara of the 4th FIW, who shot down his fourth

Senior Lieutenant Kum Sok No, North Korean Air Force who defected to the UN side in a MiG-15 (pictured under guard at Kimpo).

MiG of the war. He had achieved his first confirmed air victory of the war on 3 April. Having downed 3.5 German aircraft in WWII, he became the first jet ace of the Korean War and the first American jet ace in history on 20 May when fifty MiGs intercepted the patrol of fourteen F-86As over Sinuiju. 'Jabby', who was in the second wave of fourteen Sabres; tacked on to three MiGs at 35,000 feet and singled out the last one. He blasted the MiG with cannon fire and the pilot bailed out at 10,000 feet just before the fighter disintegrated. He climbed back to 20,000 feet and bounced six more MiGs. He fired at one and the enemy fighter began to smoke and catch fire before falling into an uncontrollable spin. He eventually scored fifteen victories, giving him the title of 'triple ace'. Jabara was ranked as the second-highest-scoring US ace of the Korean War after Joe McConnell, Jr. who was credited with shooting down 16 MiG-15s while flying F-86 Sabres.[21]

By the summer of 1951 it was estimated that the CPAF had 1,050 Soviet-built combat aircraft, including 445 MiG-15s (when only 89 F-86A Sabres were available) and new airfields were under construction in the Antung area to accommodate 300 of the jet fighters. The enemy pilots sometimes now flew in singles and pairs with drop tanks fitted to their MiG-15s as far south as the 38th Parallel. Their attacks bore all the hallmarks of being carried out either by Red Chinese instructors or Soviet pilots - 'Honchos' (from the Japanese word meaning 'boss') as the Americans called them. A worried General Otto P. Weyland, who assumed command of the FEAF on 10 June, saw the immediate need for four more Sabre wings. At this time there were only eighty-nine F-86A Sabres in the Far East and just forty-four of them were in Korea against over 400 MiG-15s. Since June-July FEAF's F-86As were being replaced by F-86Es on a one-for-one exchange basis, but this was a very slow process. (Beginning in September, a few F-86Fs filtered through to the 4th FIW but the F-86A was not completely replaced in the 4th FIW inventory until July 1952). Weyland wanted two F-86E wings to be sent immediately to Korea and two to Japan, where they would help deter possible Chinese attacks on Japanese bases

F-86Es of the 4th FIW in revetments in Korea. On 1 May 1952 51-2786, now in the 51st FIG, 51st FIW, was shot down by a MiG. Colonel Albert W. Schinz, ejected near the coast of Cholsan Peninsula. He was faced with the problems of exhaustion, damp clothing, a broken radio, lack of food and a month long existence on a island before he was rescued on 1 June.

should the Soviets supply the CPAF with Il-28 jet bombers. However, Weyland's requests for F-86Es fell on deaf ears in Washington who viewed the CPAF build-up as being purely defensive and argued that any major increase in UN air reinforcements would be seen as a prelude to all-out air warfare against China. In any case, the USAF did not want to weaken an already below strength Air Defense Command. Weyland received one F-84 Wing, no other Sabre wings were forthcoming. By September when a new Communist air offensive began, there were no less than 525 MiG-15s in the enemy inventory.

Sabres continued to knock down MiGs at a good rate. That month the 4th FIW sighted 1,177 MiG sorties over North Korea and engaged 911 MiGs in combat. Even though the odds were usually stacked against them the Sabres scored some impressive victories. On 2 September 22 F-86s battled with 44 MiGs between Sinuiju and Pyongyang and shot down four. Seven days later in a battle between 28 Sabres and seventy MiG-15s, Captains Richard S. Becker and Ralph D. 'Hoot' Gibson claimed a MiG each to become the second and third aces of the Korean War. Three F-86s were lost in these two air battles. Despite the successes, by the end of September the Communist air force posed a very real threat to American fighter-bomber operations in the North and Weyland once again requested an additional Sabre Wing, or at least the conversion of one of the existing F-80 Wings to F-86Es. His request was rebuffed and as a result, General Frank F. Everest, commander 5th AF since 1 June, had no option but to withdraw his fighter-bombers from MiG Alley and ordered them instead to concentrate on a zone between Pyongyang and the Chongchon River.

In October patrols over MiG Alley were stepped up and in the first two weeks of operations the 4th FIW claimed nineteen MiGs (including nine on 16 October) destroyed. During October 1951 no less than 2,573 MiG sorties were sighted and of these, 2,166 were intercepted and thirty-two MiGs were claimed destroyed but the

Lieutenant Colonel Thomas A. Hudson Jr. standing beside his Sabre.

Major 'Gabby' Gabreski (left) and Lieutenant Colonel George Jones congratulate Major William Whisner. Gabreski was the top American fighter ace in Europe during WWII, flying 166 combat sorties and credited with twenty-eight aircraft destroyed and three on the ground. His six-and-a-half MiG-15 kills make him one of only seven US pilots to become an ace in more than one war (the others being Whisner, Colonel Harrison Thyng, Colonel James P. Hagerstrom, Colonel Vermont Garrison, Major George A. Davis, Jr. and Lieutenant Colonel John F. Bolt USMC.) William T. Whisner, Jr., destroyed five and a half MiGs and damaged six others.

Two F-86Fs in the 334th FIS with many MiG kills in a revetment at Kimpo. (Hendel via Larry Davis)

USAF lost ten jet fighters and five B-29s. Flushed with success, the Communists relocated their fighters further south of the Yalu and based fleets of bombers at Sinuiju. The Communists also boasted a new fighter, the MiG-15bis, which had an uprated VK-I turbojet in place of the original RD-45. In good hands, the new jet easily outclassed the F-86A. The 4th FIW, including the 335th Squadron in Japan, moved up to Kimpo but they could not stave off the threat posed by the MiGs alone. Unless more F-86Es arrived soon then the United Nations would lose air superiority in Korea.

General Hoyt S. Vandenberg, USAF Chief of Staff arrived in the Far East late in October. The Chinese air force had, he said, 'almost overnight become one of the major air powers of the world'. Vandenberg ordered the transfer from Air Defense Command of seventy-five F-86Es together with air and ground crews and full supporting equipment to the Korean theatre to re-equip two squadrons of F-80Es of the 51st FIW. On 1 and 9 November the seventy-five F-86Es were shipped from Alameda, California on the escort carriers *Cape Esperance* and *Sitkoh Bay* to Korea. The 51st FIW re-formed at Suwon on 6 November and an equal number of F-80E crews returned Stateside in exchange. That same day, legendary WWII fighter ace Colonel Francis S. 'Gabby' Gabreski, who had twenty-eight confirmed German aircraft kills and had added three MiGs to his score while flying missions as deputy CO of the 4th FIW in Korea, assumed command of the new Sabre wing. (Gabreski went on to add three and a half victories while commanding the 51st. The half MiG was shared with Major Bill Whisner, another WWII ace, who finished the Korean War with five and a half kills).

In November 1951 the 4th FIW, now commanded by Colonel Harrison R. Thyng, another WW II ace, with eleven enemy aircraft to his credit, claimed fourteen MiGs destroyed.

Colonel Thyng was to recall: 'Like olden knights the F-86 pilots ride up over North Korea to the Yalu River, the sun glinting off silver aircraft, contrails streaming behind, as they challenge the numerically superior enemy to come on up and fight. With eyes scanning the horizon to prevent any surprise, they watch avidly while MiG pilots leisurely mount into their cockpits and taxi out onto their runways for a formation take-off.

'Thirty-six lining up at Antung,' Black Leader calls.

'Hell, only twenty-four taking off over here at Tatungkou,' complains Blue Leader.

'Well, it will be at least three for everybody. I count fifty at Takushan,' calls White Leader.

'I see dust at Fen Cheng, so they are gathering up there,' yells Yellow Leader.

'Once again the Commie leaders have taken up our challenge and now we may expect

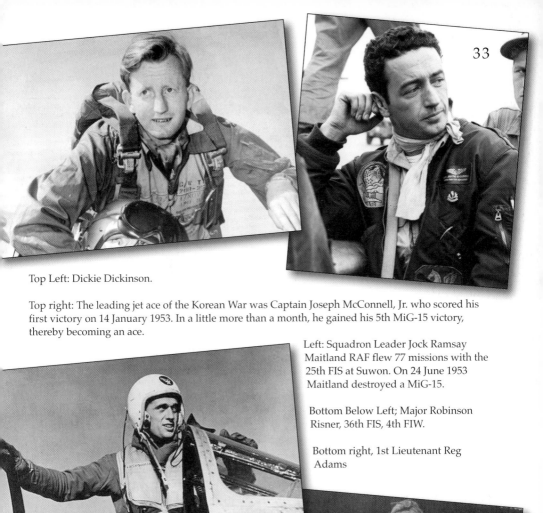

Top Left: Dickie Dickinson.

Top right: The leading jet ace of the Korean War was Captain Joseph McConnell, Jr. who scored his first victory on 14 January 1953. In a little more than a month, he gained his 5th MiG-15 victory, thereby becoming an ace.

Left: Squadron Leader Jock Ramsay Maitland RAF flew 77 missions with the 25th FIS at Suwon. On 24 June 1953 Maitland destroyed a MiG-15.

Bottom Below Left; Major Robinson Risner, 36th FIS, 4th FIW.

Bottom right, 1st Lieutenant Reg Adams

F-86E-10-NA 51-2832 *Karen's Kart* of the 25th FIS, 51th FIW was flown by several pilots including Colonel John W. Mitchell and Major (later Major-General) John C. Giraudo, who claimed two MiGs in this aircraft (now named *NINA II*) on 13 and 14 May 1953. On 16 June 51-2832 was shot down by AAA 6 miles SE of Cholsan. Giraudo ejected and was taken prisoner.

the usual numerical odds as the MiGs gain altitude and form up preparatory to crossing the Yalu.

'Breaking up into small flights, we stagger our altitude. We have checked our guns and sights by firing a few warm-up rounds as we crossed the bomb line. Oxygen masks are checked and pulled as tight as possible over our faces. We know we may exceed eight gs in the coming fight and that is painful with a loose mask. We are cruising at a very high Mach. Every eye is strained to catch the first movement of an enemy attempt to cross the Yalu from their Manchurian sanctuary into that graveyard of several hundred MiGs known as 'MiG Alley.' Several minutes pass. We know the MiG pilots will become bolder as our fuel time limit over the Alley grows shorter.

'Now we see flashes in the distance as the sun reflects off the beautiful MiG aircraft. The radio crackles, 'Many, many coming across at Suiho above 45,000 feet.' Our flights start converging toward that area, low flights climbing, yet keeping a very high Mach. Contrails are now showing over the Antung area, so another enemy section is preparing to cross at Sinuiju, a favourite spot.

1st Lieutenant Gene Kranz of the 69th Fighter Bomber Squadron beside *My Darling Marta*. Kranz later became NASA flight director for the Gemini and Apollo Space Programmes and assistant flight director on Project Mercury.

'We know the enemy sections are now being vectored by GCI and the advantage is theirs. Travelling at terrifically high speed and altitude, attackers can readily achieve surprise. The area bound by the horizon at this altitude is so vast that it is practically impossible to keep it fully covered with the human eye.

Our flights are well spread out, ships line abreast and each pilot keeps his head swiveling 360 degrees. Suddenly MiGs appear directly in front of us at our level. At rates of closure of possibly 1,200 miles an hour we pass through each other's formations.

'Accurate radar range firing is difficult under these conditions, but you fire a burst at the nearest enemy anyway. Immediately the MiGs zoom for altitude and you break at maximum g around towards them. Unless the MiG wants to fight and also turned as he climbed, he will be lost from sight in the distance before the turn is completed. But if he shows an inclination to scrap, you immediately trade head-on passes again. You 'sucker' the MiG into a position where the outstanding advantage of your aircraft will give you the chance to outmanoeuvre him.

'For you, combat has become an individual dogfight. Flight integrity has been lost, but your wing man is still with you, widely separated but close enough for you to know that you are covered. Suddenly you go into a steep turn. Your Mach drops off. The MiG turns with you and you let him gradually creep up and out-turn you. At the critical moment you reverse your turn. The hydraulic controls work beautifully. The MiG cannot turn as readily as you and is slung out to the side. When you pop your speed brakes, the MiG flashes by you. Quickly closing the brakes, you slide onto his tail and hammer him with your '50s.' Pieces fly off the MiG, but he won't burn or explode at that high altitude. He twists and turns and attempts to dive away, but you will not be denied. Your 50s have hit him in the engine and slowed him up enough so that he cannot get away from you. His canopy suddenly blows and the pilot catapults out, barely missing your airplane. Now your wing man is whooping it up over the radio and you flash for home very low on fuel. At this point your engine is running very rough. Parts of the ripped MiG have been sucked into your engine scoop and the possibility of its flaming out is very likely. Desperately climbing for altitude you finally reach forty thousand feet. With home base now but eighty miles away, you can lean back and sigh with relief for you know you can glide your ship back and land,

F-86E-1s of the 25th FIS, 51st FIW in Korea, 1952. FU-649 is F-86E-5 50-649 *Aunt Myrna* flown by 1st Lieutenant Walter R. Copeland in which he scored his sole MiG-15 victory, on 9 September 1952. The leading Sabre is F-86F-10-NA 51-2793 *Jackie's Jag* flown by 1st Lieutenant Julius Negler.

gear down, even if your engine quits right, now. You hear over the radio, 'Flights reforming and returning - the last MiGs chased back across the Yalu.' Everyone is checking in and a few scores are being discussed. The good news of no losses, the tension which gripped you before the battle, the wild fight and the g forces are now being felt. A tired yet elated feeling is overcoming you, although the day's work is not finished. Your engine finally flames out, but you have maintained forty thousand feet and are now but twenty miles from home. The usual radio calls are given and the pattern set up for a dead-stick landing. The tower calmly tells you that you are number three dead-stick over the field, but everything is ready for your entry. Planes in front of you continue to land in routine and uninterrupted precision, as everyone is low on fuel. Fortunately this time there are no battle damages to be crash landed. Your altitude is decreasing and gear is lowered. Hydraulic controls are still working beautifully on the pressure maintained by your windmilling engine. You pick your place in the pattern, land, coast to a stop and within seconds are tugged up the taxi strip to your revetment for a quick engine change.

'This mission is the type most enjoyed by the fighter pilot. It is a regular fighter sweep, with no worries about escort or providing cover for fighter-bombers. The mission had been well planned and well executed. Best of all, the MiGs had come forth for battle. Our separate flights had probably again confused the enemy radarscope readers and, to an extent, nullified that tremendous initial advantage which radar plotting and vectoring gives a fighter on first sighting the enemy. We had put the maximum number of aircraft into the target area at the most opportune time and we had sufficient fuel to fool the enemy. Our patrolling flights at strategic locations had intercepted split-off MiGs returning toward their sanctuary in at least two instances. One downed MiG had crashed in the middle of Sinuiju and another, after being shot up, had outrun our boys to the Yalu, where they had to break off pursuit. But they had the satisfaction of seeing the smoking MiG blow up in his own traffic pattern. Both instances undoubtedly did not aid the morale of the Reds.'

On 18 November 1951 four Sabre pilots sighted twelve MiG-15s in dispersals on Uiju airfield and while two of them provided top cover the other two, Captain Kenneth D. Chandler and Lieutenant Dayton W. Ragland, made a low-level strafing attack that destroyed four MiGs and damaged several others. Four MiGs were shot down in a major air action on 27 November, one of them by Major Richard D. Creighton, who became the fourth jet ace of the Korean War. In the afternoon of 30 November the biggest air combat success so far took place when 31 Sabres of the 4th FIW, led by Colonel Benjamin S. Preston, sighted a formation of twelve Tupolev Tu-2 bombers escorted by sixteen piston-engined La-9 fighters and sixteen MiG-15s heading for the island of Taehwado in the Yellow Sea, where ROK forces were fighting North Korean marines. Major George A. 'Curly' Davis Jr., CO 334th FIS and Major Winton W. 'Bones' Marshall CO, 335th FIS, became jet aces this day. Davis destroyed three of the bombers, damaged another and downed a MiG. Marshall shot one bomber down, damaged another and downed a La-9. All told, the Sabres destroyed eight Tu-2s, three La-9s and a MiG-15.

The 51st Wing's F-86E Sabres went into action on 1 December. On 2 and 4 December Sabre pilots claimed ten MiGs, two of them being claimed by 51st FIW pilots. 'Curly' Davis destroyed two more MiGs on 5 December. On the 13th he claimed another four MiGs - a Korean record - when the 4th FIW Sabres took on 145 MiG-15s in air battles along the Yalu and destroyed thirteen of them in a bitter engagement. Although MiG-15s continued to appear over North Korea in large numbers, they avoided combat below 30,000 feet. Just three more MiGs were destroyed by the end of December. One was claimed by the 4th FIW on 14 December and the other two by the 51st FIW on 15 and 28 December. A total of 28 MiGs were shot down in December for the loss of seven Sabres.

In January 1952 the Communists launched a New Year air offensive, sending as many as 200 MiGs across the Yalu at up to Mach 0.99 at any one time. Just five F-86s were lost in the air but during January-February 4th FIW F-86A Sabres downed only eleven MiGs, the Communists having raised their operational altitude to avoid battle with the F-86As which still mainly equipped the 4th FIW. The F-86Es of the 51st FIW meanwhile, could climb to 45,000 feet before engaging the enemy. They took on the MiGs on equal terms and shot down 36 aircraft during the same period for the loss of only two F-86s. One of them occurred on 10 February. Major George Davis Jr, who was the leading jet ace with twelve kills, was leading eighteen Sabres on an escort mission to the railway yards at Kumu-ri when he spotted a formation of MiGs at 32,000 feet closing on the fighter-bombers he was protecting.

Camera-gun footage of a MiG fighter going down in flames after an attack by a Sabre.

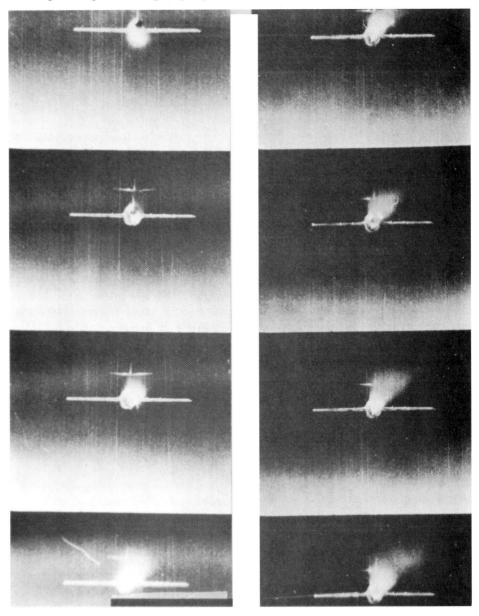

He turned to meet the threat, joined only by his wingman, intending to break up the attacking force before it could get among the bombers. Davis destroyed two of the MiGs to take his score to twelve victories and he was closing on a third when his Sabre was hit and it crashed into a mountainside near Tong-Đàng-Đông. Davis was awarded a posthumous Medal of Honor for his heroic action.

On 23 February Major William T. Whisner of the 51st FIW destroyed his fifth MiG to become the Wing's first ace and the seventh of the Korean War. Whisner, who commanded the 25th FIS 'Assam Dragons', had scored 15.5 confirmed victories in WWII.

Another reason for the dearth of 4th FIW victories during January-February was the lack of sufficient numbers of trained combat pilots to replace the experienced 4th FIW career pilots, many of whom had by now been rotated home after one hundred missions. The situation only improved in March when increased serviceability permitted more combat operations and the Sabre Wings began to receive young fighter pilots fresh from training in the US. By now FEAF had 165 Sabres in the Far East and 127 of these were available for combat in Korea but a lack of spares and poor maintenance grounded many Sabres. On average 45% of the Sabres were unserviceable, 16.6% because of lack of spares and 25.9% because of maintenance problems. Supplies of external fuel tanks were in very short supply and Sabre pilots were forced to fly combat patrols with only one tank. Further supplies of fuel tanks were flown to the combat area direct from the contractors in the USA but in February, the 4th and 51st FIWs had to reduce their combat sorties to a minimum. Air Materiel Command launched a crash program called 'Peter Rabbit' to raise stocks of spares to an acceptable level and by April 1952 the unserviceability rate for lack of spares was down to 2.4%.

In March 1952 the Sabre formations now entered the combat area stacked down from 40,000 feet to obtain a better chance of engaging the MiG-15s and pilots claimed thirty-nine MiGs for the loss of only three Sabres and two F-84s. April was even better, with 44 MiGs claimed destroyed for the loss of four F-86s and one F-80 although the total would have been higher if the American pilots had been allowed to cross the Yalu into Manchuria. Instead, they were restricted to making strafing and bombing attacks on Communist airfields south of the Yalu. On 22 April Captain Iven C. 'Kinch' Kincheloe, 25th FIS, 51st FIW, who had become an ace on 6 April and Major Elmer W. Harris, destroyed two Yak-9s at Sinuiju airfield in strafing runs. They returned on 4 May to strafe 24 Yak-9s and five were destroyed in the attack, Kincheloe accounting for three of them.[22]

Captain James Jabara had begun to think he was never going to get his fifth MiG. He had got his fourth on 22 April 1952 but the pickings had been pretty lean since that time. 'Then, about five o'clock in the afternoon of 20 May, fourteen of our F-86 Sabres from the 4th Fighter Interceptor Group were jumped by fifty Commie jets over Sinuiju, near the Yalu River. I was in the second wave of fourteen. I tacked on to the three MiGs at 35,000 feet, picked out the last one and bored straight in. My first two bursts ripped up his fuselage and left wing. At about 10,000 feet the pilot bailed out. It was a good thing he did because the MiG disintegrated. Then I climbed back to 20,000 feet to get back into the battle. I bounced six more MiGs. I closed in and got off two bursts into one of them, scoring heavily both times. He began to smoke. Then when my second burst caught him square in the middle he burst into flames and fell into an uncontrolled spin. All I could see was a whirl of fire. I had to break off then because there was another MiG on my tail. That was my bag for the day and it made me feel pretty good to know that I was the first jet ace in the history of aerial warfare.

'We fight a private little war up in MiG Alley - maybe the first time in history that two fighter outfits have engaged in such a peculiar type of warfare. On our side of the Yalu River is the 4th Fighter Interceptor Wing. On the other side are the Red MiG-15s. The capabilities and general characteristics of the two airplanes are just about the same. The battle tactics of

Lieutenant Kermit Keeley pilot of *My Darling Patricia*, 36th FBS 'Flying Friends', K-13, was in Korea from April 1953 until December that year and flew 73 combat missions.

the enemy are quite similar to our own. And he holds many advantages which I'll discuss later in some detail. Here's where the puzzle comes in. We've knocked down or damaged several score of MiGs - exactly how many I honestly don't know. We've lost exactly one of our planes to enemy action and one from causes unknown. We're not magicians. We're just average fighter pilots with some previous combat time, sound tactical training and a little patience to wait for the other guy to make a mistake. But the score is lopsided and I guess the enemy is wondering why. I'm not going to tell him, except in general terms, for this test between the best jet planes in the world is only in its first phase. The end isn't in sight yet and the score could change. But I don't believe it will.

'We're in Korea for one main reason - I'm speaking of the F-86 Sabre jets. That's to shoot down as many MiGs as we can, to help retain air superiority for our side and protect our battling ground troops from enemy air attacks. But there are a few ground rules in this private war of ours. We have to go up to their ball park - MiG Alley, in far north-western Korea, near the Yalu River that splits North Korea and Manchuria - or the enemy won't play. That means a one-way trip of 250 miles or more, depending on where we're based. That's a lot of distance, measured in jet fuel. And any fan can tell you the home team has a big advantage.

'While we're burning up a third of our fuel on the trip to MiG Alley, we have to save the amount to get home again. That leaves us a third to stay in the area, hunt for the enemy and fight him. Dogfights really eat up fuel, whether you're diving, climbing, or just manoeuvring at high speed. And we have all the normal worries: 'flame-outs' (engine failures), weather and surprise by an enemy who knows when we're on our way through his early-warning radar or GCI (Ground-Controlled Intercept).

'He has all these advantages, plus the fact that he almost never fights more than fifty miles from his base. He is near friendly territory in case he gets shot down or bails out and he can cruise at high speeds at all times, with no extra fuel tanks to slow him down. But the

The Torii Gate (a traditional Japanese gate most commonly found at the entrance of or within a Shinto shrine, where it symbolically marks the transition from the profane to the sacred) leading to the Sabre flight line at Kimpo Air Base (K-14). Under orders from their leaders and limited by the range of their aircraft, MiG-15 pilots rarely flew south of Sinanju or the Chunchon River. These limitations created the boundaries of 'MiG Alley.'

biggest ground rule of all is his sanctuary in Manchuria, across the Yalu River, where he can run any time the fight gets too hot for comfort. The traffic light changes to red the minute he darts across the river and it never changes to green no matter how long we wait. Our Sabre is a shade faster, but not enough to make a big difference. Sometimes I've wished it had a little more speed. We can out-dive the MiG at any altitude. The radius of turn is about the same, but we seem to execute it with more finesse. The MiG has a slight superiority in rate of climb and heavier firepower, with its three cannon. Fortunately they don't seem to be able to hit us with it. Note please that I say heavy firepower - not rate of fire. In general characteristics, the planes are similar and both damn good. It's hard to tell one from the other in our 600 mph plus dogfights and we have to use R/T (radio telephone) and code words to maintain air discipline.

'The Sabre is slightly larger and heavier and carries six .50-calibre forward-firing machine guns with a total of 1,800 rounds of ammo. The MiG carries one 36mm cannon and two of either 20 or 23mm. When the calibre of a gun increases, the rate of fire usually decreases. Maybe that's one reason the MiGs haven't been able to hit us. But the puffs of smoke from their guns scare the hell out of me. The MiG is rugged, make no mistake. It can soak up a lot of battle damage. I still don't know why some of the planes I damaged didn't go down. I could see the armour-piercing phosphorus-loaded incendiary bullets sparkle on impact as they hit the wings and fuselages. I guess it's almost as rugged as our Sabre and next to the Sabre I would rather fly the MiG than any other fighter.

'I can't get too technical about tactics, for the game is still going on and the team that gives away its signals doesn't usually win. But I can discuss a few general points, especially what we've learned from their tactics. Early in the air war - we were fighting the MiGs back in December - they would split up into elements of single planes, unprotected and generally at our mercy. Maybe they had no planned tactics, for they were certainly easy pickings. Now they generally stick closer together and we have to bounce twos instead of singles - unless they get panicky and forget the direction of their Manchurian sanctuary. If desperate they loop, roll and split S. When we're fighting on the deck, they frequently try to lure us across the North Korean flak areas hoping their ground gunners will pick us off like geese on the wing. That's an old Luftwaffe trick I learned to avoid while flying two tours in P-51s in Europe with the Eighth and Ninth Air Forces.

'At times we see the MiGs pulling vapour trails. Then they duck below the contrail level and we can't see them. They hope we think they've left the area. Actually they're waiting to bounce us. We haven't fallen for that trick so far and I can tell them now we don't intend to.

'The escort work we've done for FEAF Bomber Command B-29s has presented tough problems in tactics, as on 12 April, when there were more than 225 planes, friendly and enemy, in the air at one time. The Superforts were levelling their demolition bombs on the important rail bridge at Sinuiju on the North Korean side to slow down Red resupply. That day the MiGs showed that they are more aggressive against B-29 formations than against

Ground personnel attaching a fuel tank to the wing of a SAAF Sabre.

fighters. We were at a disadvantage because of slowing down for proper escort. By the time we drop our external tanks and get up speed, a MiG can be roaring through the bomber formation with his cannons blazing. We counter this by keeping four plane elements together and take our chances on superior gunnery. The MiGs feint, hoping we'll follow and leave the bombers unprotected. We stick. And shoot. In that 12 April battle our F-86s, plus escorting F-84s and the B-29 gunners, got eight MiGs for sure, probably destroyed seven and damaged eighteen. We lost some Superforts but no fighters.

'We had good air discipline in that fight and flew a good solid formation. The wing men protected the element leaders who did the firing. The enemy made mistakes and we capitalized on them. We only had seconds to do this, so we moved fast. But the tactics when we're escorting B-29s aren't exactly typical.

'Consider a fighter vs. fighter mission. We take off in four-plane formations and enter the target area, maybe thirty minutes later. We patrol MiG Alley, the Yalu River area. The enemy spots our calling card on his GCI and can bounce us first. He initiates the bounce about 70 percent of the time and our tactics naturally evolve around this fact. We try to spot the MiG and anticipate his actions. Fortunately our group commander, Colonel John C. Meyer[23] and my squadron commander, Lieutenant Colonel Glen T. Eagleston, are a couple of the shrewdest fighter-pilot tacticians in the world. They figure out our tactics for us and we stay alive by following orders.

'We drop our extra fuel tanks as we sight the MiGs so we can gain speeds almost up to Mach one. Then we manoeuvre to get into firing position. After all a fighter is simply an airborne gun platform. The pilot must turn, dive and climb to get into position to fire. At the same time he has to watch for other planes, both his own and the enemy's.

'The fight usually starts at 35,000 to 40,000 feet. It can wind up fifty feet above the ground. If the MiGs strike first and we're not in firing position, we break hard to the left or the right and down, so we can manoeuvre for a better position. A wing man covers each element leader. The wing man doesn't fire unless he has specific instructions, or gets separated. It's a tough assignment and as far as I'm concerned half my victories should go to good wing men like Lieutenants Gill Garrett, Roy McLain, Bill Yancey (who also has done some fine shooting himself while flying element leader) and Dick Becker.

'When I'm concentrating on my sights, trying to handle the Sabre smoothly and following the enemy's gyrations, I don't have time to look around and protect myself. The wing man acts as an extra set of eyes for me. He watches for MiGs and friendly planes and gives me radio warnings or signals. To me he's worth his weight in .50-caliber ammo if we're outnumbered, or the fighting gets too rough, then we manoeuvre around and wait for the enemy to make a mistake. Thank God he makes more than his share of them. Like the one he made in the big scrap on 12 April. I was at 25,000 feet and he was 5,000 feet beneath me,

Joe McConnell of the 51st Fighter Squadron, 20th Fighter Group taking off in *Beauteous Butch*.

Lieutenant Colonel George A. Davis.

Lieutenant Colonel Bruce Hinton, CO, 336th FIS, 4th FIW.

heading for the B-29s. That advantage in altitude was my break and I used it to get speed. I caught him just as he was in range of the B-29s. The bullets saddle-stitched his fuselage, but he went into loops and rolls. He was badly crippled. Another burst got his engine and I saw him crash trying to leg it across the Yalu.

'The numerical odds were against us on 22 April when our twelve Sabres were out-numbered three to one. With Captain Norbert W. Chalwick flying protection for me, I took my time about getting behind a couple of MiGs and hit them both with short bursts. I had to pop my dive brakes to keep from running into one. I was still firing as he rolled on his back. I followed him down but I didn't realize how close to the ground I was until he crashed. I had a hell of a time pulling out of my dive. The cockpit dial showed nine gs before I blacked out. Fortunately my eyes focused in about three seconds and by instinct, I guess, I was headed upward.

'That was my fourth kill. The first one was on 3 April, when Becker was flying wing man. We were two against two. We saw the MiGs first at 7,000 feet and I used 1,200 rounds, damaging the engine of one MiG that flamed out and crashed about ten miles from its home field. I damaged the other.

'On 10 April we were MiG hunting again in the Alley. We let down from 36,000 feet through the undercast and broke out in the clear at 10,000. We saw six of them at 5,000 and bounced them from the seven o'clock position. Four of the MiGs broke up into the overcast and two broke down toward the ground. They just shouldn't have done it. I took after them. The leader scampered away, leaving his wing man wide open. After three Lufberys (360-degree turns) I scored hits on the wing man. I used up my 1,800 rounds of ammo but stayed with the MiG for about thirty seconds, meanwhile radioing my wing man, Lieutenant Otis Gordon, to start shooting. This proved unnecessary, as the enemy pilot suddenly bailed out about thirty miles south of Sinuiju. I was flying almost at the

Lieutenant Colonel George Inkerman 'Shakey' Ruddell (right), CO, 39th FIS at K-13 on 18 May 1953 after becoming the 30th ace of the Korean War. Ruddell ended the war with 8 victories. (via Larry Davis)

speed of sound and couldn't see much, but he had a light blue parachute, black helmet and light grey oxygen mask.

'All of us would like to know who's actually flying the MiGs. It's good bull-session material, especially after a mission. The consensus is that the enemy has two teams. The first team, a lot of people think, is made up of highly-trained Communists and ex-Luftwaffe pilots. The second stringers are Chinese and possibly North Koreans. To me they're all tough. The best ones are aggressive, they can manoeuvre the MiG and they usually know what to do in case of trouble.

'I learned some lessons early in the game in MiG Alley. I flew seven missions between December 23 and January 2 and didn't get a crack at the enemy until the fifth one, when I bagged a probable kill. I was flying Lieutenant Commander Paul E. Pugh's wing (he's a Navy pilot flying with us on the inter-service exchange programme and has two victories over the MiGs). He took out after the leader of a flight of four. An enemy plane got on Pugh's tail and I radioed him to break as he was being attacked from six o'clock. I didn't know it until later, but his radio receiver wasn't working. The fight had gone down from 35,000 to 1,500 feet. There was nothing to do but try to get the MiG off Pugh's tail. I started shooting from 1,500 and had plenty of strikes on the wings and tail section by the time we reached 800, with the enemy making no evasive manoeuvres. Suddenly he did a split S. Two MiGs were after me from the stern position and I couldn't watch the crippled plane any longer. I almost laid myself wide open and never made the same mistake again.

'What does all this add up to? To me, we've come a long way and done a lot of good in the Korean air war since being alerted back to New Castle, Delaware, last November. We've done our bit to keep enemy air off the backs of our ground troops.

F-86As of the 4th FIW at Suwon in June 1951.

F-86A-5 49-1272 *Wham Bam,* flown by Lieutenant Martin Bambrick and F-86E-10 51-2769 *Bernie's Bo* (with two kill markings), of the 335th FIS, 4th FIW, were photographed at K-14 Kimpo. Bambrick destroyed a MiG while flying *Wham Bam* on 4 September 1952. *Bernie's Bo* was flown by Captain Robert J. Love (later the 11th jet ace of the war with 6 kills) and subsequently by Captain Clifford D. Jolley (7 kills), who had to eject from the aircraft on 4 July 1952. (via Robert Jackson)

'I'm glad to be in combat again. I like to fly jets at high speeds, although it takes something out of a guy - even at twenty-seven! I don't get nervous anymore. I outgrew that in the last war. But the strain is greater now because of the high speeds, split-second timing and the fact that the Sabres and MiGs look alike. To me fighting for thirty minutes in the F-86 is equivalent to ten times that in an F-51. We have good equipment, superior leadership and training and I know our pilots are better than theirs, whomsoever they may be. As Colonel Meyer says, the nucleus of our wing is composed of the champions of the greatest air battles of history - between the US and Germans in World War II. There are at least eleven aces among us and our wing had the highest score in the last war, 1016 enemy planes destroyed. Colonel Meyer says we're the champs of that war and I guess that applies to this one, too. At least the score thus far would indicate as much.'

Others who became aces in April 1952 were Captains Robert H. Moore and Robert J. Love and Major Bill Wescott. In May Captain Robert T. 'Cowboy' Latshaw, Major Donald E. 'Bunny' Adams, Lieutenant James H. Kasler and Colonel Harrison R. Thyng also became aces and James Kasler later increased his score to six. On 13 May 4th FIW Sabres, each carrying two 1,000lb bombs below their wings, made their first dive-bombing attack on Sinuiju. In another attack, on the railway yards at Kumu-ri, Colonel Walker H. 'Bud' Mahurin, 4th FIW CO, was shot down by flak and taken prisoner. (This was the second time in his career that Mahurin had been shot down, the first being on 27 March 1944, when he managed to evade capture. Flying P-47s in the 63rd Fighter Squadron, 56th Fighter Group, he was credited with nineteen and three quarters German aircraft destroyed and he also shot down a Japanese bomber in the Pacific). Mahurin was credited with three and a half MiGs, one probable and one damaged, at the time of his capture in Korea. He was not released until September 1953.

On 14 May on his first encounter with an enemy aircraft, Lieutenant Edwin 'Buzz' Aldrin of the 51st FIW shot down a MiG. (He ended his tour with 66 missions after shooting down another aircraft and damaging a third. In the late 1950s Aldrin became an astronaut

Captain Bruce Cunningham of the 335th FIS, 4th Fighter Wing in 1951.

Lieutenant Edwin Eugene 'Buzz' Aldrin of the 51st FIS. Born 20 January 1930, he was commissioned as a Second Lieutenant in the USAF and flew sixty-six combat missions in F-86 Sabres, shooting down two MiG-15 aircraft. The 8 June 1953 issue of *Life* magazine featured gun camera photos taken by Aldrin of one of the Soviet pilots ejecting from his damaged aircraft. Second person to walk on the Moon, he was the Lunar Module Pilot on Apollo 11, the first manned lunar landing in history. He set foot on the Moon on 21 July 1969 following mission commander Neil Armstrong.

and on 20 July 1969 Buzz became the second man after Neil Armstrong to walk on the surface of the moon in the climax to the Apollo 11 lunar landing). In May 1952 the enemy lost 27 MiGs while the Americans lost five Sabres, three F-84s and one F-51 in combat during a record 5,190 sorties. This total was unsurpassed by the time hostilities ended.

Though an expansion programme had been under way to increase Sabre strength from the five Wings on hand in June 1951, due to the time it took to increase production just seven Sabre Wings were active in June 1952. Only two of these were allotted to Korea because of USAF commitments but early in June, the 51st FIW was strengthened with the arrival, of the 39th FIS, 18th FIW, which was equipped with the latest F-86F model. The new fighter showed considerable improvement over the E model. Sabre pilots had reported that intermittent opening of wing slats on the F-86E caused them gun-sighting problems during combat. The wing slats were omitted on the F-86F version and a new wing leading edge, extended by 9 inches, was added to improve manoeuvrability at high altitudes. In June, Sabre pilots claimed twenty MiGs destroyed for the loss of three F-86s. Lieutenant James F. Low of the 4th FIW became an ace during the month. On 4 July fifty MiGs crossed the Yalu and UN pilots claimed thirteen destroyed for the loss of two Sabres. That month nineteen MiGs were shot down while four Sabres failed to return. Captain Clifford D. Jolley, 335th FIS, 4th FIW shot down a MiG-15 on the 8th to take his score to five. In August, thirty-five MiGs were shot down, including six, which were destroyed in a battle between thirty-five Sabres and fifty-two MiGs on the 6th.

In September 1952 the 335th FIS, 4th FIW received F-86Fs to replace the F-86Es. One of the heaviest battles of the year took place on 4 September when thirteen MiGs were shot down in seventeen separate air battles for the loss of four Sabres. Captain Frederick C. 'Boots' Blesse of the 334th FIS, 4th FIW destroyed one of the MiGs to become an ace. He notched a further four victories before the end of the month and one more in October to take his score to ten confirmed victories. On 9 September, F-84s attacked the North Korean

Military Academy at Sakchu and some of the 175 MiGs broke through the Sabre screen and shot down three fighter-bombers. Two more Thunderjets and six Sabres were destroyed in air combat during the rest of the month but the UN pilots claimed a record total of 63 MiGs. On 21 September Captain Robinson Risner destroyed his fifth MiG near Sinuiju to become the Korean War's twentieth jet ace. The heavy losses made the communist pilots more cautious during October. Sabres destroyed twenty-seven MiGs for the loss of four F-86s and one Thunderjet. In November only the more experienced MiG pilots dived down from the safety of numbers at 40,000 feet to take on the American formations. On occasions, smaller formations of up to 24 MiGs took on flights of four Sabres and tried to box them in. The Americans responded by increasing the flights to six or eight, with the higher-performance F-86Fs operating at 40,000 feet covering the more vulnerable F-86Es at lower altitudes. The new tactics worked, for only four Sabres were lost in combat while 28 MiGs were destroyed in the air.

In November 1952 three more Sabre pilots - Colonel Royal N. 'The King' Baker CO, 4th FIW, Captain Leonard W. Lilley of the 334th FIS, 4th FIW and Captain Cecil G. Foster of the 16th FIS, 51st FIW became aces during the month. In December 1952 MiG pilots ignored the Sabre screen and headed south to the Chongchon River where they ambushed Sabres returning home short of fuel. At least four Sabre pilots had to bail out when their fuel was exhausted but only two F-86s were lost in air combat that month, while UN pilots claimed twenty-eight MiGs.

In 1952 UN pilots included a small number of RAAF and RAF jet pilots who were specially chosen to fly the F-86 Sabre. Twenty-one pilots operated with USAF fighter squadrons. Foremost among them was fifty-five-year old Wing Commander John Robert 'Johnny' Baldwin DSO* DFC* AFC from the Central Fighter Establishment at West Raynham who had been posted on attachment to the USAF in early 1952. In

Lieutenant Colonel Vermont 'Pappy' Garrison was a career officer in the USAF and an ace with 17.33 credited victories in aerial combat. He was one of only seven Americans to achieve ace status during WWII, then again against jet fighter opposition during the Korean War. In 1966 Garrison participated in his third war, as vice commander of the 8th TFW and flew a tour of bombing and fighter missions over North Việtnam. During all three of his combat tours, Garrison was consistently older than his peers, becoming an ace in WWII at the age of twenty-eight, in Korea at the age of thirty-seven and flying 'Rolling Thunder' missions at the age of fifty-one.

Lieutenant Colonel Glenn T. Eagleston. He scored eleven and a half kills in WWII flying Mustangs. In Korea he flew 84 missions and commanded the 4th FIW. He destroyed two MiG-15s. On 22 December 1950 he downed a MiG-15 over the Yalu. On 22 April 1951, a day of very heavy aerial combat (Jabara claimed four), Eagleston shot down his second MiG. It was his last aerial victory, in a fighter pilot career that had spanned ten years, two aircraft types and two continents.

World War II he was credited with fifteen and one shared aerial victories destroyed, four damaged and five damaged on the ground as well as many ground vehicles. Flying F-86 Sabres with the 16th Squadron of the 51st Fighter Interceptor Wing, he had flown eight sorties by 15 March, when he failed to return from a weather reconnaissance in the Sariwon area.[24] After this the USAF demanded that CFE pilots should be properly trained in the United States. In addition to the twenty-one RAF pilots who operated with USAF fighter squadrons, Twenty-nine RAF pilots served on 77 Squadron RAAF. Five MiG-15s were confirmed shot down by five RAF pilots. Ten RAF pilots were lost flying while attached to the USAF and RAAF. One RAF pilot was lost flying with the FAA.

In May 1952 Flight Lieutenant Swifte, an Australian serving with the UN forces, was jumped by MiGs over Chongchon and his jet was shot down in flames. Swifte floated down. As he neared the ground he heard a rattle of fire and the whine of bullets. He hit the rocky ground on the side of a hill and rolled into the undergrowth. After releasing the harness, he got to his feet and moved in a crouching run to the other side of the valley from where the shots had come. The flight leader reported to Ops Control that Swifte was down safely and supplied the map reference. Then he warned the controller that he and the other members of his flight were running out of fuel and would have to turn for home within the next four minutes. Control told him: 'Baker Flight now approaching your position.' At this point, six piston-engined fighters from Dumbo's escort flight arrived on the scene, flashing low over the hills and a further formation of Sabres was coming in from 'MiG Alley'.

'Green Six to Able Leader.'

Swifte, crouching behind an outcrop near the base of the hill, was using his small armpit radio. Able Leader answered him.

Swifte described his position and warned him about the presence of enemy troops.

The F-86F-35-NA had the capability of carrying a 1,200lb Mk 12 'special store' or atomic bomb with a yield of up to 12 kT under the port wing, while drop tanks were attached under the starboard wing. Conventional weapons that could be carried included a pair of 1,000lb or smaller bombs, two 750lb napalm tanks, or eight 5-inch HVAR rockets.

'Some fired on me as I landed.'

The flight came low over the area and climbed away so as not to draw attention to Swifte's hide-out. Some of the pilots saw troops moving across the hillside towards the spot where he had landed.

Meanwhile, a US helicopter had taken off from a forward base and was moving north under cover of six fighters. The distance to be covered was at extreme helicopter range and a second helicopter was standing by, ready to follow at a moment's notice. If events made it necessary, it would take off and rendezvous at a point over the sea in Korea Bay, where the first helicopter carrying the rescued pilot would ditch. The second helicopter would then hoist up the crew and the pilot and bring them back to base.

The second flight of Sabres appeared in the distance now and Able Flight banked steeply in their turn for home. Swifte watched them go, their noses gently dipping, their silver canopies shining in the sun. He knew that they had over-stayed their limit and that most of them would 'flame out' before they reached base, meaning they would have to cover the last fifty miles and make their approach and landing without power. It was eight minutes since Swifte's plane had been shot down and presently the helicopter came on the air. Baker Leader, who had located Swifte, gave the American pilot the map position and warned him to expect enemy ground fire. Then he led his Sabres in on a strafing run to keep the Communists pinned down. The chopper came in from across the sea, preceded by six escort fighters. They flashed in low with their guns churning up the ground on both sides of the hill. The helicopter came quickly over the hills and set down gently on a flat spot at the bottom of the slope. Swifte stepped from behind the boulders and ran full tilt towards it, as the enemy troops opened fire. Dumbo's six piston-engined fighters made their run one at a time, their guns blasting, at the same time as the Sabres attacked the troop positions. Swifte reached the helicopter and was pulled

Captain Lonnie R. Moore, 335th FIS, 4th Fighter Wing, Korea 1953 who flew 54 combat missions in Martin B-26 Marauders during WWII and who in the Korean War, downed ten MiG-15s and one probable. He was killed in the crash of a new fighter type at Eglin AFB, Florida, at the age of thirty five.

James 'Jabby' Jabara flew two tours of combat duty in Europe during WWII as a P-51 Mustang pilot and scored 1.5 air victories. He achieved his first confirmed air victory of the war on 3 April 1951. A month later he scored his fifth and sixth victories, making him the first American jet ace in history. He eventually scored 15 victories, giving him the title of 'triple ace'. Jabara was ranked as the second-highest-scoring US ace of the Korean War.

Sabre gun camera footage of a MiG 15 being pursued over Korea.

aboard and a second later the chopper was off again, its great blades whirling, lifting off, lurching forward as it cleared the hills and swept away seawards. Baker Leader reported back to Ops Control and the show was over. The rattle of guns in the air and on the ground ceased. The chatter on the radio subsided to routine exchanges. The helicopter carrying Swifte, with its umbrella of fighters, moved south-west over the sea, then swung south towards the UN air-base and safety. Swifte was one of the fortunate pilots who survived being shot down in North Korea. Others were not so lucky - over 1,000 pilots, most of them Americans, were to die in that remote country. Whether they played a decisive role in ending the war is difficult to determine. Certainly the jet gave both sides immense striking power, but, just as in World War II, the ground forces and civilian population demonstrated that they could withstand this new and terrible weapon. Partly, of course, it was the rugged terrain which blunted the edge of the air-strikes. In such inhospitable country, it was impossible to come to grips with the enemy - a situation which was to be repeated in Viêtnam.

Late in 1952 Group Captain R. J. F. 'Dickie' Dickinson AFC was among another 'batch' of experienced RAF jet pilots to serve with the USAF Sabre wings. 'Volunteers were called from experienced day fighter pilots in RAF Fighter Command then filtered down to a number agreed with the USAF. Air Marshal Sir Basil Embry at HQ Fighter Command then interviewed the selected pilots in November 1952, before flying out to Nellis AFB in January 1953. The RAF did not have a suitable fighter at that time to match the MiG 15. Magnificent though the Meteor F.8 was, it could not cope with high Mach numbers and the very high ceiling of the MiG. In February 1953 a small group of pilots and I commenced a very intensive six weeks conversion to the F-86E: dog-fighting - tail chasing - formation flying - dive bombing - rocketing - air-to-air flag firing - night flying - and simulated sweeps of four aircraft, the latter with experienced bouncers. The staff pilots on all these training sorties were all highly experienced and most had completed 100 missions on F-86s in Korea. They were all very good and put us though our paces. After completion of the course it was off to Japan, where we were allocated to our future squadrons in Korea. I was posted to the

Right: Captain Kenneth D. Critchfield of Fort Madison, Iowa mounting 54-2321.

Below: Lieutenant 'Buzz' Aldrin of the 16th Fighter Squadron, 51st Fighter Wing with a Pluto cartoon denoting the first of his two MiG kills during the Korean War.

25th FIS at Suwon where there were already two RAF pilots - Flight Lieutenant Jock Maitland and Flight Lieutenant John Lovell. On arrival, we were made very welcome and commenced our introductory flying programme before being let loose on Yalu sweeps. Amongst my mentors for my first few sorties were Lovell and Maitland who gave me an excellent initiation into the local inhospitable terrain as well as more dog-fighting, tail chasing and sticking in as a wingman through every type of manoeuvre.

'The prime purposes of the F-86 were to maintain air superiority over the Korea peninsula and to destroy as many MiG-15s as possible in aerial combat. Air superiority involved escorting ground-attack and recce aircraft. My first Yalu sweep was on 13 May, involving 48 Sabres, but no MiGs sighted in our sector. This was repeated on 15 May, but although many MiGs sighted they were all well to the east of our area and flying above 50,000 feet so no contact was made. Things were to change on 16 May; another Yalu sweep was planned. I was to fly No.2 to Jock Maitland; we were part of 24 aircraft from our Squadron. We climbed up to 35,000 feet and toggled off our drop tanks - which we did on every mission. As we got to about fifty miles from the Yalu we checked our guns. My guns worked but my gunsight was u/s. I had a quiet word with Jock who said he had fuel feed problems and in view of this we were going to abort and return to base. He then called a 'turnabout left'. When we had passed through 90° I saw four MiGs barrelling down on us

Formation of F-86s of the 51st FIW peeling away over Korea in 1952.

from 8 o'clock high. I immediately called 'break left'. As I did this I saw three of the MiGs shoot past my tail unable to hold the turn, but the fourth MiG pulling like hell managed to get almost between Jock and myself. I thought he was going to collide with me so I slapped out my airbrakes and throttled back. By this time the MiG was filling my windscreen at about 50 yards. I pulled my trigger - still no gunsight but fired up his tailpipe aiming on my tracer. I got a number of hits upon which he broke hard left and dived steeply in a left spiral. I followed him down still firing. I was so stunned by everything that had happened in seconds that I failed to tell my leader what was happening and advising him to come out of his turn and cover me.

'Whilst still firing at the MiG who by now was really smoking, I heard Jock call me to break left as there was a MiG firing at me. I then broke off my attack and turned hard left. A quick look all around confirmed there was no MiG behind me and that I was alone. My MiG was still spiralling down vertically still smoking heavily. By chance I saw Jock orbiting to the south of me 10,000 feet above. I joined up with him and we returned to Suwon. On our debrief Jock quite rightly chewed me up for not keeping him informed and at the same time told me that after he had seen me disappear down, he thought it was a MiG on my tail whilst in fact it was me on the MiG's tail! I learnt my lesson from that engagement. In a lame excuse it was the first MiG I had ever seen close up - so nearly a disastrous mid-air collision and a lost opportunity to get a positive kill. I was credited with a probable.

'I only fired my guns twice more in anger; once when flying wingman to my Squadron Commander Major Giraudo. He was chasing a MiG about 1,500 yards ahead when two MiGs at 7 o'clock high bounced us. I called a break left, but no reaction from my boss. I could see the lead MiG firing and his 37mm cannon shells streaking towards my leader like flaming red tennis balls. He then switched over to me. I broke hard left then reversed on the MiG as he dived down and back to the Yalu River. I opened fire and got in a long burst but he was by now out of range.

'On 18 June I was briefed to fly No. 3 in a formation of four aircraft led by Colonel Robert P. Baldwin, our Group Commander. My No.2 had to abort on the R/W so the boss said, 'Okay let's go as a three.' We climbed up through cloud and then descended back though cloud to 20,000 feet over the Yalu. As we came out into the clear I saw two MiGs right behind us at about 1,000 yards. I called break left and one MiG flew past my tail and another followed my leader in a very hard turn. I managed to get on his tail and started firing. He turned on to a North heading before straightening out and starting to burn. My leader was then covering me. I fired every round in my aircraft; the MiG started to spiral down and crashed near Oick-Tong. This was the last time I fired my guns in anger. I was credited with a kill.

'The next three weeks I was involved in escorting F-84s on interdiction missions

Colonel Walker Melville 'Bud' Mahurin was the first American pilot to become a double ace in the ETO in WWII and the only US Air Force pilot to shoot down enemy planes in both the European and Pacific Theatres and the Korean War. He was credited with 20.75 aerial victories in WWII, making him the sixth-highest American P-47 ace, and was credited with shooting down 3.5 MiG-15s in Korea, giving him a total of 24.25 aircraft destroyed in aerial combat.

Colonel John C. Meyer was the fourth highest scoring American ace in Europe with twenty four confirmed air-to-air victories and thirteen destroyed on the ground. In August 1950 he assumed command of the 4th Fighter Wing and in Korea he destroyed two MiG-15 aircraft, bringing his total of enemy aircraft destroyed (air and ground) to 39½.

and US Navy Banshees on photo sorties. On 15 July I was detailed to lead four aircraft on a low-level recce mission of the Antung MiG airfield complex at 1,500 feet. We flew up the west coast at 40,000 feet until over the mouth of the Yalu, then put our noses down in 'Finger Four' formation at about .95 Mach arriving near Antung doing over 600 knots. I had staggered my four at varying heights to avoid the flak, which was intense. I had binoculars round my neck to look out for new revetments on some of the airfields planned to receive Il-28 light bombers. Lieutenant Aaron, my wingman, was getting rather excited calling out very accurate flak near Taku-Shan. I then turned slightly right. As I did this everything turned black followed by a very loud bang after which my aircraft turned on its back. I then realised my wingman had hit me as he was trying to cross under me. My aircraft decelerated from 610 knots to 180 knots but still continued to fly. I saw my wingman climbing away and disappear heading south. (Aaron got back home with a missing tailplane). My 3 and 4 had to return to base because of fuel shortage. My mayday had brought a few sympathetic calls of good luck etc. To my surprise, my aircraft continued to fly although it would go no faster than 175 knots at full throttle. As I crossed the coast still with no MiGs around and no flak I made preparations to eject. I knew there was a small island (Pyongyang-Đo) about fifty miles to the south west so I plodded down the coast well out to sea. After a while I saw the Island with its long beach and which I knew was manned by US Marines.

'I once again prepared to eject but my aircraft still handled okay and the engine kept going. To cut a long story short, I managed a successful wheels-down on the hard sand. As I came to a stop, a few Marines emerged from dugouts near the beach and greeted me. I was returned to Suwon by light aircraft the next day and back on ops the day after. My wingman had returned safely without knowing he had lost half a tail plane. The war ended on 27 July, twelve days after this incident, so I suppose I was very fortunate in not ending up in a North Korean PoW Camp.

'I believe it is worth recalling that I was leading eight Sabres on 12 August (after the war) up the west coast of Korea on an early morning mission, well out to sea, when we were recalled because of bad weather approaching our base. On arrival overhead it was obvious that Suwon was weathered out and that we had no diversions. I had advised the operations staff that this might happen, but was firmly told to get airborne. After an abortive approach to Suwon I climbed back through terrible weather and rejoined the rest of my formation whom I had left at altitude and carted them off to Pyongyang-Đo Island where all except my wingman who had damaged his undercarriage, completed successful wheels-down landings on the beach. A Dakota flew up that afternoon with fuel and ground crew and we all flew back to Suwon the next day with the exception of my No. 2 who returned in the Dakota.

'At the same time as this drama was unfolding, Jock Maitland was leading eight Sabres on a similar mission up the east coast of Korea and was faced with an identical problem. After the weather recall he saw a small gap in the clouds with an airstrip visible. He dived his formation and under very heavy rain landed them all safely on a South Korean airfield with no damage other than some aircraft sliding off the end of the runway.

'Another interesting mission took place after the war on 28 August, when I was included in a twelve aircraft escort for two Banshee recce aircraft to photograph some Soviet airfields close to Vladivostok. We put on 200-gallon drop tanks and joined up with the two recce aircraft and headed across Korea to the East Coast then up to Vladivostok at altitude. The Banshees dropped into 1,000 yard lines astern at about 25,000 feet for the photo run and we flew Top Cover at 35,000 feet. We expected swarms of MiGs and possibly flak but surprisingly saw neither. The mission was of course completed out to sea and took 2¼ hours.

'The Sabre was a truly magnificent aircraft and a delight to fly. Sitting up in that excellently positioned cockpit, I felt I was king of the castle and would survive in any situation and perhaps immodestly get a few more MiGs if the war had continued a little

Top right: Major (later lieutenant colonel) John Franklin Bolt USMC in the cockpit of *Darling Dottie*, named after his wife Dorothy E. Wiggins. He remains the only US Marine to achieve ace status in two wars and was also the only Marine jet fighter ace. He scored six victories during fights along the northern border of North Korea, commonly known as 'MiG Alley,' giving him a total of 12 victories over his career.

Left: 2nd Lieutenant Philip A. Redpath of 335th FIS 4th Fighter Wing, Korea, 1953.

Centre left: 1st Lieutenant Lloyd Irish and 2nd Lieutenant Richard Laidley of Mike Flight, 36th FBS.

Below right: Joe McConnell with his F-86 *Beauteous Butch II* following his last mission in Korea. He was later killed in a 1954 training accident.

Below left: Captain 'Hal' Fischer, 39th FIS, 51st FIW in Korea in 1953. On 7 April 1953 he was shot down by Han Decai, a Chinese pilot whom he later met in 1996. Fischer who ejected from his F-86 north of the Yalu, was taken captive by Chinese military personnel and imprisoned near Shenyang, Liaoning Province. After a thwarted escape attempt nine months into his captivity, he was routinely tortured and ultimately admitted to trumped up charges that he had been ordered to enter Manchuria and that he had participated in germ warfare. A mock trial led to his release in May 1955. Fischer was returned to active service two months later. He served in the Viêtnam War, mainly as a helicopter pilot, flying more than 200 missions.

Mig Maulers

KOREAN WAR 1950-1953

CAPT. J.D. McCONNELL, JR.
51 TH JET ACE
16 MIGS

MAJ. J. JABARA
1ST JET ACE
15 MIGS

CAPT. M.J. FERNANDEZ
334 TH JET ACE
14 MIGS

CAPT. R.N. BAKER
51ST JET ACE
13 MIGS, 1 LA-9

MAJ. G.A. DAVIS
5TH JET ACE
11 MIGS

LT. H.E. FISCHER
25TH JET ACE
10 MIGS

COL. J.K. JOHNSON
25TH JET ACE
10 MIGS

CAPT. R.S. PARR
335D JET ACE
10 MIGS

LT. JAMES F. LOW
17TH JET ACE
9 MIGS

MAJ. F.C. BLESSE
19TH JET ACE
9 MIGS, 1 LA-9

CAPT. L.R. MOORE
34TH JET ACE
5 MIGS, 1 LA-9

CAPT. R. RISNER
20TH JET ACE
8 MIGS

MAJ. V. GARRISON
32ND JET ACE
8 MIGS

CAPT. C.D. JOLLEY
18TH JET ACE
7 MIGS

CAPT. L.W. LILLEY
22ND JET ACE
7 MIGS

LT. H. BUTTLEMAN
36TH JET ACE
7 MIGS

COL. F.S. GABRESKI
51TH JET ACE
6 1/2 MIGS

CAPT. D.E. ADAMS
14 TH JET ACE
6 1/2 MIGS

MAJ. J.P. HAGERSTROM
18TH JET ACE
6 1/2 MIGS

COL. G.L. JONES
50TH JET ACE
6 1/2 MIGS

CAPT. I.C. KINCHELOE
10TH JET ACE
6 MIGS-4 YAK 9

CAPT. R.J. LOVE
11TH JET ACE
6 MIGS

MAJ. J.F. BOLT
37TH JET ACE
6 MIGS

LT. J.H. KASLER
6TH JET ACE
6 MIGS

MAJ. W.T. WHISNER
7TH JET ACE
5 1/2 MIGS

CAPT. R.S. BECKER
8 JET ACE
5 MIGS

CAPT. R. GIBSON
3RD JET ACE
5 MIGS

LT. COL. R.D. CREIGHTON
4 TH JET ACE
5 MIGS

CAPT. R.H. MOORE
9TH JET ACE
5 MIGS

MAJ. W.H. WESCOTT
12 TH JET ACE
5 MIGS

CAPT. R.T. LATSHAW
13 TH JET ACE
5 MIGS

COL. H.R. THYNG
15 TH JET ACE
5 MIGS

LT. C.L. FOSTER
32ND JET ACE
5 MIGS

CAPT. D.W. OVERTON III
31 TH JET ACE
5 MIGS

LT. COL. G.L. RUDDELL
33ST JET ACE
5 MIGS

COL. R.P. BALDWIN
35 TH JET ACE
5 MIGS

CAPT. C.A. CURTIN
38 TH JET ACE
5 MIGS

MAJ. G.L. DETTINGER
39 TH JET ACE
5 MIGS

MAJ. W.H. MacDONNELL
40 TH JET ACE
5 MIGS

longer. One of its greatest assets was the all-flying tail. One could take it up to 40,000 feet, turn it on its back and pull through still maintaining full elevator control with the Mach indicator hovering just over Mach 1. The bubble canopy with its superb rear view was an invaluable asset. The ailerons were crisp at all altitudes and speeds. It was very docile in the circuit and landing. Its constraints lay in its slight lack of engine power. As far as armament was concerned, the .5 machine guns did very well, but two or four 20mm cannons would have been much more lethal - just recalling the later Spitfires and Me 109s.

'We would often start off a sweep with 48 aircraft sub-divided into fours. Once MiGs were sighted, the fours would spread out until close contact was made then split into pairs during combat covering each other if possible. It was the wing men's task to cover their leaders and only shoot in extreme circumstances. On a number of occasions, we sighted MiGs flying in trains of about sixteen aircraft at heights of above 50,000 feet. They would sometimes detach four or more aircraft and dive down on us - have a quick burst often out of range and then 'high tail' it off to the North for the sanctuary of China. On these occasions we had few alternatives other than wait until we were bounced then break at the appropriate time - reverse quickly as they shot past our tails and have a going away shot. Once they turned and tried to tangle with us, they usually lost out and were shot down.

'One of our biggest problems was fuel. We had to cover 200 miles of hostile territory to get to the combat area of the Yalu; this left us with only fifteen minutes for combat before 'bingo' time and the return 200 miles to Suwon.

'Our kill ratio was about twelve to one; the total number of MiGs destroyed in combat was about 790. I finally completed 42 missions before the war ended.

'The quality of pilots was excellent and similar to those I had known on RAF Squadrons but this, of course, was the testing of USAF pilots in a real hot war. I would like to pay tribute to those RN, Army and RAF pilots who lost their lives in Korea and those who suffered as PoWs of a voracious and cruel enemy. With many thanks to the USA and the USAF who made us so welcome as 'Brothers in Arms'.'

In January 1953 meanwhile, thirty-seven MiGs were destroyed. Captains Dolphin D. Overton III of the 16th FIS and Harold E. Fischer of the 39th FIS, 51st FIW became aces, Overton destroying five MiGs and damaging another in just four missions. On 18 February, four Sabres attacked forty-eight MiGs, shooting down two and forcing two more to spin and crash. In all, twenty-five MiGs and four Sabres were lost in combat during February. On 3 February at Osanni

Ground crew personnel re-arming a 4th FIW Sabre in Korea.

airfield the 18th FBW's three squadrons, the 12th and the 67th and 2 Squadron SAAF, finally began conversion from Mustangs to F-86Fs. The Wing flew its first combat mission with F-86Fs on 25 February on a fighter sweep to the Yalu. Colonel Frank S. Perego, 18th FIW commander, was not satisfied with the many of the ex-Mustang pilots and he reassigned them to other 5th AF units replacing them with pilots from the United States and they were fully operational by early April. On 22 February the 35th and 36th Squadrons, 8th FBW at Suwon also began conversion, from F-80Cs to F-86F Sabres and the 8th FBW flew its first Sabre mission on 7 April when four Sabres joined a fighter sweep to MiG Alley. The 80th FIS began conversion to the F-86F on 30 April. On 13 April the F-86Fs were fitted with bomb shackles, special 200-gallon drop tanks and a gun-bomb-rocket sight. The 8th FIW flew the first F-86F fighter-bomber mission and were followed by the 18th FIW on 14 April.

In March 1953 34 MiGs and three Sabres were lost and in April Sabres claimed 27 MiGs destroyed for the loss of just four F-86s. A fifth Sabre was shot down by flak. On 12 April Captain Joe McConnell of the 16th FIS, 51st FIW was forced to eject to safety over the Yellow Sea after his Sabre was hit badly by enemy anti-aircraft fire (other sources state that he was shot down by a Chinese pilot named Daoping Jiang). He was rescued within minutes by a H-S helicopter of the 3rd Air Rescue Squadron. He was back in action within 24 hours and shot down his ninth MiG. Captain McConnell flew at least three different F-86 Sabres, all named *Beautious Butch*. The name referred to the nickname of his wife, Pearl 'Butch' Brown. His final Sabre in combat was repainted following his final mission, with the name being changed to *Beauteous Butch II*. McConnell's tenth victory came on 24 April, putting him level with Captain Manuel J. 'Pete' Fernandez of the 334th FIS, 4th FIW. On 27 April Fernandez shot down his eleventh enemy fighter to lead the table of Korean aces. May 1953 was a highly successful month for marauding UN fighter pilots who no longer faced Soviet and Chinese pilots in combat. During 8-31 May 1,507 MiGs were sighted and in engagements with 537 of them, fifty-six MiGs were shot down. On 18 May Captain Joseph McConnell scored his sixteenth and final victory when he destroyed two and damaged one of twenty-eight MiG-15s over North Korea. Both he and Fernandez, who finished the war with 14.5 kills, were pulled out of the war on 19 May and sent Stateside. McConnell's score remained unbeaten making him the leading ace of the Korean War.[25]

In June 77 enemy fighters were shot down, eleven probably destroyed and forty-one damaged without loss to UN forces. Sixteen of the victories were claimed on one day, 31 June - a new record. The June victories saw five new aces: Lieutenant Colonel Vermont Garrison, Captain Lonnie R. Moore and Captain Ralph S. Parr of the 335th FIW, 4th FIW and Colonel Robert P. Baldwin and Lieutenant Henry 'Hank' Buttelmann of the 51st FIW. 1st Lieutenant (later Lieutenant Colonel) Reg W. Adams in the 39th Squadron at K-13 (Suwon) in central South Korea recalls a full-blown Yalu sweep on 19 June:

'It was a beautiful flying day in Korea with unlimited visibility. No less than 48 Sabres from the 16th, 25th and 39th Squadrons were lined up on the runway. The air to ground boys across the field (the 8th FBW) were scheduled to launch soon afterward. Leading my flight was Colonel (later General) George 'Shakey' Ruddell, 39th Fighter Squadron commander. I was flying No.4 as wingman to Lieutenant Wade 'Killer' Kilbride. We were 'Cobra Flight', which coincidentally was also the emblem of the 39th Squadron. Flying with the squadron commander was not exactly every pilot's dream, because he was always the most demanding. We also suspected that the engine in his F-86 was a little 'souped up', so to speak. The only setting that Colonel Ruddell knew on the throttle was full forward from takeoff to landing.

'Our mission was to intercept any MiGs attempting to cross the Yalu River and attack the F-84 and F-86F fighter-bombers that were working targets in North Korea. Soon after arriving at our patrol station on the Yalu River, we spotted six MiGs in formation attempting to slip into North Korea at low altitude. Colonel Ruddell immediately began a dive, which put us right on

Iven Carl 'Kinch' Kincheloe, Jr. (right with two other pilots in the 25th FIS, 51st FIG in Korea in 1951) spent a year as a test pilot flying the F-86E at Edwards AFB, California before being promoted to First Lieutenant and transferred to Korea in September 1951. During the war, he flew F-80s on 30 combat missions and F-86s on 101 combat missions, downing five MiG-15s before returning to the US in May 1952. Kincheloe joined the Bell X-2 programme and on 7 September 1956, flew at more than 2,000 mph and to a height of 126,200 feet. He was killed in the crash of an F-104A at Edwards AFB on 26 July 1958. He was only 30 years old.

top of and directly behind the MiG formation, i.e. the perfect 'bounce' from 6 o'clock high. The Colonel and his wingman took on the MiG leader. Kilbride set his sights on the leader of the second element. The other two MiGs broke their formation and disappeared for the moment. Though we lost sight of Ruddell, he eventually shot down the MiG that he had engaged. He was already an ace and this was his eighth victory of the war.

'Kilbride, my leader, engaged his MiG in a tight turn, firing continuously and scoring numerous hits on the Russian fighter. F attempted to stay on his wing, protecting his tail and watching the MiG Wade had staked out. Thank God for the 'G' suit, because I was holding a constant four 'Gs' trying to stay with Wade and the MiG in the turns. In the course of all this action, the enemy wingman appeared on my left side attempting to get into a firing position on Kilbride. As the MiG pulled up on my left, I held my 'G' forces until I felt that it was time for me to do something to prevent his firing on Wade.

'I relaxed just enough stick pressure to put me in position to fire. My .50 calibre tracers laced through the canopy of the MiG, which immediately did a lazy roll and headed for the ground. In spite of my gun camera film confirming this part of the action, I didn't see any type of explosion. I suspect that my bullets may have killed the MiG pilot, as my tracers penetrated the fuselage where the MiG had very little armor protection.

'However, the intelligence people would not confirm the victory. Many times I have wondered if I should have broken off and followed that MiG down to get the confirmation. But, needless to say, as a wing man I was committed to staying with my leader and protecting his tail. Shortly thereafter, Kilbride 'fired out' (expended all his ammunition) and called on me to continue the engagement with 'his' MiG. I pulled in behind the MiG Wade had been firing on. The MiG pilot, thinking the engagement was over, rolled out straight and level, turned north and headed for the Yalu and safety. I very deliberately pulled in right behind the MiG, put my pipper on his tailpipe and almost counted a kill. Suddenly I noticed what appeared to be flaming ping-pong balls floating past my Sabre. Cannon shells! Really big 37mm cannon shells! I heard a frantic call from Wade, 'Cobra 4, break right NOW!' I had no choice but to break off from a certain victory and head for home.

'Later Wade and I determined that the two MiGs we thought had abandoned the fray after our initial bounce had decided to come back and help their comrades. We also figured they had received a bit of 'encouragement' from the MiG that Wade and I were firing on, i.e. Chinese for 'Get these guys off my tail!' My hard right break saved my life, as the MiGs didn't give chase, which allowed us to return to Suwon safely. There were a lot of hairy stories floating around the bar that night because we, the 51st Group, had several confirmed kills that day. Kilbride bought me a drink!'

In July 1953 Sabres alone shot down 32 enemy fighters. On 11 July Major John F. Bolt USMC in the 25th FIS, 51st FIW shot down his fifth and sixth MiGs to become the only USMC ace of the Korean War. Major John H. Glenn Jr. USMC another exchange pilot scored three victories while with the squadron. The 'MiG Mad Marine' as he was known, later became an astronaut and became the first man in space. Major James Jabara had returned to the USA with six kills before returning to combat in January 1953. By 26 May Jabara had destroyed three MiGs and on 10 June the 4th FIW ace shot down his tenth and 11th MiGs. He added three more that month before claiming his 15th and final MiG victim on 15 July. On 19th and 20th two more 4th Wing pilots, Captain Clyde A. Curtin and Major Stephen L. Bettinger, also became jet aces. Bettinger was the 39th and last jet ace of the war but it was several months before his status could be confirmed because he was shot down and captured and the UN kept his kills secret until his safe repatriation. At 1700 hours on 22 July, three Sabres of the 51st FIW led by Lieutenant Sam P. Young entered MiG Alley at 35,000 feet on an offensive patrol. It was Young's 35th mission and he had yet to fire his guns in anger when ahead and below he saw four MiG-15s sweep across his path at right angles. Young dived down and destroyed the No.4 with a long burst of fire. It was the last time that Sabre and MiG met in combat. On 27 July an Armistice was signed. That same day Captain Ralph S. Parr of the 335th FIW, 4th FIW destroyed an Il'yushin Il-12 transport. It was the last aircraft to fall in the Korean War and Parr's tenth victory.

On 29 July a 5th AF communiqué stated that the war had cost 58 F-86s shot down and that 808 MiGs had been destroyed by Sabres; a ratio of 13.79:1. These totals had been

Captains Joseph McConnell Jr. and Harold Fischer stand before Captain McConnell's F-86 Sabre jet, *Beautious Butch.* McConnell was the top ace of the war with 16 kills. Fischer was the first double ace, but was shot down and captured in April 1953. Both were assigned to the 39th Fighter-Interceptor Squadron of the 51st FIW.

achieved despite the Sabre pilots having to operate over enemy territory the whole time at the extreme limit of their range, which restricted patrol time along the Yalu to under fifteen minutes. MiG pilots chose the time and place and broke off combat when it suited them. So how did Sabre pilots (who were usually vastly outnumbered in combat) manage to knock down so many MiGs for a relatively low combat loss rate of F-86s? UN airmen were experienced pilots while the majority of Chinese flyers were greenhorns by comparison. Often they would panic and fire wildly. Many put their fighters into unnecessary spins and in the last resort some chose to eject rather than stay and fight. (In the last four months of 1952 a fifth of the Sabre victories were achieved without the F-86 pilots firing their guns! 32 MiGs were seen to snap suddenly into spins while manoeuvring to escape and eight pilots ejected, twenty-two crashing with their aircraft). A FEAF study in March 1954 declared that '…68% of pilots who had destroyed MiGs were over twenty-eight years old, while 67% of the pilots who had scored no kills were less than twenty-five years old. Pilots with MiG kills had flown an average of eighteen missions in WWII, while pilots with no kills had flown an average of four missions in WWII. Some 810 enemy planes were claimed destroyed by Sabres and the thirty-nine Sabre pilots who became jet air aces destroyed 305.5 aircraft. Whether or not a pilot was flying as an element leader and the conditions under which he sighted MiGs affected his chances for scoring victories, but the more experienced pilots apparently had the best chance for shooting down the enemy…'

Sources since have lowered the number of MiGs shot down by Sabres to as low as 379 and Russian archives admit the loss of 345 Soviet-piloted MiG-15s, while other sources reveal that the Sabre kills ratio was between 10.32:1 and 14:1 with the higher score the more likely. Whatever the scores, unquestionably, without the Sabre the Communists would have gained air superiority in Korea and the war would have been lost.

On 27 July 1953 the Communists signed the Armistice and the thirty-eight-month war was over. Peace reigned once again in the 'Land of the Morning Calm'.

Endnotes for Chapter 2

20 Senior Lieutenant Kum Sok No joined the Communist Party and assumed the role of a super communist. In July 1952 he was made vice-chairman of his battalion Communist Party and, in August, promoted to Sanwi - senior lieutenant - and named squadron leader of four MiGs. He escaped from North Korea in September 1953.

21 On 17 November 1966 Colonel Jabara was travelling with his family in two cars to their new home when his daughter crashed the car she was driving and he was riding in, killing them both.

22 In September 1956 Kincheloe took the experimental Bell X-2 to Mach 2.93, He was killed flying a F-104A at Edwards AFB on 26 July 1958.

23 Colonel John Meyer destroyed a MiG-15 near Sinuiju on 12 April 1951 and was also credited with damaging another. It took his final score to 26 victories in two wars. He was promoted to Brigadier General on 1 August 1959.

24 *Aces High.*

25 On 25 August 1954, while testing the fifth production F-86H-1-NA at Edwards Air Force Base, McConnell was killed in a crash near the base following a control malfunction. Fernandez died in a plane crash on 18 October 1980.

Chapter Three

The Indo-Pak Wars

'....close to the area, we descended fast, looking all around and below us for the enemy aircraft. At about this time we also learnt that the C-in-C was flying around the area in a L-19. We did not see him; we later on discovered that he left well before we got there. Our search succeeded and I saw two enemy aircraft. They were crossing underneath us and I informed Rafiqui about it. He immediately acknowledged it '... contact'. Rafiqui said he was going for them. While covering his tail, I spotted two Canberras 9 o'clock from me at 5,000-6,000 feet. Then I spotted another two Vampires trying to get behind Rafique. I instinctively broke off and positioned myself behind these two. In the meantime, Rafiqui had knocked down one of his two targets and was chasing the other. About now I had my sights on one of my own and was holding my fire. I was anxiously waiting for my leader to bring down his second and clear out of my way. When the Vampire I had targeted closed in on Rafiqui too dangerously, I called out to him break left. Within the next moment Rafiqui shot down his second, reacting to my call and broke left. Simultaneously I pressed my trigger and hit one of them. Having disposed of one I shifted my sight on the other and fired at him. In the chase I had gone as low as 200 feet off the ground when I shot my second prey, he ducked and went into the trees. We had bagged four in our first engagement with the Indians...'

Flight Lieutenant Imtiaz Bhatti, F-86 Sabre pilot, 5 Pakistan Air Force (PAF) Squadron, 1 September 1965. As an exchange pilot in the UK his OC, Squadron Leader Sarfraz Ahmed Rafiqui flew Hunters for two years. Sarfraz's OC on 19 Squadron RAF, reporting on his flying abilities, wrote: 'In the air his experience and skill combine to make him a very effective fighter pilot and leader who creates an impression of disciplined efficiency in all that he does'. On return to Pakistan in 1962 he was given command of 14 Squadron. A year later, he was given command of the elite 5 Squadron. He became well known for his highly assertive and effective control of the unit as much as for his spirited attitude towards flying.

Sunset was only about an hour and a quarter away on 1 September 1965 when a forward airfield in the Punjab suddenly came to life with the noise of jet engines starting up. In sections of four, with a few minutes interval between each section, twenty-eight fighter-bombers of the Indian Air Force took off for the Chamb sector in the Jammu and Kashmir area, to help stem the unexpected thrust of Pakistani armour which had crossed the international border into Jammu. This was the start of the air action by the Indian Air Force which, when it ended on 23 September, had cost the Pakistan Air Force seventy-three aircraft destroyed in the air and by ground fire. This figure does not include aircraft destroyed or damaged during the numerous night attacks carried out by Indian bombers on Pakistani air bases. Indian losses during the same period were only thirty-five aircraft. The need for the Indian Air Force to go into action had been made imperative by the Pakistani action in spearheading its attack across the international border and the cease-fire line with almost two regiments of tanks in the Chamb sector. In this first strike by the Indian Air Force, fourteen tanks were destroyed or damaged; eleven were actually seen burning. In addition thirty to forty heavy vehicles were also destroyed. After this engagement, however, two Indian Vampires were missing and two more had been damaged.[26]

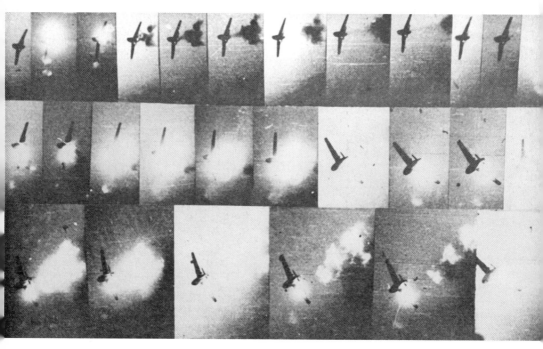

Camera-gun sequence showing the destruction of a PAF F-86 over Halwara on 6 September 1965 by Flying Officer V. K. Neb of 27 Squadron IAF who was flying a Hunter F.56 on a dusk patrol with Flight Lieutenant D. N. Rathore when an emergency call that Halwara airfield was under attack made them rush to base. About the same time two Sabres flown by Flight Lieutenants' Yunus Hussain and Cecil Choudary were exiting the raid. As the Hunters jumped them Neb latched onto Hussain's Hunter and destroyed it with a one and a half second cannon burst, earning his first Sabre Kill. Neb had to wait another six years until he could claim another IAF Hunter.

On 3 September 1965 an IAF Gnat (seen in left with a F-86 Sabre) flown by Squadron Leader Brijpal Singh Sikand surrendered to a 9 Squadron F-104 Starfighter during an air combat. The Indian pilot landed at Pasrur airfield near Gujranwala and was taken prisoner. Later Squadron Leader Saad Hatmi flew the captured Gnat from Pusrur to Sargodha and it is now in the PAF museum in Karachi.

On 13 September 1965 Squadron Leader Alauddin 'Butch' Ahmed of 32 Wing, PAF was flying an F-86 in a low level raid against the freight wagons in the goods yard at Gurdaspur Station. On a second pass at very low level through smoke from previous strikes his aircraft was hit by fragments from the exploding trucks and twelve miles away from Pakistani territory he reported that his cockpit was full of smoke. He continued to fly his damaged aircraft westwards before finally ejecting from his burning Sabre. He did not survive. There is conjecture as to whether he was shot while descending in his parachute in the combat area.

Captain (later Air Commodore) Rahat Hussain PAF.

Since Partition of British India in 1947, Pakistan and India remained in contention over several issues, not least the disputed region of Kashmir. On 5 August 1965 between 26,000 and 33,000 Pakistani soldiers crossed the Line of Control dressed as Kashmiri locals headed for various areas within Kashmir. Indian forces, tipped off by the local populace, crossed the cease fire line on 15 August. Initially, the Indian Army met with considerable success, capturing three important mountain positions after a prolonged artillery barrage. At that time the Pakistan Air Force had about 140 combat aircraft, mostly American-built, including the F-104As of 9 Squadron. Pakistan acquired its Starfighters as a direct result of the Soviet downing of an American Lockheed U-2 spy plane that had been based at Badaber (Peshawar Air Station) on 1 May 1960. The aircraft, flown by Central Intelligence Agency pilot Francis Gary Powers, was performing aerial reconnaissance when it was hit by an S-75 'Dvina' (SA-2 'Guideline') surface-to-air missile and crashed in Sverdlovsk.[27] Understandably annoyed at the Pakistanis for allowing the Americans to use their country as a base for espionage missions, the Soviets threatened to target Pakistan for nuclear attack if such activities continued. Taking the threat seriously, the United States agreed to provide Pakistan with enough surplus F-104A interceptors to equip one squadron. Although the F-104As were intended to defend Pakistan against high-flying Soviet bombers coming over the Hindu Kush Mountains, their actual combat use would be under quite different circumstances. The PAF's fighter force comprised 102 F-86F Sabres and twelve F-104 Starfighters, along with 24 Martin B-57 Canberra bombers.[28] B-57s flew 167 sorties, dropping over 600 tons of bombs. Three B-57s were lost in action, along with one RB-57F electronic intelligence aircraft. However, only one of those three was lost as a result of enemy action. During the war, the bomber wing of the PAF was attacking the concentration of airfields in north India. In order to avoid enemy fighter-bombers, the B-57s operated from several different airbases, taking off and returning to different bases to avoid being attacked. They would arrive over their targets in a stream at intervals of about 15 minutes, which led to achieving a major disruption of the overall IAF effort. The unknown Pakistani flying ace, '8-Pass Charlie', was named by his adversaries for making eight passes in the moonlight to bomb different targets with each of the B-57's bombs.

Facing the PAF was the Indian Air Force (IAF), with about 500 aircraft of mostly British and French manufacture.[29] In January 1957 India placed a large order for the Canberra; a total of 54 B(I)58 bombers, eight PR.57 photo-reconnaissance aircraft and six T.4 training aircraft were ordered, deliveries began in the summer of that same year. Twelve more Canberras were ordered in September

IAF Gnat pilots in front of one of their aircraft.

1957; as many as thirty more may have also been purchased by 1962. First used in combat by the IAF in 1962, the Canberra was employed during the UN campaign against the breakaway Republic of Katanga in Africa. The most audacious use of the bomber was in the raid on Badin when the IAF sent in the Canberra to attack a critical Pakistani radar post in West Pakistan. The raid was a complete success, the radars in Badin having been badly damaged by the bombing and put out of commission. A later raid by the IAF was attempted on Peshawar Air Base with the aim of destroying, amongst other targets, several Pakistani American-built Canberras. Due to poor visibility, a road outside of the base was bombed, instead of the runway where PAF B-57 bombers were parked. The IAF had also begun to acquire MiG-21Fs, new Soviet interceptors capable of Mach 2, but only nine of them were operational with 28 Squadron in September 1965 and they saw little use.

On 1 September Pakistan launched a counter-attack, called Operation 'Grand Slam' with the objective to capture the vital town of Akhnoor in Jammu, which would sever communications and cut off supply routes to Indian troops. Attacking with an overwhelming ratio of troops and technically superior tanks, Pakistan made gains against Indian forces that were caught unprepared and suffered heavy losses. India responded by calling in its air force to blunt the Pakistani attack. That evening saw hectic and desperate attempts by the IAF to stop the rapid advance of PAK Army's 12th Division offensive against Akhnoor. Vampire Mk 52 fighter-bombers of 45 Squadron, which moved from Poona to Pathankot were hastily called into action. The obsolescent Vampires had been considered suitable for providing close support in the valleys of Kashmir but though they were put on high alert during the Sino-Indian War of 1962 they did not see any action, as the air force's role was limited to supply and evacuation. The grim situation on the ground found the Vampires at work immediately. Three strikes of four Vampires each (along with some Canberras) had been launched in succession that evening and were successful in slowing the Pakistani advance. Major General G. S. Sandhu in his book *'History of Indian Cavalry'* recounts how the first Vampire strike of four 'leisurely proceeded to destroy three AMX-13 tanks of India's own 20th Lancers, plus the only recovery vehicle and the only ammunition vehicle available during this hard-pressed fight. The second flight attacked Indian infantry and gun positions, blowing up several ammunition vehicles'. One was shot down by ground fire. Then an element of two Sabres armed with air-to-air missiles arrived on the scene; in the ensuing dogfight, the outdated Vampires were outclassed.

Squadron Leader Sarfraz Rafiqui, the plucky and outstanding OC of 5 Squadron, and Flight Lieutenant Imtiaz Bhatti were patrolling at 20,000 feet near Chamb. On being vectored by the radar, they descended and picked up contact with two Vampires in the fading light. Rafiqui closed in rapidly and before another two Vampires turned in on the Sabres, made short work of the first two with a blazing volley from the lethal 0.5 Browning six-shooter. Then, with a quick-witted defensive break he readjusted on the wing of Bhatti, who got busy with his quarry. While Rafiqui cleared tails, Bhatti did an equally fast trigger job. One Vampire nosed over into the ground which was not too far below; the other, smoking and badly damaged, staggered for a few miles before its pilot, Flying Officer Pathak, ejected. The less fortunate Flight Lieutenants A. K. Bhagwagar, M. V. Joshi and S. Bhardwaj went down with their Vampires in full view of the horrified Indian troops. The IAF immediately withdrew from front-line service about 130 Vampires, together with over fifty Dassault Ouragan 'Toofani' jet fighter-bombers.[30] The IAF was effectively reduced in combat strength by nearly 35% in one stroke, thanks to Rafiqui and Bhatti's marksmanship.

Chandrakant Nijanand Bal, a young pilot on 31 Squadron IAF who flew the Mystère IVa fighter bomber during the 1965 war, distinguished itself operating from Pathankot on 1 September.

'Time 1730 hours. Twenty odd faces could be seen in the briefing room. The Officer-in-charge flying entered the room and closed the door behind him. He paused, head cocked to one side in his usual fashion. 'Boys, we have got the green light. The Pak army, with 90 tanks crossed the border this morning in the Chamb Sector' and he indicated a small bulge on the quarter inch map. 'Your job is to stop them. The Ground Liaison Officer will take over from now.' The GLO completed his briefing and the pilots took down the details on their maps and hurried to their respective squadrons. I had been recalled from leave some days previously. I had just spent about three weeks at home. The daily newspaper used to bring news of 'kills' by our security forces. One could feel the mounting tension. I reached my squadron on 27 August. Sethi was

Footage captured by Flight Lieutenant Imtiaz Bhatti's gun-camera on 1 September 1965 of Squadron Leader Sarfraz Ahmed Rafiqui reacting to Bhatti's 'break' call near the River Tawi at the foothills of the Parmandal Range after he had shot down two Vampires.

the first to meet me. 'You missed some sorties over the valley while on leave" he said. I knew he meant the Srinagar Valley. I was looking forward to some good flying. However, things worked out differently. Flying was stopped and the airmen worked feverishly to get the maximum number of aircraft on the flight line. The Navigation Officer of the Squadron was burdened with the number of maps being issued. We were giving the final touch to the 'cutting edge.'

'Early morning, 1 September I was standing by for a patrol sortie in the Valley. I listened to the briefing, inwardly wishing I were in the formation. The sortie went off without a hitch. It's 10 o'clock and Tony passes the word that Gurdaspur has been shelled. We celebrated our Squadron's second anniversary by a special lunch. There is a cake for the occasion baked by 'Mrs Boss' [Wing Commander Jimmy Goodman's wife] and we made short work of the ceremony. Five o'clock and the word goes around. I leapt to my feet and made it towards the briefing room. Tony reminded me that I have forgotten my map. I ran back and fetched it, not wishing to miss any part of the briefing.

'I was once again standing by for the first section, and felt bad about it. It must have shown on my face for Tony said that I could join the second section. I went to my aircraft well before time and inspected it. Under each wing is a pod containing rockets. I had never fired this before and mentally go through the briefing, 'Circuit breaker IN, Wing Master ON, lift flap and press.' I was pleased with myself. I now saw the first section of Vampires getting airborne. It was time to strap-up. My section took off and I switched off the engine. Peachy came on my scooter and asked me to hop on. I am to fly another aircraft. I strap-up for the second time. Just as I started the engine Tony came running to my aircraft. He was supposed to be in the first section but I did not think of that then. He signalled me to get out. Something must have gone wrong. I did as I was told and cursed, and went back fuming to the Squadron. I must have looked a sight.

Squadron Leader Amjad Yunus Hussain Khan fought in air battles aggressively, fearlessly and with great professional skill. During one such engagement he fought singly against six IAF aircraft and claimed two Hunters. Though his own aircraft was damaged in this encounter, he managed to bring it back to base safely. On 6 September 1965, while attacking Halwara airfield, his small formation was intercepted by a large number of IAF and, although his aircraft was hit, he refused to break off the engagement, in complete disregard of personal safety, and was reported missing from this mission. For his gallantry, valour, professional skill and devotion to duty he was awarded the Sitara-e-Jurat.

Gun-camera sequence showing a PAF Sabre going down in flames.

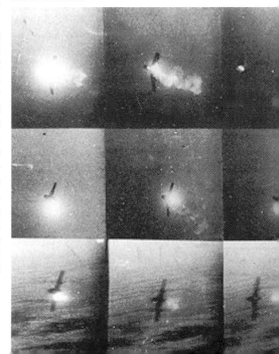

'That day twenty-eight sorties were flown. That must have been a good blow to the advancing tanks, for their progress was slowed down. We lost Horsey Bharadwaj that day. News of three others was yet to come.'

The next day, Pakistan retaliated; its air force attacked Indian forces and air bases in both Kashmir and Punjab. Chandrakant Bal started the next day early. 'The duty bearer woke me up at three o'clock. I dressed quickly and reported to Wing Commander Goodman in the Mess, as instructed. Both the Station Commander and he had been busy during the night. I could see that plainly, as fatigue is quite visible on their faces. The Station Commander explained the situation to me. I am to go with the Boss to Chamb at first light for a reconnaissance of yesterday's battlefield. We are to have escorts for our protection. A final briefing and a time check and we were off to our aircraft. We took off at dawn and made for the target area, flying low, just above the trees to avoid enemy radar detection. As we neared Chamb I spotted four Sabres but kept quiet, as there was no immediate danger. The Sabres were orbiting the battle area. A quick check on the sabres and we started our reconnaissance 'literally under their noses.' The enemy aircraft had not yet seen us and Boss called 'Buster port' and all of us veered sharply to the left and opened up power. We are now on our way back. After reaching base I climbed out of the cockpit soaked in sweat. I breathed in the cool morning air and felt good. A few words of praise to the airmen and I was on my way for the debriefing. I met Sethi after the debriefing. He had flown yesterday and got a tank. He asked how the mission had gone and I narrated the tale. The next three days saw little other activity except more strikes in the Chhamb Sector. Every day the scores went up a little. We were hitting anything on wheels. Even a few camps were detected and fired upon. These especially were very difficult to see from the air as they were well camouflaged.'

On 3 September came the break-through, which marked the start of the superiority which the Indian Air Force maintained throughout the rest of the campaign. At 7 am that day a formation of Pakistani fighters was reported to be circling over Indian Army positions in the Chamb sector. A section of Gnats was scrambled to intercept the enemy. Thirty-four year old Squadron Leader Trevor Keeler VSM,[31,] born on 8 December 1934 in Lucknow who was leading the section, sighted the enemy and identified them as F-86 Sabres. Trevor, who had an elder brother, Denzil, who would also be honoured for his service in the IAF, immediately engaged them. While Keeler was jockeying for position, the F-86s were joined by some Pakistan Air Force F-104s. But in spite of being face to face with reputedly superior aircraft, Keeler refused to break off and finally lining up a Sabre in his sights, shot it down. The next day another two Pakistani Sabres were shot down over the same area.

On 6 September when the Indian Army marched into the Lahore sector to forestall an attack in the Punjab the IAF was called upon to give ground support and try to disrupt the logistics of the Pakistani Army. Until then the IAF had not attacked any air bases. Chandrakant Bal recalled:

'We woke to the sound of artillery guns. The western horizon was aglow and we were informed about the advances being made by our ground forces in the various sectors. The very same evening PAK Sabres visited our Base with unfriendly intentions. We were all sitting outside our crew room talking shop. One of our missions was seen returning. For a few moments aircraft were seen all over the circuit and they landed one behind the other. We were about to resume our discussions when Tony spots an unfamiliar looking aircraft rolling into a dive. 'Here they come!' he said and strode into the crew room. There was more than a little confusion with bodies colliding with one another as an effort was made to head for protection. I ran for a trench, tripped over, fell, scrambled on all fours and finally dived into it. This is done to the tune of machine gun fire from the Sabres.

'Others later remarked that this reminded them of a scene from the film *'From Here to Eternity.'* A moment later I felt a heavy weight crushing my legs. Looking back I saw Chandru who sheepishly said, "I hope your leg is not hurting.' Roundy, the Squadron's only pilot attack instructor was coolly assessing the Sabre tactics and score, sometimes saying with a frown

"That's not how it should be done." After the raid was over we trickled out of hiding, all dusty, but with false smiles on our faces.

'Back after our day's work I was in the bath and have just about soaped myself when I heard the anti-aircraft guns firing. I grabbed a towel and was in a trench in no time. It turns out to be a false alarm and a kind soul gives me a handkerchief to wipe the soap out of my eyes. The soapy episode was followed the same night by the first night raid of the war. Though it stood nowhere when compared with the London or Berlin air raids of the last war, it still qualified to be classed as an air raid by virtue of the fact that a bomb fell a little to one side of the runway, causing a high degree of excitement among us. Those still clinging to the bar by candle light managed to reach the nearest trench, not forgetting to bring their glasses with them. The sky filled with red fireballs, which indicated the individual lines-of-fire of the anti-aircraft guns. In the dim light of a rising quarter moon we had a glimpse of the B-57. The raid did no damage other than disturb our sleep. This practice was to follow in all future night raids. During one such night we were disturbed three times within an hour or two in between. These raids demonstrated the unique human quality of adaptation. Never did anyone feel that this was his last day in spite of heavy odds against him. We used to sleep with one ear tuned to the siren and could sprint to the trenches in total darkness if called to do so.

'The war had been going on for over a week now. The army was fighting a determined enemy on the ground while the Air Force battled for air superiority. Many a pilot made a 'Nylon descent' to safety or captivity. In this grim struggle one of our tasks was to find out what was going on behind the enemy lines. On one such mission the pilots returned and excitedly reported seeing a railway train carrying a load of tanks. This vital information was used later in an extremely successful strike on the train, thus denying to the enemy these tanks at a critical time.'[32]

That evening Pakistani aircraft attacked two Indian air bases. One of these attacks was on Halwara and was carried out by four F-86 Sabres. It was to prove an extremely costly venture for the Pakistanis, for none of the four Sabres returned; three F-86s were shot down by IAF Hunters and one fell victim to anti-aircraft fire. When the Pakistanis raided Kalaikunda in the Eastern sector, again with a section of four F-86s, the story of Halwara was repeated; all four were shot down, two by Hunters and two by AA. After that, the Pakistanis never ventured to

IAF Hawker Hunter F.Mk.56s of 14 Squadron with BA209 in the foreground before delivery to India.

attack Indian air bases in daylight. But these raids did open the way for Indian pilots to attack Pakistani airfields in retaliation. The first to be attacked by the Indian bombers were Sargodha and Chaklada on the night of 6/7 September. From then on until the cease-fire on 23 September a heavy toll in the air battles, Indian Army gunners were doing wonders with their anti-aircraft guns. Taking only one example of a single battery at Amritsar, the first attack by the PAF against this installation came on the evening of 5 September; it was driven off. In the next attack, on the 8th, one PAF aircraft was shot down. Further successes followed and by the time hostilities ceased this battery had a 'bag' of ten Pakistani aircraft confirmed, including B-57 bombers.

While the Pakistanis had been effectively deterred from carrying out daylight attacks on Indian airfields and installations and targets inland, the IAF fighter-bombers ranged far and wide, attacking military targets and air bases. Sargodha airfield was attacked several times in broad daylight by Indian Mystère IVAs and Hunters. Considerable damage to the installations was done and, besides other aircraft, at least two F-104 Starfighters were destroyed or damaged. In offensive fighter sweeps, tanks, heavy guns, armoured vehicles, anti-aircraft guns, heavy motorised transport and formation headquarters fell victim to Indian rockets, bombs and cannon. During the twenty-three days' fighting the IAF destroyed no fewer than 120 Pakistani tanks alone. In one particularly effective strike on 8 September four IAF Hunters destroyed a goods train - which action eventually resulted in the blunting of the Pakistani armour attack in the Khem Karan sector and, in addition, knocked out four tanks and over sixty vehicles. While the IAF fighter-bombers continued to give ground support to the Army, Indian fighters were busy clearing the skies of the Pakistani Sabres. Every time the F-86s were engaged by Gnats or Hunters, the Sabres were never able to get away without loss. The reputedly deadly Sidewinder air-to-air missiles, on which the PAF depended so heavily for air combat, proved ineffective because of the low altitudes at which most of the air battles were fought. More often than not, the enemy fighters had to jettison these missiles when engaged by the Gnats.

In fact the greatest single deterring factor in the air battles proved to be this British-designed lightweight high-performance fighter which has been under licence-manufacture in India since 1956. It was soon nicknamed 'Sabre Slayer' and not without reason. Its performance in the air battles was so impressive that even the supersonic F-104s refused to engage it and almost invariably decided to break off combat by cutting in their afterburners, when chased by a Gnat.

Learning that daylight operations against Indian airfields were costly, the enemy started visiting these places at night with their Martin B-57 Canberras. But here again accurate anti-aircraft fire usually made the Pakistani pilots drop their bombs in a hurry and scuttle away. While the fact was that the B-57 night raids failed to hit any worthwhile installation, Pakistan continued to churn out fantastic claims of aircraft destroyed and airfields put out of action. For example, after a night raid on Ambala the enemy claimed twenty-seven Indian aircraft destroyed on the ground, whereas in reality, except for a section of the old flying control tower, none of the airfield installations, let alone a single aircraft, had even been damaged. All the enemy bombs had fallen on non-military targets. Then again, the airfields at Pathankot, Adampur and Halwara were claimed to have been put out of action.

The Air Attachés of foreign countries who were taken round all the airfields in the Punjab after the cease-fire were able to see at first-hand that none of these airfields had been put out of commission or rendered inoperative for even a single day.

The destruction of MiGs was another fantastic claim, which was floated by the Pakistani propagandists. They claimed that the Pakistan Air Force had destroyed nine MiG-21s. In fact the IAF started the operations with only nine MiG-21s and was prepared to show eight of these aircraft at the end of the campaign. On the other hand, the destruction of seventy-three Pakistani aircraft in air battles and by ground fire has been conclusively corroborated by cine gun film records, supported by eye-witness accounts of pilots and recovery of wrecks on the ground.

After the first few skirmishes PAF efforts flagged and resistance to Indian daylight attacks declined. The last raid put in by the IAF, for example, with a section of Canberras on the vital

Ground personnel re-arm the 20mm cannon service on this PAF Sabre.

radar installation at Badin in Sind, did not meet any aerial resistance at all, but only ack-ack - which did not, however, stop the Canberras from destroying this installation with rockets.

Mohammad Mahmood Alam was a scrap of a man who appeared almost lost in the none-too roomy cockpit of a Sabre. Yet on 7 September, this Pakistani squadron commander established a combat record which has few equals in the history of jet air warfare. Alam was born on 6 July 1935 to a well-educated family of Kolkata, British India. Although born and raised in the Bengal region, Alam was not ethnically Bengali, contrary to common perception. Alam's family was of Urdu-speaking Bihari origin, having emigrated from Patna and settled in the Bengal province of British India for a long time. The family migrated from Calcutta to eastern Bengal which became East Pakistan (now Bangladesh) following the formation of Pakistan in 1947. Alam completed his secondary education in 1951 from Government High School, Dhaka in East Pakistan. He joined the then RPAF now PAF in 1952 and was granted commission on 2 October 1953.

Many pilots have scored several air victories in one sortie and have equalled or exceeded Alam's claim of shooting down up to five enemy aircraft of superior performance within a few minutes. But few are likely to be able to match his record of destroying at least three opponents-Hunters of the Indian Air Force - within the space of somewhere around 30-40 seconds. Admittedly, confirmation of Alam's claims had been difficult to obtain, despite close-range observations of this encounter by several PAF pilots and some gun camera evidence. Nearest of these observers was his wingman, Flying Officer Masood Akhtar, who, protecting his leader's tail, clung like a leech throughout the action. Another section of PAF Sabres, led by Flight Lieutenant Bhatti, was attempting to engage the Hunters but Alam got there first. Flying top cover in an F-104 was Arif Iqbal who, with intense fascination and frustration watched the brief combat.

On this basis, Alam was originally credited with five IAF Hunters destroyed, although the wreckage of only two could be found in Pakistani territory, within two or three miles of Sangla Hill railway station. The bodies of the pilots - one Hindu and one Sikh - were reportedly burnt beyond recognition. The area of the main engagement however, thirty miles east of Sargodha airfield, was only about fifty-five miles inside the Pakistan border - seven or eight minutes at jet speed. Thus only the IAF is in a position to verify, some day, its actual losses on the second day of its war with Pakistan. The clear ascendancy established by the PAF pilots in this encounter and those that would follow on that fateful day was a powerful factor in heightening both morale and fighting spirit in Pakistan's outnumbered but resolute air arm. Alam takes up his account of that engagement:

'As we were vectored back towards Sargodha, Akhtar called, 'Contact - four Hunters' and I saw the IAF aircraft diving to attack our airfield. So I jettisoned my drops (underwing tanks which can be quickly released, for greater combat agility, before going into action) to dive through our own ack-ack after them. But in the meantime I saw two more Hunters about 1,000 feet to my rear, so I forgot the four in front and pulled up to go after the pair behind. The Hunters broke off their attempted attack on Sargodha and the rear pair turned into me. I was flying much faster than they were at this stage - I must have been doing about 500 knots - so I pulled up to avoid overshooting them and then reversed to close in as they flew back towards India.

'I took the last man and dived behind him, getting very low in the process. The Hunter can outrun the Sabre - it's only about fifty knots faster - but has a much better acceleration, so it can pull away very rapidly. Since I was diving, I was going still faster and as he was out of gun range, I fired the first of my two Sidewinder air to air missiles at him. In this case, we were too low and I saw the missile hit the ground short of its target. This area east of Sargodha, however, has lots of high tension wires, some of them as high as 100-150 feet and when I saw the two Hunters pull up to avoid one of these cables, I fired my second Sidewinder. The missile streaked

Napalm bombs dropped by two PAF F-86 Sabres exploding on target.

ahead of me, but I didn't see it strike. The next thing I remember was that I was overshooting one of the Hunters and when I looked behind, the cockpit canopy was missing and there was no pilot in the aircraft. He had obviously pulled up and ejected and then I saw him coming down by parachute. This pilot (Squadron Leader Onkar Nath Kakar, commander of an IAF Hunter squadron) was later taken prisoner.

'I had lost sight of the other five Hunters, but I pressed on thinking maybe they would slow down. (There were, of course, still only two Sabres pitted against the remaining five IAF aircraft). I had lots of fuel so I was prepared to fly 50-60 miles to catch up with them. We had just crossed the Chenab River when my wingman called out, 'Contact Hunters 1 o'clock' and I picked them up at the same time - five Hunters in absolutely immaculate battle formation. They were flying at about 100-200 feet, at around 480 knots and when I was in gunfire range they saw me. They all broke in one direction, climbing and turning steeply to the left, which put them in loose line astern. This, of course, was their big mistake. If you are bounced, which means a close range approach by an enemy fighter to within less than about 3,000 feet, the drill is to call a break. This is a panic manoeuvre to the limits of the aircraft's performance, which splits the formation and both gets you out of the way of an attack and frees you to position yourself behind your opponent. But in the absence of one of the IAF sections initiating a break in the other direction to sandwich our attack, they all simply stayed in front of us.

'It all happened very fast. We were all turning very tightly-in excess of 5g or just about on the limits of the Sabre's very accurate A-4 radar ranging gunsight. And I think before we had completed more than about 270 degrees of the turn, at around twelve degrees per second, all four Hunters had been shot down. In each case, I got the pipper of my sight around the canopy of the Hunter for virtually a full deflection shot. Almost all our shooting throughout the war was at very high angles off - seldom less than about thirty degrees. Unlike some of the Korean combat films I had seen, nobody in our war was shot down flying straight and level. I developed a technique of firing very short bursts-around a half second or less. The first burst was almost a sighter, but with a fairly large bullet pattern from six machine guns, it almost invariably punctured the fuel tanks so that they streamed kerosene. During the battle on 7 September, as we went around in the turn, I could just see, in the light of the rising sun, the plumes of fuel gushing from the tanks after my hits. Another half second burst was then sufficient to set fire to the fuel and, as the Hunter became a ball of flame, I would quickly shift my aim forward to the next aircraft. The Sabre carried about 1,800 rounds of ammunition for its six 0.5 inch guns, which can therefore fire for about fifteen seconds. In air combat, this is a lifetime. Every fourth or fifth round is an armour piercing bullet and the rest are HEI - high explosive incendiary. I'm certain after this combat that I brought back more than half of my ammunition, although we didn't have time to waste counting rounds.

'My fifth victim of this sortie started spewing smoke and then rolled on to his back at about 1,000 feet. I thought he was going to do a barrel roll, which at low altitude is a very dangerous manoeuvre for the pursuer if the man in front knows what he's doing. I went almost on my back and then realised I might not be able to stay with him so I took off bank and pushed the nose down. The next time I fired was at very close range-about 600 feet or so - and his aircraft virtually blew up in front of me.' [33]

According to Fizaya in *Psyche of the Pakistan Air Force* by Pushpindar Singh and Ravi Rikhye, 'In the Pakistan-India conflict of 1965, the first 48 hours established the superiority of PAF over its much larger adversary. The major successes which contributed towards the PAF getting the better of IAF are its lightning action on the Grand Trunk Road by F-86s of 19 Squadron, when on 6 September the Indian Army was prevented from crossing the last defence before Lahore, the BRB Canal just in time as the lead brigade of Indian 15th Infantry Division was about to throw a bridgehead across the BRB Canal when it was attacked by the F-86s that strafed it and other elements of the Division up and down the Grand Trunk Road, throwing the Indians into confusion, delaying the advance and thus allowing Pakistan's 10th Division to assume its forward positions, which ended the Indian hope of a quick victory.

'The other missions which deserve special credit along with PAF's successful defence of Sargodha on 7 September are the attacks on Kalaikunda, where 14 Squadron F-86s from Dhaka destroyed numerous Canberras lined up on the tarmac; 19 Squadron's famous raid on Pathankot in which IAF MiG-21s, Gnats and Mystères were caught off guard on the ground; and 5 Squadron's ill-fated strike over Halwara, which ended in tragedy but had far reaching consequences.

Having set off to a flying start by enabling the destruction of the Indian Vampires on 1 September, Squadron Leader Sarfraz Ahmed Rafiqui had set very high standards. On 6 September, when the Indian Army launched its three-pronged offensive, like the other squadrons at Sargodha, Rafiqui's pilots too were kept busy in ground support sorties to stop the Indian onslaught. At 1300 hours, tasking orders were received for the implementation of the pre-designated strike plan. For a Time Over Target (TOT) of 1705 hours, Squadron Leaders Mohammad Mahmood Alam and Rafiqui were to attack Adampur and Halwara with F-86s from Sargodha while from Peshawar, Squadron Leader Sajad Haider's squadron was to strike Pathankot with eight F-86s and two as armed escorts. Halwara was situated southwest of the industrial township of Ludhiana, Punjab, not far from the border and surrounded by numerous agricultural fields. At this airbase were Nos. 7 and 27 Hunter Squadrons. 7 Squadron had moved to Halwara from Ambala in August. The war was expected to come so from the second half of August Combat Air Patrols (CAP) were flown regularly.

All the three Pakistani F-86 squadrons got busy in preparing for the strikes. When Rafiqui learnt that only four Sabres would be available for the strike on Halwara, he detailed himself as Leader with Flight Lieutenant Cecil Chaudhry as No.2, his Flight Commander Flight Lieutenant Younus Hussain, Sitara-e-Jurat, another outstanding pilot as No.3 and Flight Lieutenant Saleem as No 4. Rafiqui reached the flight lines along with his pilots at 1600 hours to get airborne at 1615 for attacking Halwara at 1705 but to his surprise, he discovered that none of the allocated

Squadron Leader Najeeb Khan, OC 7 Squadron during the 1965 war walks away from his B-57 after a sortie. He was leading a flight of two B-57 bombers to Ambala on the night of 18 September, one of the heavily defended air base of the Indian Air Force. (Air Commodore (Retd) Rais A Rafi).

aircraft was ready. The morning's defence of Lahore had taken its toll and there were minor unserviceabilities or the aircraft had landed late and were yet to be turned around. He informed the Station Commander of the delay and was advised to make good whatever TOT was possible. The same was the case with Mohammad Mahmood Alam as his aircraft were not ready on time either. Meanwhile, Squadron Leader Sajad Haider struck Pathankot exactly on time and achieving complete surprise, carried out textbook pattern attacks and devastated his target.

Alam's formation got ready before Rafiqui's and he took off with Flight Lieutenants' Syed Saad Akhtar Hatmi, Sitara-e-Jurat, Alauddin 'Butch' Ahmad[34] and Murtaza to attack Adampur. As Rafiqui approached the aircraft to start up at 1715 hours, his heart was full of remorse. He was not concerned about himself but realizing the suicidal nature of his mission, he was thinking of Younus, who had been blessed with a second son the previous week but had not been able to go home to see him and Cecil Chaudhry who had recently been married. With grief in his eyes but determination on his face, Rafiqui tapped them on the shoulders and wishing them luck, climbed aboard his aircraft. During taxi, No 4's generator packed up and Saleem was ordered by Rafiqui to abort the mission.

About the time of the attack on Pathankot, four Hunters of 7 Squadron were on patrol near Taran Taran. This formation code-named 'Grey' was led by the Squadron's CO, Wing Commander A. T. R. H. Zachariah and consisted of Squadron Leaders A. K. Rawlley and M. M. Sinha and Flight Lieutenant S. K. Sharma. The patrol reached Taran Taran when they spotted some Sabres coming in at low level. The Sabres, led by Squadron Leader Mohammad Mahmood Alam, had been unable to reach Adampur as there was stiff opposition by the Indian Air Force, who were alerted by the raid on Pathankot. Down to only three aircraft, the formation had pressed on in the fading light. The Sabres on spotting the Hunters, shed their drop tanks and

Martin B-57B 33-941 call-sign 'Zulu 6' on 8 Squadron, 31 Bomber Wing based at Pakistan Air Force Station Mauripur (now Base Masroor) at Karachi, flown by 31 year old Squadron Leader Mohammad Shabbir Alam Siddiqui and the 32 year old navigator Squadron Leader Muhammad Aslam Qureshi which was shot down on the night of 6/7 September 1965.

Squadron Leader Shabbir Alam Siddiqui, pilot of the Martin B-57 Canberra on the night of 6/7 September 1965 and Squadron Leader Aslam Qureshi, navigator who did not return from their third bombing mission when they were shot down shortly before dawn on 7 September after dropping two bombs on Jamnagar airfield. They were in the circuit to drop the remaining load when they were hit by AAA fire and crashed. Both crew died on impact and were buried in nearby fields.

Squadron Leader Aslam Qureshi, navigator of the Martin B-57 Canberra on the night of 6/7 September 1965.

started gaining height, while the Hunters did the same. In the fight that followed, Rawlley was shot down and killed by Alam who then aborted the attack and extricated his aircraft from the fight. Alam's Sabre formation exiting out of the area crossed the Sabre formation led by Squadron Leader Sarfraz Rafiqui. Alam had warned Rafiqui's formation about the presence of the Hunters but Rafiqui carried on with his strike mission on Halwara airbase. The Hunters being low on fuel left the Sabres and started making it back to the base. Zachariah reported the loss of Rawlley and the two Hunters on the Operational Readiness Platform were ordered to take off.

That evening, two pairs of Hunter CAPs (Combat Air Patrols) were airborne, one from 7 Squadron with Flying Officers A. R. Gandhi and Prakash Sadashiv Rao Pingale[35] and the other from 27 Squadron with Flight Lieutenant D. N. Rathore and Flying Officer V. K. Neb. Gandhi who joined 7 Squadron in May 1965 was flying his fourth sortie of the day and Pingale was on his first. The two Hunters took off for their CAP over Halwara. Ten minutes later Halwara Air Control informed them that they were under attack by F-86s. The Hunters arrived over the airfield and could not figure out anything in the confusion. The airfield's ack-ack guns shot down one of the F-86s which dived headlong into the ground near the airfield. Rafiqui's formation had reached Halwara at 1800 hours. By then visibility had reduced considerably and they were having difficulty in locating the target. As they were positioning themselves to execute the attack, they spotted the two Hunters being flown by Gandhi and Pingale in front of them, Chaudhry and Younus who were criss-crossing behind their leader to keep them clear of the enemy threat from the rear, saw the Hunters as soon as Rafiqui called contact with them. Rafiqui positioned himself behind them and called to Chaudhry to take the Hunter on the left while he would take the one on the right. Since Younus was in a better position and Chaudhry had lagged slightly behind, Younus suggested that the leader should take the one on the left and he could take the one on the right. Rafiqui agreed and while Chaudhry cleared the tails of both the Leader and No.3, Rafiqui's guns found their mark before Younus could shoot. The first indication the Hunter pilots had that the Sabres had jumped them was when bullets fired out of nowhere slammed into Pingale's Hunter. Pingale suffered systems failure and loss of engine power. He ejected from his stricken aircraft safely and was picked up later. Younus saw his target break viciously to the right.

He followed him in the turn and just then two more Hunters appeared from the right. Both Chaudhry and Rafiqui spotted them and as Rafiqui manoeuvred to position himself for the kill, Chaudhry took up a defensive position behind him. Chaudhry was wondering why the leader hadn't commenced firing, when Rafiqui's calm and confident voice called out that his guns had jammed and Chaudhry should take over lead. At that time they were heading west and could have easily disengaged from the combat taking advantage of the fading light heading into the setting sun. This would have meant abandoning Younus, whom they had lost in the melee while he was chasing his target.

Rafiqui attacked Gandhi's aircraft and overshot him. Presented with a nice target, Gandhi manoeuvred behind it and started firing his cannon. Even though he did not take good aim, the 54 foot spread of the Hunter's four 30 mm cannon shells took care of the Sabre. Gandhi could see the Sabre was streaming smoke and was at 150 feet, when the cockpit canopy flew off. The Pakistani pilot had pulled his ejection lever and before the ejection sequence began, the Sabre nose-dived into the ground and blew up. Flying Officer Gandhi had got the first kill for the 'Battleaxes'. Before he could revel in his triumph, the remaining three Sabres made a beeline for his aircraft. His right wing got hit repeatedly. The Hunter lazily rolled to the right and entered into a spin. Gandhi ejected and landed on the outskirts of Halwara. Chaudhry overshot from the left, throttling forward. As he positioned himself behind the trailing Hunter, he saw the Hunter Leader pull away but by then he had opened fire and to his satisfaction he saw the enemy aircraft streaming smoke and the pilot eject. Chaudhry suddenly became aware of the eerie silence surrounding him. He looked around for his Leader and called him on the RT but received no response. The next instant he observed an F-86 in a classic scissors manoeuvre with a Hunter and thought it was Rafiqui but when he saw its guns blazing, he realized it must be Younus since Rafiqui's guns had jammed. Before Younus could get his target, another Hunter

Flying Officer Waleed Ehsanul Karim, Shaheed (Martyr) born July 1944, Harbang, Chakaria, Cox's Bazar, British India in front of his F-86 54989, one of the youngest Sabre jet pilots in the world was killed on 19 April 1965 when his recently repaired aircraft (which was hit by anti-aircraft guns at Rann of Kutch in the morning sortie) developed engine trouble and plunged into the Arabian sea about 10-15 miles off the south coast of Karachi when he was returning from a reconnaissance mission over Gujarat.

pounced on him and Younus was shot down. Left alone and running short of fuel, Chaudhry bravely fought his way out and managed to reach base to narrate the details of the courage and determination displayed by Rafiqui and Younus.

The last two Sabres were continuing their strafing when the two Hunter F.56s, flown by Flight Lieutenant D. N. Rathore and Flying Officer V. K. Neb as No.2, returning from a sortie, were directed towards the Sabres at about 18.40 hours, when the sun had gone down and the horizon was lit only by twilight. Rathore, who was about three miles from Halwara airfield, caught a flash in the air in the vicinity of the base. A second look confirmed that the base was under attack by Pakistani Sabres and that a dogfight was in progress with another section of two Hunters led by Gandhi. Rathore, warning Neb, immediately turned towards the airfield. The remaining two Sabres were strafing the airfield and bombing it from a very low level. Jockeying for position was not difficult as the two Pakistani pilots were concentrating on their ground attacks. Getting behind the Sabre, which was on his right, Rathore closed in to 1,000 yards, at the same time instructing Neb to take on the Sabre on the left. Overtaking his victim fast, Rathore closed in to 650 yards before opening fire. He saw the hits, registering on the Pakistani Sabre and it abandoned its ground attack. Closing in still further, Rathore fired again, from 500 yards. This time the Sabre was mortally hit. It started banking to the left and then turned into the ground, exploding in a huge sheet of flame five or six miles away from the airfield. Meanwhile, Neb had closed in behind the second Pakistani Sabre which, like the first one, was intent on strafing the airfield below. Neb, incidentally, had not carried out any air-to-air firing before and at the time of this engagement was still under operational training. Aiming and firing he lost no time closing in on the Pakistani Sabre to about 400 yards. The Pakistani pilot at once abandoned his attack on the airfield and pulled up sharply. Neb, unsure of his accuracy because of lack of any practice, rapidly closed in to less than 100 yards and fired again on the sharply climbing Sabre, which presented a much better target this time. He saw pieces fly off the Sabre, as his cannon shells found their mark and shredded the Sabre's left wing in an instant. There was a puff of smoke which rapidly turned into a sheet of flame as the last of the four Pakistani Sabres disintegrated in mid-air and fell to the ground. Both the Hunters formed up and flew back to base.

It has been said that it was difficult to assess how many Indian aircraft were in the air to defend Halwara when Rafiqui's strike formation arrived and that 'it is beyond comprehension that after being alerted by the successful PAF attack with ten F-86s on IAF Base at Pathankot they would have only two in the air and later divert two more.' Sarfraz Rafiqui's determination to lead the attack on Halwara, deep inside enemy territory, being heavily outnumbered and having lost the element of surprise, speaks volumes for his sense of duty and courage. Although he would have been perfectly justified to leave the battle area, his decision to continue the engagement with the enemy despite his guns being jammed is in the highest traditions of chivalry. For him the end was never in doubt. [36]

Sarfraz Rafiquis' parents' grief over the earlier loss of their elder son Ijaz in a Hawker Fury crash many years ago had not quite subsided when a poignant message addressed to Mr. B. A. Rafiqui arrived by telegram at 22 ILACO House, Victoria Road, Karachi. It read, Regret to inform, your son Squadron Leader Sarfaraz Rafiqui failed to return from a mission against enemy…Any further news about him will be conveyed immediately. Letter follows. His fate was officially known only after the war when, dreadfully, he was not amongst the PoWs being exchanged.

On 8 September four IAF Hunter pilots were briefed to carry out an offensive sweep over the Raiwind-Khem Karan sector. Composition of the formation was: Flight Lieutenant C. K. K. Menon, leader; Flight Lieutenant A. S. Kullar, No. 2; Flight Lieutenant D. S. Nagi, No. 3 and sub-section leader; and Squadron Leader. B. K. Bishnoi, No. 4. The planes were armed with rockets and 30mm cannon. The section of four took off at 1800 hours for the target area. The aircraft kept low, flying between fifty and one hundred feet above the ground, the fertile green countryside of the Punjab passing under their wings as a blur. As the section approached

A formation of IAF Hawker Hunter F.Mk.56s BA360A and A489 on patrol over Ladakh.

Raiwind railway station, all four pilots saw a goods train which had pulled in. Menon decided that it was carrying military stores because the locomotive was attached to that end of the train which pointed towards Kasur, in the battle area. Simultaneously the layout of the station and the area around the train was firmly implanted in his memory. All this had to be assimilated in about a second as the aircraft swept past.

Menon as the leader asked his pilots whether they should take on the train. The reply was a unanimous affirmative. As the section had passed over the station, anti aircraft guns had opened up. To confuse the Pakistani gunners and also to utilise the section of Hunters to the best effect against the train, Menon decided to approach the goods train from a different direction. He therefore led the section well past the railway station till he was quite certain that the aircraft would be out of sight of those watching from the station. He then put his section in a wide left-hand turn. This ruse was to give the impression that the Hunters had missed seeing the goods train. The wide turn also enabled him to place his pilots in the best position for attack.

Coming out of the turn, Menon led his section on a course parallel to the length of the train, but still low. Judging the section's position to be abreast of the goods train, Menon pulled up his aircraft signalling the start of the attack. Almost simultaneously the other three Hunters pulled up. At the same time, the Pakistani anti-aircraft guns, sighting the Hunters, opened up again. At the top of their climb the aircraft were in their most vulnerable position, their speed having fallen off, before diving for their rocket attack. The positioning of the section by Menon had been excellent. As they pulled up and rolled to the left in the attacking dive, the section faced the train broadside and was evenly spaced out along the entire length of the target. Going in first, through the mushrooming flak, Menon concentrated on the extreme left of the train. He released his rockets at about 500 feet and levelling out from the dive a bare 100 feet above the ground he flashed over the train. He could not see his rockets hit the target. But Bishnoi, who as No. 4 was the last to go in, could see clearly the effect of the other three pilots' strikes. Bishnoi saw Menon's rockets strike the wagons on the extreme left. The explosion lifted them off the rails and set fire to them.

Kullar attacked the middle left of the target and Bishnoi saw his rockets also hit their mark and turn that section of the train into a blazing inferno. As Kullar hurtled low, over the train with ack-ack puffs chasing him, Nagi's rockets hit home in the middle right of the goods train. A powerful explosion ripped through the wagons, although as in all rocket attacks Nagi was not able to see the result of his attack. Bishnoi however, being the last in, saw Nagi's rockets hit home. Putting the extreme right end of the train in his sights, Bishnoi then fired his own rockets from about 400 feet. He watched their smoke trails heading towards the target, but then he too was very low and had to level out of the dive. He went over the train at about 100 feet and then turned to see the effect of his attack. Bishnoi's rockets had also found their mark and the wagons at the extreme right were also burning furiously.

By now explosions had started ripping the train apart and the whole area was enveloped in smoke and flames. Bishnoi called up his leader, Menon, on the R/T who also turned to see the success of their attack. Kullar and Nagi too had a glance at the now completely destroyed goods train and then the section turned to fly up the railway line from Raiwind towards Kasur. Menon and Kullar still had some rockets left and all four had their front-gun ammunition intact.

Nearing Kasur the pilots noticed a huge cloud of dust slightly to one side, so Menon led his section, flying very low, in that direction. Menon and Kullar picked up two groups of tanks as their target and pulled up to attack them. As their aircraft gained height rapidly, a murderous fire opened up on them from the ground. Undeterred, Menon went into a dive, latching on to one group of tanks and fired his remaining rockets. Three tanks burst into flames. Kullar who had followed Menon in the attack concentrated on the second group of tanks and fired. He could not confirm the damage caused by his rockets but was certain that he had damaged a few. While Menon and Kullar were attacking the tanks, Nagi and Bishnoi, who had expended all their rockets in the train attack, took on some armoured vehicles with their cannon. Despite the very heavy ack-ack fire, they made two passes each at the armoured vehicles and saw a considerable number catch fire and blow up.

All this while the four aircraft were being subjected to very heavy ground fire. Not only were the regular ack-ack guns firing, but also the anti-aircraft guns mounted on Pakistani tanks and other automatic weapons were blazing away at the Hunters. Nevertheless, Menon, after attacking the tanks, spotted two convoys of vehicles. Pulling up, he engaged the nearest with his cannon. Then, pulling up again, he attacked the second convoy. In these two attacks, he saw that he had set fire to thirty vehicles which, with their inflammable stores, were now bursting and exploding. Kullar, the No. 2, after his rocket attack on the second group of tanks, pulled up again in the teeth of heavy ack-ack fire, ranged another tank in his gunsight and went for it with his cannon. He managed to disable it.

With their ammunition almost expended, the section turned back to base at very low level,

F-86 Sabre and B-57 bombers of the Pakistan Air Force.

re-forming at the same time. Assessing the damage to their own aircraft, Menon found that his fuel state was lower than it should have been; ack-ack had punctured his port wing tank and the fuel had leaked out. Another bullet had damaged his airspeed indicator. Kullar had been slightly more unlucky, a bullet had found his main fuel tank and punctured it, so his reaching the base was a touch-and-go affair. However, all four pilots reached base safely, although Menon had to be shepherded in because of his unserviceable ASI.

He had gathered an impressive tally of one-quarter goods train destroyed, three tanks destroyed and thirty vehicles set on fire - all in about half an hour. How important that goods train was to the Pakistanis only came to light later. The train was carrying petrol and ammunition for the Pakistani tanks in the Khem Karan area and the enemy armour was depending for replenishment on this train. With its destruction, the Pattons in the Khem Karan sector were forced to go into battle with only thirty shells each and a limited amount of petrol. When their initial thrust was stopped by Indian armour, the Pakistani tanks had to withdraw, suffering heavy losses, because they did not have the fuel or ammunition to continue the fight.

On the morning of 9 September the Pakistanis were building up for an armoured thrust in the Khem Karan area and Indian troops were under great pressure. To relieve this pressure IAF Hunters had been called upon for ground strikes against Pakistani gun and armoured positions; two sorties had already gone out for this purpose.

For the third strike of the day, four pilots had been briefed. The section was to be led by Squadron Leader. B. K. Bishnoi, who only the previous evening had taken a hand in destroying the goods train at Raiwind station. The other pilots assigned were Flight Lieutenant G. S. Ahuja as No. 2, Flight Lieutenant S. K. Sharma as No. 3 and sub-section leader and Flying Officer Parulkar as No. 4. During the briefing these pilots were told to attack enemy tanks, armoured vehicles and gun positions in the Khem Karan area.

The take-off in sections of two was smooth. Bishnoi and Ahuja pulled up sharply after getting airborne to enable Sharma and Parulkar to avoid the jet blast on their take-off run. Settling down at about one hundred feet above ground, in tactical formation, they proceeded towards their target. Ahuja was on Bishnoi's left and slightly behind him, while Sharma and Parulkar came up on their leader's right about 500 yards away and slightly behind. This loose formation enabled everyone to concentrate on accurate low-level flying, navigation and at the same time keep a look-out for enemy aircraft and ground targets.

As the section approached the target area, still maintaining 100 feet above ground, Bishnoi spotted well to his left the tell-tale cloud of dust which indicated tank and vehicle movement. Bishnoi warned the others in the section that they were approaching enemy armoured concentrations and that everyone should choose his target. Ahuja, Sharma and Parulkar acknowledged the transmission. All four pilots switched on the electrical circuits for releasing their rockets and tested their front guns by firing a short burst. Bishnoi from his previous day's experience over the same area was expecting enemy anti-aircraft fire - but not the kind of concentration that opened up as the four Hunters approached the tanks. The familiar black puffs of 40-mm. ack-ack almost blackened the sky around them and the Patton-tank-mounted guns sprayed the airspace with their lethal loads. There was one favourable factor, however. The 40-mm. shells were bursting above the Hunters. The enemy gunners had not got the correct height, but then they were anticipating the pilots' next move. The aircraft would have to pull up for a rocket attack and that would take them to a height where the sky was already pock-marked by ack-ack puffs. There was such a concentration of tanks, armoured cars and other vehicles that choosing targets was not difficult. Bishnoi selected a group of three tanks which were in a 'U' formation a little to his left. He pulled up to 300 feet and rolled into his attacking dive. Now the ack-ack fire seemed to be all round him and at the same height. Ignoring this Bishnoi settled his gunsight on this group of three tanks and then from about 400 yards distance, fired a salvo of eight rockets. Levelling out at about 50 feet he hurtled over the tanks and then turned to have a look. All three tanks had been hit and had blown up; they

Mohammed Shaukat-ul-Islam of the Pakistan Air Force. (Group Captain Mohammed Shaukat-ul-Islam)

Muhammad Mahmood Alam (known as M.M. Alam), a F-86 Sabre flying ace and one-star general who served in the PAF, commanding 11 Squadron and was awarded the Sitara-e-Jurat ('The Star of Courage') for his actions during the Indo-Pakistani War of 1965. Alam holds the record of having downed five Indian aircraft in less than a minute.

were burning furiously.

Following their leader's example, the other three, Ahuja, Sharma and Parulkar, also selected tanks as their targets and pulling up, one by one, in the deadly danger zone of exploding anti-aircraft shells, delivered their rocket attacks. Between the three of them, they hit and destroyed seven more tanks. Having expended their rockets, all four Hunter pilots now decided to take on the armoured cars and other vehicles with their nose-mounted cannon.

After attacking the tanks Bishnoi had spotted a group of vehicles, to which he now turned his attention. Leaving the safety of low altitude, he pulled up again before engaging his new target. With heavy ack-ack fire following him, Bishnoi rolled into his attack from the apex of his pull-up and fired his cannon. He saw his shells hit and explode on the vehicles; in an instant the vehicles were on fire and the ammunition in them started exploding. By this time, however, Bishnoi had levelled out and, hugging the ground, had sped past the target. Ahuja in the meantime engaged some armoured cars with his cannon, while Sharma and Parulkar took on some more vehicles carrying supplies. Again and again pulling up in the face of murderous flak, all four went in for their strafing attacks until their ammunition was exhausted. After their last attack, the section remained low and sped out of the enemy area. Once out of range of the enemy ack-ack, the Hunters formed up again in tactical formation and set course for base.

Just as they were clear of the target area, Parulkar called up his leader, Bishnoi and told him that he had been hit in his right arm. Bishnoi was really concerned because, although Parulkar could probably manage to fly with his left hand till they reached their base, on landing he would need both hands and especially the right for coaxing the fighter down on to the runway. Throughout the flight back to base, Parulkar, who incidentally was on his first operational sortie, kept on assuring Bishnoi that he was all right. The section reached their base and immediately the first three landed.

All were now waiting for Parulkar. He made a normal turn on to the final approach and started coming lower and lower. With a sigh of relief, everyone saw him make a perfect touch-down and hurtle down the runway on his landing run. If his right hand was badly hurt, his troubles were not yet over. He would have to apply the brakes with his right hand to stop the aircraft. This too, Parulkar managed and, ignoring the ambulance and crash tender, turned on to the taxi track and taxied back to dispersal. It was only when he got out of the aircraft that his fellow pilots and his ground crew saw the seriousness of his wound. A bullet had hit his right upper arm and torn through the flesh, baring the bone. His overall was drenched with blood. He must have been in extreme pain and it was a wonder that he had not fainted due to lack of blood. Parulkar was of course rushed to hospital where the doctors put in nine stitches to close the wound. But such was his excitement that he was soon in the crew room recounting the day's adventure to his squadron mates.

Low-level dogfights in the modern jet age are said to be impossible - or at least improbable. But in the heat of battle even the improbable comes to pass. Such was the case on 19 September when an air battle was fought over the Chawinda Sector between Indian Gnats and Pakistani Sabres which started at about 1,500 feet and ended at tree-top height. Squadron Leader Denzil Keelor, born 7 December 1933 and his section of four Gnat aircraft was detailed to provide cover to four IAF Mystère IVAs which were going out for a close-support sortie to Chawinda. With Keelor were Flying Officer Rai his No. 2, Flight Lieutenant V. Kapila as sub-section leader and Flight Lieutenant Maya Dev as the No. 4. Taking off in their Gnats, they followed the Mystères at low level towards Chawinda. As they arrived over the target the enemy flak opened up and being very low, they could see the flak bursts near and above them. Suddenly Maya Dev called out a warning that four Pakistani Sabres were approaching to attack the Mystères. The four Gnat pilots spotted the Sabres on their left above them at about 4,000 feet. Denzil Keelor and his pilots were a bare 300 feet above the ground. He put his section into a shallow left-hand climbing turn so as to place himself behind the Sabres. As the distance between the two formations closed rapidly, Keelor saw that Kapila, with Maya Dev looking after his tail, was in the best position for an attack on the Pakistanis. He ordered Kapila to engage the nearest Sabre. As Kapila with commendable adroitness latched on behind one of them, the Pakistani became aware of this threat and started taking violent evasive action. He went into a hard turn to the left and Kapila followed him, but still could not get into a favourable firing position. Suddenly the Sabre reversed his turn and went into a steep turn to the right. This was the opportunity Kapila was waiting for. Jettisoning his drop tanks, he easily slipped into a firing position and, reducing the distance to 500 yards, gave a short burst, which at once went home.

The engagement which had started at about 1,500 feet was now getting lower and lower as the Sabre, in order to get away, was executing descending turns. With Kapila's first burst striking the Sabre, it slowed down a bit. Getting nearer still, Kapila fired again from 300 yards. Again his shells found their mark. But by now being a bare 300 feet above the ground, he had to pull up; he did not see the Sabre spin and crash to the ground. But Keelor with Rai - who had been following Kapila and Maya Dev through this engagement to guard them against possible rear attacks - watched the end of the Sabre, which after Kapila's second burst spun and hit the ground, exploding on impact. Keelor called out to Kapila confirming his kill. Just as Keelor had finished transmitting to Kapila he saw a Sabre which had been separated from his section in the melee, trying to get away from the scene. The Sabre apparently had not seen Keelor, as it did a hard turn to the right. This was a manoeuvre which gave Keelor the opportunity of quickly slipping behind the Sabre in a favourable firing position. Reducing the distance to less than 500 yards, Keelor fired a couple of bursts which were enough to send the Sabre crashing to the ground. It was only when the Sabre hit the ground that Keelor realised that he himself was skimming the tree tops. [37]

India's decision to open up the theatre of attack into Pakistani Punjab forced the Pakistani army to relocate troops engaged in the operation to defend Punjab. The war saw aircraft of the Indian Air Force (IAF) and the Pakistan Air Force (PAF) engaging in combat for the first time since independence. The IAF was flying large numbers of Hawker Hunter, Indian-manufactured Folland Gnats, de Havilland Vampires, English Electric Canberra bombers and a squadron of MiG-21s.

Pakistan used the F-104As primarily for combat air patrols, usually consisting of two Sidewinder-equipped F-86F Sabres, with a Starfighter to provide top cover. The F-104s occasionally provided escort to PAF Martin B-57B Canberra bombers or reconnaissance aircraft and sometimes flew high-speed photoreconnaissance missions themselves. No other aircraft in the history of aviation has engendered more controversy such notoriety and suffered such a high loss rate over a short period as the Starfighter. Pakistan, which remained an important ally of the United States through the Cold War, was the first non-NATO country to equip with the Starfighter. By September 1965 the Pakistan Air Force (PAF) had only 150 aircraft (including 102 F-86Fs), while the Indian Air Force (IAF) possessed approximately 900 aircraft. Twelve of the aircraft in the PAF inventory were Starfighters, the bulk of which were received in August 1961. These consisted of ten refurbished F-104As and two F-104Bs, all supplied under the US Military Defense Assistance Programme (MAP). At PAF's request, all its F-104s were refitted with the M-61 gun, whereas the USAF had removed the weapon on the assumption that air combat after Korea would occur at high speeds where only AAMs would be effective. This and the more advanced GE-J-79-II engine made the PAF F-104s unique - they had the gun and being the lightest of the F-104 series therefore enjoyed the best thrust-to-weight ratio. All were used to equip 9 Air Superiority Squadron. This became an elite unit, its personnel handpicked from F-86 Sabre squadrons. The PAF Starfighters, which were each armed with two AIM-9B Sidewinder AAMs, were the first Mach 2 capable aircraft in Asia. Even in Europe at this time, most countries were still flying subsonic aircraft. Even before its introduction to combat, the Starfighter had gained such a reputation in the IAF that it was known as the 'hadmash', 'scoundrel' or 'wicked one'.

Many questioned Pakistan's ability to fly and maintain such a sophisticated aircraft as the F-104A/B. (The in-commission rate of the F-104 during the first five years of service was over 80 per cent and all systems performed with high reliability). 9 Squadron lost only one Starfighter during training, when Flight Lieutenant Asghar 'pitched up' and went into an uncontrollable

spin during an air combat training sortie. This F-104A was replaced under the MAP programme. Also, Flight Lieutenant Khalid managed a 'dead stick' landing after an engine flame out in another F-104A. PAF Starfighters were used throughout the wars with India in 1965 and in 1971.

During the 1965 conflict the PAF was out-numbered by around 5:1. The PAF's aircraft were largely of American origin, whereas the IAF flew an assortment of British and Soviet aeroplanes. It has been widely reported that the PAF's American aircraft were superior to those of the

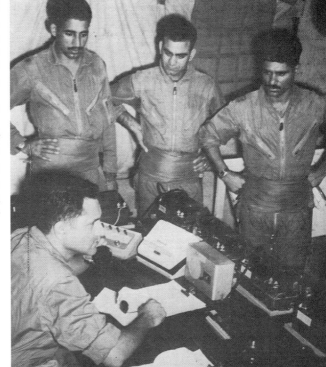

Group Captain Zafar Masud the PAF station commander at Sargodha debriefing some of the pilots of 32 Wing.

IAF, but according to some experts this is untrue because the IAF's MiG-21, and Hawker Hunter fighters actually had higher performance than their PAF counterpart, the F-86 Sabre. Although the IAF's de Havilland Vampire fighter-bombers were outdated in comparison to the F-86 Sabre, the Hawker Hunter fighters were superior in both power and speed to the F-86 according to Air Commodore Sajjad Haider, who led the PAF's 19 Squadron in combat during the war.

Group Captain Mohammed Shaukat-Ul Islam recalls: 'In November 1964 I was posted to 11 (F) Squadron, commanded by Squadron Leader Mohammad Mahmood Alam at Sargodha. I became operational in August 1965 and was allowed to take part in the 6-23 September 1965 war with India. I considered myself very lucky to have taken part in the war as a Flying Officer with only about eighty hours on the F-86F with a grand total of about 400 hours. At the outbreak of the war 11 Squadron was tasked to carry out a dawn strike against the Indian Army in Chamb-Jurian sector with two formations of eight F-86 aircraft. Each aircraft carried 32 x 5.75-inch rockets and 1,800 x .50 inch ammunition. We exhausted all the weapons on the convoy of the Indian army and returned to Sargodha safely. As it was a surprise dawn strike we faced only small arms fire from the enemy. By the time I landed and cleared the runway my aircraft flamed out because of shortage of fuel.

'On 9 September four F-86Fs were tasked to provide a low level escort mission for three B-57 bombers attacking a train carrying ammunition at Gadro. The bombers carried out four attacks each and all seven aircraft remained within heavy ack-ack fire for about fifteen minutes. All aircraft exited low level after the successful delivery of weapons. The three bombers recovered at Peshawar and we four fighters came back to Sargodha safe and sound. It was my first experience of remaining within such heavy anti-aircraft fire for such a long time.

'On 11 September, I was in a formation of four F-86Fs who took part in an escort mission at day time to give air protection to a train carrying ammunitions from Lahore to Sialkot sector. It might sound very easy but to give protection to such a slow moving train by so fast moving aircraft at low level by four aircraft for such a long time was very demanding. The train reached its destination and got its cargo off-loaded.'

On the night of 13/14 September Squadron Leader Mervyn Leslie Middlecoat achieved the first blind night interception in an F-104, firing a Sidewinder at a Canberra from a distance of 4,000 feet and reporting an explosion, but failing to obtain a confirmation. Another Starfighter was lost on 17 September, when Flying Officer G. O. Abassi tried to land in a sudden dust storm, undershot the runway and crashed in a ball of fire. Miraculously, he was thrown clear, still strapped in his ejection seat and he survived with only minor injuries.

On 16 September Group Captain Mohammed Shaukat-Ul Islam took off from Sargodha as Squadron Leader Mohammad Mahmood Alam's wingman to carry out a high level offensive patrol mission deep inside Indian territory.

'We were flying in battle formation at 23,000 feet between two Indian Air Bases, Halwara and Adampur. The aim was to invite the Indian fighters to come and fight with us. We could take such a venture because by then the PAF already had established air-superiority over the IAF. It was about 2 pm with clear blue sky when our ground controller from a radar station transmitted that two IAF Hunters had taken off from Halwara and were approaching to intercept us. When they came in sight we jettisoned our drop tanks and entered into close air combat. The air battle became intense and under such high 'g' manoeuvres I could not stay on the tail of my leader. As it turned out, my leader shot the No.2 of the other formation and their leader shot me. My aircraft caught fire and I ejected through the shattered canopy at about 12,000 feet. I lost consciousness for a couple of seconds and by the time I got my senses back I was floating in the air and that the small parachute was pulling out the bigger one. As I settled down with my parachute I saw a Hunter with streaming fuel and crash with a big explosion. The Hunter pilot was shot in the cockpit. When I looked down to locate my probable landing spot, I noticed with horror that a man in uniform was pointing a .303 rifle at me and a civilian was aiming a double barrel shot gun. I heard three shots and within seconds my feet touched the ground. I got up, released the parachute and was surrounded by a crowd of people. The name of the place was Taran Taran. The local police rescued me from the crowd and took me quickly to a nearby police station and then to a hospital. I was bleeding profusely from my back. A doctor operated on me and showed me a .303 bullet taken out of my back. Next day I was taken to IAF Base, Adampur and flown to Delhi in an Antonov An-32 and admitted to the Combined Military Hospital (CMH). The cease-fire was declared on 23 September when I was still in the CMH. Later, I joined another pilot and a navigator of the B-57, which was shot down by AA fire on 15 September in a night raid over IAF Base Adampur. We three returned to Pakistan after being released in a prisoner exchange in February 1966.

'In the war of 1965 I flew a total of nineteen missions including the Air Defence missions day and night up to 16 September. The story of my time as a PoW was a different chapter of my life. However, I can say that the IAF treated me very well. In the later days when I joined the Bangladesh Air Force in 1972, I had the opportunity to visit the IAF as official guest and met many friends whom I came in contact as a PoW. After returning from India, I was posted back to 11 Squadron. From then on it became my passion to be a master in the air combat. In my later days I could fly the F-86 like a toy and used to manoeuvre it to its design limits. In the early sixties we used to comment by saying that a pilot who had not flown the F-86 did not enjoy the charm of fighter flying. I was later posted to 14 Squadron, Dhaka and 26 Squadron, Peshawar where I continued flying the F-86F. In 1968 the PAF introduced the F-86E and soon it became a very popular fighter aircraft. I continued flying both models till 1970 and logged about 1200 hours on the F-86F and E combined. In total I had flown thirteen types of aircraft in my career including the MiG-21MF and the F-5.'

India claimed that the F-86 was vulnerable to the diminutive Folland Gnat, nicknamed 'Sabre Slayer.' The PAF's F-104 Starfighter was the fastest fighter operating in the subcontinent at that time and was often referred to as 'the pride of the PAF'. However, according to Sajjad Haider the F-104 did not deserve this reputation. Being 'a high level interceptor designed to neutralise Soviet strategic bombers in altitudes above 40,000 feet' rather than engage in dogfights with agile fighters at low altitudes it was 'unsuited to the tactical environment of the region.' In combat the Starfighter was not as effective as the IAF's far more agile, albeit much slower, Folland Gnat fighter. Yet it zoomed into an ongoing dogfight between Sabres and Gnats, at supersonic speed, successfully broke off the fight and caused the Gnats to egress. In their first aerial encounter on 3 September, two PAF F-86s battled six IAF Gnats while an F-104A, flown by Flying

The Martin B-57B Canberra in PAK service had an ejection seat for both the pilot and navigator whereas in IAF service the Canberra had only an ejection seat for the pilot, which meant certain death in combat for a navigator.

PAF Martin B-57 Canberra, two F-86F Sabres and a RT-33 photographed from another RT-33 from Masroor AB before the 1965 war with India. (Taimur Khan)

Officer Abbas Mirza, darted around above, vainly trying to get a shot at one of the elusive Gnats. When a second F-104A arrived, however, one of the Gnats, flown by Squadron Leader Brij Pal Singh Sikand, suddenly descended and landed at an abandoned Pakistani airstrip at Pasrur and was captured by the Pakistan Army. The pilot claimed that most of his equipment failed and even if he could get some chance on that, the star-fighters snuffed it. This Gnat is displayed as a war trophy in the Pakistan Air Force Museum, Karachi. Squadron Leader Saad Hatmi who flew the captured aircraft to Sargodha and later tested and evaluated its flight performance was of the view that the Gnat was no 'Sabre Slayer' when it came to dog fighting.

India and Pakistan made contradictory claims of combat losses during the war and few neutral sources have verified the claims of either country. The PAF claimed it shot down 104 IAF aircraft and lost nineteen of its own, while the IAF claimed it shot down seventy-three PAF aircraft and lost fifty-nine. According to one independent source, the PAF flew eighty-six F-86 Sabres, ten F-104 Starfighters and twenty B-57 Canberras in a parade soon after the war was over. Thus disproving the IAF's claim of downing seventy-three PAF fighters, which at the time constituted nearly the entire Pakistani frontline fighter force. Indian sources have pointed out that, despite PAF claims of losing only a squadron of combat craft, Pakistan sought to acquire additional aircraft from Indonesia, Iraq, Iran, Turkey and China within ten days of the beginning of the war. But this could be explained by the 5:1 disparity in numbers faced by the PAF. India retained much of its air force in the East, against the possibility of Chinese intervention and, as a result, the air forces were quite evenly balanced in the West.

During the 1965 war, 9 Squadron was commanded by Squadron Leader Mervyn Leslie Middlecoat who, as a flight lieutenant, was, with Squadron Leader Mian Sadruddin, one of the two pilots to land the first pair of PAF Starfighters at Sargodha in 1962. India had radar cover above 5,000 feet, which made it virtually impossible for the Starfighter to achieve surprise, while subsonic aircraft operating under radar cover could easily defend themselves. At first, most thought that the chance of a real war breaking out between the two countries was high and a morning Combat Air Patrol (CAP) was flown before dawn. The F-104s would fly to 30,000 feet and patrol the area near the disputed territory of Indian-held Kashmir.

On 3 September, before the war began, a single PAF F-104A, flown by Flight Lieutenant Hakimuilah, was vectored at supersonic speed to intercept an IAF Gnat, whose pilot, Squadron Leader Brijpal Singh Sikand, promptly lowered his undercarriage in surrender and landed at the abandoned PAF airfield of Pasrur. Sikand was made a PoW. On 6 September two Starfighters from Sargodha, with Flight Lieutenant Aftab Alam Kahn leading and Flight Lieutenant Amjad

Hussain Khan as his wingman, were vectored by Sakesar radar towards four IAF Mystères engaged in bombing and rocket attacks against a stationary passenger train at Gakkhar railway station near to the border with Kashmir. What followed was the first combat kill by a Mach 2 aircraft and the first missile kill for the PAF when a PAF F-104A shot down an IAF Mystère IV. It was also proven that the F-104 and the Sidewinder missile were an effective weapon system at low altitude. Flight Lieutenant Aftab Alam Kahn recalls:

'I was informed that the IAF had crossed the Pakistan border and were attacking ground positions approximately 80 nautical miles south of us. This meant that India had actually decided to start an all-out war. We were immediately vectored and were soon over the site where the Indian aircraft were attacking. While dawn was breaking at 15,000 feet, it was still dark down below and I asked for permission to descend to ground level, but was denied. The reason given was that radio contact would he lost. I, however, decided to descend and, leaving my wingman at 15,000 feet to act as radio relay, I dived down and headed towards some flashes. As I reached the area, I was surprised to see that I was flying head-on into a formation of four IAF Mystère IVA aircraft that were attacking ground targets. I was shocked more than I was surprised, as I felt a wave of anger leap through me. I had to shoot down these aircraft. I jettisoned my external fuel tanks and started to engage the Mystères as they turned into me. Manoeuvring started at treetop level. I kept my eves 'glued' on the target. I could feel the strain under high Gs, looking over the tail of the aircraft, keeping the enemy in sight and skimming the trees at high speed. One mistake and I would have hit the ground. If I had lost sight of the Mystères the fight would have been over. The F-104, with the afterburner blazing, at low altitude, was responding very well. I used the high-speed take-off flaps to improve the turning capability as required. The 'stick shaker' was a big help in flying the aircraft to its limit. The Mystères would have no problem keeping the F-104 in sight because of its afterburner.

'After some hectic manoeuvering, I was positioned behind two aircraft, but the other two were still not visible. I then spotted them, further ahead. Joy leapt though me. I aimed my weapons and decided to shoot the first two with missiles and the next two with guns. I fully realized that a confidential order prohibited me from using the missile below 10,000 feet. However, I was sure the missile could he used effectively at any height provided the targets could he discriminated from the background heat sources. A distant increase in missile tone ensured this. I set the wingspan of the Mystère IVA and started to recall the missile-firing checklist: 'Check Ranger, Check Tone, Check G's, Squeeze the trigger and hold.'

'I aimed the missile at the nearest aircraft and heard the loud pitched missile tone. The sight indicated that I was in range. With all the other requisite firing conditions met, I squeezed the trigger and kept it pressed. I waited, only to note that the missile had not fired. As I looked towards the left missile, I saw a big flash and the missile leaving the aircraft. The missile had taken, as stipulated in the manual, approximately 8/10ths of a second to fire after the trigger had been pressed but in combat, this seemed like an eternity. The flash of the missile blinded me for a few seconds. The radar controller [Flight Lieutenant Farooq Haider from Sakesar radar] who was also monitoring the radio of the Mystères immediately informed me that one Mystère had been shot down and that another had been damaged. I was then at once instructed to tutu tight and pick up visual contact with the other Mystères, which were exiting. I turned as directed but could not see them. On landing back, I was informed that the dogfight had taken place overhead the Rahwali airfield where low-powered radar was located. The Mystère wreckage had fallen close by. The other three had got away.'

In one of the early attacks, Flight Lieutenant Arif Iqbal in an F-104 was about to fire at a Mystère IVA, when he suddenly saw a PAF F-86 flight appear between him and the IAF aircraft and shoot down the Mystère. During an Indian attack on Sargodha air base, however, Flight Lieutenant Amjad Hussein Khan, who had missed his chance the day before, made amends. He made visual contact with the IAF Mystères and headed toward them. By the time he caught up with them, the Indian aircraft were 6-8 miles away from Sargodha, flying at 150-200 feet in

Two PAF F-104 Starfighters of 9 Squadron in formation.

a south-easterly direction towards India. As the Mystères jettisoned their drop tanks, Khan positioned himself behind one of them and released a Sidewinder missile, which went straight into the ground. The Mystère then began to dogfight with the Starfighter, which used its superior climb and acceleration to raise the combat from ground level to about 7,000 feet to gain room for manoeuvre. Khan fired his cannon and was delighted to see the shells hit the Mystère. The IAF pilot, Squadron Leader A. B. Devayya of 1 Squadron IAF, showed commendable courage in staying with the F-104 and despite being mortally wounded, scored several cannon strikes on the Starfighter. Hussain Khan managed to eject at low altitude. He had reason to be grateful that his F-104 did not have the original downward-firing ejection seat - otherwise, his subsequent award of the Sitara-e-Jurat would probably have been posthumous. (Six F-104 pilots received gallantry awards during the 1965 war). This was the only Starfighter to be lost to enemy action in the 1965 war. During attacks on Rawalpindi and Peshawar by IAF English Electric Canberras that night, three F-104s tried to intercept them but failed to get a target acquisition because the bombers were too low.

At around 0515 hours on the morning of 7 September a large number of PAF F-104s and F-86s flew CAP in the vicinity of Sargodha waiting for the IAF to attack. The F-104s were assigned the outer perimeter, while the F-86s were kept closer to the airfield. The first IAF attack, at 0530, by six Mystère IVAs of 1 Squadron, got through without being intercepted. Six Hawker Hunter F.56s of Nos. 7 and 27 Squadrons IAF carried out the second attack on Sargodha, at 0610 hours. The third attack was made at 0947 hours, by four Mystères of 1 Squadron IAF and a fourth and final attack on Sargodha was carried out by two Mystères at 1030 hours.

Flight Lieutenant Aftab Slam Khan continues:

'The pilots of 9 Squadron competed fiercely; to undertake as many combat missions as they could, never missing a chance to close with the enemy looking for combat. In the days that followed, the F-104 pilots noted that whenever they got airborne, the IAF grounded all its aircraft. This made it very difficult for the F-104 pilots to engage the enemy during the day. Flight Lieutenant Muchtaq, my brother, flying an F-104 in the same squadron, made contact with the enemy, only to note that as he approached the target, the IAF Hunters disengaged well in time. Flight Lieutenant 'Mickey' Abbas in an F-104 had a similar episode. This experience would be repeated for the F-104 pilots for all daytime interceptions. I personally patrolled in a lone F-104, at 30,000 feet, deep inside Indian Territory over the two Indian fighter airfields of Adamput and Halwara for one hour and there was no response from the Indian side. This was total air superiority and it displayed the supremacy of the Starfighter.

'At medium and high altitudes the F-104 ruled the sky. The IAF refused to challenge the Starfighter. But below 5,000 feet a fierce battle raged between the F-86 and the IAF fighters, mainly the Hunters and Gnats. The F-86 was the workhorse of the PAF. It was under-powered, outnumbered and outgunned. Nevertheless, the F-86 pilots showed great courage as they fearlessly engaged their opponents and displayed an unusual skill for air combat, achieving an excellent kill ratio. The F-104, by controlling the sky at medium and high altitude, had reduced the workload for the F-86s to the extent that the numbers were manageable. The F-86s could now hold their own against the enemy at low altitude.

'Immediately after the start of the war there was an urgent need for a high-speed reconnaissance aircraft. The PAF RT-33 was rendered obsolete with a speed of less than 400 knots. It was liable to be shot down as it crossed the border. At night we did standby duties, one bout in the cockpit and one bout off. In the off time I would go and receive the B-57 pilots returning from their bombing missions over Indian airfields. The battle damage from these missions needed to be assessed. I suggested to the Base Commander that if he authorized a recce mission by the F-104, I would have a photograph on his table by noon next day. He ordered the mission.

'Low flying was not a part of the F-104 war plan - no training had been conducted, but while demonstrating the aircraft, I noticed that the Starfighter flew very well at low level. I planned the mission at 600 knots (10 miles/minute). Low flying was normally done at 420 knots in the F-86 squadrons. For the photograph I went to town early morning and bought a film for my personal Yashica 120 camera. I then requested Squadron Leader Middlecoat, the squadron commander, if he would allow me to fly while he took the pictures. He agreed. The mission was flown in an F-104B dual seater [57-1309]. Ten miles a minute made the DR navigation very easy. Over flat terrain, the height of the aircraft was lowered until Squadron Leader Middlecoat said that downwash was hitting the ground. This height was then maintained - a thrilling experience. We pulled up, slightly offset from the airfield. Pictures were taken and a visual recce made. The photographs were placed on the Base Commander's table, as promised. The missions that followed were with bigger and better cameras but I was always told to fly. The F-104 had a new role.

'The reconnaissance flights revealed that the forward IAF bases had only approximately forty aircraft each at Adampur and Halwara and even fewer than that at Pathankot. Where were the rest of the IAF aircraft? This got me thinking and I went on to study the map. Moving further east from the Indian airfields of Adampur and Halwara were Agra and Delhi. These airfields were 350 nautical miles from Sargodha. There was no attack aircraft in the PAF inventory that could reach these airfields flying at low level. If an aircraft approached at a high altitude level, it could easily be intercepted. I therefore presumed that the Indians would have the bulk of their aircraft at these bases and because they were sure they could not be attacked, the aircraft would be in the open. The F-104A's J-79-11A engine, was very fuel-efficient. This gave the PAF F-104's an extended range capability.[38] I marked the route and was surprised to note that if we took off with four tanks and jettisoned them as they went empty, we could reach these bases while maintaining a speed of 540 knots at low level. It would also allow us to make two gun attacks, exit at 600 knots to the border; climb to attain height and land back with 1,000lbs of fuel remaining. The plan looked like a very exciting possibility to me. I thought of 'Pearl Harbor'; complete surprise could be achieved. I stayed up all night, made the Flight plan and next morning made the proposal to my Squadron Commander. He told me that he was against submitting the proposal, as it was too risky. I then took the plan to the Wing Leader who had been my instructor on the Harvard T-6G. He said that it was a good plan but refused to take it any higher. I then went to the Base Commander. He said he liked it, but he would not make the proposal to the high command. There was nobody else to go to. Immediately after the war, the Air Chief ordered a high altitude recce mission of the airfields at Agra and Delhi. This was to be flown by the B-57F 'Droopy', a fanjet modified B-57 that had replaced the U-2 and was flown by Pakistani pilots. The recce flight revealed that Agra and Delhi were sprawling with aircraft. If the F-104 had attacked Delhi and Agra, it could have been a historic day for the PAF, as well as for the IAF to remember. This was the greatest chance missed by the PAF and the F-104. After the war I had a chance to discuss the plan with the Air Chief; he said that he would have definitely ordered the attack if it had been brought to his notice.'

During the 1965 war, the F-104s flew a total of 246 hours 45 minutes. Mostly; the missions flown were Air Defence and Air Superiority operations, but 42 were at night against IAF Canberra B (I) 58s. The Starfighter's rudimentary AN/ASG-14T1 fire-control radar system met the Soviet high altitude bomber threat of the Cold War era for which it was designed, but it could not illuminate small targets against ground clutter. The standard high-speed intercept tactic employed by PAF F-104 pilots was to approach their targets from below, with a typical height differential of 2,000-3,000 feet, against a target they wished to acquire at a range of 10-15 kilometres. This limitation was well known to the Canberra jet bomber pilots of the IAF. They adopted a standard hi-lo-hi profile to minimize the threat of interception. During most of their inbound and outbound flight over Pakistani territory the IAF Canberra B (I) 58s of Nos. 5 and 35 Squadrons would stay below about 1,000 feet during their approach and exit phases. This posed a difficult night interception problem. The PAF F-104s had, in these circumstances, to be used in an unconventional low-altitude intercept profile that severely challenged the capabilities of its airborne radar. To pick up low-flying bombers on their scope, the F-104 pilots had to get down to about 300-500 feet ASL to point their radars upward and clear of the ground clutter at the IAF bombers. The problem was exacerbated by the Canberra's tail warning audible alarm that would go off the moment an F-104 got to near astern position and enable the bomber to take timely evasive action to shake off its pursuer.

'The F-104 was the only night fighter the PAF had' says Flight Lieutenant Aftab Alam Khan. 'Its radar was good for high altitude, line astern missile attack, but was unusable below 5,000 feet, because of ground clutter. Also, if the target started to turn, it was not possible to deliver a missile attack. These were the limitations of the system. The IAF Canberra bombers would operate at night, usually below 500 feet. One aircraft would drop flares while others bombed the targets. After delivering their ordnance they would exit at low altitude, but as they approached the border, the Canberra's would start climbing. At this time the F-104s would be vectored for the intercept. The IAF had also installed tail warning radars on their Canberras. As the F-104 started to get into a firing position, the bombers would start a defensive turn and radar contact would be lost. Twice, I had made radar contact but as I closed into missile range, the aircraft executed a defensive manoeuvre. On the night of 21 September Squadron Leader (later ACM) Jamal A. Khan, flying F-104A 56-874, intercepted an IAF Canberra B (I) 58 at about 33,000 feet. He executed a perfect 'textbook' attack and shot it down with a Sidewinder near Fazilka, inside Pakistani territory. The bomber pilot, Flight Lieutenant Manmohan Lowe, ejected and was taken prisoner but the navigator, Flying Officer A. K. Kapor, who could not eject, was killed in the action. (The British-built Canberra B (I) 58, unlike

Squadron Leader Mohammad Mahmood Alam PAF who claimed nine IAF aircraft and two damaged in the 1965 Indo-Pak war.

its American counterpart, the Martin B-57, which the PAF used, had no ejection seat for the navigator). The Canberra pilot stated that the tail warning radar made very annoying beeping sounds at low level. Therefore, he had switched it off and he had forgotten to switch it on again as he had climbed out. This was the first kill achieved by an F-104 at night after a number of near misses. Although the F-104 made only one night kill, it did prevent the enemy from doing damage. The threat or fear of the F-104, forced the Canberras to operate at low altitude levels, once over Pakistani airspace. This prevented the attacking pilots from making determined attacks. They did not, or could not properly identify their targets and thus dropped their bombs at random, doing little or no damage.

'As the war progressed' continues Aftab Alam Khan, 'a radar controller assigned to the army gun radar unit told me that the army radar could see the IAF Canberras very clearly at night, but the track length was limited to approximately twenty nautical miles. I realized that this was good enough for the F-104 to make an interception. With its high speed it could position behind the target very fast. Once this was done, the F-104 could be aligned with the help of its infrared (IR) gun-sight for a missile or a gun attack. The Canberra tail warning radar was ineffective at low altitude. To get the system working only a radio had to be installed in the army radar unit. The war ended before the system was made effective and put into practice.

'Flying the high speed F-104 at night in wartime conditions was hazardous. The environment was as hostile and dangerous as the enemy. When there was no moon, the nights were pitch-

The remains of a PAF Sabre shot down over the Punjab.

dark, as the blackout was complete. Haze and poor visibility were common. The runway lights were switched on once the aircraft was about to pitch out for a landing. We were lucky if we could see the airfield lights on downward and turning base. The landing conditions were severe. The TACANs were not aligned with the runways. There were no approach lights, IFS or VASI. It was under these conditions that Flight Lieutenant Abbasi, while making an approach, crashed short of the runway. The F-104 was destroyed, but miraculously, he escaped and survived to fly again.

'A cease-fire had been agreed and the fighting was to stop at 3am on 23 September 1965. I was told to confirm the same from the air. The visibility was excellent but it was like a dark night. From 30,000 feet I could see the firing along the bomb-line. It looked like a ping pong match. Exactly at 3am the firing started to slow down and then it stopped completely. I made the report and was ordered to land back at the home base. As I came on final approach, I noticed the runway was tilted to the left. I turned left and I was no longer aligned with the runway. I approached in a zigzag manner and decided to go-around and try again. I guess the stress, fatigue and landing conditions were creating illusions. I asked for my squadron commander, who came immediately. I explained the problem and he gave me the necessary instructions. The next approach was worse, after which I had fuel left for two attempts. I tried again and I was told to overshoot. My squadron commander then told me to eject on the downwind. He was getting the helicopter airborne. Now, I had only 200lb of fuel left, just enough for one last approach. At this time the air traffic controller requested permission to switch on the entire airfield lights, as the war was over. As soon as this was done, my senses returned to normal and a safe landing was carried out. Thus ended the 1965 Indo-Pak War. The F-104 and myself had seen the start and we saw the finish; a lucky and historic coincidence.

'Pakistan got the better of the IAF, with odds of 1:6 or 150:900. Air superiority was maintained day and night. The genius and courage of Air Marshal Nut Khan and F-104/F-86 team had made this possible. Undoubtedly the F-86 was the workhorse, but the F-104 had a very special task. The PAF pilot/F-104 team had created a situation where the IAF pilots did not have the will to fight the F-104. When the F-104 was up, the IAF was 'Down on the Ground'. This removed a major portion of the threat. The Starfighter and its pilots had contributed immensely to achieving this victory. The pilots fought very aggressively, never losing an opportunity to engage the enemy by day or night. Working long hours and flying under difficult flight conditions, the maintenance crews and the F-104s deserve a special accolade: not one technical abort or snag affected a mission! The F-104 was flown by determined pilots, maintained by efficient crew and supported by dedicated radar controllers. This made a tremendous team that helped win the battle for air superiority for the PAF. The F-104 Starfighter was in a 'class of its own'; 'superlative' to say the least. Without the dozen Starfighters the outcome of the war may not have been so good. It definitely was a pleasure, a thrill and the ultimate experience to fly the F-104 in combat.'

The 1965 Indo-Pak war lasted barely a month. The PAF lost twenty-five aircraft (eleven in air combat), while the Indians lost sixty (twenty-five in air combat). Pakistan ended the war having depleted 17% of its front line strength, while India's losses amounted to less than 10%. Moreover, the loss rate had begun to even out and it has been estimated that another three week's fighting would have seen the Pakistani losses rising to 33% and India's losses totalling fifteen percent. Air superiority was not achieved and was unable to prevent IAF fighter bombers and reconnaissance Canberras from flying daylight missions over Pakistan. Thus 1965 was a stalemate in terms of the air war with neither side able to achieve complete air superiority. Most assessments agree that India had the upper hand over Pakistan when ceasefire was declared. The war proved that Pakistan could neither break the formidable Indian defences in a 'blitzkrieg' fashion nor could she sustain an all-out conflict for long. Pakistan Air Force on the other hand gained much credibility and reliability among Pakistan military and international war writers for the successful defence of Lahore and other important areas of Pakistan and heavy retaliation to India on the next day. Some pilots were scrambled six times in less than an hour on indication of Indian air raids. Pakistan Air Force along with the army is celebrated on Defence Day and Air Force Day in commemoration of this in Pakistan (6 and 7 September respectively). Another negative consequence of the war was the growing resentment against the Pakistani government in East Pakistan (present day Bangladesh), particularly for West Pakistan's obsession with Kashmir. Bengali leaders accused the central government of not providing adequate security for East Pakistan during the conflict, even though large sums of money were taken from the east to finance the war for Kashmir. Despite some PAF attacks being launched from bases in East Pakistan, India did not retaliate in that sector, although East Pakistan was defended only by an under strength infantry division, sixteen aircraft and no tanks. Sheikh Mujibur Rahman was critical of the disparity in military resources deployed in East and West Pakistan, calling for greater autonomy for East Pakistan, which ultimately led to the Bangladesh Liberation War and another military conflict between India and Pakistan in 1971.[39]

Once again, the IAF outnumbered the PAF by nearly five to one. More significant, however, the qualitative advantage enjoyed by the PAF in 1965 had been considerably reduced. Indian, Bangladeshi and international sources consider the beginning of the war to have been Operation 'Chengiz Khan' (inspired by the success of Israeli Operation 'Focus' in the Arab-Israeli Six Day War) when Pakistan launched pre-emptive air strikes on eleven Indian airbases in north-western India, including Agra, 300 miles from the border on the evening of 3 December (the Moslem Sabbath) at about 1740 hours. Though PAF put up no more than fifty aircraft a total of 183 bombs were dropped rendering the Indian airfields useless for six hours to six days. At around 1743 hours in the twilight hours of 3 December a Mirage III of the PAF came over Pathankot airfield to drop bombs and strafe the Hawker Hunter Mk.56 base. Pathankot is a mere sixty seconds flying time from the border and offered the least amount of early warning to India. In 1965 the PAF managed to do considerable damage to the airfield in a surprise attack but this time all the aircraft were dispersed to rear airfields like Ambala, Palam and Hindon. Wing Commander Cecil Vivian Parker the 20 Squadron OC, was in a meeting with Air Commodore T. S. Brar, at the time of the PAF pre-emptive attack. All detachments returned to Pathankot in the early hours of 4 December. As the Commanding Officer, Parker exercised his privilege of mounting the first mission which was to attack Peshawar airfield. The attack was a classic in the air war of 1971. Erstwhile, only Canberras had dared to fly to Peshawar and bomb it.

During the 1965 War, Canberras of 5 Squadron managed a solitary raid on the night of 13/14 September to Peshawar. Canberras were chosen, as no other aircraft had the range to fly the distance. The Hunter Mk.56 was equipped with four 100 imperial gallon tanks to extend its range but even so and with no external weapons load, the aircraft did not have the range to fly to Peshawar and back. Between the wars, the Hunter Mk.56A was acquired which could carry two 100 gallon outboard and two 230 gallon tanks on its inner pylons, thus extending its range. Trials were made before the war, testing the aircraft's range. On one occasion two Hunters were flown lo-hi-lo all the way from Pathankot to the Jamnagar firing range, overflying Agra and Ahmedabad, so the pilots had sufficient confidence in the Hunter's ability to reach Peshawar and back. Even then, the aircraft would have to carry only cannons, dispensing with any external stores such as bombs or rockets. The allowance for air combat and evasive manoeuvres was marginal if non-existent. There being no Hunters on 20 Squadron at Pathankot on 3 December, Parker was authorised to borrow two aircraft from the neighbouring unit, the 27 'Flaming Arrows' Squadron and the mission launch time was fixed at around 0430 hours on 4 December to enable both the pilots to reach Peshawar at first light.

Wing Commander Cecil Parker took Flight Lieutenant C. S. Dhillon as his No.2. When they went over to 27 Squadron's dispersal area to pick up the Hunters, the OC was dismayed to find that the Hunters had rocket rails fixed under their wings. Flying at extreme range, the rocket rails would have been a tremendous drag on the aircraft's performance. But time did not permit the ground crew to turn around the aircraft for their removal and Parker was eager

F-86 Sabre of the Pakistan Air Force.

Survivors of the section of four F-86F Sabres which attacked Amritsar radar on 11 September 1965 seen after their return. They are, from L-R: Flight Lieutenant Cecil Chaudhry, Wing Commander Anwar Shamin (now Air Marshal and C-in-C PAF) and Flight Lieutenant Imtiaz Bhatti. Note the smoke-blackened gun panel of the Sabre.

to start at 0430 hours to avoid spending too much time in hostile territory in daylight. Both Hunters took off on time and after almost seventy-five minutes of flying, pulled up over Peshawar airfield, as dawn was breaking. Parker and Dhillon noticed three Sabres were already in the air at a distance. But due to the probability of the sun shining in the Pakistani pilots' eyes, the Hunters were not spotted. After identifying the airfield, both Parker and Dhillon went in for the first strafing run. Dhillon noticed a Bulk Petroleum Installation (BPI) and made it a target for his second run. Parker identified two Sabres on the ground refuelling from a bowser and in his second run totalled it, with big plumes of black smoke confirming his hits. Two strafing runs were all that were allowed for this mission and both the Hunters rendezvoused to fly back to Pathankot, when the three Sabres which were noticed earlier vectored towards the returning Hunters. The Sabres slowly caught up with the Hunters and some hits were scored on them. With still a long way to go and the Sabres slowly making some headway in hitting the Hunters, Parker called for a break. Till then his objective had been to get himself and his wingman out safely, but with his Hunter already having bullet holes in its tanks and fuselage, the prospect of Parker rushing to help Dhillon was dim. On the order to split, Dhillon banked his aircraft hard port and headed towards Jammu. The F-86s split too, with one peeling off to chase Dhillon, while the other two stuck to Parker's tail.

'This' Parker recalls, '...was a godsend. If they had sent two Sabres to chase the less experienced Dhillon, they might have got him!'

With two Sabres on his tail, Parker arrived over the twin cities of Islamabad and Rawalpindi. The chase was at a low level. And just south of the two cities, Parker noticed some high ground approaching rapidly. He was faced with a dilemma, to increase power and pull up and in the process exhausted his reserves even more, or to turn around. He chose a manoeuvre which would probably have meant death in a dogfight; he turned his aircraft around, dropping half flaps and losing speed. The Hunter cleared the obstacle in a tight turn. The Sabre that was chasing him was flying too fast to follow a tight turn and the Pakistani pilot pulled back into a high-speed turn. Parker, on coming out of the turn, noticed that the Pakistani pilot had in fact overshot him and, having lost sight of his adversary, was searching frantically in the skies by jinking his aircraft around. Parker could not let go of this opportunity and he closed in and fired his little remaining ammunition into the Sabre which plunged into the ground and blew up. The second Sabre was nowhere to be seen and Parker never knew what happened to the second Pakistani pilot, who probably was lost in the chase. Now devoid of any adversaries on his tail, he set course for Pathankot. Parker received some sporadic ground fire just near the border, which could have come from either side. He had radioed to Pathankot about his precarious fuel situation and Pathankot ATC cleared him to land 'at any runway, any place.'

Meanwhile Dhillon was coming in from the direction of Jammu, to Pathankot. He had received several hits from the Sabre but all the same shook him off and lost him. Dhillon too made a similar call to Pathankot and was approaching it with his fuel reserves at the minimum. Parker, being nearer to the airfield, landed first; his engine flamed out due to lack of fuel. Dhillon too landed with empty tanks. Both the aircraft had numerous bullet holes. Parker's aircraft received twenty-two hits from the tail controls right up to the cockpit area. Two Sabres on the ground were confirmed destroyed, as was one Sabre in air combat.

Both the damaged aircraft were returned to 27 Squadron with gratitude as well as apologies. Meanwhile the aircraft of 20 Squadron had returned to Pathankot. One aircraft was fired at eagerly by the Indian air defence gunners. Luckily no damage was done.

The second strike of the Lightnings was already underway by the time the first strike had landed. Squadron Leader Jal Maneksha Mistry, the senior most pilot of the squadron after the CO, along with Squadron Leader Bajpai, flew to attack Kohat, which was also at the extreme range of the aircraft. Bajpai's Hunter started too late, so Mistry flew alone to attack Kohat airfield. The target was identified and attacked, the aircraft being recovered successfully. Lieutenant Arun Prakash, Indian Navy, led the third mission with Karumbaya as his wingman to attack Chaklala Airfield. The aircraft arrived over Chaklala to find a number of unidentified aircraft,

Air Marshal Nur Khan, 6th chief of the PAF 23 July to 31 August 1969 prior to his first flight in a 9 Squadron F-104 Starfighter.

from light executive aircraft to C-130s. Arun Prakash identified and destroyed a C-130, with his colleague attacking and hitting several hangers and installations. Squadron Leader A. A. D. Rozario, another senior flight commander, led the attack to Murid airfield with Flying Officer Balasubramanian as his No.2 and Kailey and Flight Lieutenant Deoskar as his No.3 and No.4. Arriving over Murid airfield, the aircraft received the now familiar response of ack-ack fire. The first pair of pilots, Rozario and Balasubramanian immediately identified several targets and attacked them. One 'needle-nosed aircraft', in all probability an F-104 or a Mirage III, which was camouflaged, was identified and destroyed. Later a sortie by a PR Sukhoi-7 confirmed the destruction of this aircraft. The second pair of Kailey and Deoskar missed the target. So they carried out some interdiction before returning safely back to base.

Back at Pathankot, the SASO, HQ WAC telephonically ordered a second strike on Peshawar airfield. Wing Commander Parker advised against it, as the gains may not be commensurate with the effort. The SASO overruled the CO and a second raid on Peshawar was launched. Two Hunters flown by Squadron Leader K. N. Bajpai and Flying Officer K. P. Muralidharan took off for Peshawar. Their standing orders were clear, at such an extreme range, all air combat was to be ignored and as feared both the pilots ran into air opposition, intercepted by Sabres as soon as they had completed their attack. Bajpai called for a break and a rendezvous to fly back to Pathankot, but Murali, instead of evading the attacking Sabres, got involved in a dogfight. Muralidharan was last seen flying north of Peshawar in combat with a Sabre. Bajpai had enough problems of his own with the Sabres taking shots at him. However Bajpai managed to shake off his pursuers, but found himself in a damaged aircraft, with diminishing fuel reserves. He knew he would never reach Pathankot. Base suggested that Bajpai land at Jammu, where a new airfield was being constructed. Jammu received the attention of the GREF just before the beginning of the war and an engineer force along with civilian labour was engaged in re-building the runway. Jammu was notified by Pathankot about Bajpai's imminent arrival and all the construction equipment was cleared off the runway to enable the Hunter pilot to land safely.

Labourers cleared the debris and equipment as the smoking Hunter came into land. Bajpai put the Hunter down neatly, but the runway proved to be too short for him; the Hunter overshot at the Tawi end and placed itself snugly on a civilian truck which was unloading masonry, at the end of the runway. He climbed down safely, none the worse for his landing experience. The GREF personnel marvelled at the unique sight of the Hunter sitting on the truck. Later a driver came and drove the truck with the Hunter on it, to the repair shop!

Thus ended the first day strikes of Lightning squadron. Five missions were flown to four different airfields and at least four aircraft on the ground and an F-86 in the air were assessed to have been destroyed. The other Hunter squadron at Pathankot, 27, flew some missions to Pakistani airfields too. However they lost two of their Hunters to PAF's F-6s on two different occasions. Both the pilots missing in action.

As dawn broke on 5 December the first raid of the day was already on the way. Squadron Leader Ravi Bharadwaj and Flight Lieutenant Gahlaut flew to attack Chaklala airfield. The pilots continued the good work done by Lieutenant Arun Prakash and his wingmen the day earlier and successfully knocked out some aircraft on the ground. Bharadwaj, adding a C-130 transport to the tally and Gahlaut, destroying a Twin Otter. The Twin Otter was admitted to have been destroyed by Radio Pakistan, but the Otter belonged to the Royal Canadian Air Force (RCAF) detachment with the UNMOGIP. Though the aircraft were observed as having been painted as white, it was difficult for the pilots to actually confirm that the aircraft belonged to the UN.

Parker was to lead the second raid of the day to Mianwali at around 1431 hours, with Dhillon as his No.2 and Balasubramanian and Arun Prakash as the No.3 and 4. Parker's aircraft failed to start and Dhillon's aircraft went unserviceable after getting airborne. Nevertheless the strike was underway with Bala as the leader. One C-130 was identified and Arun Prakash knocked the aircraft out, destroying it completely. Some other light aircraft too were destroyed. The attack on Mianwali was timed to coincide with another mission to Sakesar radar station. Sakesar was the air defence centre of the PAF which was instrumental in directing the air defence fighters of the PAF. Squadron Leaders Jal Mistry and Karumbaya were designated to take off for the mission, which was at the same time as the other raid on Mianwali. Karumbaya's Hunter failed to start. Jal Mistry again decided to fly alone to Sakesar. The Indian Air Force strongly discourages pilots to fly on solitary missions alone. But Mistry decided to go alone. Parker himself was not available, being in the air himself. Mistry flew alone to Sakesar and successfully rocketed it. Bala and Arun Prakash, who were returning from Mianwali, got a radio call from Mistry announcing the damage to Sakesar. It was the last they ever heard from him. Mistry was intercepted by a Mirage III flown by Flight Lieutenant Safdar. The PAF pilot scored a hit with an air-to-air missile and reported the Hunter going down. Mistry was killed in the crash. Sakesar was to become a death trap for Hunters that day.

Much earlier in the day, another mission of two Hunters from 27 Squadron struck at Sakesar. These two Hunters were intercepted in the return leg by two MiG-19s from Mianwali and shot down, both the pilots being killed. Mistry was the third pilot to be shot down attacking the same target. Back at Pathankot, Mistry was declared missing. Later, a Pakistani broadcast was picked up specifying that Mistry was shot down over Pakistan. It appeared that either Mistry was a PoW or that the Pakistanis had recovered something to identify him, most probably his Identity Card, which incidentally pilots were not supposed to carry with them. However, much later on, the pilots at the Lightning Squadron came to know that Mistry was killed in the combat. Four Hunters flown by Flying Officers' DeMonte, Suraj Kumar, 'Bond' Heble and Kailey flew a sortie to Lahore and Walton in search of opportunity targets. They found and attacked some railway installations and a train somewhere near Walton. They came back without damage. The last mission of the day was a two ship strike against Chak Jumra by Deoskar and A.K. 'Bomber' Sharma. By end of the second day of operations, No.20 Squadron had flown nine missions and destroyed more than six Pakistani aircraft on the ground for the loss of two Hunters and their pilots.

From 6 December onwards, 20 Squadron turned its attention from counter air to economic targets. Those were targets whose destruction would prove to be damaging to the Pakistani industry. Top of the list was the Attock oil refinery, which was situated South East of Rawalpindi. This target was defended by a good network of anti-aircraft guns controlled by the nearby airfield of Chaklala which was about twenty miles away. Destruction of the refinery or, at the very least, hampering its operations, would impose a severe crunch in the POL reserves of the Pakistanis. It was planned to send a four ship strike to Attock. Wing Commander Parker, along with Squadron Leader Bajpai, Flying Officers DeMonte and Karumbaya were the pilots on this mission. Technical snags prevented Karumbaya's Hunter from starting. Finally Parker, DeMonte and Bajpai took off to attack the refinery. The actual routing of the Hunters took them over for a diversionary attack on to Chaklala, then executing a turnabout and hitting the Attock Oil Refinery from the west. The AA guns were caught napping at first. The refinery was shrouded in camouflage and the AA guns were defending it to the last inch. Parker was the first to dive in. The Hunters carried cannon ammunition and the first burst set fire to the fuel tanks. The fire spread quickly through the refinery fuelled by the vapours. The blaze spread so fast that their height was reaching the Hunters which were making their second run. The ack-ack fire could not make its presence felt and all the aircraft were recovered safely. Gun camera pictures of the raid prove the accuracy of the damage to the facilities. PR recce confirmed the damage to the refinery. The fire in the refinery resulted in a 'beautiful blaze' lasting several days and nights. Indian bombers flying in the stealth of the night reported the flames which served as a navigational aid for some days to come.

The first effort to attack a economic target was a success for the squadron. Focus soon shifted towards interdiction. A strike was launched against railway targets on the Wazirawali-Lahore railway axis and the raid was uneventful in terms of opposition encountered.

The next economic target on the list of 20 Squadron was the Mangla Hydel Dam which was attacked in the morning of 7 December. The strike was scheduled to be a four aircraft mission. Squadron Leader R. N. Bharadwaj led the raid, with Dhillon, Chowfin and Heble as his wingmen. All the Hunters were equipped with two 68mm rocket pods. Mangla Dam has been assigned as a target for the squadron as far back as October. Parker was briefed about the position and location of the dam and the objective was given as the destruction of the Hydro Electric Station at the foot of the dam. With no pictures to go by and instructions to knock out the Hydel Station, a trip for Parker was arranged to the Joginder Nagar Dam in Punjab. This dam was supposed to simulate the actual layout of Mangla dam and Parker was allowed to study the area in detail. Later, Parker and Bharadwaj, flew a dummy sortie to the Joginder Nagar Dam, to try and test their tactics. All the training paid off, when Bharadwaj led the actual raid on the Mangla Dam, he found the target exactly as they imagined it, with the Hydel station at the foot of the dam, with two AA guns on top of it. Again the enemy AA defences were caught napping. They could not respond effectively to stop the Hunters which, by that time, had set fire to and damaged the Hydel Station. The Hunters suffered several cannon stoppages and failure of the rocket pods to fire, but all in all, the power station was badly knocked about.

A second strike was planned later in the day. Bharadwaj deputed to lead the aircraft again, accompanied by Dhillon, Sharma and Chowfin. But Bharadwaj's aircraft suffered problems, the engine refusing to start, and the remaining three carried out the raid, without damage or loss. Squadron Leader Rozario led a four-aircraft mission to Kohat, with DeMonte and Karumbaya as his wingmen. The fourth aircraft flown by Deoskar, returned to base as soon as it suffered some technical snags after takeoff. The raid was successful.

Meanwhile, Wing Commander Parker led a mission to Murid airfield, a forward station for a MiG-19 squadron and some Sabres. Arun Prakash and Bajpai flew with Parker on this mission. Gremlins made their presence felt yet once again, when the fourth aircraft, being flown by Balasubramanian was rendered unserviceable due to snags before takeoff.

Parker arrived over Murid and, identifying two Sabres on the ground, made a strafing run on them. One of the Sabres burst into flames emitting smoke, while the other did not. This left a doubt in the pilots' minds that the aircraft could have been some dummy/decoy aircraft.

As the aircraft were pulling out of the raid, one of the pilots noticed an aerial mast dead

Squadron Leader Munirudda 'Munir' ud-Din Ahmed PAF who was KIA while attacking a high-powered heavily defended radar station near Amritsar on 11 September 1965 when his F-86F was shot down by ground fire. Before his last sortie, 'Munir' flew eight combat missions and shot down an IAF Gnat on 10 September. He was posthumously awarded the Sitara-e-Jurat.

ahead in their path, with wires dangling from it. This mast was not marked out in the map and its presence slightly unnerved the pilots, who thought it was some anti-aircraft measure.

The aircraft had to take drastic evasive measures to avoid crashing into the mast or its wires. In all probability, it was an unmarked aerial on the Indian maps, but it did unnerve the formation for a brief moment. A second strafing run was made over Murid, including the hangers and installations which looked like housing some aircraft, was carried out. But the damage if any was difficult to assess.

Murid received further attention the very next morning. This time Squadron Leader Bharadwaj was leading the mission, with Heble, Karumbaya and Deoskar. This time they struck gold. A transport was destroyed by Bharadwaj, while Karumbaya and Deuskar attacked and destroyed two fighters, later identified as MiG-19s.

The squadron flew its next major number of sorties on 10 December. In response to the Indian Army's call for close support in the Chamb sector, the Lightnings contributed to the support requests of the ground forces. First among the aircraft was a two-aircraft strike by Squadron Leader R. N. Bharadwaj and Karumbaya. They engaged some Pakistani tank and gun positions across the Manawar Tawi.

It was during one such attacking run that Karumbaya felt his Hunter shudder under the impact of bullets from a Sabre that had bounced him. Karumbaya broke left, with his tanks and aircraft holed, but Bharadwaj who was coming behind Karumbaya engaged the Sabre and shot it down. The aircraft, which crashed in Indian territory, confirmed the kill. Bharadwaj then shepherded Karumbaya who flew his damaged aircraft back to Pathankot.

PAF Sabres were very much active that day over Chamb. Hunters of 27 Squadron too flew missions to Chamb. One Hunter flown by Squadron Leader M. K. Jain was hit by ground fire and was lost along with the pilot. Ground fire also hit and damaged one of 20 Squadron's aircraft. Squadron Leader Rozario and Heble were flying over the area when Rozario's Hunter was hit repeatedly by ack-ack fire. Rozario with great difficulty flew the aircraft back to Pathankot, with Heble acting as a shepherd.

When Rozario put the aircraft onto the runway, he discovered that the tyres were punctured by ack-ack and the resultant force on the undercarriage sheared the landing gear off, as the aircraft hit the runway on its belly and slithered out of control over a distance. It finally came to a stop after some distance and Rozario walked out of the Hunter unscathed. The belly landed Hunter was badly damaged and was sent for repairs, flying only after the war. Meanwhile Heble had safely returned and landed.

The squadron carried out about ten sorties on 11 December. After a week of hectic operational flying from 4 to 10 December, the squadron was withdrawn from the forward base to Hindon, where it was to take a break from operations and give the pilots some rest. All the pilots were pulled back to Hindon, leaving behind the ground crew and about five of them. 20 Squadron was relieved by aircraft of 7 'Battle Axes' Squadron and MiG-21s from 30 Squadron. The 'Battle Axes' in fact shared the ground crew facilities of the 'Lightnings'. For the remaining six days of the war some of the five pilots left behind at Pathankot flew missions along with 7 Squadron in their aircraft. The Hunters also flew some air defence sorties from Hindon during the remaining days of the war. The general mood of the squadron was that after a brief rest period of a week or so the squadron would again be sent to the frontline. All the pilots were very eager to fly back to Pathankot and start operations again. But as the days went by the probability of the war coming to an end increased with the imminent collapse of the Pakistan Army in the Eastern Sector; the pilots felt somewhat disappointed at an opportunity being lost.

They would not know it, but fate had decried that the 'Lightnings' would soon face a bigger challenge and instructions were already being issued in that direction. Soon after the move to Hindon, Wing Commander Parker was brought to Air HQ for some top secret discussions. There at the meeting, he was asked, whether his Hunters would be able to operate out of an airfield in Visakhapatnam, off the coast of the Bay of Bengal in Andhra Pradesh. Parker had

Above: On 4/5 December 1971 Flight Lieutenant Naeem Atta of 5 Squadron flying a Mirage IIIEP shot down a IAF Canberra B(I) 58 with a Matra R.530 AAM during a night interception near Skardu, Pakistan. Flight Lieutenants Lloyd Moses Sasoon, pilot and Ram Netharam Advani navigator were killed.

Top right: Flying Officer (later Air Chief Marshal) Mushaf Ali Mir Shaheed a F-6 Shenyang pilot with one air-to-air victory in the 1971 war.

Middle: Squadron Leader Sarfraz Ahmed Rafiqui.

Bottom left: on 5 December 1971 Flight Lieutenant Safdar Mahmood flying a Mirage shot down a IAF Hunter (A 1014) of 20 Squadron piloted by Squadron Leader Jal Maneksha Mistry. The pilot ejected but it was too late.

Below: On the 6 December 1971 when Flight Lieutenant Salimuddin Awan of 5 Squadron at Sargodha shot down a IAF Su-7 over Jammu sector. In total Flight Lieutenant Salimuddin flew 17 sorties during the war, including two Air Test flights to certify the airworthiness of the aircraft.

neither heard of Visakhapatnam's airfield, nor had he ever been there, but by the demands of the situation, felt that the Hunters could land on the runway employing their drag chutes to cut their run short. The advent of the cease-fire made such a move unnecessary.

When a tally was compiled for the 'Lightnings' at the end of the war, the squadron turned out to be the highest scoring unit in the IAF during the 1971 conflict. Since its primary objective had been counter air, the unit had a total of thirteen enemy aircraft destroyed on ground. Two F-86 Sabres were also downed in air combat. There was one occasion when a hapless Mirage III found itself for a brief moment in the sight of one of the Hunters. The gun camera film is a treasured souvenir in the squadron reminding them of the discomfort of the Pakistani Mirage pilot, who jinked and weaved to get out of the firing line of the Hunter flown by A. K. 'Bomber' Sharma who had no ammunition left!

Including the eight days of operational flying, 20 Squadron had flown a total of 121 sorties throughout the war amounting to about 115:30 hours. In this period, they fired about 15,000 rounds of cannon ammo, dropped about 17,000 lbs of HE bombs, 1720 litres of napalm and 548 rockets at enemy targets. The claim of thirteen enemy aircraft destroyed on the ground included four C-130 Hercules, one Twin Otter, one Viscount and a light-executive aircraft. Renowned US pilot, Brigadier General Charles E. Yeager, who was then on deputation to the PAF as an Advisor,[40] lost his USAF Beech Queen Air aircraft in Chaklala, which might well have been lost to the Lightning's onslaught. [41]

As the war progressed, PAF B-57s carried out many night missions. There was a higher attrition rate than in 1965, with at least five B-57s being put out of service by the end of the war. They were retired from PAF service in 1985.

The F-104 was used for deep penetration strikes against airfields and radars on 11 December. Two F-104s

Squadron Leader Shabbir Hussain Syed in front of PAF F-86 Sabre 55-4029 a veteran of the 1965 and 1971 war with India. During this conflict, while flying with 14 Squadron, it saw heavy combat and scored several air-to-air and air-to-ground confirmed victories. It also participated in the decisive strike against IAF Base Kalaikunda, thus earning the unit the distinguished title of 'The Tail Choppers'.

Squadron Leader Mervyn L. Middlecoat (right) with AM Nur Khan, who led 9 Squadron Sabres of the PAF.

attacked Amritsar and Faridkot IAF radars. Wing Commander Arif Iqbal, who not only damaged the radar but also shot down a HAL HAOP-27 Krishak military observation aircraft, led the attack on Faridkot. The PAF admitted to losing just three aircraft and the onset of night prevented any further advantage the attackers may have had. In an address to the nation on radio that same evening, Prime Minister Indira Gandhi held that the air strikes were a declaration of war against India and the Indian Air Force responded with initial air strikes that very night. These air strikes were expanded to massive retaliatory air strikes the next morning and thereafter, which followed interceptions by Pakistanis anticipating this action. This marked the official start of the Indo-Pakistani War of 1971. Indira Gandhi ordered the immediate mobilisation of troops and launched the full-scale invasion. This involved Indian forces in a massive coordinated air, sea and land assault. Indian Air Force started flying sorties against Pakistan from midnight. The main Indian objective on the western front was to prevent Pakistan from entering Indian soil. There was no Indian intention of conducting any major offensive into West Pakistan.

After the initial pre-emptive strike, PAF adopted a defensive stance in response to the Indian retaliation. When the IAF struck back the next day, two of 9 Squadron's F-104As flown by Squadron Leaders Amanullah and Rashid Bhatti attacked Amritsar radar. They met with stiff resistance but managed to shoot down two aircraft, an IAF Gnat and a Sukhoi Su-7 'Fitter' over Sargodha. The pilot of the Gnat, Flight Lieutenant J. Preira, was killed.

The Gnats most notable action was the Battle of Boyra on 22 November, where the first dogfights over East Pakistan (Bangladesh) took place. Intruding PAF Canadair Sabre Mk.6s of 14 Squadron 'Tail-choppers' inadvertently crossed into Indian airspace while performing a close air support mission against the Mukti Bahini, the Bengali Guerrilla freedom fighters and a Battalion sized detachment of the Indian Army which were fighting in the Battle of Garibpur against the PAF as part of the Bangladesh Liberation War. The first intrusion of four Sabres was picked up in the Jessore area on Indian radar at 0811 hours. Four Gnats of 22 Squadron 'Swifts' based in Kalaikunda Air Force Station and tasked with the Air Defence of the Calcutta Sector were scrambled from Dum Dum but the Sabres had flown back to their territory by the time the Gnats could make it to Boyra. A second raid by the Pakistanis followed at 1028 hours. An interception again could not be carried out in time and the Sabres were able to escape to safety.

At around 1448 hours, Indian radar picked up the four Sabres as they pulled up in a north westerly direction to about 2,000 feet above ground level. Within a minute, the ORP at Dum Dum was scrambled. Four Gnats took off by 1451 hours led by the formation leader Flight Lieutenant Roy Andrew Massey. It was less than three minutes from the time the Sabres were detected by the radar. The Fighter controller in the sector was Flying Officer K. B. Bagchi who vectored the gnats to the Sabres and directed the interception. The Sabres already having carried out several attack runs in the eight minutes it took the Gnats to reach the Boyra Sailent, were commencing to start another dive - they were at about 1,800 feet and diving down to 500 feet in an attack run. The four Gnats separated into two sections and dived into the attack to bounce the Sabres. The first section of Gnats was of Massey and Flying Officer S. F. Soarez as his wingman. The second section consisted of Flight Lieutenant M. A. Ganapathy and Flying Officer D. Lazarus. As the Gnats dived in, a section of two Sabres pulled out of the attack and placed themselves in an awkward position, just in front of Ganapathy and Lazarus. Ganapathy called out on the R/T the Brevity code 'Murder-Murder-Murder'. Both the pilots opened fire with 20mm cannon fire and both the Sabres were badly damaged. The Pakistani pilots Parvaiz Mehdi Qureshi and Khaleel Ahmed ejected over Boyra and parachuted down safely and were taken prisoner. The wreckage of the abandoned Sabres fell near the village of Bongaon in India. Simultaneously Massey pulled up over Ganapathy and Lazarus to latch onto another Sabre piloted by Wing Commander Chaudhury, who, in a skillful dog-fighting move, broke into Massey's attack forcing him to take a high angle-off burst which missed his target. After manoeuvering back into firing position and taking aim, Massey let off another burst at 700 yards

Pilots of 14 Squadron PAF at either Masroor or Sargodha. L-R: Pilot Officer (later Wing Commander) Badrul Hassan Khan; Flying Officer (later Squadron Leader) Sarfraz Ahmed Rafiqui, Squadron Leader Gul Ahmed; Flying Officer (later Wing Commander) Hamid 'Harry' Anwar (who flew as an exchange pilot at Phoenix, Arizona.; the RAF as a member of the world-famous 'Blue Diamonds' aerobatic team and the Royal Jordanian Air Force where he formed his own team 'The Hashemite Diamonds'); Flight Lieutenant (later Air Marshal) Abdul Azim Daudpota.

and hit him in the port wing. By that time, Massey's starboard cannon had stopped firing, but the Sabre streaked back into Pakistani territory billowing smoke and fire. Massey, realizing that he was well over East Pakistani airspace in his chase, turned around and regrouped with the rest of his formation which then proceeded back to base. Early on it was thought that the badly damaged Sabre must have crashed soon after. Once the war had ended, however, reports confirmed that Chaudhury, showing considerable courage, had managed to fly his badly damaged Sabre back to Tezgaon airfield near Dhaka. Chaudhury himself claimed to have shot down one of the Gnats, which was later proved false as all four Gnats landed safely.

Another notable dogfight involving a Gnat was over Srinagar airfield on 14 December where a lone Indian pilot, twenty-eight-year old Flying Officer Nirmal Jit Singh Sekhon of 18 Squadron 'The Flying Bullets' held out against six Sabres of 26 Squadron from PAF base Peshawar, scoring hits on two of the Sabres in the process, before being shot down. Sekhon was on readiness duty at that time. As soon as the first aircraft attacked, Sekhon rolled for take-off as No.2 in a two-Gnat formation, with Flight Lieutenant Ghumman in lead, just as the first bombs were falling on the runway. Only delayed due to dust kicked up by the preceding Gnat, Sekhon lost no time in singling out the first Sabre pair, which was re-forming after the bombing run. The Gnat Leader, Ghuman, lost visual with his wingman just after take-off, and remained out of the fight. In the ensuing air battle, Sekhon scored a direct hit on one Sabre and set another ablaze, though it has been denied by all the sources of PAF. The latter was seen heading away towards Rajauri, trailing smoke. Sekhon, after being hit, was advised to return to the base. He is said to have flown in straight, wings level for some time, before inverting and plummeting down, probably due to failure of the control system. He attempted a last-minute ejection, which did not prove successful, as his canopy was seen to fly off. The wreckage of the Gnat was found in a gorge, near the road coming from Srinagar town to the base, a few miles from the base. Despite many search efforts by Army and Air Force, his body was never found due to the mountainous terrain over which his fighter went down. Sekhon was posthumously honoured with the Param Vir Chakra (India's highest gallantry award), becoming the only member of the IAF to receive it.

During an attack on the radar installation at Amritsar on 5 December, 9 Squadron suffered its first loss of the war to anti-aircraft fire. Flight Lieutenant Amjad Hussein Khan ejected from his F-104 and was taken prisoner. As the war progressed, the Indian Air Force continued to battle the PAF over conflict zones, but the number of sorties flown by the PAF gradually decreased day-by-day. The Indian Air Force flew 4,000 sorties while the PAF offered little in retaliation, partly because of the paucity of non-Bengali technical personnel. This lack of retaliation has also been attributed to the deliberate decision of the PAF High Command to cut its losses as it had already incurred huge losses in the conflict. Though PAF did not intervene during the Indian Navy's raid on Pakistan's naval port city of Karachi, it retaliated with bombing the Okha harbour, destroying the fuel tanks used by the boats that attacked. In the east, the small air contingent of 14 Squadron was destroyed, putting the Dhaka airfield out of commission and resulting in Indian air superiority in the east. While India's grip on what had been East Pakistan tightened, the IAF continued to press home attacks against Pakistan itself. The campaign settled down to a series of daylight anti-airfield, anti-radar and close-support attacks by fighters, with night attacks against airfields and strategic targets by B-57s and C-130 (Pakistan) and Canberras and An-12s (India).

By 1971 the MiG-21 had become numerically the most important fighter in the IAF, with 232 in service, enough to equip nine squadrons. Hindustan Aeronautics Ltd had been producing improved model MiG-21FLs under license. In addition, the IAF had six squadrons of Soviet-built Sukhoi Su-7BM supersonic fighter-bombers. The PAF had three squadrons of French-built Mirage IIIEJs from an unidentified Middle Eastern ally (who remains unknown) and three squadrons of Shenyang F-6s (illegal Chinese copies of Russia's supersonic MiG-19F), which the Pakistanis had improved with British Martin-Baker ejection seats and American Sidewinder missiles.[42] In addition, the Pakistanis had replaced their older model F-86Fs with five squadrons of a far more potent version; the Canadair Sabre Mark 6, acquired via West Germany and Iran. The F-6s were employed mainly on defensive combat air patrols over their own bases, but without air superiority the PAF was unable to conduct effective offensive operations and its attacks were largely ineffective. During the IAF's airfield attacks, one US and one UN aircraft were damaged in Dhaka, while a Canadian Air Force Caribou was destroyed at Islamabad, along with US military liaison chief, Brigadier General Chuck Yeager's USAF Beech U-8 light twin.

Sporadic raids by the IAF continued against Pakistan's forward air bases in the West until

In 1971 the PAF had three squadrons of Mirage IIIEJs, Pakistan having purchased 18 Mirage IIIEs and three Mirage IIIRs and three Mirage IIIDs from France in 1967. An additional ten Mirage IIIRs were delivered in 1977.

the end of the war and large scale interdiction and close-support operations and were maintained. Indian Canberras flew a strategically important sortie against the Karachi oil tanks; this had the effect of helping the Indian Navy in their own operations, a series of missile boat attacks against the Pakistani coast.[43]

On 8 December Flight Lieutenant Manzoor Bokhari intercepted an IAF Canberra B (I) 58 and shot it down during a low-level chase. On 10 December, while attacking the Indian harbour at Okha, Wing Commander Arif Iqhal shot down a Breguet Alizé ASW aircraft of the Indian Navy (one of twelve supplied for 310 Squadron aboard the carrier Vikrant) into the sea over the Gulf of Kutch. Lieutenant Commander Ashok Roy, Lieutenant H. S. Sirohi and ACO Vijayan, were killed. On 12 December the PAF became the only nation to use the Starfighter in air-to-air combat, when two F-104s flying at low level towards Indian airfields or port installations bordering the Gulf of Kutch were intercepted by two MiG-21FLs of 47 Squadron from Jamnagar. One of the F-104As broke off and fled northward. The other Starfighter, which was flown by Wing Commander Middlecoat, one of the veterans of the 1965 War, was pursued over the Gulf by one of the MiG-21s, flown by Flight Lieutenant Bharat B. Soni. Applying full afterburner, Soni fired a K-13 missile, but the F-104 evaded it and then turned sharply to the right. Cutting inside the Starfighter's turn and closing to 300 metres, Soni fired three bursts from his GSh-23 cannon and then watched the stricken F-104 pull up. Middlecoat ejected and parachuted into the shark-infested Gulf of Kutch. Soni called for a rescue launch, but no trace of his opponent was found. Flight Lieutenant Arun K. Dutta, another MiG-21 pilot, was awarded the claim of having shot down Flight Lieutenant Samad Changezi. Both Wing Commander Middlecoat and Flight Lieutenant Samad Changezi were awarded the 'Sitara-e-Jurat' (approximately equivalent to the British DFC).

On the last day of the war, 17 December, when 9 Squadron's Starfighters clashed with MiG-21s of 29 Squadron, Squadron Leader I. S. Bindra claimed an F-104, though in fact it escaped with damage. In a later fight over Umarkot, Flight Lieutenant N. Kukresa made a similar premature claim on an F-104, but when he was attacked in turn by another Starfighter, Flight Lieutenant A. Datta blew it off his tail, killing Flight Lieutenant Samad Ali Changezi. While no MiGs were downed by Starfighters during the war, one was reportedly shot down by an F-6 on

Formation of four PAF F-86 Sabres on patrol during the 1975 Indo-Pak war.

MiG 21 of the IAF taking off. By 1971 the MiG-21 had become numerically the most important fighter in the Indian Air Force with 232 in service, enough to equip nine squadrons.

14 December and another MiG-21 lost a dogfight with a Sabre flown by Flight Lieutenant Maqsood Amir of 16 Squadron on 17 December. The Indian pilot, Flight Lieutenant Harish Singjhi, bailed out and was taken prisoner.

Although the PAF scored a three-to-one kill ratio, destroying 102 IAF aircraft and losing 34 aircraft of its own, the war was only three days old when East Pakistan fell. After just thirteen days, on 16 December, the war between India and Pakistan ended when Pakistan agreed to Indian demands for an unconditional surrender. The Indian victory was achieved with significant help from the Soviet Union. Although there was a US Government embargo on arms sales to both India and Pakistan (which had been in force ever since the 1965 war began), no consideration was given to the fact that India, a long-time ally of the soviet Union, barely used any American military equipment and the sanctions exclusively degraded the combat potential of only the Pakistani armed forces. At least one Tupolev Tu-126 'Moss' AWACS (Airborne Warning and Control System) aircraft, which would effectively have observed every move the PAF made or intended to make, was detached, with its crew, to serve with the IAF during the 1971 war. Indian ECM effectively knocked out the Pakistani ground radar and communications network.

Hostilities officially ended at 1430 GMT on 17 December, after the fall of Dhaka on 15 December. India claimed large gains of territory in West Pakistan (although pre-war boundaries were recognised after the war), though the independence of Bangladesh was confirmed. India flew 1,978 sorties in the East and about 4,000 in the West, while PAF flew about thirty and 2,840 respectively. More than 80% of the IAF's sorties were close-support and interdiction and about sixty-five IAF aircraft were lost (fifty-four losses were admitted), perhaps as many as twenty-seven of them in air combat. Pakistan lost seventy-two aircraft (fifty-one of them combat types, but admitting only twenty-five to enemy action). At least sixteen of the Pakistani losses fell in air combat (although only ten air combat losses were admitted, not including any F-6s, Mirage IIIs, or the six Jordanian F-104s which failed to return to their donors). But the imbalance in air losses was explained by the IAF's considerably higher sortie rate and its emphasis on ground-attack missions. The Instrument of Surrender of Pakistani forces stationed in East Pakistan was signed at Ramna Race Course in Dhaka on 16 December 1971.

The United States supported Pakistan both politically and materially. President Richard Nixon and his Secretary of State Henry Kissinger feared Soviet expansion into South and Southeast Asia. Pakistan was a close ally of the People's Republic of China, with whom Nixon had been negotiating a rapprochement and where he intended to visit in February 1972. Nixon feared that an Indian invasion of West Pakistan would mean total Soviet domination of the region and that it would seriously undermine the global position of the United States and the regional position of America's new tacit ally, China. Nixon encouraged Iran and Jordan to send their F-86, F-104 and F-5 fighter jets in aid of Pakistan while also encouraging China to increase its arms supplies to Pakistan. Ironically, late in 1972 the PAF decided to phase the F-104 out of service after the inventory had been decimated as a result of a US Government arms embargo which made it increasingly difficult to maintain a reasonable in-commission rate on the F-104A/Bs.

Endnotes for Chapter 3

26 Review of IAF operations against Pakistan by the Indian Ministry of Defence, New Delhi.

27 Initially the United States government tried to cover up the U-2's purpose and mission, but was forced to admit its military nature when the Soviet government came forward with the U-2's intact remains and captured pilot as well as photos of military bases in Russia taken by the aircraft. Coming roughly two weeks before the scheduled opening of an East-West summit in Paris, the incident was a great embarrassment to the United States and prompted a marked deterioration in its relations with the Soviet Union. Powers was convicted of espionage and sentenced to three years of imprisonment plus seven years of hard labour but would be released two years later on 10 February 1962 during a prisoner exchange for Soviet officer Rudolf Abel.

28 A licence-built version of the English Electric Canberra that entered service with the USAF in 1953. The Glenn L. Martin Company later modified the design to produce several unique variants.

29 The first thirteen Folland Gnats for the IAF were followed by partly completed aircraft and then sub-assemblies as Hindustan Aircraft slowly took over first assembly and then production of the aircraft. The first flight of an IAF Gnat was in the UK on 11 January 1958. It was delivered to India in the hold of a C-119 and accepted by the Air Force on 30 January 1958. The first Gnat squadron was 23 (Cheetah), which converted from Vampire FB.52 on 18 March 1960 using six Folland-built Gnats. The first aircraft built from Indian-built parts first flew in May 1962. The last Indian-built Gnat F.1 was delivered on 31 January 1974.

30 While not equal in performance to the Soviet-built MiG-15/17 the Dassault MD.450 Ouragan ('Hurricane' or 'Toofani' (Hindi) had proven itself in action during the 1956 conflict. On 25 June 1953, India ordered 71 Ouragans with the slightly uprated Nene 105 engine, with deliveries starting that year and completed in March 1954. An additional order for 33 second-hand Ouragans in March 1957 brought the total to 104. Selection of the Ouragan at this time reflected the decision to initiate diversification of supply sources. The Indian 'Toofanis' faced combat in 1961 when they performed air strikes against the Portuguese territory of Diu on the western coast of the Indian sub-continent. They were also used in ground attack missions against anti-government rebels in Assam and Nagaland, and in 1962 for reconnaissance missions in the Sino-Indian War. One 'Toofani' strayed over the border with Pakistan on 24 April 1965 and was forced to land by a PAF F-104 Starfighter. While the pilot was returned to India the aircraft was retained and ended up being displayed at the PAF Museum at

Peshawar. As was the case in France, the Ouragan started to be replaced in front-line service by the Mystère IVA in 1957, being withdrawn fully from front line service in 1965, although it continued in use for some years as advanced trainer and target tug.

31 Keelor had been awarded the Vayu Sena in 1964. On 5 February 1964 he was detailed to ferry a Gnat from Poona to Palam in a formation of five aircraft. The last part of the flight had to be undertaken at a height of 41,000 feet. While descending to land at Palam, he discovered, at a height of 15,000 feet that there was no response from the engine to the throttle movements. After informing the leader Kellor immediately broke off the formation and attempted a landing at Palam, knowing full well that previous attempts to force land a Gnat had resulted in fatal or serious injury to the pilot. With great presence of mind and careful handling, he accomplished the forced landing successfully without any damage to the aircraft.

32 'On 10 September we came to know that our Boss had been awarded the Maha Vir Chakra 'for gallantry in the face of the enemy.' We were all proud of him and there was much rejoicing. He in turn had taken the news with utmost modesty, reminding us of the unfinished task ahead of us. We felt all the more glad for it indicated that we were as a unit an efficient fighting force.'

33 Squadron Leader Onkar Nath Kacker, 27 Squadron (PoW); Squadron Leader A. B. Devayya, 7 Squadron (also claimed by Flight Lieutenant Amjad Hussain); Squadron Leader Suresh B. Bhagwat, 7 Squadron; Flight Lieutenant B. Guha, 7 Squadron; Flying Officer Jagdev Singh Brar, 7 Squadron (KIA), near Sangla Hill. The PAF figures have been disputed by Indian sources which claim that Alam made four kills, attributing one of the losses (Squadron Leader Onkar Nath Kacker's aircraft) to technical failure or some other cause, including the possibility of ground fire. They also claim that gun camera footage of Alam's kills is yet to be made public and therefore some of the kills cannot be confirmed. On 16 September Alam claimed his seventh and final victory of the war, a Hawker Hunter near Amritsar. Flying Officer Farokh Dara Bunsha of 7 Squadron was KIA. In 1967 Alam was transferred as the Squadron Commander of the first squadron of Dassault Mirage III fighters procured by the PAF. He was removed from Staff College based on a false pretext in May 1969. His family moved to West Pakistan in around 1971, after the secession of East Pakistan. Being the eldest among eleven siblings in his family, Alam never married as he had to share the financial responsibilities of his younger sisters and brothers. In 1972 he commanded 26 Squadron for two months. In 1982 Alam retired as an Air Commodore and took up residence in Karachi. Since retiring, The Air Force legend was admitted to Pakistan Naval Station Shifa Hospital in Karachi. He died in Karachi on 18 March 2013. He was 77. He had been under treatment for respiratory problems for about 18 months.

34 On 16 September Ahmed was flying an F-86 in a low level raid against raid against the freight wagons in the goods yard at Gurdaspur Station. On a second pass at very low level through smoke from previous strikes his aircraft was hit by fragments from the exploding trucks. Twelve miles away from Pakistani territory he reported, 'My cockpit is full of smoke." He continued to fly his damaged aircraft westwards and added, 'It seems alright now.' It was not and Ahmed ejected from his burning Sabre. He did not survive. There is conjecture as to whether he was shot while descending in his parachute in the combat area.

35 Later Air Vice Marshal Prakash Sadashiv Rao Pingale VrC.

36 All three participants of the ill-fated Halwara Strike were awarded Sitara-e-Jurat while Sarfraz Rafiqui Shaheed was also awarded Pakistan's highest leadership award, the Hilal-e-Jurat for his outstanding qualities of Leadership and solidarity. The Government awarded 77 acres of prime agricultural land as recompense with the awards of HJ and SJ which was most generously bequeathed by Rafiqui's parents to the Sarfraz Rafiqui Welfare Trust administered by the PAF to benefit widows, orphans and the needy. Younus Hussain Shaheed's widow brought up her sons Sajjad and Fawad who later served in senior positions in PAF. Later, the PAF base at Shorkot Road was named after Rafiqui, a fitting tribute to a brave and dedicated young Pakistani. On the Indian side, Flying Officers Gandhi and Pingale were awarded the Vir Chakra and rose to the rank of Air Marshal. As narrated by Cecil Choudhry, he met Gandhi many years after the 1965 war in Iraq where both were on deputation. Gandhi duly acknowledged Choudhry as the victor and introduced him as such to his wife.

37 Review of IAF operations against Pakistan by the Indian Ministry of Defence, New Delhi. The Sabre kill by Denzil (later Air Marshal Denzil Keelor PVSM, AVSM, VrC, KC) earned the Keelor family a unique distinction. Both he and his brother Trevor now had Sabres to their credit and both earned the Veer Chakra, making it the first time brothers had been awarded the Veer Chakra for identical feats. Wing CommanderTrevor Keelor VrC died on 27 April 2002.

38   'The J-79-11A engine was sophisticated and complicated. It had inlet guide vanes in front of the engine and a variable nozzle system in the rear. These were liable to fail, but the PAF maintenance crew had mastered the equipment. We only had one engine flame out and the pilot Flight Lieutenant Khalid managed to make a 'dead stick' landing. This was a difficult manoeuvre requiring precise judgement. The pattern was flown at 240 knots and the landing flare started 300 feet above ground level, to make a touch down at 190 knots on a 9,000 feet long runway. Only one F-104 was lost during training - a training air combat sortie - in which Flight Lieutenant Asghar 'pitched up' and went into a spin. He ejected safely at high speed and received major bruises. The aircraft was replaced under the MAP programme. Operational training was fun. Flying at Mach 2 was an incomparable experience. The thrill of coming under radar control, attacking F-86 formations, that were denied radar help, was a fighter pilot's dream come true. The F-104 zoomed out of nowhere and before the F-86 pilots could start their defensive manoeuvres, the F-104 had completed its simulated missile launch and was breaking off.'

39   East Pakistan had officially seceded from Pakistan on 26 March

40   In all, during and after the 1971 war PAF claimed the destruction of 107 IAF aircraft. Of these 51 were shot down in air engagements, 5 destroyed on the ground and 28 downed by airfield ack ack. The basis of the awards was stringent: each claim had to be confirmed by either gun camera film or an identifiable wreckage or a reliable eyewitness. Yeager who was at that time the US defence representative in Islamabad and who volunteered to join the PAF's helicopter teams documenting downed IAF aircraft says in his autobiography: '...the Pakistanis scored a three-to-one kill ratio, knocking out 102 Russian-made Indian jets and losing 34 airplanes of their own. I'm certain about the figures because I went our several times a day in a chopper and counted wrecks on Pakistani soil, documented them by serial numbers, identified the components such as engines, rocket pods and new equipment on newer airplanes like the Soviet Su-7 fighter-bomber and the MiG-21J, their latest supersonic fighter.' Of the 107 aircraft claimed the wreckages of 31 were documented and photographed, the destruction of 21 was recorded on gun camera films and 27 were seen to go down by reliable eye witnesses (i.e. accompanying pilots and/or ground witness). Nine of the latter categories were also confirmed by radio transmissions of IAF aircraft and ground stations. Nothing can be said with certainty about the fate of IAF fighters damaged in air engagements, but post-war intelligence indicated that the IAF had lost a further 20 aircraft due to battle damage including a MiG-21 shot down by another who took it to be a PAF fighter. Today, 20 Squadron is equipped with Sukhoi Su-30MKI and based at Lohegaon Air Force Station, Pune.

41   For this impressive performance Parker and Bharadwaj received the Maha Vir Chakra (MVC). Five pilots earned the Vir Chakra award. Arun Prakash, S. Balasubramanian, Jal Maneksha Mistry (posthumous), B. C. Karumbaya and A.L. Deoskar received the Vir Chakra. C. S. Dhillon recieved the Vayu Sena Medal (VSM). There were two Mentioned-in-Dispatches and ten commendations from the CAS/AOC. The 'Lightnings' take pride in the fact that Lieutenant Prakash was awarded the Vir Chakra under the 'Air Force List' rather than the 'Navy List'. 20 Squadron moved back to Pathankot immediately after the rest period of the war. Parker handed over command to Wing Commander Lele in December 1972 and left to DSSC, Wellington as a Directing Staff (Air). The squadron stayed at Pathankot till 1975 when it moved back to Hindon. In 1981, a decision was taken to move the squadron to the East to Hashimara, where they formed the first formation aerobatics team of the Indian Air Force under Wing Commander Ben Brar. Then started almost a decade of flying as the IAF's showpiece till March 1989, when the Thunderbolts flew their last public display. The Squadron received the President's Colours in 1992, when it was based in Kalaikonda. In 1997 the Hunters were replaced with the MiG-27ML 'Flogger', the remaining 'Lightning' aircraft being dispersed as gate guardians around the country or kept in storage in Tezpur.

42   Libyan F-5s were reportedly deployed to Sargodha, perhaps as a potential training unit to prepare Pakistani pilots for an influx of more F-5s from Saudi Arabia.

43   On 21 May 1999, prior to the commencement of the Kargil War, the IAF Air HQ assigned a Canberra PR.57 aircraft on a photographic mission near the Line of Control, where it took a severe blow from a FIM-92 Stinger infrared homing missile on the starboard engine; the Canberra successfully returned to base using the other engine. The Canberra fleet was grounded and then retired following the crash of an IAF Canberra in December 2005. After 50 years of service, the Canberra was finally retired by the IAF on 11 May 2007.

Chapter Four

QRA

NORAD (originally known as the North American Air Defense Command), was recommended by the Joint Canadian-US Military Group in late 1956, approved by the United States JCS in February 1957 and announced on 1 August 1957; the 'establishment of [NORAD] command headquarters' was on 12 September 1957, at Ent Air Force Base's 1954 blockhouse. The 1958 international agreement designated the NORAD commander always be a United States officer (Canadian vice commander) and 'RCAF officers ... agreed the command's primary purpose would be...early warning and defense for SAC's retaliatory forces.' In late 1958 Canada and the United States started the Continental Air Defense Integration North (CADIN) for the SAGE air defense network (initial CADIN cost sharing agreement between the countries was on 5 January 1959) and two December 1958 plans submitted by NORAD had 'average yearly expenditure of around five and one half billions', including 'cost of the accelerated Nike Zeus program' and three Ballistic Missile Early Warning System (BMEWS) sites.

'It all began with a blip on a screen in a lonely radar outpost near Sioux City Lookout, Ontario, about 150 miles north of the Canadian border in 1962. The blip wasn't there before and it appeared in a place it wasn't expected. Because it did, it set in motion a chain reaction that involved hundreds of men, many millions of dollars worth of equipment and the security of the North American Continent. It also brought into focus the mission of a defensive network spread over two nations and three oceans. Finally, it took me higher and faster than I had ever been - past the speed of sound and nearly ten miles above the earth.

'I flew a mission with NORAD'.

The NORAD Command Centre inside Cheyenne Mountain.

'The North American Air Defense Command (NORAD, the joint Canadian-American military system for guarding against manned attack over the top of the world, consists basically of three lines of defence. The first, longest and farthest north is the familiar DEW line (distant early warning), a radar screen manned by the US Air Force along the northern coast of Canada and Alaska which looks for targets far out into the Arctic. Its flanks are extended into the Pacific and Atlantic by US Navy radar aircraft which fly between the Aleutian and Midway Islands and between Greenland and the British Isles. South of the DEW line is the Mid-Canada line, an east-west line across Canada about half-way down from its northern border. The third line is the Pinetree system of radars, which straddles the Canadian-American border and is operated jointly by the armed forces of both nations. This line is divided into regions and each region is divided again into smaller sectors for purposes of defence.

'It was in one of these sectors - the Duluth sector of the 30th NORAD region - that our mission was flown. It covers parts of Minnesota, Wisconsin, Michigan and Ontario. Like all NORAD sectors, the Duluth sector has radar to detect all aircraft flying within its boundaries, computers that store information on which aircraft have been authorized to fly within these boundaries, supersonic fighters to intercept those that cannot be identified and missiles to destroy those that are identified as hostile.

'This the NORAD mission, to detect all aircraft, to identify them, to intercept the unidentified and, if necessary, destroy them. At this writing, of course, no aircraft have had to be destroyed, but virtually every day several have to be intercepted and given an 'eyeball' identification.

'I flew on one of these intercept missions and it all began with that blip...

'The Duluth sector is spotted with radar sites that sweep the skies and overlap one another. Radar specialists sit in semidarkness, staring at scopes, waiting for new blips to appear, watching the old ones follow their planned course.

'The blip that started my mission appeared at the top of the scope of a radar console in an Air Force station at Sioux Lookout. It was easily interpreted as a high-flying jet north of the site and heading south, toward Duluth and Minneapolis. It alerted the specialist because no flight plan had reached him calling for an aircraft at that spot at that time, nor had any warning of an unidentified aircraft come from either the DEW or Mid-Canada lines.

'What was it and how did it get there?

'The jet's location, speed and altitude were relayed to sector headquarters...

'Sector headquarters is a massive windowless building with walls four-feet thick, located at an airbase on the outskirts of Duluth, Minnesota. Inside are the men and equipment that process and control the operation of the entire sector. In the bowels of the building are giant computers - the brains of the system - which, with astronomical speed, receive, store, correlate and answer questions on all data fed into them by radar sites, air bases, guided missile stations, the DEW, Mid-Canada and Pinetree lines, flight-control centres and weather stations. They memorise information on weather conditions, the status of jets and missiles, projected flight plans of all aircraft authorised to fly through the sector, authorised or not.

'The report on the blip from Sioux Lookout came into the computers and the data was automatically relayed, in code form, to scopes in the identification room. The identification officer (IDO) already knew which planes should be flying where at what time. This new track was a stranger.

'Reaching for his light gun, an electronic device that triggers responses from the computers, he aimed it at the blip and fired.

'There was no flight plan.

'The IDO picked up his direct line to the Winnipeg, Manitoba flight-control centre and gave it the location and altitude of the jet and the direction and speed of its track.

'The IDO, thirty seconds after the track appeared, signalled the weapons room that it had

A two-seat F-106B.

an unidentified aircraft.

'In the weapons section, lights flashed and bells rang on the console of the senior weapons director. This too, was superfluous insurance because he had already seen the track and translated its code. By the time he received the IDO's signal, confirming that it was as an unknown, he had selected a weapons team to direct the mission. A radio frequency was assigned, the scramble button was pushed and the horn went off in the pilots' ready room...

'My day began early that morning. Pilots of the 11th Fighter Interceptor Squadron - those who are not on 24-hour alert - report for duty at 7.30 am. So did I. After passing the security check at the gate, I was escorted to squadron headquarters by Lieutenant Bernard Hartman, one of the 11th's jet pilots.

'In the squadron lounge I met the rest of the pilots, including the man who was to fly me, Captain Charles Pugh. A few of the others told me, not in his presence, that Pugh was 'a damn good pilot.' In Air Force languages, it means the same thing it does in any other language.

'After coffee at the snack bar, we went into the briefing room. At these morning sessions, the day's activities are outlined. I was scheduled for an afternoon alert, so I spent the rest of the morning getting suited up and checked out.

'A pressure suit is no place for anyone with claustrophobia. All Air Force jets have pressurised cabins but, for high-altitude missions these king-size corsets are worn, too. I felt like I was being squeezed to death and, when they put the helmet on, I thought I was in a custom-made coffin. A parachute goes on over all that and, when we found one to fit, I hobbled out to the plane for the cockpit check.

'The first close-up sight of an F-106 is a shocker. No fact sheet coldly listing its size and performance (28 feet high, 70 feet long, speed more than 1,500 mph) can prepare you for it. They are big, beautiful birds.

'I sat down in the back seat of an F-106B, the two-seat version and got a short course in how to panic. The first thing that strikes you is the smallness of the area and the maze of instruments that surrounds you. Already near-motionless from the pressure suit, I was crippled still further as they tightened the parachute straps until the suit wrinkled ('If they're loose the jolt will break your leg when the chute opens,' Hartmann said amiably.) Over that came the shoulder straps and the seat belt, with an extra lanyard hooked up to the seat itself.

'Now nearly paralyzed, I thought, 'I'm going to break the damn sound barrier and I'll be too numb to feel a thing.' And a trickle of sweat ran down my back.

'When they closed the canopy momentarily I knew how Lazarus must have felt. Hartmann then taught me how to bail out.

'Reach down along both sides of the seat and you'll find two handles'' he said. 'When you bail out, just yank them hard. The rest is automatic. The canopy goes, the seat rockets go; you go. The seat stays strapped until, you fall to 14,000 feet and then it blasts loose. The lanyard initiates a one-second delay and your chute opens.'

'Then he made the most tasteless comment of the day. 'You have to go first. If the man up front bails out ahead of you his seat rockets will burn you up. He won't wait very long, so you better be ready.'

'There was still one more thing, a subject referred to only vaguely. Some NORAD fighters are armed with atomic-warhead missiles. As I sat there, I knew the missiles bay was just a few feet below and behind me. I asked Captain Pugh if he knew what was in our bay, but he just smiled vacantly and changed the subject. I never did find out but it's a weird feeling sitting there and wondering what it is you're sitting on.

'After lunch, we suited up again and went to the alert room to sweat it out. One pair of pilots pulls a five-minute alert - they have to be off the ground five minutes after the horn goes - and another pair is on 30-minute alert. I was with the first pair.

'About one o'clock we began a card game. At 1:40, as I was dealing, that man at Sioux Lookout spotted the blip. Before I had made two discards, the horn went off...

'Scrambling is old hat to most Air Force pilots and they can tell some hilarious tales about it. Like punch-drunk fighters primed to answer the bell, they are conditioned to jump up and start running when the horn goes. At one air base, so they say, the alert room had been remodelled and one pilot jumped up and crashed into a wall where the door used to be. Another leaped out of bed and started running in his pyjamas when his six-year-old son sneaked into the bedroom and blew a toy horn in his ear.

'When the horn blew in our ears,

Kevin V. Brown who wrote the accompanying article *I Chased a Bogie in a NORAD jet* in *Popular Mechanics*, August 1962, is squeezed into his pressure-suit before boarding the F-106B (left) with his pilot, Captain Charles Pugh of the 11th Fighter Interceptor Squadron. The Convair F-106 Delta Dart was the primary all-weather interceptor aircraft of the United States Air Force from the 1960s until the 1980s. Designed as the so-called 'Ultimate Interceptor', it proved to be the last dedicated interceptor in US Air Force service. The 11th Fighter-Interceptor Squadron's last assignment was with the 343rd Fighter Interceptor Wing at Duluth Airport, Minnesota, where it was inactivated on 30 June 1968.

Pugh and I and the pilot of the second ship started running. In that pressure suit, it was more like controlled stumbling. I came in third but Pugh had other things to do while I finished strapping myself in. When he started the engine and closed the canopy, I could feel the sweat along my spine again. There was no turning back now.

'Luckily, Pugh began his check-in routine while taxiing out and I had to stop feeling sorry for myself and start taking notes.

'Duluth Tower. Victor November Red. Scramble two F-106s.'

(Translation: Pugh called the airport tower, identified himself by code name and asked for take-off instructions.)

'Roger, Victor November Red. You are Victor November Zero One and Zero Two. Cleared TACAN scramble, two-nine-three radio outbound. Contact Majority, channel three. Gate climb, angles four-five.'

'(For the flight, our planes would be identified as VN-01 and 02. We were cleared for a tactical air-navigation flight, with a 293-degree heading after takeoff - a standard westerly heading at Duluth to avoid the congested areas to the east. We were to contact sector headquarters on channel 3 and climb at full throttle to 45,000 feet.)

'By that time we were in take off position. Pugh revved it up, released the brakes and my head snapped back against the seat rack. If thunder could hum, it would sound like a jet fighter on takeoff.

'We were off the ground within 3,000 feet and Pugh was on the air. 'Hello Majority. VN-01 and 02 climbing 293, gate.'

'The intercept director answered. 'Roger Zero One. Turn starboard to three-six-zero. Dolly check.'

'(Turn right and fly straight north. Check the data link. This last is the fantastic system by which the intercept director sitting in front of a console, inside a building with walls four foot thick, can fly a supersonic plane hundreds of miles away. His computer feeds information to the computer aboard the aircraft which, in turn, controls the plane's autopilot. The pilot except for takeoff and landing and firing the missiles - NORAD still wants human control over these - can fly 'hands off.')

'Pugh checked his instruments.

'Dolly sweet.'

'Roger, follow dolly.'

'And not another word was spoken. Under actual combat conditions, voice communication could be jammed, but the data-link system is impossible to jam. I could hear the engine hum behind me and the air whistle as we streaked through it, climbing close to the speed of sound.

'The instruments meanwhile, kept up a running account of the battle, the dials clicking constantly, giving our position and the target and the relative bearings of both. We were climbing straight north at Mach .95, slightly below the sonic barrier. The target was at 45,000 feet, heading 175 degrees, at a 45-degree angle from us, 95 miles away and closing fast.

'Down below the intercept director had both tracks on his scope. He was pointing us, appropriately, for 'offset point,' a pinpoint place in the sky that his computer told him would bring us broadside to the target.

'In the plane, as we levelled out at 45,000, I could see vapour trails ahead of us.

'Several of the instruments flipped to new readings and the 106 banked gracefully into a right turn. Our new heading was to be 90 degrees and - look out! - our new speed, Mach 1.25.

'Pugh took over the controls and the plane leaped forward with a new roar as he slammed the throttle into afterburner.

'They told me earlier that breaking the sound barrier would be a disappointment; that nothing much happens. The Mach gauge hung momentarily at .95 and then jumped to 1.1 and kept rising and the plane kept right on flying.

'Pugh broke the spell and the silence with the first words since takeoff. 'Hello, Majority. VN-01. Contact!'

The target was looming up fast on the left and, at the second 'offset point,' our plane banked again to the right, sliding in behind the target but closing the gap fast. Finally, I got some sensation of our speed as the vapour trails poured out behind the target's eight jet engines. There was no mistaking it as an Air Force B-52. Pugh, I'm sure, had identified it earlier.

'He slid right in behind it smoothly, slightly below it and to the right, in perfect position to read the tail number. He called it in and then broke off. The mission was over.

'Pugh climbed sharply to 53,000 feet to kill the speed and startled me over the interphone with the ridiculously casual question: 'Want to fly it a while?'

'The B-52, it turned out, had been on a routine training mission, slightly off course and its flight plan had been misfiled - two of the most common causes for intercept missions. A trace located the plan and the bomber was contacted and told to get back where it belonged.

'If it had been identified as hostile, Pugh would have armed his missiles, used his radar to line up the target, fired and broken off. The second 106, which stayed fifteen miles behind us, could have made its pass while Pugh circled and the two would have kept it up until the bogie was destroyed.

'If both failed - which is highly unlikely with homing missiles - the two ships on 30-minute alert would have taken off and intercepted the target all over again. And, by that time the whole NORAD system would have been alerted, including the Bomarc and Nike missile bases.

'The sky was clear the day I flew, but they tell me that the date-link system can fly a plane in a pea-soup fog close enough to a target to get the colour of the pilot's eyes. They also told me that, from the time Sioux Lookout spotted the blip until Pugh called in the tail number, less than twenty minutes had elapsed. Most missions take less than fifteen.

'This was just one simple mission against one target in one sector of NORAD. Multiply it by all the sectors in all the NORAD regions and then by all the men and the equipment, all the way up to the Arctic Ocean and from Midway to Scotland and you have an idea of the saturation surveillance that is going on every day over the North American continent.

'Everything that flies is detected. Everything detected must be identified. Anything unidentified is intercepted. Anything that's intercepted could easily be destroyed.

'So far, this has not been necessary.

'But if it ever should be, it is comforting to learn by flying a mission with NORAD that the system for tracking and finding these targets has been worked out to such a fine point and that the men who man the electronic equipment and fly the planes are such artists at their trade.'

In America by 1973 the General Dynamics/Convair F-106 Delta Dart had been the USAF's first-line interceptor for the previous fifteen years. But like a fine wine, some aircraft - the F-106 among them - actually improve with age. Captain Donald D. Carson USAF described what it was like to fly the 'Six' in both intercept and air-superiority roles and told about some of its improved capabilities.

'How does an aircraft perform after fifteen years of hard use? The men who fly the F-106 Delta Dart think it has improved with age. Many say the 'Six' is one of the truly great airframe designs of modern aviation. The 'Six' can perform its mission far better today than it could when introduced in 1959 because the systems have been continually refined.

'The physical beauty of the F-106 is immediately apparent. Its sleek fuselage and its tall, sweptback tail give an indication of the aircraft's great speed. The F-106 established several altitude records and, in 1959, set a world's official speed record of 1,525.9 mph, which is impressive even today. The F-106 has been the first-line interceptor of ADC and NORAD since 1959.

F-106A 57-2494 of the 101st Fighter Interceptor Squadron, 102nd Fighter Interceptor Wing of the Massachusetts Air National Guard based at Otis Air Force Base, Massachusetts, intercepting a Soviet Tu-95 'Bear-D' bomber off Cape Cod near Yarmouth, Nova Scotia on 15 April 1982. All it took was just one wrong course correction and the Cold War would have gone 'hot' and then combat would begin.

'To give you an idea of what it is like to fly the F-106, let me take you along on two typical training missions. The first demonstrates its abilities as an interceptor. The second shows its potential in aerial combat.

'Externally, the 'Six' has remained basically unchanged from its beginning and has not been fattened with the added weight and drag of 'bolt-on modifications,' which so often plague fighter aircraft with sloth-like performance as they grow older.

'Our walk-around inspection starts with the lance-like pitot tube at the very front of the aircraft. This provides an air-pressure input for the central air data computer (CADC) which in turn provides accurate airspeed and altitude information to the (light instruments and main aircraft computer. Behind the pitot tube is the large black conical radome - the nose of the aircraft. Housed here are the radar antenna and a nose full of 'magic black boxes' to power the radar, infrared (IR) and fire-control systems. The huge delta wing is the most prominent feature of the F-106. A delta-winged aircraft is unique. It has no horizontal stabilizer or elevators. The movable portion of the wings serve as both elevator and aileron and are appropriately called 'elevons.' The elevons operate differentially (in opposite directions) to produce roll and together for pitch control. A delta-wing aircraft feels much the same as any conventionally designed aircraft during flight. Its advantages are its excellent performance at high altitudes and an agile turning ability at lower and medium altitudes. The very large wing enables the 'Six' to cruise efficiently at high subsonic and supersonic speeds. The aircraft's cruise performance can be even greater when external fuel tanks are removed.

'Passing under the wing, we continue the inspection, stopping to open the missile bay to inspect our weapons load. Today, we'll be firing live AIM-4 Falcon missiles on the air-to-air range over the Gulf of Mexico near Tyndall AFB, Florida. A full weapons load consists of two IR and two radar-guided missiles and an AIR-2A Genie rocket. Today's firing load is two AIM-4F radar missiles. The three types of air-to-air weapons give the F-106 an excellent capability against either manned bombers or manoeuvering fighters at both high and low altitudes. All armament is carried internally.

'Our exterior inspection complete, we climb the ladder into the cockpit. Our first check is the vertical tape instruments, which are used instead of conventional round gauges. Once you've flown a 'taped' bird, you are forever spoiled. Tapes present all necessary information in such a clear manner that it is almost impossible to misread altitude or airspeed.

'Centred above the aircraft instruments is a special 'daylight' radarscope. The scope background is a bright green with white target returns, easily visible in broad daylight. Older scopes needed a hood to shade them, or else the pilot had to lean forward to see the scope displays. Flying with your head in a radarscope while trying to conduct a low-altitude intercept is not the way to gain another cluster for your longevity ribbon.

'A unique feature of the 'Six' is the 'annunciator' for the armament, computer and navigation systems. A small, round indicator window tells the status of each system. There is never any doubt as to whether they are operating or not.

'On the lower pedestal, between my feet, is one of the most remarkable pieces of navigation equipment ever put into a fighter - the Tactical Situation Display (TSD). It resembles a TV screen and shows a map corresponding to the TACAN navigation station I've selected. A triangle, called the interceptor symbol, which represents my aircraft, is positioned over this map at our exact location. The advantages of this versatile system become evident especially during a night weather penetration.

'After we're strapped in, I depress the engine ignition button and move the throttle outboard and then back in to fire the starter motor and provide ignition. The engine can be started without external power by using internally stored high-pressure air and the aircraft battery. This enables the F-106 to operate from dispersed airfields with a minimum of support. Once started, I turn on the single MA-1 fire-control power switch, which operates all of the weapons, radar, computer, navigation and communication equipment. I dial in a grid reference setting to tell my computer the location and aircraft heading. The aircraft computer has tremendous capabilities and one of them is dead-reckoning navigation. Once the grid reference setting has been inserted, I can fly to any predetermined fix on my TSD without receiving information from a TACAN station or any other type of navigation aid.

'I close the canopy and taxi to the runway. Everything looks good, so I, 'hack' the clock, release the brakes and put the throttle in afterburner. Suddenly, everything gets quiet for a moment as the EPR drops while the engine eyelids open. I'm jolted forward by a solid kick in the back and a loud bang as I get the 'hard light' so characteristic of the J75 engine. This is the same engine found in the F-105, making the 'Thud' and 'Six' the two most powerful single-engine aircraft in the world. The J75 puts out 24,500lbs of thrust in full afterburner (26,500 for the F-105 during a water-injection takeoff). The hard light is even more apparent than in the F-105, as the 'Six' is several tons lighter.

'Acceleration is extremely rapid. I ease back on the stick at 135 knots to raise the nose wheels off the runway. Holding this takeoff attitude, the aircraft flies off the runway at 184

A F-106A Delta Dart from the California ANG fires an AIR-2 Genie rocket.

knots. At 250 knots, I come out of afterburner long before crossing the end of the runway. Moving almost 42,000lbs from a standing start to more than 250 knots in about 7,000 feet is quite impressive. The F-106 is a thrill to fly and the novelty never wears off. I accelerate out to 400 knots and begin to climb at a steeper rate, maintaining this speed until reaching Mach .93, which I hold to level off. I kick my rudders to fishtail the aircraft - a signal to my wingmen that I want them to move out into route formation.

'After contacting the ground-controlled intercept (GO) director who will control the mission, I separate my flight. Each aircraft begins to follow the 'Data Link' commands sent from the intercept director. Under Data Link direction, the computer at the Semi-Automatic Ground Environment (SAGE) or Backup Interceptor Control (BUIC) centre transmits information to each aircraft. The MA-1 aircraft computer displays data as heading, airspeed and altitude commands. I also receive target heading, speed, altitude, range and bearing information.

'Once I've checked in with my intercept director, giving my armament safety check, the remainder of the intercept can be conducted without either of us saying a word. I receive all commands on my 'tapes' in the form of white markers that appear over the speed, altitude and heading I'm to fly. There is also information displayed on the Tactical Situation Display (TSD), which depicts the entire intercept on my map display. I can see my position in relation to that of the target and the type of intercept I'll be conducting. Today, for range safety, I'll call my contact with the target and get verbal clearance to fire from my GCI controller.

'When the target-marker indicator moves up ON the altitude tape and I begin to receive target range, I know I've been committed against a specific target. At this time I arm my missiles.

'I search the sector of my radarscope that corresponds to the target bearing and distance being sent by the Data Link. I position my radar antenna elevation to search the altitude at which my target is flying. Today, I'll be directed to make a 10,000-foot front 'snap-up' attack against a Firebee drone target flying at 40,000 feet.

'I'm turning toward the drone, which is now thirty miles ahead, coming directly at me. I select afterburner to gain speed for the snap-up. The snap-up manoeuvre is used against targets at very high altitudes. This drone will not be above 45,000 but I'll still use a snap-up since it is a more demanding intercept and provides very realistic training. The afterburner quickly pushes me through the transonic area into supersonic flight. There is no difference in the feel of the aircraft as it goes supersonic. Your only indication is a slight movement in the altitude tape, which quickly settles back down to normal.

'I spot my target five degrees left at the top of my scope and call a 'contact.' Grasping the left half of the 'split stick.' which controls both the aircraft and the radar system, I'm positioning the antenna beam and 'range gate' over the radar return. The radar locks on. 'Red Lead...Judy,' I call to the GCI controller to indicate I'm assuming full control of the intercept.

'The MA-1 computer now takes over and computes the intercept steering geometry. I can either select the 'auto-attack' mode, which will take the computer inputs and steer me to the target, or fly it manually. The autopilot doesn't need the practice! I'm turning to centre the steering dot depicted on the radar attack displays. The target is moving rapidly down the scope. I'm selecting the expanded sixteen-mile radarscope display, which gives more precise information.

'At approximately fourteen miles, the scope tells me it's time to begin the snap-up. I'm smoothly pulling the nose above the horizon into a steep climb as the outer radar range circle on the radarscope begins to shrink. When this circle shrinks to the same size as the smaller steering circle, the missiles will fire. A steering dot and another smaller circle on the scope provide directional information. The aircraft is turned to put the 'dot in the hole,' thus positioning the aircraft for an accurate missile launch.

'Looking up, I see the drone dead ahead and well above me. Squeeze the trigger! Wait for the computer to fire the missiles at the correct moment! The steering dot is 'pegged' directly in the centre of the steering circle. When the fire signal appears on the scope, there is a loud rush of air as the weapons bay doors rapidly slam open.

'Now a roar as two Hughes Falcon missiles accelerate away from me as if I were sitting still. They're heading toward the drone with a closure rate almost three times the speed of sound. It's a hit!

'My fascination is interrupted by the jolting realization that I must execute my breakaway manoeuvre to avoid flying through the debris of the target. I begin following the Data Link commands for RTB (return to base). I look down and follow the parachute attached to the crippled drone, now thousands of feet below, slowly falling into the Gulf of Mexico.

'Back in the airfield traffic pattern, I'm reminded of one disadvantage of the delta wing - the absence of wing flaps. This causes the 'Six' to have relatively high final approach and landing speeds. A normal weight final approach (2,000lbs of fuel remaining) is flown at 181 knots, with touchdown at 149 knots. Landing speeds can exceed 200 knots on final with a heavy fuel load on board. However, the drag chute and high drag generated by the delta wing during aerodynamic braking enables you to stop the F-106 in very short distances. Aerodynamic braking is accomplished by slowly raising the nose of the aircraft - up to a maximum of seventeen degrees - once your main landing gear have touched the runway. It gives you the feeling that you're going to topple over backwards.

'All F-106 live armament firings are done on the Tyndall AFB ranges under direction of the Air Defense Weapons Centre. Each F-106 squadron deploys to Florida annually for at least a week of weapons firing. Daily training missions are flown against high- and low-altitude targets, using chaff and electronic countermeasures (ECM). The chaff and ECM emitted by target aircraft test the anti-jamming capabilities of the F-106, which are second to no other interceptor flying. Countering the ECM of a well-equipped bomber is beyond the ability of most fighters, but not the F-106. There is almost always a way for the 'Six' to get an 'MA' (mission accomplished) or a kill!

'The aerial-refuelling modification added in the late 1960s gave the F-106 unlimited range and the ability to respond to emergencies anywhere in the world. In 1968, F-106s were flown across the Pacific to Korea in response to the North Korean seizure of the USS *Pueblo*. This worldwide capability increased the possibility that the F-106 will come in contact with enemy fighters. To prepare for this contingency, all F-106 pilots are given extensive training in air combat tactics (ACT), a mission at which the 'Six' excels.

'To demonstrate what it's like to fly an F-106 during an ACT engagement. I'd like to now take you to the 48th Fighter-Interceptor Squadron at Langley AFB Virginia, where you will observe a mission flown against a flight of Navy fighters from Oceana Naval Air Station, Virginia. Much of the ACT training in the F-106 is conducted against different types of fighters, to obtain more realistic training and expose the pilots to the tactics of others.

'As I lead my flight of two into the ACT training area just west of Cape Hatteras, North Carolina I check in and wait for the Navy flight to come up on my frequency. I usually arrive in the training area first since the F-106 normally flies with external fuel tanks and has approximately forty minutes more fuel than the Navy fighters, which fly without external tanks.

'I set up an orbit at the western edge of the training area and spread my wingman out into patrol formation. The Navy flight checks in on my frequency - their call sign is 'Ripper.' I answer, 'Hello, Rippers. This is Red One... We are in an orbit over lake at twenty thousand.'

'Ripper lead answers, 'Roger, Red... we are heading east to the Cape.' With one flight positioned over Cape Hatteras and the other over Lake Matamuskeet, we have a fifty-mile separation for the first setup.

'Red flight, vector, 120 degrees,' directs the GCI controller. 'Ripper flight, go port to 300 degrees. Ripper, you will be the first bogey.' You pick up the heading and push up the throttle to gain a little speed.

'On an ACT mission, the initial setup is either 'head on' or from the beam. The flights alternate being the bogey (target flight) and the interceptor flight. The flight acting as bogey will receive only one heading and altitude to fly until they obtain visual contact with (he interceptors. At this time, they are free to manoeuvre to defend or, if possible, take the offensive during an ensuing engagement. The interceptor flight receives full GCI support and is vectored toward the bogeys under radar control.

'Red flight is steady 120.' I transmit.

'Roger, Red... target is five degrees right at thirty miles.'

'I pick up a radar blip five degrees right at about thirty miles on my scope and lock on to it. The radarscope indicates 1,200-knot overtake on the bogeys. I advise the GCI controller that we have a 'Judy' (radar lock on).

'Go, Gate,' I call to my wing-man, to select afterburner. The Mach tape rapidly climbs to 1.4 as we nose over to unload and let our aircraft accelerate while maintaining zero G. By 'unloading' and flying with less than one G. The aircraft is free from the drag caused by producing lift with its wings. All engine thrust is now used to propel the aircraft forward, greatly increasing acceleration. The discomfort of hanging against the lap belt as you float under a lack of gravity is well worth the speed gained during the few moments of this manoeuvre. We are now closing at almost 2,000 mph. Turning into their beam, we visually pick up two F-4s at eight miles.

'I call, 'Tally ho!...twelve o'clock... about 5,000 feet high.' My wingman answers that he's got them in sight too. The bogeys are flying straight ahead, so we know that they haven't spotted us as we slide into their stern at four miles, closing quickly.

'The bogeys see us and suddenly begin a defensive turn into us. As we close, the Navy flight is still in a turn when they call their 'split.' Ripper lead dives in afterburner to pick up speed and keep us out of range. His wingman climbs to gain separation and cover the leader. If we follow his leader, the wingman will be in a good position to come in from behind and sandwich us between them.

'I decide to drive the low man out of the flight and then double-team the high man. 'Red, let's take the low man,' I call to my wingman, as I head down after Ripper lead. Ripper leader sees us getting into good firing position and breaks into a very hard spiral to get us off his tail. I pull back on the stick. The G meter climbs to six Gs and the air-craft shudders slightly as I climb rapidly.

'OK, Two. He is out of the fight for a while - let's take the high man,' I call. When the low man 'broke,' he killed off his airspeed in order to make an extremely hard turn. This got him out of his immediate predicament, but also temporarily destroyed his ability to get back up into the fight to support his wingman, who stayed high. We had used our speed to climb back up to Ripper Two, rather than bleed it off in an attempt to turn with the leader.

'Ripper Two is now three miles at our two o'clock and slightly high. This gives us a 'two-on-one' situation, which was what we had pre-briefed to attain.

'Red Two; stay high - I'm going in on Ripper Two,' I call to my wingman.

'Roger, lead,' he answers.

'I know from where Red Two is flying that he'll be able to cover my six o'clock during the attack. Ripper Two starts a turn into us. We pass almost head on with only a few hundred feet separating our aircraft. I start a steep climbing turn into him. We pass canopy to canopy. Every time I pass that close to an aircraft, I'm amazed at the sensation of speed you feel. The other aircraft is only a blur as you pass him at over 1,200 mph.

'Ripper Two continues in a level turn as I climb rapidly almost straight up. As the airspeed begins to bleed off, I roll my aircraft on its back and hang inverted, watching our bogey still in his turn below. Putting in full left rudder and pulling back on the stick, I rapidly roll straight down behind Ripper Two, picking up the airspeed I had lost in the climb.

'Red One is sliding into Ripper Two's six-o'clock... Where is Ripper lead?' I ask my wingman.

'My wingman answers, 'He's low and still out of it... no threat. I'll keep him out of the fight.'

'The perspiration runs down into my eyes as I increase the Gs to more than five to cut Ripper off in his turn. I move my left hand from the throttle over to the radar hand control. It's a struggle. G-forces always seem to add to the tension of a dogfight. This added weight requires that you exert an extra effort to make any movement. You're also squeezed tightly through your legs and stomach as your anti-G suit inflates, to prevent all the blood from rushing to your legs.

'Continuing to close on Ripper Two. I get an infrared head-up lock-on without looking into the radar-scope. This is a great system. It enables an F-106 pilot to get a quick lock-on to a hard manoeuvering target without taking his eyes from the fight. Moving closer. I squeeze the firing trigger at three-quarters of a mile and feel the weapons bay doors open as the inert missiles are extended into the airstream and quickly retract after tracking the target.

'Red One'... 'MA' on Ripper Two.' I transmit as I pull the throttle out of afterburner. Easing off the Gs, I 'roll off' and head away from Ripper Two. 'Red is disengaging and heading toward the lake,' I call. Looking right, I see my wingman still in excellent position. We head west to the lake to set up for another engagement. This time it will be our turn to be the bogeys and to be on the defensive.

'Checking fuel, we both have 5,500 pounds remaining. Enough for two more engagements and the return trip home of more than 100 miles. It is now that the long legs of the F-106 become of value. You can get in a lot of good flying in the 'Six' and still have plenty of fuel for the trip home.

'We're finally seeing long-overdue changes in the F-106. Many 'Sixes' are now flying with a new clear bubble canopy that eliminates the great visibility problem presented by the old canopy. The F-106 fleet is also getting the composite boresight modification. This is the head-up lock-on capability mentioned earlier. There will also be greatly increased reliability built into the MA-1 fire-control system as it is up dated to increase its capabilities and accuracy. Many MA-1 components have already been converted to solid-state technology, replacing the older and less reliable equipment.

'The present F-106 engine accessory drive and generator system is made up of four separate and independent generators. This will soon be replaced by the single multiphase F-111 generator. It has proved to be extremely reliable and will provide all F-106 electrical power, with a saving in total aircraft weight.

'Probably the most significant modification since 1959 is installation of the M-61 Vulcan, 20-mm cannon 'Six-Shooter' package in the missile bay of the aircraft. It will not interfere with the Falcon missiles, which will be retained along with the gun. The only noticeable change will be a slight bulge along the centreline of the weapons bay doors where the M-61 rotating gun barrels exit the fuselage. All F-106s will soon have the gun. The 'Six-Shooter' package will also include the 'Snap-Shoot' gun sight, one of the most advanced and accurate sights ever developed. This system, specially designed for the F-106, has proved to be deadly accurate in more than a hundred firings against drone and dart airborne targets.

'With this renewed interest increased emphasis on upgrading F-106, it will be around for many years to come. Together with an improved manned interceptor (IMI), the over-the-horizon backscatter (OTH-B) radar and the Airborne Warning and Control System (AWACS), the F-106 will continue to provide a viable deterrent to airborne aggressors. There are many good years left for the F-106. It is an even better interceptor today than when it entered the ADC inventory fifteen years ago.'

In Britain meanwhile, Hunter 6 and Javelin jet fighters had been replaced in 1960 in the interceptor role by the English Electric Lightning. The Lightning presented a major challenge. It was the RAF's first supersonic, night/all-weather interceptor. In speed alone it doubled the performance of the Hunter. But more than that - with its combination of AI23 (airborne interception radar) and Firestreak air-to-air guided weapons - the Lightning had a genuine interception capability against high-performance bomber aircraft. With the introduction of the Lightning, air defence was at last being given an appropriate degree of priority which many fighter experts thought was long overdue. QRA, or Quick Reaction Alert, was the Lightning's raison d'etre. RAF Fighter (later Strike) Command stationed Lightnings and later, Lightnings and Phantoms on a special 'ready' pan, armed and ready to go at a few minutes' notice. The pilots' task was to intercept, supersonically any aircraft approaching the UK without a flight plan or who crossed into the air defence zone without warning and, if ordered, shoot them down with missiles and cannon fire. In the UK the permanent state of high

Left: Scramble! Air and ground crew race to their waiting and fully armed F.2A at the start of another intercept sortie. (Richard Reeve)

Below: A 11 Squadron Lightning F.6 on QRA. The Q Shed, a self-contained unit which housed aircrew and ground crew in an adjacent bungalow, was built away from the airfield hangars, next to the main runway, so the aircraft minimised taxiing time prior to take off. (Malcolm English)

RAF Illuminated plotting board in the early part of the Cold War.

readiness is called QRA (Quick Reaction Alert) and in RAF Germany it was known as Battle Flight. In the UK the readiness state was ten minutes and in Germany it was five minutes. Air- and ground crew waited in their ready rooms at the same notice 24 hours a day, 365 days a year. The Q Shed, a self-contained unit which housed both aircrew and ground crew in an adjacent bungalow, was built away from the airfield hangars, adjacent to the main runway, in order that the aircraft minimised taxiing time prior to take off. Ground crew could stay for a week at a time - all living in accommodation just a few feet from their aircraft in the Q shed. It was a popular duty because a Lightning pilot was almost certain to get a training scramble during each period and always had the next day off. The reason for the frequent training scrambles was that 5 minutes really was not very long to run to a Lightning, climb the ladder, strap in, start engines, taxi to the runway and take off. If the pilot were asleep when the 'Scramble' bell sounded the time allowed was even tighter.

Once an alert sounded the two pilots would belt for their transport and drive across to the pan, where, strapped in, they were ready to be airborne within two minutes. Ground crew supplied external power to the Lightnings during these waiting periods and the pilots got their briefing via a plug-in telebrief direct from the relevant operations room. Many of the Lightning alerts were practices - intruders simulated by Canberras from RAF Germany - but there were "quite a few" visitors from Russia, some of them long-range maritime flights from the far north, which flew past Norway and turned over the Shetlands. Visual identification of strange targets was practiced by the Lightning pilots making an approach to an intruder from behind and at 300 yards range identifying the intruder visually. At night this had to be done in whatever light was available. On all occasions a radar lock-on had to be achieved. The aircraft, which were put up against the QRA force, included Canberras, Phantoms, Buccaneers and Sea Vixens. All Lightning pilots had an intensive aircraft recognition course at OTU and when they arrived on the squadron they were kept in practice by continuous refresher training both simulated and live. Some visitors clearly tested the readiness of the QRA force with some intruders' playing 'cat and mouse' with the Lightnings, flying close enough to wake up pilots and then turn away before they were scrambled. Others listened for the signatures of NATO ECM devices and there were the electronic-intelligence gatherers, which flew around listening to radio and radar frequencies. There were even some practice bombing runs. Whatever the intruders were doing the Lightnings intercepted, identified and accompanied them out of the area, armed with cameras and live missiles. Nobody has ever refused to go.

Normally the Lightnings on QRA operated with the local air-defence radar network, which would vector the interceptors on to a target until the Ferranti Airpass AI23B radar had picked it up. The AI23B was a pilot-interpreted system, which meant that the pilot must position himself within brackets, which were displayed in order to make an effective missile firing. To do this he could fly a computed flight path, also displayed, or position himself manually. The technique in an attack was to approach a target either very high or very low so that the intruder could easily be seen without the Lightning itself being spotted. For very high-level attacks the technique was to accelerate to supersonic speed near the tropopause and then climb at attack speed to the height required. The Lightning was still able to climb to height quicker and accelerate to supersonic speeds faster than the Phantom and was therefore ideal for the QRA role. The Lightning's greatest attribute was said to be its handling qualities. It was highly manoeuvrable particularly in the transonic bands. By the early 1970s, Northern

Publicity photo of two Lightning pilots on QRA running to their Lightnings. (MoD)

High above the North Sea on 15 September 1972, one of the Soviet's long-range Tu-95RT 'Bear-D' Maritime reconnaissance model with multi-sensor pallets is intercepted and shadowed by F.6 XR753/A of 23 Squadron, from Leuchars. (MoD)

and Southern Air Defence Regions had been established, the Northern being patrolled by aircraft from Leuchars and Binbrook and the Southern from Coningsby and Wattisham. The McDonnell Douglas Phantom was the next aircraft to hold QRA, serving with 43 and 111 Squadrons at RAF Leuchars. [44]

NATO countries maintain a round-the-clock vigil by coordinated QRA jet fighter teams, ready to implement a process that has been evolving since the advent of aircraft. A QRA response involves the fighter aircraft being scrambled to investigate an infringement of the NATO country's airspace. [45]

Endnotes for Chapter 4

44 Strike Command's air defence of the UK in 1980 consisted of two Lightning and five Phantom squadrons.

45 A total of eight Russian warplanes were intercepted by the RAF over the North Sea and Atlantic Ocean on one day in January 2015. The two Bears intercepted had originally been part of a larger formation of eight aircraft - including four Il-78 tankers - intercepted by Royal Norwegian Air Force F-16 fighters in international airspace over the Norwegian Sea. While six of the planes returned back towards Russia, the two Bears carried on towards the UK where they were picked up by RAF Boulmer. They continued on over the Atlantic to the west of Portugal, where they were intercepted by Portuguese Air Force F-16s before turning back. On the same day, there were a series of similar incidents over the Black Sea and the Baltic where Russian military formations were intercepted by Turkish fighters and Portuguese jets assigned to the NATO Baltic air policing mission. In November 2015 during operations in Syria against the Islamic State a Russian Su-24 bomber was shot down by Turkish F-16s over the Turkish-Syrian border after violating Turkish air space and ignoring ten warnings. One of the two pilots was killed in the air by fire from the ground.

Republic F-84B-21-RE Thunderjets of the 14th Fighter Group at Dow AFB, Maine in formation in 1948.

F-86F Sabres of the 56th Fighter Wing in formation.

A F9F-2B Panther taxies in on USS *Philippine Sea* (CV-47).
Inset: LSO (Landing Signals Officer) directing operations
for landing aboard the *Philippine Sea*. (Roland H. Baker) '.

Below: F9F Panther lands on USS *Valley Forge* (CV-45).
By October 1952 the USS *Valley Forge* had become the
only US carrier to return to the Korea combat zone four
times. On 2 January 1953 the 'Happy Valley' began the
New Year with strikes against Chinese supply dumps
and troop billeting areas behind the stalemated front
lines.

Above: F-86Fs of the 35th FBS, 8th FBW at Suwon, South Korea, 1953 with Miss Tena, Colonel W. B. Wilmot's aircraft in the foreground.

Middle: Troy Gordie Cope on the wing of F-86 Rosie in September 1952 before he was last heard from.

Below: Colonel Benjamin O. Davis Jr., commander of the 51st FIW leading a formation of F-86F Sabres over Korea in January 1953.

Top: Indian Air Force Gnat. India claimed that the Pakistan Air Force F-86 Sabre was vulnerable to the diminutive Folland Gnat, nicknamed 'Sabre Slayer.'

Below: In 1954 Pakistan began receiving the first of a total of 120 F-86F Sabres. The Canadair Sabre Mk.6, acquired from ex-Luftwaffe stocks via Iran, were the mainstay of the PAF's day fighter operations during the Indo-Pakistani War of 1971.

Above: Heyl ha' Avir (Israeli Air Force, IAF) A-4H Skyhawks.

Right: The Dassault Super Mystère B.2 was the first Western European supersonic aircraft to enter mass production and were well liked by the Israeli pilots. In 1958 24 B.2s were purchased by the IAF and saw action in the 1967 Six-Day War and the 1973 Yom Kippur War.

Below: IAF F-4E Phantoms in formation.

Above: Vulcan scamble!

SAC B-52Ds armed with AGM-28 Hound Dog Missiles on Ground Alert Duty on the flight line in 1967. The supersonic, turbojet-propelled, air-launched cruise missile with a W28 Class-D nuclear warhead was developed in 1959 and was primarily designed to be capable of attacking Soviet ground-based air defence sites prior to a potential air attack by B-52s during the Cold War.

USAF F-4 Phantoms and a 388th TFW F-105 'Wild Weasel' refuelling with a KC-135 on a mission to North Vietnam in 1970.

Middle: A-4E 150032 of VMA-121 which was shot down by small arms fire over South Vietnam on 30 May 1967. The pilot, 1st Lieutenant Walter Thoennes, was killed.

Bottom: F-8Es of VF-33 being launched from the USS *Enterprise* (CVAN-65) in 1964.

MiG-21U in Việtnam People's Air Force (NVNAF) livery, similar to the type used by the the North Việtnamese Air Force.

F-4D in the 435th TFS armed with LAU-3 rocket launchers approaching a KC-135A tanker over Vietnam.

Below: Grumman A-6A Intruders of VA-196 aboard the USS *Constellation* during the squadron's second combat cruise (May 1968-January 1969) releasing Mk.82 bombs over Vietnam.

Chapter Five

The Six Day War

On 4 November 1966 the Soviet Union vetoed a six-Power resolution inviting Syria to prevent incidents that constituted a violation of the General Armistice Agreement. Between 1966 and 1967 Israel's borders saw repeated Arab terrorist attacks and Syrian military activity. During 1965-1967, Israel's armed forces staged numerous provocations along the Israeli-Syrian border area. On 7 April 1967 a serious incident broke out between Israel and Syria, after Israel had begun to cultivate more westerly tracts in the Ha'on sector of the demilitarized zone. Israel took military action against Syria and eventually both sides employed artillery, tanks and mortars. During this clash Israeli airstrikes were launched a few miles from Damascus. Israel bombed both Syrian border villages and military targets. After several hours the United Nations Truce Supervision Organization managed to arrange a ceasefire. Following this confrontation, Arab governments pledged their support to Syria. In May 1967 the Egyptian leader, President Nasser, received false intelligence reports from the Soviet Union that an Israeli attack on Syria was imminent. These false reports followed Israeli officials threatening military action against Syria if the Syrian authorities did not stop Palestinian guerrillas from crossing the border into Israel. Nasser declared full mobilisation in Egypt as of 14 May, citing the joint defence agreement with Syria. On 22 May Nasser declared the Straits of Tiran closed to Israeli shipping and on 27 May stated 'Our basic objective will be the destruction of Israel. The Arab people want to fight.' Israel reiterated declarations made in 1957 that any closure of the Straits would be considered an act of war; or a justification for war. On 30 May 1967 Jordan and Egypt signed a defence pact. On 4 June Israel's National Unity Government took the decision to go to war. Israel's defence forces were confident of victory in any conflict with the Arab states and military leaders provided Prime Minister Eshkol with alarmist information to persuade him to support an attack.

Since the end of the Sinai Campaign in 1956 the IAF had its share of combat and between 1958 and 1967 claimed a single Hunter, two MiG-17s, two MiG-19s and eight MiG-21s in air combats. The beginning of April 1967 saw Israel ready to resume cultivation of three plots near Kibbutz Ha'on, in the southern demilitarized zone, south of the Sea of Galilee. Although initially planned

President Abdul Nasser and Egyptian pilots on 22 May 1967 at Bir Gifgafa.

for 3 April, bad weather prevented work from beginning on that date and it was delayed until 7 April. Israel, meanwhile, put the Israel Defence Forces (IDF) on alert, fully aware that deterioration along the border was not unlikely. Tanks, artillery and mortars were moved into positions around the Sea of Galilee, while at various Heyl ha'Avir (Israeli Air Force, IAF) bases aircraft were fuelled and armed for the day's possible combat. Search-and-Rescue helicopters, light observation aircraft and the Heyl ha'Avir's command and control structure were put on alert as well, all in anticipation of events on the border. On the morning of 7 April two Israeli tractors began their work on the disputed plots, overlooked by Syrian posts on the Golan Heights. The work had received the go-ahead despite continued bad weather, after the Israeli Defence Force had learned that the weather was to clear up later in the day, allowing Heyl ha'Avir aircraft to participate in whatever fighting erupted. The day's hostilities began shortly after when cannon and gunfire opened up on the tractors from the Syrian post at Amrat Az-El-Din. Israeli ground forces returned fire and deterioration was quick to follow, tank and artillery fire erupting as well.

By late morning, Syrian shells began falling in Kibbutz Tel-Katzir and the IDF Chief-of-Staff, Itzhak Rabin, asked the Israeli government to authorize IAF strikes against four Syrian posts along the frontier. The Heyl ha'Avir received its orders at 1214 and quickly launched its aircraft. Yet only when shelling of the Israeli tractors resumed were these permitted to carry out their attacks. Commencing at 1332, the attack was led by 110th Squadron Vautours,[46] followed by 107th Squadron Ouragans[47], 105th Squadron Super Mystères B.2s, 116th and 109th Squadron Mystères and by 117th Squadron Mirage IIICs.[48] The attack was broken off however, when Syrian MiGs were spotted making their way towards the combat zone. The attacking aircraft were therefore pulled back and 101st 'First Fighter' Squadron Mirages were vectored in to engage the new arrivals. The day's first two dogfights began at 1358 with Captains Iftah Spector and Benyamin Romah engaging a pair of MiG-21s over the Syrian town of Kuneitra. The high-speed approach between the two pairs soon turned into a tight twist and turn dogfight, the Israeli Mirages attempting to close in on the MiGs from behind. Spector was first to achieve this and downed one MiG after manoeuvring slightly above his opponent and then sinking in for the kill. Romah however, found himself on a parallel course with the other fighter. Breaking towards the MiG at full throttle and with his afterburner, he managed to cut off his opponent and then approach him from the rear. Already over Damascus and pressured to turn back, Romah only managed a short burst from 400 metres away. This was sufficient for the kill and the MiG was seen going down, exploding a few seconds later after taking hits from Spector's aircraft as well.

The dogfight had just ended when more Syrian MiGs were spotted in the vicinity of the southern demilitarized zone. Kibbutz Ein-Gev on the eastern shore of the Sea of Galilee soon

IAF Commander-in-Chief Mordechai Hod (right) with Shimon Peres before the Independence Day Parade in Jerusalem on 15 May 1967. A third-generation Sabra (native-born Israeli), Hod had taken his first flight training in Czechoslovakia in 1948 and then converted to jets in England. (Moshe Milner).

Israeli pilots running to their Mirage IIICJ fighters.

came under fire, apparently from four MiGs which had overflown the settlement unnoticed by the Heyl ha'Avir. A pair of 117th 'First Jet' Squadron Mirages flown by Squadron commander Major Amihay Shmueli and Captain Shlomo Nir, on patrol over the western shore of the lake, were directed eastwards towards the intruders. Contact was made at 1453 when the two Mirages spotted a lone MiG-21. Nir fired a single Shafrir air-to-air missile but missed completely. Retreating back to Syria by this point, the MiG was shielded by the cloud cover over the Golan Heights and managed to elude the Israeli fighters. It soon became apparent however, that the shells falling in Ein-Gev did not originate from the MiGs but rather from one of the Syrian posts on the Heights. Shells, meanwhile, began falling on another Israeli settlement, this time Kibbutz Gadot in the central demilitarized zone. Within fifteen minutes a new attack plan was formed and the IAF initiated strikes against the posts overlooking Gadot. After an hour-long-attack that began at 1525, the Syrians ceased their shelling of the kibbutz.

By the time the shelling was over, another Syrian MiG had fallen prey to Israeli Mirages, this time from the 119th 'Bat' Squadron. At 1552 a dogfight took place between another pair of MiG-21s and two Mirages flown by Squadron leader Major Ran Peker and Captain Avraham Shalmon. Once again both pilots went after separate foes in dogfights that took them into Syrian territory. Peker's first Shafrir launch was a near miss, the missile's proximity fuse failing to detonate. The MiG pilot, upon spotting the missile, attempted to evade Peker by engaging his afterburner, the effect of which was actually providing Peker's second Shafrir with a near-perfect heat signature of the aircraft's engine. Peker however, in his eagerness, launched the missile out of envelope and the MiG managed to evade the missile. Now it was Peker's turn to engage his afterburner and close in for a cannon kill. A two second burst was sufficient to detonate one of the MiG's fuel tanks, turning the aircraft into a ball of fire. Shalmon, meanwhile, was chasing the other MiG at full afterburner having jettisoned his underwing fuel tanks. From 1,000 meters away he fired his first Shafrir but the missile failed to hit its target. The second missile proved to be a miss as well, fired from 700 metres away. Shalmon then closed in to within 400 metres before firing his cannons. Although apparently hitting his opponent, he was directed to disengage. While the Mirages were making their way back to Tel-Nof, the stricken MiG made its way back to Syria's Dumayr air base.

The Heyl ha'Avir's afternoon strikes ended at 1616 and only six fighters remained on the scene, a pair from each Mirage squadron: the 101st, 117th and 119th. But while IAF aircraft were making their way back to base, four MiG-21s were taking off from Dumayr and making their way to the front at low altitude. The four MiGs aircraft appeared over the southern Golan

Heights at 1627, taking a route that took them from south to north over the frontier. By this time the two 117th Squadron Mirages, flown by Major Ezra Dotan and Captain Avraham Lanir had teamed up with the 119th Squadron aircraft, flown by Majors Mordechai Yeshurun and Oded Sagi, while the 101st Squadron Mirages, flown by Captains Avner Slapak and Amnon Shamir, were patrolling elsewhere. At 1630 ground control informed the six pilots of the enemy aircraft in their vicinity. The time of day was ideal for the Israeli pilots, with the afternoon sun at their backs, providing them with excellent visibility while blinding their opponents.

Ezra Dotan was first to spot the MiGs, west of Pik, a Syrian village near the Jordanian-Israeli-Syrian tri-border area. Spotting the Syrian formation's rear guard lagging behind the leading pair, Dotan and Lanir proceeded to take on the rear pair, Dotan taking on the formation's No. 3 and Lanir engaging No. 4. An attempt by Dotan to launch one of his Shafrir failed and he was forced to chase his opponent at low altitude through the canyons of the Yarmouch, a tributary of the Jordan River. A burst of cannon fire from 400 metres away failed to hit the MiG and Dotan continued his pursuit to within 250 metres. A long burst from his cannon and the MiG went down, Dotan breaking westward to locate Lanir and the other Mirages. The Syrian pilot managed to parachute to safety, his aircraft crashing in Jordanian territory.

Lanir, meanwhile, was on the heels of his own opponent. Unlike Dotan, Lanir had jettisoned his underwing fuel tanks and had closed the distance between himself and the fleeing MiG-21 to within 200 metres. He had barely pressed the trigger when the MiG disintegrated into a ball of fire. Lanir's first bullets had apparently hit a fuel tank and the MiG had immediately detonated, without affording Lanir a chance to break away. Lanir's Mirage flew right through the fireball created by the destroyed MiG, comprising of burning fuel alone by now and not of any debris, much to Lanir's good fortune. The Mirage was scorched black however, including the canopy, effectively blinding its pilot. Escorted by Major Yeshurun, leader of the 119th Squadron pair, Lanir managed to make his way back to Israel. The soot was soon swept away from the canopy and Lanir was able to bring his aircraft to a landing in Ramat-David AFB.

The two 101st Squadron Mirages flown by Slapak and Shamir had flown a separate patrol route from the other aircraft. Leading the pair, Captain Avner Slapak knew of other Mirages in the air but not of their number nor of their location. Upon spotting four unidentified aircraft, Slapak turned to his ground control, inquiring whether any enemy aircraft were known to be in his vicinity. Despite receiving a negative answer, Slapak dismissed the possibility that the

A pair of Egyptian Air Force MiG-17 fighter-bombers strafing an Israeli supply convoy.

Three IAF Sud Aviation SA-4050 Vautour light bombers in formation.

aircraft were Mirages and began to give chase. He tried to inform others of his actions but mistook the right radio frequency and could not get his message across. Soon the four MiGs split into two pairs, the rear pair turning left and the leading pair right. Slapak began chasing the rear pair, closing within 500 metres of one of the aircraft when he saw another Mirage descend on him from above! Breaking away, Slapak went after the other MiG when once again the other Mirage got in his way. Despite his protests on the radio, he saw the other fighter open fire and down the MiG. As it turned out, Slapak had gone in after the same pair Lanir and Dotan had engaged, the interfering Mirage being none other than Dotan's.

Breaking away, Slapak suddenly noticed another MiG closing in on a Mirage, later identified once again as Dotan's. Having gone in after the MiG, Slapak was infuriated to see the other Mirage return to engage the MiG, getting in his way again. Descending lower to avoid a collision, Slapak engaged his afterburner and broke ahead of Dotan. Closing to within 250 metres, he fired his cannons and soon saw a number of small explosions rock the MiG, before a huge explosion totally destroyed the fighter. Turning away to team up with Shamir again, Slapak spotted a parachute descending away from the wreckage and then the empty MiG crashing into the ground. Of the four MiG-21s, only one managed to make it back to Dumayr, all three others falling inside Jordan.

The Heyl ha'Avir had carried out 171 sorties during 7 April 1967, of which eighty-four were attack sorties and fifty-two were interception and patrol sorties (the remaining thirty-five were aircraft that were launched but did not get a chance to participate in the fighting). Seventeen Syrian targets were attacked; bombs dropped weighing a total of sixty-five tons. Israeli aircraft fired approximately 700 20mm rounds and 2,900 30mm rounds, five Shafrir AAM, one Matra 530 AAM and ninety-three T-10 rockets. The Syrian air force had carried out 28 MiG-21 sorties and six MiG-17 sorties, all patrol and interception sorties except for the four which had over-flown Ein-Gev. Beginning at 1440 the Syrians had also operated four helicopters on Search-and-Rescue missions to locate their downed pilots. Syria admitted the loss of four of its aircraft, three of them having gone down in Jordan while another was destroyed right over Damascus, in view of its public. Yet it claimed the destruction of five Israeli fighters and heralded the day as a Syrian victory.

The events of 7 April did nothing to dissipate tensions along the border and both militaries remained on a high state of alert. On 13 May Syria informed Egypt of an Israeli plan to attack Syria and the following day saw the Egyptian military enter a high state of alert as well. Dusk on 14 May saw the beginning of Egyptian troop movements into the Sinai Peninsula.

The countdown to the Six-Day War evoking the days of creation had begun.[49]

A period of high tension preceded the war. In response to PLO (Palestine Liberation Organisation) sabotage acts against Israeli targets, Israel raided into the Jordanian-controlled West Bank and initiated flights over Syria, which ended with aerial clashes over Syrian territory, Syrian artillery attacks against Israeli civilian settlements in the vicinity of the border followed by Israeli responses against Syrian positions in the Golan Heights and encroachments of increasing intensity and frequency into the demilitarized zones along the Syrian border and culminating in Egypt blocking the Straits of Tiran, deploying its troops near Israel's border and ordering the evacuation of the UN buffer force from the Sinai Peninsula.

On the evening of 1 June 1967 Moshe Dayan, Israel's newly-appointed Minister of Defence, called Chief of Staff Yitzhak Rabin and the General Officer Commanding (GOC), Southern Command Brigadier General Yeshayahu Gavish to present plans against Egypt. Dayan had not taken part in most of the planning before the Six-Day War. He was covering the Viêtnam War to observe modern warfare up close and was on patrol as an observer with members of the US Marine Corps. War was nothing new to the general who at age fourteen had joined the newly formed Jewish militia known as the Haganah. His trademark black eye patch which covered his left eye was a result of enemy action on 7 June 1941, the night before the invasion of the Syria-Lebanon Campaign, when a French rifle bullet fired by a marksman from several hundred yards away propelled metal and glass fragments into his left eye, causing it severe damage. By late October 1949 he was a Major-General. As Chief of Staff of the Israeli Defence Forces, he had personally commanded the Israeli forces fighting in the Sinai during the 1956 Suez Crisis.

Rabin had formulated a plan in which Southern Command forces would fight their way to the Gaza Strip and then hold the territory and its people

Above: One of a sequence of pictures taken through the gunsight of an Israeli Mirage fighter showing the last moments of a Syrian MiG-21.

Centre: A MiG explodes on the ground seen through the gunsight of a IAF jet.

Below: IAF pilots at a briefing.

hostage until Egypt agreed to reopen the Straits of Tiran; while Gavish had a more comprehensive plan that called for the destruction of Egyptian forces in the Sinai. Rabin favored Gavish's plan, which was then endorsed by Dayan with the caution that a simultaneous offensive against Syria should be avoided. With the exception of Jordan, the Arabs relied principally on Soviet weaponry. Jordan's army was equipped with American weaponry and its air force was composed of British aircraft. Israeli weapons were mainly of Western origin. Its air force was composed principally of French aircraft. Israel's first and most critical move was a surprise attack on the Egyptian Air Force. Initially, both Egypt and Israel announced that they had been attacked by the other country. Egypt had by far the largest and the most modern of all the Arab air forces, consisting of about 420 combat aircraft, all of them Soviet-built and with a heavy quota of top-of-the line MiG-21s. Of particular concern to the Israelis were the thirty Tu-16 'Badger' medium bombers, capable of inflicting heavy damage on Israeli military and civilian centres.

On 2 June, to create the illusion that war was not near, General Moshe Dayan had thousands of soldiers released for the weekend. Their appearance back at their homes and on beaches and in café's seemed to confirm that tensions were relaxing. Some reporters gave up their vigil and left Israel in search of more pressing stories. By this time Egypt had 210,000 troops ready for deployment, with 100,000 of them equipped with 930 tanks ready in the Sinai. They had thirty Tu-16 bombers, which were a threat to Israel's cities. Overall the Egyptian Air Force, by far the largest and the most modern of all the Arab air forces, consisted of about 450 combat aircraft, all Soviet-built and relatively new. The Arabs (at the time the neighboring states of Egypt were known as the United Arab Republic) had far more combat aircraft than Israel (682 compared to Israel's 286). Israel would need to rely on the training and motivation of this largely civilian army to counter the numeric superiority of the Arabs in manpower and weaponry.[50]

At 0755 on 5 June an air-raid warning sounded over the Israeli capital, Tel Aviv. When Israel had declared Independence on 14 May 1948, the population of Tel Aviv was over 200,000. By the early 1960s it had peaked at 390,000. Surprisingly, for Israel, 5 June did not bring total mobilization. Somewhere between 20,000 and 30,000 men and women had not been called up. Excluded was the civil-defence organization, a highly significant omission. While the alarm went on, a radio newscaster continued his scheduled report, completed it, then on the stroke of 0800, added quietly: 'We are at war.' In that way some of the public got the word. Early morning in Tel Aviv was otherwise almost normally calm, except at military headquarters. The sky was bright and cloudless. Following the all-clear, men and women proceeded on their routine rounds. Motor traffic had kept rolling, disregarding the alert. School had recessed with the mobilization so that students could take over the tasks of delivering mail, digging ditches, harvesting and performing other work appropriate to older hands now in military service. So when the clock struck eight, the only certainty was that this war would be unlike 1956. Egypt alone could field more tanks than Israel and Arab air bases on Israel's borders could put up enough jet bombers, such as the Tu-16 'Badger' and Il-28 'Beagle', along with MiG-21 transonic fighters and MiG-17s, to outnumber the Israeli Air Force's comparable types, like the Vautour fighter-bomber and the Mirage IIIC, by better than two to one. With four air bases in Sinai, two of them new, Egypt could put MiGs over Tel Aviv in seven minutes, the flight time from El Arish.

Jordan launched immediate multiple attacks on Israel: civilian suburbs of Tel-Aviv were shelled by artillery; Israel's largest military airfield, Ramat David, was shelled; Jordanian warplanes attacked the central Israeli towns of Netanya and Kfar Sava; thousands of mortar shells rained down on West Jerusalem hitting civilian locations indiscriminately, including the Hadassah Hospital and the Mount Zion Church; Israel's parliament building (the Knesset) and the Prime Minister's office, each in Israeli-controlled West Jerusalem, were targeted. Twenty Israelis died in these attacks; 1,000 were wounded; 900 buildings in West Jerusalem were damaged. 'Jerusalem is totally engulfed in war…' reported the British Consul-General that morning. All this happened before Israel reacted militarily against Jordan, or moved at all into

Right: An undamaged Tu-16 in a pen on an Egyptian airfield while smoke billows from another destroyed Badger.

Left: Burnt out MiG-17 on an Egyptian airfield.

the West Bank. Israel responded to Jordanian shelling of Jerusalem with a missile strike that devastated Jordanian positions.

At 0745 Israeli time, as civil defence sirens sounded all over Israel, the IAF launched Operation 'Moked' ('Focus'), a large-scale surprise air strike by all but twelve of its nearly 200 operational jets against Egyptian airfields that was the opening of the Six-Day War. The Egyptian defensive infrastructure was extremely poor and no airfields were yet equipped with hardened aircraft shelters capable of protecting Egypt's warplanes. And, the Egyptians hindered their own defence by effectively shutting down their entire air defence system: they were worried that rebel Egyptian forces would shoot down the aircraft carrying Field Marshal Abdel Hakim Amer and Lieutenant General Sidqi Mahmoud, who were en route from al Maza to Bir Tamada in the Sinai to meet the commanders of the troops stationed there. In any event, it did not make a great deal of difference as the Israeli pilots came in below Egyptian radar cover and well below the lowest point at which its SA-2 'Guideline' surface-to-air missile batteries could bring down an aircraft.[51]

One hundred Iraqi tanks and an infantry division were readied near the Jordanian border. Two squadrons of fighter-aircraft, Hawker Hunters and MiG 21, were rebased adjacent to the Jordanian border. The Arab air forces were aided by volunteer pilots from the Pakistan Air Force acting in independent capacity and by some aircraft from Libya, Algeria, Morocco, Kuwait and Saudi Arabia to make up for the massive losses suffered on the first day of the war. PAF pilots shot down several Israeli aircraft.

It was 0145 in New York and Washington when the attack order sent Israel's war planes winging toward the Nile, Suez and Sinai - fifteen minutes before the armour was directed to roll for the borders. Those cities slept on, not knowing until 0330 that a new war was underway. By then its outcome was already virtually decided. Eleven bomber and MiG-21 bases - El Arish, Bir Gifgafa, Bir Tamada and Jebel Libni in Sinai; Abu Suer, Kabrit and Fayid in the Canal Zone, Imshas, Cairo West, Beni Sueir and Luxor in the Nile Valley were targeted because their destruction was expected to shock Egypt and create in its air arm a state of near-paralysis. Such MiGs as remained intact in Egypt would not have range enough to menace any city in Israel.

All the IAF aircraft in the synchronized strike on the eleven main bases took off from the runways near Tel Aviv. Pilots were extensively schooled about their targets and were forced to memorize every single detail and rehearsed the operation multiple times on dummy runways in total secrecy. The Egyptians had constructed fortified defences in the Sinai. These designs were based on the assumption that an attack would come along the few roads leading through the desert, rather than through the difficult desert terrain. The Israelis chose not to risk attacking

MiGs destroyed on the ground in Egypt.

the Egyptian defences head-on and instead surprised them from an unexpected direction. Only four unarmed Egyptian training flights were in the air when the strike began. Most of the Israeli warplanes headed out over the Mediterranean for a short distance, flying low to avoid radar detection, before turning toward Egypt. Others flew over the Red Sea. Those bound for the targets along the Nile then flew on a direct southwest course to their objectives. The Sinai-bound fighters, which are certain to have staged out last because of the short distance, flew almost due south.

First to take off was a formation of Vautour fighter-bombers of the deep penetration group. Theirs was to be the farthest journey, their target the bomber base at Luxor on the Nile, far to the southwest of Sharm-el-Sheikh and almost twice the distance to Cairo. It would be a synchronized attack, directed against eleven bases only. The lift-offs were timed and staged so that each formation fronting the first wave would go at its target in the same minute. Thereafter the same eleven bases would be pounded steadily for eighty minutes.

The pilot leading that formation, an older colonel, in civilian life a specialist in aviation, selling his wares and ideas abroad, had been on a business trip to the United States when, on 25 May, he received an informal greeting relayed by his wife: 'Come home, dear, defence needs you.' With radios silent, the 5 June formation flew on toward Egypt. During the approach, as well as in striking the target, the twin-jet Vautours flew at their maximum speed of 600 mph - none of the war-loaded medium bombers or fighters were unable to fly at trans-sonic speed. A few minutes past eight and they were crossing the Egyptian coastline at tree-top level. Without sign of any reaction below, the Vautours flew on to Luxor without incident, rose 500 feet in the air to bomb the runways and strafe the un-bunkered Tu-16s, which were neatly, evenly spaced on the apron and alongside the runways. At Luxor the four 30mm cannon on the Vautours were the big killers of Egypt's Soviet-built aircraft. Much the same sort of thing was occurring at the other ten bases by the time the farthest-south Vautours were heading for home. At Israel's insistence, the French-built Mirages and Super Mystères had been modified to carry two 30mm guns instead of their original rockets. Thus, Israeli pilots destroyed Egypt's air force with cannon fire. Thus for eighty minutes, more of the same was delivered against the seven airfields in the Canal Zone and along the Nile. It was judged soon after the first strike that the MiGs based on Sinai were all burned to ash and wrecked metal. There followed a respite of perhaps twenty minutes. Then for eighty minutes more, the air force went at Egypt again. Syrian and Iraqi bases went untouched throughout the morning. Only twelve fighting aircraft were left at the Tel Aviv bases to defend Israel. None was put up as a screen to the north or east and when at last that was deemed advisable, only eight took to the air.

The mastermind of this plan sat in his unpretentious command post at Tel Aviv, supremely confident that it would work. At age thirty-nine, about one year earlier, Brigadier General Mordechai Hod had taken command of an air force that weight-for-weight was probably the most effective fighting machine anywhere, made so largely by his predecessor, Brigadier General Ezer Weizman, now Deputy for Operations.[52] Weizman shaped the tools and trained the men.[53] There were some simple reasons for Hod's conviction that he could win the battle for Israel over Cairo. He calculated that it would take the Egyptians one hour to assess what had happened and a second hour to agree on what could be done about it. He was convinced that when hit, they would not tell the truth to their allies. Instead, they would proclaim a victory, disarming in its effect. Syria and Iraq he could not take seriously; they were just an inconvenience. But instead of a lag of two hours, the Egyptians gave him four hours. Long before that it was all over.

Although the powerful Jordanian radar facility at Ajloun detected waves of aircraft approaching Egypt before it was destroyed in an Israeli airstrike and reported the code word for 'war' up the Egyptian command chain, Egyptian command and communications problems prevented the warning from reaching the targeted airfields. The Israelis made bombing and strafing runs against aircraft on the ground, bombing the runways with special tarmac-shredding penetration bombs developed jointly with France to disable them and leave surviving

IAF Mirage IIICJ and a Egyptian Air Force MiG-17 in Israeli markings.

aircraft unable to take off. The runway at the Arish airfield was spared, as the Israelis expected to turn it into a military airport for their transports after the war. Before the war, Israeli pilots and ground crews had trained extensively in rapid refitting of aircraft returning from sorties, enabling a single aircraft to sortie up to four times a day (as opposed to the norm in Arab air forces of one or two sorties per day). This enabled the IAF to send several attack waves against Egyptian airfields on the first day of the war, overwhelming the Egyptian Air Force and allowing it to knock out other Arab air forces on the same day.

The fighter-bombers of the first wave all returned to home base by 0900. It was then that Hod put up the screen to the north. The surviving aircraft were later taken out by several more attack waves. The operation was more successful than expected, catching the Egyptians by surprise and destroying virtually all of the Egyptian Air Force on the ground, with few Israeli losses. A total of 338 Egyptian aircraft were destroyed and 100 pilots were killed, although the number of aircraft actually lost by the Egyptians is disputed. Among the Egyptian planes lost were all thirty Tu-16 bombers, twenty-seven out of forty Il-28 bombers, twelve Su-7 fighter-bombers, over ninety MiG-21s, twenty MiG-19s, 25 MiG-17 fighters and around thirty-two assorted transport aircraft and helicopters. In addition, Egyptian radars and SAM missiles were also attacked and destroyed. The Israelis lost nineteen planes, including two destroyed in air-to-air combat and thirteen downed by anti-aircraft artillery. One Israeli aircraft, which was damaged and unable to break radio silence, was shot down by Israeli Hawk missiles after it strayed over the Negev Nuclear Research Centre. Another was destroyed by an exploding Egyptian bomber. The attack guaranteed Israeli air superiority for the rest of the war.

By the time the operation had been going for two hours fifty minutes, or at approximately

1100, he was able to report to Minister of Defence Moshe Dayan: 'I am certain that there is not another bomber left in Egypt.' Knowing that he had won the air battle in Egypt, Hod began shifting bombers and fighters to Sinai to support the attack by the armoured columns. Around noon he began the air attack on the bases of Jordan and Syria and continued it throughout most of 5 June. But they were in effect finished after one hour. The small Royal Jordanian Air Force consisted of only twenty-four Hawker Hunter F.6 fighters, six transports and two helicopters. According to the Israelis, the Hunter was essentially on par with the French-built Dassault Mirage III. At 1150 sixteen Jordanian Hawker Hunters attacked Netanya, Kfar Sirkin and Kfar Saba, killing one civilian, wounding seven and destroying a Noratlas transport at Sirkin. Shortly before 12:30 am, the IAF attacked Jordan's two airbases. The Hawker Hunters were refuelling at the time of the attack. The Israeli aircraft came within two waves, the first of which cratered the runways and knocked out the control towers and the second wave destroyed all of Jordan's Hawker Hunters, along with six transport aircraft and two helicopters. One Israeli jet was shot down by ground fire. Israeli Fouga Magister jets attacked the Jordanian 40th Brigade with rockets as it moved south from the Damiya Bridge. Dozens of tanks were knocked out and a convoy of twenty-six trucks carrying ammunition was destroyed. Hod was above all elated by the performance of the Fougas. Built in Israel, the Fouga Magister was the basic trainer for jet pilots but this relatively slow training aircraft had been armed with two machine guns and thirty-six rockets to operate as a tank-killer over Sinai. Older men - El Al pilots and others from civilian life - had been called back to man these aircraft. They destroyed more than seventy Egyptian artillery pieces; took on the enemy armour wherever they found it and softened the base camps before the armoured spearheads arrived. Their overall contribution to a speedy victory is incalculable.

The only Iraqi base strafed was H-3, in western Iraq along the pipeline, just east of the border of the Jordan panhandle. During the attack, twelve MiG-21s, two MiG-17s, five Hunter F6s and three Ilyushin Il-28 bombers were destroyed or shot down. A Pakistani pilot stationed at the base managed to shoot down an Israeli fighter and bomber during the raid. Habbaniya, near Baghdad, was not attacked, being beyond range of Israel's bombers. Three Iraqi Hawker Hunters strafed civilian settlements in the Jezreel Valley and an Iraqi Tu-16 attacked Afula and was shot down near the Megiddo airfield. The attack caused minimal material damage, hitting

A MiG-17 destroyed on the ground at an Egyptian air base.

Ilyushin Il-14 transport burning at Kabrit airbase after the surprise attack by IAF Mirage IIICJ jets.

Above: Wrecked Il-14s at Kabrit after the devastating Israeli air attack.

Mil Mi-6 helicopters on fire at Bir Gifgafa airfield in the Sinai, 90 kilometres east of the Suez Canal. This Egyptian base was subsequently overrun by the Israelis.

only a senior citizens' home and several chicken coops, but sixteen Israeli soldiers were killed, most of them when the Tupolev crashed.

Attacks on other Arab air forces took place later in the day as hostilities broke out on other fronts. A third or more of Nasser's warplanes remained in condition to fight. Well aware of it, Hod had no intention of renewing the assault on the bases. There had been no dogfights; not one MiG had risen to challenge a Mirage. So Egypt's pilots would always have an excuse for themselves: 'We were given no chance to show what we could do.' If their morale was to be shattered irreparably, it would have to be done in the air east of Suez. So here was the implicit invitation to come on and try. The air-to-air duelling started that Monday afternoon somewhat west of the Bir Gifgafa-Jebel Libni line and continued into Tuesday. There were growls and gripes from Israel's soldiers fighting below when the MiGs first appeared above them. Hod heard rumbles like this: 'Look, you said you destroyed their air force; it's still around.' Until cured, it had to be endured. Egypt threw SAM missiles into the air fight from the park west of the Mitla Pass. An Israeli pilot said casually: 'Hey, one of those blazing telephone poles is after me.' No harm was done by the SAMs; Israel's fighters were flying too low.

On the evening of 5 June the IAF attacked Syrian airfields. The Syrian Air Force lost thirty-two MiG-21s and twenty-three MiG-15 and MiG-17 fighters and two Il-28 bombers, two-thirds of its fighting strength. The Syrian aircraft that survived the attack retreated to distant bases without playing any further role in the ensuing warfare. Israeli aircraft continued strafing Arab airfield runways to prevent their return to usability. Meanwhile, Egyptian state-run radio had reported an Egyptian victory, falsely claiming that seventy Israeli

Egyptian Air Force MiG-17 on a ground attack sortie in the Sinai.

aircraft had been downed on the first day of fighting. The Israeli plan was to surprise the Egyptian forces in both timing (the attack exactly coinciding with the IAF strike on Egyptian airfields), location (attacking via northern and central Sinai routes, as opposed to the Egyptian expectations of a repeat of the 1956 war, when the IDF attacked via the central and southern routes) and method (using a combined-force flanking approach, rather than direct tank assaults). President Nasser, having learned of the results of the air strike, decided to pull out the troops from Sinai within 24 hours. As Egyptian columns retreated, Israeli aircraft and artillery attacked them. Israeli jets used napalm bombs during their sorties. The attacks destroyed hundreds of vehicles and caused heavy casualties.

The numbers of Arab aircraft claimed destroyed by Israel were at first regarded as 'greatly exaggerated' by the Western press. However, the fact that the Egyptian Air Force, along with other Arab air forces attacked by Israel, made practically no appearance for the remaining days of the conflict, proved that the numbers were most likely authentic.

On 7 June Israeli forces seized Bethlehem, taking the city after a brief battle. Again, the air superiority of the IAF proved paramount as it immobilized the Jordanians, leading to their defeat. False Egyptian reports of a crushing victory against the Israeli army and forecasts that Egyptian forces would soon be attacking Tel Aviv influenced Syria's willingness to enter the war. Syrian artillery began shelling northern Israel and twelve Syrian jets attacked Israeli settlements in the Galilee. Israeli fighter jets intercepted the Syrian aircraft, shooting down three and driving off the rest. In addition, two Lebanese Hunter jets, two of the twelve Lebanon had, crossed into Israeli airspace and began strafing Israeli positions in the Galilee. They were intercepted by Israeli fighter jets and one was shot down.

By 10 June Israel had completed its final offensive in the Golan Heights and a ceasefire was signed the day after. IAF losses were more than 10 per cent of the force - four Magisters, four Mirages, four Mystères, five Ouragans, four Super Mystères and two Vautours - but Israel claimed to have destroyed 418 Arab aircraft for the loss of just twenty-seven of their own. Although the remains of the Arab air forces continued to operate, the IAF achieved total air supremacy which allowed the IDF to capture the Gaza Strip and the Sinai Peninsula from Egypt, the West Bank of the Jordan River (including East Jerusalem) and the Golan Heights from Syria - an area larger than Israel itself - within just six days of fighting. Some of the story is told in statistics. By the end of the war the number of IAF losses amounted to a total of forty-six, about 25% of the force, which included nine Mirages, ten Super Mystères, five Vautours, six Mystères, nine Ouragans, six Magisters and a single Noratlas. As the total number of combat aircraft sorties was 3,279 the IAF loss ratio was one per seventy-three sorties. In air-to-air combat the IAF claimed 60 kills in the course of 66 air combats while 391 enemy aircraft were claimed to have been destroyed on the ground. The IAF flew only 492 sorties to destroy 402 enemy aircraft on the ground. All told, Israel's forces destroyed 452 aircraft; some were gunned down by anti-aircraft batteries. There were thirty-one dogfights near Suez and above western Sinai; five Egyptian aircraft were shot down and not one Israeli warplane. Hod lost twenty-five pilots, twenty-four of them when their ships were shot down by ground fire; the other man died as a forward observer with the army. Yet the 492 sorties were the lesser part of the work load; airmen flew nearly a thousand sorties in support of the armoured advance into Sinai.

Hod learned that he had sorely underestimated the resources of his men and their machines. He had expected three to four sorties a day from the average pilot; he got an average of seven and some went as high as ten. He figured the standard of gunnery established in peacetime training would drop during combat; instead, it rose. He anticipated that the serviceability of aircraft would slip steadily downward once fighting started. To begin, it was ninety-nine per cent and it held that way through six days.

One young pilot shot down four enemy aircraft. In between number two and number three he was hospitalized for a wound, then ducked back to duty without permission. But for the wasted time, he might have become Israel's first ace.

The blow dealt Egypt by General Hod's men and machines on the morning of 5 June doomed President Nasser's hope for any military success against Israel. Defence Minister Moshe

Israeli Mirage pilots walk towards the camera after a mission sortie.

Dayan was quick to point out that decision was never in doubt thereafter. For the first time, air power had effectively won a war.

Speaking three weeks after the war ended, as he accepted an honorary degree from Hebrew University, Yitzhak Rabin gave his reasoning behind the success of Israel: our airmen, who struck the enemies' planes so accurately that no one in the world understands how it was done and people seek technological explanations or secret weapons; our armoured troops who beat the enemy even when their equipment was inferior to his; our soldiers in all other branches ... who overcame our enemies everywhere, despite the latter's superior numbers and fortifications-all these revealed not only coolness and courage in the battle but ... an understanding that only their personal stand against the greatest dangers would achieve victory for their country and for their families and that if victory was not theirs the alternative was annihilation.

Endnotes for Chapter 5

46   In 1957 Israel purchased eighteen Sud Aviation Vautour IIA aircraft to form a fighter-bomber squadron to replace aging Mosquito and B-17 bombers. A large, twin-engine, swept-wing aircraft, the Vautour IIA was armed with four 30-mm cannon. The aircraft could also carry more than 4,000lbs of weaponry in its internal bomb bay and on underwing pylons. The French Air Force operated several versions of the Vautour, including fighter-bomber, reconnaissance and radar-equipped fighter models. The Vautour could fly at nearly 700 mph and had a radius of action in excess of 750 miles. Satisfied with the performance of the attack version, the IAF purchased seven two-seat Vautour UN all-weather fighters. These specialized jets served with the remaining NF.13 Meteors in the single IAF night/all-weather fighter squadron. This special unit had the responsibility for night and bad weather air defence of Israeli airspace. Later the IAF purchased four two-seat Vautour HBR aircraft with a glazed nose and internally mounted sensor pallet in the weapons bay. These planes were used on reconnaissance missions. About thirty Vautour aircraft were eventually delivered to the IAF. Until mid-1958 their existence in Israel was a matter of utmost secrecy. *Fighters Over Israel: The Story of the Israeli Air Force from the war of Independence to the Bekaa Valley* by Lon Nordeen (Greenhill Books, 1990).

47   Seventy-five Ouragans (24 new and 51 ex-Armée de l'Air aircraft) were acquired by Israel from 1955 and were used to form two squadrons.

46   By the late 1950s, the IAF had received in excess of sixty Dassault Mystère IVA fighters. During the late 1950s and early 1960s, the two Mystère IVA squadrons were responsible for the air defence of Israel. The Mirage IIIC fighter entered service with the IAF on 7 April 1962 and by 1967 the Mirage force had expanded to 72 aircraft, which equipped three IAF fighter squadrons. Three Mirage IIIB train versions were also acquired for the IAF.

49   This account is based on an IAF History branch publication called *The War for the Water.*

50   Syria had 63,000 troops and Jordan 55,000 - totalling 328,000 troops ready to fight Israel. The Arabs had twice the number of tanks compared to Israel (2,330 against 1,000) and 1,845 armoured personnel carriers compared to Israel's 1,500. However, by fully mobilizing Israel could muster 250,000 men. On 5 June seven to eight Egyptian division, two of them armoured, now deployed in Sinai: 200 tanks opposite Eilat, with the aim of cutting off the Southern Negev. Along Israel's Eastern border were 60,000 Jordanian soldiers and 300 tanks. The Jordanian army placed under Egyptian command units, as well as Iraq forces which had entered its territory. On Israel's Northern border with Syria, 50,000 Syrian soldiers dug in, fortified and protected by concrete and steel. Some 600 Egyptian, Jordanian, Syrian and Iraqi planes ready.

51   Developed in the mid-1950s, the V-750 Dvina was the first effective Soviet surface-to-air missile. The Soviets used it to shoot down Gary Powers' U-2 over the USSR in 1960 and Major Rudolph Anderson's U-2 over Cuba in 1962. The missile was better known by the NATO designation SA-2 Guideline. The Soviets began exporting it to many countries worldwide in 1960, with many remaining in use into the 21st century.

52   Now Deputy of Operations of the entire Israeli Defence Force.

53   Hod belonged to the first class of pilots ever to win wings in Israel, on 14 March 1949.

Chapter Six

A Hostile Peace

'The United States Strategic Air Command is a deterrent of the highest order in maintaining ceaseless readiness. We owe much to their devotion to the cause of freedom in a troubled world. The primary deterrents to aggression remain the nuclear weapon and trained United States Strategic Air Command [combat crews] to use it.'

Sir Winston Churchill, speech to British Parliament, spring 1955. In the early post-war years a marked deterioration in relations between East and West intensified and a new phrase, Cold War, was coined. Winston Churchill, speaking at Westminster College in Fulton, Missouri on 5 March 1946 first used the term 'iron curtain' in public. 'Iron curtain' was the guarded border between the Soviet Bloc (territories recently liberated by the Soviet Union) and the rest of Europe. 'This is certainly not the liberated Europe we fought to build up', Churchill declared. 'Nor is it one which contains the essentials of permanent peace.' The Soviet Union was a great land power whose forces were quite capable of overrunning the Western Democracies in Europe. While America could until the late 1950s obliterate the main centres of the Soviet Union, the US was relatively invulnerable to a Soviet counter. The Soviet Union detonated its first fission bomb on 29 August 1949 to end the USA's nuclear monopoly. By the early 1960s 'Massive Retaliation' had given way to 'Mutually Assured Destruction' (MAD) which was all that stood between fragile co-existence and Armageddon. Both sides knew that any first strike by an aggressor would have to be met by a retaliatory strike in kind.

Development of the Boeing B-52 had begun in June 1945 after the USAAF had directed Air Material Command to consider second generation intercontinental bombers to eventually replace the B-36 Peacemaker in post-war service. The B-52 formed the backbone of the manned bomber strategic deterrent in Strategic Air Command (SAC) which was created on 21 March 1946 under the command of General George C. Kenney with a directive to build an organization capable of conducting long-range offensive operations in any part of the world. In-flight refuelling was introduced, giving SAC's bombers true intercontinental range. Lieutenant General Curtis E. LeMay, who transferred from the US Air Forces in Europe (USAFE) to assume command of SAC (CINCSAC) on 19 October 1948 came out strongly in favour of the B-52 project. Never one for half measures, during his nine-year tenure (1948-57) SAC became the world's most powerful military force operating on a global basis. On arrival at SAC headquarters LeMay had demanded to see the war plan. There was no war plan he was informed. Within weeks of taking over LeMay had replaced SAC's deputy commander, chief of staff, director of operations and director of plans and replaced them with generals who were all veterans of the Pacific strategic bombing campaign. As he said in his memoirs:

'My determination was to put everyone in SAC into this frame of mind: We are at war now. So that, if actually we did go to war the very next morning or even that night, we would stumble through no period in which preliminary motions would be wasted. We had to be ready to go then…' In March 1949 LeMay proposed that SAC's capabilities be increased to the point where it was possible to deliver 133 atomic bombs against seventy major Soviet cities in a single, all-out strike. This plan was accepted in December 1949 by the Air Force. On 12 January 1954 John Foster Dulles, the Secretary of State, declared, 'Local defences must he reinforced by the further deterrent of massive retaliatory power' and that the defence of the West depended 'primarily upon a capacity to retaliate instantly by means and at places of our own choosing'. During Operation 'Redwing Cherokee' on 21 May 1956, B-52B 52-0013 of the Air Research and Development Command dropped a Mk.15 hydrogen bomb capable of producing a yield of 3.75 megatons at the Bikini Atoll in the Pacific. Now any act of aggression by the Communist bloc could result in strategic nuclear strikes on Soviet or Chinese targets. SAC further demonstrated strategic bombing capability in spectacular fashion on 24 and 25 November 1956. Four B-52Bs of the 93rd Bombardment Wing and four B-52Cs of the 42nd Bombardment Wing made a non-stop flight around the perimeter of North America

General Curtis E. LeMay, seen here at an awards ceremony, assumed command of SAC on 19 October 1948 and came out strongly in favour of the B-52 project which otherwise might never have reached production. His proposal that SAC's capabilities be increased to the point where it was possible to deliver 133 atomic bombs against 70 major Soviet cities in a single, all-out strike was accepted in December 1949. When he left on 30 June 1957 to become Air Force Vice-Chief of Staff, his legacy to SAC was a strategic air force that had become the only nuclear deterrent to prevent a pre-emptive Communist strike on the USA. And it was the B-52 that formed the backbone of the manned bomber strategic deterrent.

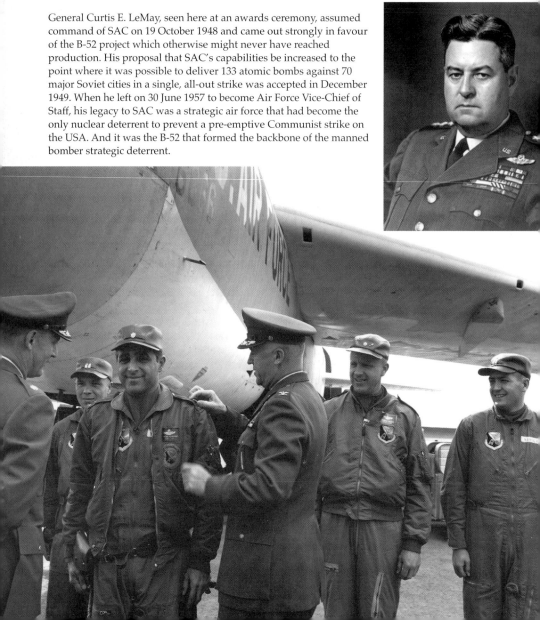

The Alert Crew of B-52D 56-0590 of the 92nd Bomb Wing run to their aircraft during a practice drill at Fairchild AFB, Washington. *Duplum Incolumitatis* is Latin for 'Twofold Security'.

in Operation 'Quick Kick'. When on 30 June 1957 LeMay left to become Air Force Vice Chief of Staff, his legacy to SAC was a strategic air force that had become the only American nuclear deterrent to prevent a pre-emptive Communist strike on the USA. In November, General Thomas S. Power, who became commander in chief of SAC, went public about his command's ground alert. He also alluded to the fact that, 'Day and night I have a certain percentage of my command in the air. These planes are bombed up and they don't carry bows and arrows.' From 15 September to 15 December 1958 exhaustive trials of airborne alert on a round-the-clock basis were conducted by B-52Ds of the 42nd Bomb Wing at Loring AFB, Maine under the code-name 'Head Start I'. In February 1959 Power told Congress. 'We in the Strategic Air Command have developed a system known as airborne alert where we maintain airplanes in the air twenty-four hours a day, loaded with bombs, on station, ready to go to target. ...I feel strongly that we must get on with this airborne alert. ...We must impress Mr. Khrushchev [the Soviet Premier] that we have it and that he cannot strike this country with impunity.'

Strategic Air Command grew so concerned about a sneak attack that it ordered a dozen B-52 bombers to be airborne 24 hours a day, loaded with thermonuclear weapons. On these intercontinental flights, code-named 'Chrome Dome' missions, the B-52s and their crews would fly their attack profiles, soaring across the ocean and angling in toward the target-rich Soviet interior before breaking away short of Soviet air space.

On 11 October 1956 a Vickers Valiant on 49 Squadron RAF carried out the first British operational atomic bomb to be dropped from an aircraft, which was released over Maralinga, Southern Australia. On 15 May 1957, a Valiant of the same Squadron dropped the first British Hydrogen bomb during Operation 'Grapple' on Christmas Island in the Pacific. The first British hydrogen bomb that detonated as planned was dropped on 8

Though Strategic Air Command's motto was 'Peace Is Our Profession' on arrival at SAC HQ at Offutt AFB near Omaha, Nebraska, General Curtis LeMay discovered that SAC had no war plan and he replaced SAC's deputy commander, chief of staff, director of operations and director of plans with generals who were all veterans of the Pacific strategic bombing campaign. LeMay's credo was: 'We are at war now' and was unchanged from WW2 - 'If you destroy the [enemy's] capability to win war, then the will to wage war disappears also.' SAC was disestablished in 1992 as part of an overall post-Cold War reorganization of the US Air Force.

November 1957. The 'Grapple' series of tests continued into 1958 and in April that year the 'Grapple Y' bomb exploded with ten times the yield of the original. Testing was finally terminated in November 1958 when the British government decided it would perform no more air-delivered nuclear tests.

Intended for operations as a high-level strategic bomber, the Vickers-Armstrongs Valiant was the first of the British V bombers to become operational and was followed by the Handley Page Victor and the Avro Vulcan. The first squadron to be equipped with the Valiant was 138 Squadron, which formed at RAF Gaydon on 1 January 1955, with 232 Operational Conversion Unit forming at Gaydon on 21 February to convert crews onto the new bomber. The crews for the Valiant were selected from experienced aircrew, with first pilots requiring 1,750 flying hours as an aircraft captain, with at least one tour flying the Canberra, with second pilots needing 700 hours in command and the remaining three crewmembers had to be recommended for posting to the Valiant by their commanding officers. In September 1956 Peter Williams penned an article entitled 'V Bombers At War!' for *RAF Flying Review*.

'One sentence by Group Captain B. P. Young OBE, Commanding Officer of 232 OCU, put the whole thing in a nutshell. 'We are ready to go to war at any moment,' he said.

On 15 May 1957 Valiant B.1 XD818 of 49 Squadron RAF dropped the first British Hydrogen bomb during Operation 'Grapple' X Round C1, which took place off Malden Island, an uninhabited atoll 400 miles south of Christmas Island (now Kiritimati) a Pacific Ocean raised coral atoll in the northern Line Islands. The test was largely a failure, as the measured yield was less than a third of the maximum expected and while achieving the desired thermonuclear explosion the device had failed to operate as intended.

Valiants of 'B' Flight, 49 Squadron used in Operation 'Grapple', on the newly constructed dispersals at Christmas Island.

That, I soon discovered, was the spirit pervading this advanced training school for V-bomber pilots. The V-force is, in effect, at war - now. For the next war, if there is one, will be fought and won not with equipment and personnel laboriously marshalled over a period of years, but with the men and machines available at the moment the balloon goes up. 'What we have at that moment will be it,' said Group Captain Young. 'We shall get no second chance.'

'Here at Gaydon, in Warwickshire, not far from sleepy, old-world Leamington Spa, men are being trained to handle the most up-to-date aeronautical equipment in the world. All of them are hand-picked - the cream of the Royal Air Force - and they are the men whose very existence constitutes the most powerful deterrent to war yet known.

'At the moment, these crews are being trained to fly Valiants. Shortly the course may include training for Victors as well. From Gaydon is emerging the nucleus of Britain's V-bomber force. And, make no mistake about it; these are the men who will be the spearhead of Britain's attack in any future conflict. Security, as is fitting with a station which already regards itself as being at war is rigorous. My pass was meticulously examined at the gatehouse and I was aware throughout my visit of the tight-lipped caution of those who had secret information. Nevertheless, thanks to the co-operation of all concerned, I am able to give this picture of a unique establishment - the very core of the V-force.

'How do you join the V-force? The answer came from Squadron Leader F. C. D. Wright, a 36-year-old pilot who is just completing his conversion course on Valiants. 'You don't apply to join the V-force,' he said. 'You are picked.' Wright himself was in Malaya when the call came and he expresses himself as 'surprised but not displeased' to join the V-force. The fact is that only the most experienced and reliable aircrews are chosen for the V-force. The qualifications needed are formidable: a Valiant captain must have 'above average' flying ability and have flown at least 1,750 hours as a first pilot. In addition, it is 'desirable' that he should have considerable experience of flying four-engined aircraft! (Though this is not- now considered essential.) Even second pilots for Valiants must have flown at least 700 hours as first pilots, including a tour on Canberras. Not surprisingly, the crews undergoing training at Gaydon are not in the first flush of youth: the average age is somewhere about thirty. Why this insistence on experience and above-average ability? Is the Valiant difficult to fly? Squadron Leader Wright gives a most definite negative. 'The Valiant is a most stable and easy-going aircraft,' he says. 'It's perfect for bad-weather landing and it's easy to handle. But it requires above all else, teamwork between all the members of the crew.'

'No, the Valiant is by no means a 'difficult' aircraft. With only a limited amount of instruction it could probably be flown satisfactorily by any man who had had experience of Canberras. The demand for experienced, veteran pilots is due not to the nature of the aircraft of the V-force but to the nature of the missions on which it will be engaged.

'We cannot say, of course, exactly how the V-bombers will be utilised in conflict. But it is pretty obvious that they are intended as long-range strategic bombers carrying nuclear bombs, or something similar, right to the heart of enemy territory. Such missions will have to be carried out with the utmost speed and with the very minimum of preparatory warning. Once mounted, these attacks must hit the mark first time. There will be no margin for error.

'There is another reason, too, why the V-bomber crews must be absolutely on top of their jobs. The aircraft itself is a pretty costly piece of mechanism - somewhere in the vicinity of a third of a million pounds. With the apparatus and bomb-load it is expected to carry, the crew will be responsible for something like a million pounds' worth of equipment. The Secretary of State for Air recently stated that to train a pilot up to V-bomber operational standard costs £55,000. All of which means that the RAF has invested a considerable amount of money in each V-bomber that flies. To insist on only the finest aircrew available is pure common sense!

'Flight Lieutenant Walton, navigational instructor, who has been at Gaydon for fifteen months, stressed the chief function of this conversion unit. 'Each member of the crew is experienced in his own job,' he said. 'What we have to do here is to weld them into a team.' Indeed, the crews are formed here at Gaydon and go on to their squadrons as a complete entity.

'Teamwork! It is the keynote of everything at Gaydon. The Valiant has two pilots, seated side by side, with dual controls. Two navigators and a signaller (now called Air Electronics Officer, as being a more apt title for the duties involved) are seated on a lower level, facing rearwards. In front of them is a large panel with a bewildering mass of instruments. Each one of this team has a vital part to play in the functioning of the whole aircraft.

'Consider the pre-take-off drill, for a start. It takes about an hour to complete. Before the captain enters the aircraft there are some 70 external items to be checked, ranging from such basic matters as the removal of the engine intake blanks to checking the setting of the tail-plane incidence. Inside the aircraft are nearly forty items to be checked before the captain reaches his seat. Then comes the actual cockpit drill. Since most of the services are operated by the engine-driven electrical generators, power for pre-take-off checks is supplied by a mobile generator, also used for engine starting. During this process the ground crew chief is in telephonic communication with the aircrew in the aircraft. Before starting up, there are another 60 items on the pilots' instrument panels to be checked! In war, of course, the checks would be carried out in rotation so that the aircraft would be ready to go at any moment. Servicing of each aircraft is carried out by a crew of eight, including a Crew Chief, who is responsible solely for the one plane. The other seven members of the ground crew are specialists in airframes, engines, instruments, electrics, wireless, radar and armament. I spoke to Master Technician D. J. Livett, who acts as 'A' Squadron Engineer Officer. (He was, incidentally, the first Master Technician Crew Chief in the Service.) On a complicated board in his office I saw how teams were allocated to each aircraft and how, if one particular item of servicing should prove difficult, additional specialist fitters are allocated to handle it. Special ladders and adjustable hydraulic platforms are used to give access to the aircraft for servicing. There is a tower ladder, for working on the tail, which has a gantry attachment capable of lifting a complete rudder. Livett told me that servicing has caused no major difficulties and the layout and accessibility of equipment in the aircraft is good. The Valiant is fitted for pressure refuelling and can be 'turned round' in a very short time.

'But to get back to the flying crew. Let's follow Squadron Leader Wright (he won his DFC with 254 Squadron shooting up enemy shipping off the Dutch coast with torpedo-Beaufighters) as he goes through his course at Gaydon. First phase of the training syllabus consists of four weeks' ground school, during which Wright is instructed on the aircraft performance and systems, with emphasis on flight planning and 'cruise control.' Wright has been on thirty courses before and he considers this one 'very practical.' The pupils' braids and medal ribbons make this an unusual 'schoolroom,' and the instruction is carried out accordingly. 'They treat you like grown-ups,' says Wright. He sees models which demonstrate all the aircraft's systems and such matters as the importance of consuming fuel from the various tanks in a correct sequence. (If he makes a hash of this in flight, he'll find the plane's centre of gravity displaced, making it unmanageable.) While all this is going on, second pilots are being instructed on their particular responsibilities, which include management of the fuel system in the air, control of the cabin pressurisation and recording engine conditions (power, jet pipe temperatures, etc.). Towards the end of this first phase, Wright is introduced to the 'Flight Simulator' - a massive, £350,000 instrument which he soon learns to call 'The Beast.' This is an exact replica of the Valiant control cabin and it reproduces faithfully all conditions of flight - even to such details as the noise made by the tyres when they meet the runway on landing! 'On The Beast,' says Wright, 'they can give you every emergency you are likely to come up against in flight - and a few more besides!'

'I went along to the Flight Simulator to try out the experience myself. Students in full flying kit were seated in the pilots' seats and the inside of the cabin looked for all the world like the control centre of a Valiant. The noise of the engines and the actual vibration was faithfully reproduced. Behind the two pilots, in the space normally occupied by the navigators, an operator sat at a control desk which was one vast array of switches. By

A B-52 crew chief checks his chart.

flicking one or more of these he was able to reproduce on the pilots' instrument panels emergency situations in various combinations. (There might, for instance, be a simple indicator failure, or something more serious like an engine fire or an undercarriage failure.) It is possible for the operator to 'feed in' a series of defects so that the situation gets progressively worse. Unless the pilot corrects matters, his instruments will soon register a 'crash'! The only flight sensation not reproduced by the Simulator is 'g' (the effects of gravity), but this is no real disadvantage. In actual flight the rate of 'g' would indicate to the pilot something unusual in the attitude of the aircraft. In the Simulator he has no such warning and must rely on the readings of instruments.

'Wright spends a total of sixteen hours in the Simulator before he actually flies the Valiant and he is by then so familiarised with the essentials of Valiant flying that he really feels he's done it all before his first solo. It works out a lot cheaper, too. The cost of operating the Simulator is about one-tenth the cost of flying a Valiant.

'On then to the second phase of instruction: two weeks of mixed ground school and actual flying. Then the last phase: six weeks' flying. The first instructional flight consists of two hours' demonstration of its handling at high altitudes, followed by landings. Then comes a short cross-country flight and demonstration of emergency systems. Wright's first solo - when he captains the aircraft for the first time, accompanied by his own second pilot - is made on the third exercise.

'And so to the end of the course. Wright has spent fifty hours flying - about half of it at night - and is ready to proceed with his crew to the squadron. They will be part of the fourth RAF squadron to be equipped with Valiants, the first three being Nos. 138, 214 and 543. Another squadron has been added to the V-force another team of the most experienced and highest qualified aircrews in the world. The strict security made it just as difficult to get out of Gaydon as to get in and I noticed on my departure a line of alert RAF police dogs and their handlers. They seemed to be symbolic of all that Gaydon stands for - watchdogs of the peace of the world.'

The article was largely prophetic, although not in the way one would have imagined. On 26 July 1956 international tensions were heightened again, when President Gamal Abdel Nasser of Egypt announced his government intended to nationalise the Suez Canal. Britain and France were determined to reverse the decision by military means.

Sèvres was a classic setting for international intrigue, wrote Wilfred P. Deac. A tile-roofed villa secluded among fog-swirled trees, ivy clinging to building wings clustered around a stunted steeple-like tower. The first group of conspirators landed at a French airfield outside Paris and reached the wall-enclosed villa in an unmarked car during the wee hours of 22 October. Later that Monday morning, French Foreign Minister Christian Pineau visited his office in Paris, then was chauffeured home to switch to his personal car. He soon was at the villa shaking hands with Israel's 70-year-old Prime Minister David Ben-Gurion, eye-patched Chief of Staff Moshe Dayan and Defence Ministry Director-General Shimon Peres. British Foreign Minister Selwyn Lloyd, a key member of the third group of plotters, called his office in London to say he was staying home with a cold. He left England shortly after, to arrive at the villa that afternoon.

By the time the tense clandestine discussions - which also included French Premier Guy Mollet and British Prime Minister Anthony Eden - ended two days later in France and England, a secret accord had been reached. Champagne glasses were raised to celebrate a tripartite pledge to pursue what one chronicler called 'the shortest and possibly silliest war in history.' The target was Gamal Abdel Nasser's Egypt, which had become the symbol of Arab nationalism.

Israel, still territorially insecure after 8½ years of existence among hostile Arab neighbours and cut off from access to the Red Sea by a blockade, had agreed to launch a pre-emptive invasion of Egypt's 24,000-square-mile Sinai Peninsula on 29 October. In response to that 'threat' to the strategically important Suez Canal, Britain and France would step in the next day to give the belligerents 12 hours to stop fighting, pull back from the strategic waterway and accept temporary occupation of 'key positions on the Canal' to 'guarantee freedom of passage.' That ultimatum, so obviously favourable to Israel, was designed to be rejected by Nasser. Then, on 31 October - following a 'decent interval' for Egypt's rejection of the ultimatum–Britain and France would launch airstrikes against the Egyptians. Invasion forces would then land long enough afterward to lend plausibility to the scenario.

As the three conspiring nations formulated their plot at Sèvres, they also set in motion military preparations. Operation 'Musketeer', a joint Anglo-French undertaking, was put into action to destroy the Egyptian Air Force. All front line stations were immediately brought to operational readiness as aircraft were prepared for the preliminary deployment to Malta and Cyprus. Meanwhile, in late October Israeli Air Force Mystères fought air-to-air combats with the Egyptian Air Force and carried out air-to-ground missions along with Ouragans and Meteors, although both latter types were also involved in air combats versus EAF MiG-15s. The IAF claimed in air-to-air combat eight victories: a single Il-14 was shot down at night by a Meteor NF.13 while the Mystères claimed four Vampires and three MiG-15s. In total, the IAF flew 1,846 sorties of which 751 were combat aircraft sorties representing a loss ratio of one combat aircraft per 63 combat sorties.

The main force of what was to be known as the Valiant Wing arrived on Malta on 26 October. It comprised 24 Valiants made up of four on 214 Squadron commanded by Wing Commander Leonard Trent VC DFC, six of 207 Squadron commanded by Wing Commander D. Haig and six on 148 Squadron commanded by Wing Commander W. Burnett while another eight were from 138 Squadron at Wittering. Flying Officer R. A. C. Ellicott on 214 Squadron recalled: 'The looks and expressions of surprise can only be imagined when, within two hours of landing at Luqa, all crews gathered in the Bomber Wing Operations briefing room for the first operational briefing and the curtains were drawn aside to reveal Egyptian airfields as the targets. Targets in Phase I were the Egyptian airfields operating Russian-built Il-28 bombers and MiG-15 fighters. The aiming points were the runway intersections and crews were briefed to avoid the camp areas. Further instructions were given that bombs were not to be jettisoned 'live' in case Egyptian casualties were caused. At dusk on 30 October operations commenced.'

Though designed to drop thermonuclear bombs the Valiants were fitted with multi carriers and six light series bomb racks to carry conventional free-fall bombs, the biggest being the 1,000 pounder. Twenty-one of these weapons could be carried. Chances of accurate delivery were poor however as many of the Valiants were bereft of their full complement of navigational and radar-operated bombing equipment. Instead they were forced to rely on the World War Two system of target marking while ex-Lincoln bomber sighting heads were fixed in temporary fittings. (As it turned out, those Valiants that carried navigation and bombing systems (NBS) most went unserviceable in the air). Bomber Command was ill prepared to undertake a 'Musketeer'-type operation. The Command was geared to a 'radar' war in Western Europe and was not constituted nor organised for major overseas operations. The majority of the Valiant force had neither Navigation Bombing Systems nor visual bombsights and was not cleared for HE stores. The Canberra aircraft forming the bulk of the force deployed were equipped only with 'Gee-H' as a blind bombing device and it was not possible to position ground-based beacons to give coverage for this equipment over Egypt. It was considered that it would be prudent for the Valiants and Hal Far- and Cyprus-based Canberras to carry out night bombing attacks on Abu Sueir, Kabrit, Almaza, Fayid and Cairo West, the main Il-28 base and this necessitated a reversion to the marking technique successfully used in WWII.

A Vickers Valiant bedecked with black and yellow Suez stripes heads off into the dusk from Malta towards its target in Egypt. On the evening of 31 October the first wave of Valiants of 148 Squadron took off at 17:20 from Malta for an attack on Cairo West, but was then ordered to abort after US transport aircraft were detected at their target. They turned back and flew straight into the aircraft of the second wave, which were just taking off. Another five Valiants and seven Canberras from Malta were diverted to bomb Kibrit. The third wave consisted of 18 Canberras from Cyprus and Malta and four Valiants from Malta, which were to hit Abu Sueir.

The plan was to crater the runways, followed up at dawn by ground attack strikes to destroy the aircraft. It was considered that the destruction of the EAF would be achieved in two days. Little opposition was expected.

On the night of 30 October/31 October the Valiants and Canberras set off to bomb eight of the nine airfields in the Canal Zone and four more in the Nile Delta with 500lb and 1,000lb bombs. Five Valiants on 148 Squadron and one on 214 Squadron plus four Canberras on 109 Squadron and three on 12 Squadron attacked Almaza airfield near Cairo at 19.00Z hours. Intelligence reports stated that there were ten Vampires, ten MiG-15s, ten Il-28 bombers, nine Meteors and 31 twin-engined transports on the airfield. Canberras on 139 Squadron operating from Cyprus did the visual marking. The first Red TI markers from a PFF Canberra went down over Heliopolis and the flares were dropped on the western hardstands 1,000 yards from the nominated aiming point. A second marker dropped TIs closer to the aiming point and called the bombers to drop on the most eastern set of TIs. Bombing was scattered, the Valiants attacking from 42,000 feet with free-fall bombs. XD814 on 148 Squadron was the first V-bomber in action. Because of the poor marking, the 50 per cent error circle was 1,550 yards and only one runway was hit, suffering superficial damage. It was a similar story at Kabrit and Abu Sueir, where although accuracy was better, damage was light. Little opposition was encountered and there was light AA fire in the target area but it was sporadic and well below the attacking aircraft. The Valiant piloted by 34-year old Squadron Leader Ellis Trevor Ware DFC was intercepted by an Egyptian Meteor NF.13 but its pilot could not hold on to the bomber, which climbed out of his range and the Meteor flew away. (On 10/11 August 1943 Ware had been shot down on the operation on Neuemberg flying a 35 Squadron Halifax. Ware and three of his crew were taken prisoner.)

The following night attacks were made on the airfields at Cairo West, Fayid and Kasfareet. Reconnaissance photographs showed that many Egyptian aircraft had escaped the initial bombing, so subsequent raids were made at lower altitude. Hunter escorts were also dispensed with, as there was so little opposition and it was felt that the fighters

Valiant crews on 207 Squadron brief for a bombing sortie during Operation 'Musketeer'.

Armourers preparing to load high-explosive bombs into Canberra B.2 WH951 of 12 Squadron at Hal Far. Malta prior to a raid on military targets in Egypt. The Canberras flew 72 missions from Malta and Valiants, 49, dropping at least 1,439 bombs. Some Canberra B.Mk.2s were stationed on Cyprus to mark targets for Valiant and Canberra bombers based on Malta.

could do a better job providing cover for the approaching naval forces. 'Six crews were briefed to carry out an attack on Cairo West airfield' reported the 138 Squadron diarist. 'Led by the squadron commander, these crews took off during the afternoon, but after roughly one hour's flight all aircraft were recalled, as it was believed that American civilians were being evacuated by air from that airfield. After burning off fuel, all aircraft brought back their bombs and landed safely. Later that evening two crews, captained by Squadron Leaders Wilson and Collins, carried out an attack on the airfield at Abu Sueir. Both crews dropped proximity markers with 11,000lb of bombs and both marking and bombing were observed to be extremely accurate. No enemy opposition, either by fighters or anti-aircraft fire, was encountered by either crew.'

Early the following morning a U-2 flew high over Cairo West Airport and carried out two photo passes over the airfield. The second set of photos showed Egyptian aircraft and buildings on fire. Telephotoed a set of pictures, the RAF responded with, 'Warm thanks for the pix. It's the quickest bomb damage assessment we've ever had.' De Havilland Venoms and Armée de l'Air F-84F Thunderstreak fighter-bombers from Cyprus attacked Canal Zone airfields and Royal Navy Hawker Sea Hawks and de Havilland Sea Venoms from the carriers *Eagle*, *Bulwark* and *Albion* struck at three airfields in the Cairo area. The flak was light and all the attackers returned. By early afternoon, the carriers were fifty miles offshore and launching a fresh sortie every few minutes. On Cyprus, aircraft were taking off or landing at the rate of one a minute. The jets were joined by turboprop Westland Wyverns from the RN carriers and propeller-driven Vought F4U Corsairs from the French carrier *Arromanches*, which was accompanied by *Lafayette*, carrying Grumman TBM Avengers and helicopters. Corsairs sank an Egyptian

Canberra B.2 WH667 of 10 Squadron being loaded with bombs at Nicosia, Cyprus during Operation 'Musketeer'. By late October 1956 there were 112 combat aircraft at Akrotiri, 127 at Nicosia and 46 at Tymbou. These included two squadrons of Hunter F.Mk.1 interceptors and one with Meteor NF.13 night-fighters, three units with 36 Venom fighter-bombers, as well as 60 French F-84Fs and 16 RF-84Fs. WH667 was written off on 7 November 1980 when an engine exploded on take-off from RAF Akortiri and the aircraft rolled, hit the ground and was destroyed by fire. Squadron Leader George William 'Paddy' Thompson and his navigator, Flying Officer Mark Wray who ejected, were killed.

torpedo boat and damaged a destroyer off Alexandria. The vessel *Akka* was attacked by Sea Hawks as it was being towed into the main channel midway down the canal and sunk. The 347-foot-long ship, filled with cement and debris for the purpose, was the first of 49 vessels scuttled to cause the canal's first major blockage in its 87-year history. British bombs also tumbled the key Firdan Bridge into the shipping lane.

About sixty Egyptian aircraft were destroyed on the ground, but airfields were not put out of action and at Cairo West, the Ilyushin Il-28 bombers had already flown to apparent safety in Syria and far-away Luxor. It was a wasted effort, as the Il-28s at Luxor were put out of action a few days later by Armée de l'Air F-84F Thunderstreaks. Opposition was slight as targets including the Cairo radio station, communication centres, Huckstep Barracks (which was attacked by seven Valiants) and transport complexes were attacked on the night of 2/3 November. Further heavy damage was inflicted on the strategically important Nfisha railway marshalling yards outside Port Said. Although AAA defended many of the targets, this was usually light and almost always well below the aircraft but a Venom was hit by anti-aircraft fire during one low-level sortie, killing the pilot. The Huckstep Barracks was bombed again two nights later together with the coastal batteries on El Agami Island. During the attacks on Huckstep the markers were well placed and bombing was reasonably concentrated but at El Agami most of the bombers failed to drop because the TIs were extinguished, probably having fallen into the sea. These attacks heralded the landing of British and French paratroops on 5 November, together with Israeli land forces crossing the border under an umbrella of continued air support.

By 3 November the EAF had virtually ceased to exist. About 260 of its aircraft had been destroyed, including most of the 120 MiGs and fifty Il-28s that were in service when the conflict began. Only eight of them had been lost in air combat. The Anglo-French airborne assault began on 5 November and the seaborne assault went ahead on the morning of the 6th when all immediate objectives had been taken. Shortly after dawn Venoms on 249 Squadron RAF flew a strike against the Egyptian artillery positions and they appeared over the Port Said just in the same moment as a EAF MiG-15 flew the one and only strike against the British paras at Gamil. Flying Officer Budd immediately tried

Above: HMS *Eagle*, HMS *Bulwark* and HMS *Albion*, which took part in the Suez operation. In total 163 fighter jets were based on them, including 117 Sea Hawks, Sea Venoms and Wyverns. The fighters from HMS *Eagle*, for example, flew 621 combat sorties and those from *Albion* 415. They dropped 229 bombs and fired 1,448 rockets and 88,000 30mm rounds. The invasion fleet of five British carriers (including HMS *Theseus* and HMS *Ocean* which acted as troop-transports), five cruisers, 13 destroyers, six frigates and five submarines, as well as 60 other ships, sortied from Malta on the evening of 30 October 1956.

Right: A Hawker Sea Hawk FGA.6 of 897 Naval Air Squadron receives its Anglo-French identification markings on board HMS *Eagle*.

Below: A Sea Hawk aircraft of 899 Squadron, armed with rockets, about to be launched from HMS *Eagle* for a strike on an Egyptian airfield.

to attack the MiG, but it managed to get away due to its higher speed. In the early afternoon the 40 Commando was stopped by Egyptian resistance south of Port Said, but the Sea Hawks from British carriers then flew a series of highly effective strikes and the advance was continued.

Mounting pressure at the UN instigated by USA led to a cease-fire on 8 November and the RAF and French crews stood down. The total Bomber Command effort during the Suez campaign amounted to 49 Valiant and 278 Canberra sorties. Post-conflict analysis determined that the destruction of the EAF was largely due to attacks by the fighter-bombers. On 17 November all the Valiants returned to the United Kingdom.

In *'Wings Over Egypt'*, Peter Williams of *RAF Flying Review* in December 1956 described the RAF's part in the Suez Campaign:

Above: Arming a Sea Hawk aboard HMS *Eagle* in preparation for a strike on an Egyptian airfield.

Right: Sea Hawk pilots being debriefed by an intelligence officer on HMS *Eagle* after they had returned from preliminary strikes on Egyptian strongpoints in preparation for the landing of British and French paratroops on 5 November when fighters from HMS *Bulwark* and HMS *Albion* flew 355 combat sorties on the day, mainly striking different Egyptian Army columns and bases and several patrol boats of the Egyptian Navy.

Sea Hawks of 800 Naval Air Squadron being re-armed between sorties, on board HMS *Albion*. On 6 November a 897 Squadron Sea Hawk FGA.6 (XE377) flown by Lieutenant J. H. Stuart-Jervis from HMS *Eagle*, was hit by flak which caused the fuel tank to catch fire shot down around the Port Said area. He ejected over the sea and was recovered. Sea Hawk FGA.6 XE400 '107' of 800 NAS was lost on 7 November whilst operating from HMS *Albion*. XE400 crashed into the Mediterranean during operations off Port Said after the engine was hit by flak. The pilot ejected safely and was recovered by SAR helicopter. On 14 November a 897 Squadron Sea Hawk FGA.6 (XE375) flown by Lieutenant Donald F. Mills was shot down over the Port Fuad-Ismailia road. He ejected over the enemy-held territory, but was recovered by a Whirlwind helicopter, covered by the rest of his flight and despite a number of Egyptian tanks nearby. Sea Hawk FGA.6 XE375 '239/B' of 801 NAS was written off when the arrestor hook pulled out of the aircraft on landing on HMS Bulwark. The pilot attempted to stop but the aircraft struck parked Sea Hawk WM985 before running over the side of the carrier into the sea. The pilot was rescued by the SAR helicopter.

'It was in many ways a 'model' air operation, the sort of large-scale exercise which is meticulously planned and which somehow goes even more smoothly than the planners could have dared to hope. But it was no mere exercise; this was the real thing. And the campaign was made more difficult by the deliberate Allied policy of sparing Egyptian life wherever possible and by broadcasting warnings in advance of every attack. As a blue-print for the sort of police-action which may be necessary in troubled areas, the offensive carried out by the British and French air forces is interesting and significant. It fell into three distinct phases: first, the destruction of the Egyptian Air Force; second, attacks on military targets; third, the dropping of parachute troops to occupy key areas. It says much for the tactical skill of those concerned that all three of the phases had been completed by the end of five days.

'It began shortly before dusk on Wednesday, 31 October. At airfields in Cyprus and Malta vast armadas of RAF aircraft - more numerous than anything we've seen since the war - were drawn up ready for action. Canberras, Hunters, Valiants, Venoms ...familiar aircraft, some of them only recently arrived from Britain, looking strangely unfamiliar in their freshly painted operational markings (black and yellow stripes on wings and

Over Almaza on 1 November this Sea Venom on 893 NAS was damaged by flak and the pilot, Lieutenant Commander Willcox, had to make an emergency landing aboard HMS *Eagle*, without undercarriage. The aircraft has been caught by the arrester wires on the flight deck.

fuselage). The whole force was under the command of the C-in-C MEAF, Air Marshal H. L. Patch. In command of the air task force bombing the Egyptian airfields was Air Marshal D. H. F. Barnett, a 50-year-old New Zealander.

'As darkness fell and the blue lights along the runways shone out brightly, the whine of the eager Canberras increased. Then, with a shrill scream, they were off. Their targets: the Egyptian airfields at Almaza and Inchass, near Cairo (where at least two MiG-15 squadrons were known to be housed) and the airfields at Abu Sueir, Fayid and Kabrit in the Canal Zone where further MiG-15s bought by the Egyptians from Czechoslovakia were believed to be stored. No one could predict just how the Egyptians would react to this challenge. How many of their MiGs would be sent up to intercept; how many, indeed, were available to be sent up? These were unknown quantities. But the intelligence available to the Allies suggested that many of the MiGs were still in crates and many more were unmanned due to a shortage of trained crews.

'As wave after wave of the attacking Canberras returned to base, the reports of the

A Westland Whirlwind helicopter taking off from HMS *Albion* to stand by for emergency rescue operations as the ship turns into the wind to fly off her aircraft on a strike. Sea Venoms of 809 Squadron are left and Sea Hawks of 800 NAS are on the right. Two Sea Hawks, two Wyverns, one Canberra (over Syria), one Venom and two Whirlwind helicopters were shot down during the fighting and over fifty other aircraft were damaged.

MiGs burning on Inchas airfield after an attack by twelve Sea Hawks of 810 Naval Air Squadron operating from HMS *Bulwark*. Within only a few hours 40% of Egyptian combat aircraft were destroyed or damaged by air strikes. Although the EAF suffered a loss of only five pilots and 200 other ranks killed and injured during the air strikes, the EAF was completely destroyed, with all its operational airfields badly damaged, control towers, hangars, radar stations, shops and depots destroyed. It was later estimated that the EAF lost 104 MiG-15s and MiG-17s, 26 Il-28s, 30 Vampires, eleven Meteors and 63 other assorted aircraft while 50 others were heavily damaged.

Original production of the DH.113 was for export and the type was ordered by the Egyptian Air Force but when the export of arms to Egypt was banned, these aircraft became surplus and were taken over for the RAF under the designation Vampire NF.10 (WP233 pictured). In order to evade the British arms embargo, 58 single-seat FIAT-built Vampire FB.52A fighter-bombers, painted in Syrian markings, were delivered to Egypt. The EAF lost three Vampires in combat with Israeli jets during the Suez Crisis.

An Armeé de'l Air F-84F Thunderstreak casts a shadow en route to its target. It is estimated that the French aircraft based in Israel flew approximately 100 combat sorties. At Luxor 13 F-84Fs of EC.1 found 20 Il-28s neatly parked in two rows. Five hours later, six F-84Fs appeared over Luxor again, this time followed by a single RF-84F of ER.4/33 based on Cyprus, to complete the destruction. In total, 17 EAF aircraft - including at least ten Il-28s - were destroyed during these two strikes. The RAF, FAA, AdA and Aéronavale flew more than 5,000 operational sorties during the short war and the counter-air offensive was the most intensive flown since Korea.

Hawker Hunter F.Mk.1 of 34 Squadron with Suez stripes on Cyprus during Operation 'Musketeer'. The overcrowded British bases on Cyprus were highly vulnerable to air attacks by EAF Il-28 bombers.

RAF Venom WR398/H of 249 Squadron taxies past RF-84F 52-7325/33-DD of ER.4/33 at Akrotiri. On 3 November, at Fayd, RAF Venoms caught two EAF Meteors during refuelling and destroyed them both and at Kibrit the last intact MiG-15 in Egypt was destroyed by the pilots of the 6 Squadron RAF. Four other Venoms on an armed reconnaissance mission at very low level near al-Qantara, suffered their first loss, as the formation overflew a concentration of Egyptian flak batteries and Flight Lieutenant Sheehan's Venom hit the water and crashed while trying to evade.

By mid-1956 the Israeli Air Force had 176 combat aircraft, of which 112 were jets. On 30 October eight Mystère IVs (pictured) fought 16 EAF MiG-15s and shot down one MiG while a second and one of the Mystères were damaged. On 31 October, two Mystères claimed a MiG-15 and a MiG-17.

Right: Israeli Dassault M.D.450 Ouragans (including this one with its large shark-mouth insignia, usually associated with '113' or 'Lion Head Squadron' IDF/AF during the Sinai campaign) were assigned to close support operations, since they could not match the performance of Egyptian MiG-15s.

Below: No British, French or Israeli fighter was capable of matching the MiG in the air but its pilots lacked air-combat manoeuvering and gunnery training. MiG-17s saw at least one air battle with Israeli fighters. Later, Soviet 'instructors' flew them in a battle against the British. (EAF)

Below: Canberra PR.7 WH799 on attachment to 13 Squadron at Akrotiri, Cyprus was shot down by Syrian Meteor F.8s (pictured) over the Syrian-Lebanese frontier on 6 November, the last day of the Suez War. Flight Lieutenants Bernie Hunter and Sam Small survived but Flying Officer Roy Erquhart-Pullen, navigator, was killed when the Canberra crashed.

crews were anxiously studied. Flight Lieutenant John Slater, the 34-year-old captain of one of the aircraft, confirmed our suspicions: the Egyptian Air Force was lying low. The Canberras had all been able to drop their full load of bombs dead on target, without any opposition from Egyptian fighters. Ack-ack fire - mostly wild and inaccurate - reached up to about 8,000 feet and continued for 105 minutes non-stop. There was no blackout in Egyptian towns until after the bombers had passed.

'Now it was the turn of the four-jet Valiants from Malta. One of them reported a 'near-interception' by an Egyptian Meteor, but this was the only instance of any night-fighter activity. The Valiants were making for Cairo West airfield in an attempt to destroy the forty-odd Il-28s known to be based there but just before they reached their target they received orders to turn back. It became known that convoys of American citizens were being evacuated from Cairo along an adjoining road and the attack was consequently called off. But the Valiants went back next morning and carried out the operation successfully.

'The emphasis had, until then, been on high-level bombing. Now it shifted to low-level attacks. On Thursday morning Venom FB.4 day-fighters made low-level raids on the airfields and they joined by aircraft of the Fleet Air Arm from carrier task forces in the Mediterranean and by French Thunderstreaks and Corsairs. Canberra PR.7s on reconnaissance flights next day reported that fifty Egyptian aircraft had been destroyed on the ground and another forty seriously damaged.

'But where was the rest of the EAF? The recce flights on Friday seem show that Nasser was hurriedly evacuating his aircraft out of the immediate danger area - to Syria, perhaps and to Luxor, 150 miles south. So that evening another force attacked Luxor, located a number of Il-28s on the ground and destroyed them.

'Phase One of the operation was on Saturday afternoon. The Allied communiqué announced the 'virtual destruction' of the Egyptian Air Force. The attack shifted to military and other targets. Now the Hunters went into operation for the first time, providing an air umbrella for Canberras attacking the Egyptian Army barracks at Aimaza. There was an attack, too, on the Cairo broadcasting transmitter, seven miles from the City, which put it out of action. Ammunition depots, tanks, radar installations, anti-aircraft batteries - all were hit. But, because of the announced intention of the Allies not to bomb populated areas, the Egyptians had begun moving their military formations and A/A guns into villages, where they were immune from attack. An indication of the complete air superiority we had achieved over Egypt was the fact that on Saturday night Hastings aircraft were able to fly, unescorted, over Cairo, dropping half a million leaflets.

'By Sunday night Phase Two was completed and all was ready for the troops to go in. At 04.44 on Monday morning the first troop transports roared into life at airfields in Cyprus and raced down the runway at twenty-second intervals. Hastings aircraft, each carrying forty troops, Valettas carrying thirty, were joined by Noratlas planes with French paratroops aboard. Close support for the landings was given by Sea Hawks, Corsairs and Avengers from the Allied carrier task force and by RAF Venoms and Hunters and French Thunderstreaks. From then on it was up to the troops...

'During the five-day campaign the Allied air losses appear to have been only one Venom aircraft which failed to pull out of a dive and a few planes which suffered minor damage. The Egyptians, on the other hand, seem to have lost at least four-fifths of their Air Force on the ground, but as the planes were mostly unmanned at the time, their loss of life must have been small. With one exception, the Egyptian Air Force failed even to make contact with our aircraft. The complete failure of Nasser's air arm must be attributed to lack of trained aircrews and possibly also to inefficient maintenance of the aircraft they had available. If they had had more time to convert to the newly-acquired Russian planes, if they had had more skilled technicians and 'volunteer' pilots from abroad, it might have been a very different story.'

Although the Egyptians did not oppose the attacks and there were no Valiant combat losses, the results of the raids were disappointing. Their primary targets were seven Egyptian airfields. Although the Valiants dropped a total of 842 tons of bombs, only three of the seven airfields were seriously damaged. It was the last time the V-bombers flew a war mission until Avro Vulcans bombed Port Stanley airfield in the Falkland Islands during the Falklands War in 1982.

The United Nations called an emergency Security Council meeting to order a ceasefire with effect from midnight on 6 November, which was adhered to by all sides and an UN Emergency Force took over from the ground forces, following which the British and French forces gradually withdrew. The evacuation was completed on 22 December. As well as the Venom already mentioned, Operation 'Musketeer' cost the RAF two Canberras (a PR. 7 shot down by a Syrian Air Force MiG-15 and a B.6(BS) crashing on take-off following battle damage repair) which represented just over one per cent of the aircraft involved. The four Valiant squadrons had a trouble-free conflict, apart from the electronic malfunctions, although one Valiant crew reported seeing an EAF Meteor NF.13 during a night sortie.

Politically, the fall-out from Operation 'Musketeer', as far as Britain was concerned, was catastrophic. Above all the United States' non-cooperative stance confirmed the urgent necessity to have an independent nuclear weapons capability together with the means of delivering it. The Valiant was noticeably less advanced than the Vulcan and Victor and several Valiants were soon converted to perform various support roles, such as aerial refuelling tankers and reconnaissance aircraft. In July 1964 a cracked spar was found in a Valiant. Following inspections of the entire fleet which showed that the wing spars were suffering from fatigue at between 35% and 75% of the assessed safe fatigue life, probably due to low level turbulence, in January 1965 the British government decided that the expense of the repairs could not be justified and the fleet was permanently grounded as of 26 January 1965. The QRA (Quick Reaction Alert) that had been in place for SACEUR was maintained until the final grounding and was then allowed to lapse.

In Britain, as the Cold War had advanced, there became an impetus for the development of a more substantial air defence system. With the advent of jet technology, QRA took on an extra dimension. Not only did it involve launching aircraft to intercept

B (K).1 Valiant XD816 which first flew on 25 July1956 and on 148 Squadron bombed targets in Egypt on 31 October and on the 1st and 4th of November. In 1958 this aircraft was transferred to 214 Squadron, in the colours of which it is pictured at RAF Abingdon in 1968.

an enemy, but also to launch waves of aircraft, such as the Vulcan bomber, to unleash a nuclear salvo upon the Warsaw Pact. From 1950 onwards, aircraft were placed on 30-minutes readiness to intercept intruders, which had been spotted by radar. Initially Meteor aircraft performed the task and then the Hunter; however, these aircraft had a very limited range and endurance. 1951 saw the advent of night jet-fighter interception flights with the introduction of the De Havilland Vampire NF.10. In addition to the Vampire, the night-fighter flights were undertaken by Meteor NF 11-14 and latterly Javelin FAW5-9 aircraft.

In October 1958 Peter Williams observed Exercise 'Sunbeam' at close quarters at Fighter Command HQ at Stanmore, Middlesex. This optimistic name was given to that year's major air defence exercise designed to test preparedness for an attack on Britain:

'In the old-world mansion where Lady Hamilton once entertained Lord Nelson, Fighter Command's Headquarters staff survey the progress of the exercise. Here, the atmosphere is tense, expectant. Notices scrawled in red crayon exhort us to KEEP QUIET! in the vicinity of the conference room. We pad softly over the thick carpets. No one knows when the next heavy raid will materialise; it is almost like the real thing. Air Chief Marshal Pike, the C-in-C, is quietly-spoken, confident. He lists the attacking forces, ranging from the three V-bombers of Bomber Command to B-47s and B-66s of the USAF. They are supported by F-84s and F-100s of the 2nd and 4th Allied Tactical Air Forces, flown by Dutch, Belgian and American pilots. Canada is represented, too - by CF-100s and Sabre 6s. Altogether some 3,500 enemy sorties are expected in this concentrated three - days - and - nights attack. Unlike the real thing, however, the 'enemy' is here with us - in the person of a smiling Bomber Command representative. The fighter boys do not know what he is cooking up. He gives nothing away, except to reveal that up to 450

A Vulcan crew at dispersal.

'enemy' aircraft may be expected on some raids.

'Fighter Command's C-in-C is unmoved by this threat. He tells us that the Hunter 6s and Javelins now in service are capable of intercepting any known bomber in the world. Bomber Command smiles still more broadly. Doubtless he is thinking of his own Command's recent statement that the V-bombers can outmanoeuvre any known fighter in the world!

'This year, for the first time, the RAF's Bloodhound missile station at North Coates is taking part in the exercise. The C-in-C assures us, however, that no missiles are actually being fired. 'At £10,000 a time,' he says, 'we can't afford to fling missiles about the sky.' '£10,000?' we query. But this is no revelation of the actual cost of the Bloodhound. The Air Chief Marshal tells us he was talking in round figures only.

'Early warning is, of course, a vital aspect of fighter defence. Exercise 'Sunbeam' is utilising the Continental Early Warning System and we are told that Fighter Command now has its own representatives in Norway, Denmark, Holland, Belgium, Germany and France to pass on by direct link the information required. Air Chief Marshal Pike reiterates that 'British radar is the best in the world.'

'To what extent is this exercise representative of the reality of a future war? We gather that this is an uneasy transition period for Fighter Command. No air-to-air missiles are yet in service and the role of ground-to-air missiles is still to be firmly established. (One obvious need is a zoning plan to keep our fighters out of the way of the ground-to-air missiles.) Enemy stand-off bombers, too, must be expected and here Fighter Command is limited by the weapons presently available. Fighters can cope with the stand-off bomber, we are assured, but only a missile will be able to deal with the stand-off bomb itself.

'We leave the conference room and Fighter Command HQ settles down to its vigil. No longer is it the nerve-centre of the defences - for nowadays these things are largely controlled from the master radar stations - but it still seems to us to be a pulsing and lively heart.'

Geoffrey Norris of *RAF Flying Review* meanwhile, flew with 617 Squadron on the Exercise: "Vulcan 483 of 617 (the Dam-Busters) Squadron, seems motionless, high in the night sky. We are crossing the east coast of England. Ahead and slightly to our left twinkle the lights of York and Leeds; further down to the south we can see Hull and Grimsby clearly; on our right Flamborough Head and Scarborough.

'As I stand on the flight deck between the captain Squadron Leader A. A. Smailes and co-pilot Flying Officer 'Harry' Hopkins, we seem to be alone in the sky. But we know that the night-fighters are out in strength. We are one of four hundred bombers attacking England on the night of October 16/17. Fighter Command are making an all-out effort to prevent us crossing the coast - but, as yet, we seem to have escaped attention. Will we be one of the few to get through?

'The answer comes a few seconds later. A white flash suddenly lights the sky above our nose. Some wonderment at first until Smailes supplies the answer. 'A night-fighter,' he says over the intercom; he's flashing his landing lights to let us know we've been intercepted.' How successful the interception was, only the night-fighter pilot knows. The crew of Vulcan 483 show little interest in what is for them a purely academic question. The time is 0110 hours. For them and for myself there are another three hours and well over a thousand miles of flying to cover before we land back at Scampton. There is plenty of work yet to be done...

'We had been briefed to take off from Scampton, Lincolnshire, at six minutes past eleven that night. Three Vulcans were flying from 617 Squadron; with over 300 other attacking aircraft we were flying out to Denmark to begin a run in on Northern England. With so many aircraft in the sky the importance of accurate navigation was stressed. At

Avro Vulcan B1A XH483 of 617 'Dam Busters' Squadron which Geoffrey Norris flew on during Exercise 'Sunbeam' in 1958. XH483 was delivered to 617 Squadron at Scampton in May 1958. When 617 received its Mk2 Blue Steels in 1961, its B.1s and B.1As reformed as 50 Squadron at RAF Waddington. 483 was flown to Manston for fire-fighting practice in September 1967.

the briefing, an air electronics officer announced radio frequencies and a met-man gave us our weather forecast. Little or no clouds with good visibility were the good news he brought. But he added that wind speeds at 40,000 feet would be 150 knots and that we could expect severe turbulence.

'Diversionary airfields were named, we were given a time check and then we went out to the aircraft. Gone are the days when a crew scrambled into the back of a truck. We climbed sedately into a special air-conditioned bus which took us out to our Vulcan. There we were met by the crew chief, Chief Technician Harper and his highly trained ground crew. They had been working all day preparing 483 for the night's flying. Pilot and co-pilot climb up to their exalted position on the flight deck and are strapped in by the ground crew. Squadron Leader Smailes, like all 'V' Bomber pilots, is an airman of the finest quality. He joined the RAF in 1941, served in fighters in the Middle East and was shot down by flak over Albania and taken prisoner-of-war. After his return to England he remained with Fighter Command until 1948 and since then has been an instructor at the Central Flying School, at the Air Ministry in London and on a year's Staff College course in Canada. He has been flying Vulcans for eighteen months. His co-pilot, Flying Officer J. D. N. (Harry) Hopkins is, at 20, probably one of the youngest pilots to sit in the right-hand seat of a Vulcan. He joined the RAF in late 1955 and went on to Vulcans straight after training in Canada.

'Finally I clamber up into my makeshift 'seat' on a raised platform on the port side. To my right as I sit facing across to starboard are the three rearwards-facing seats of navigators and AEO, on my left, the ladder leading up to the flight deck and beyond it the dark cavern of the visual bomb-aiming position. The flight deck is screened by a canvas curtain. Oxygen on, intercom plugged in and I listen to the intricate pre-flight checks carried out between captain, co-pilot and crew chief who is on the outside intercom. These begin at 2215 hours. By 2230 we are ready to start the four Bristol Olympus engines. So efficient is the drill that, within two minutes, Squadron Leader Smailes is able to report: 'All four engines started and running normally. At 2242 hours the door is closed. The engine noise dwindles to a distant rumble. The crew chief comes off the intercom and stands clear and we are on our own. There is strict radio silence and we will speak to no one except other crew members until the exercise is over. Dead on the second we begin to taxi and by 2300 hours are standing at the end of the runway. More checks. Then the green light from control and at 2306 hours we are off. The co-pilot has already worked out the exact weight of our aircraft and he knows at exactly what speed and how far down the runway we should unstick. As we race off into the night he chants out the speed for the captain and, at precisely the calculated position, we are airborne. Wheels up, an alarming drop in engine noise and acceleration as we reduce to climb power and we are well on our way. In a very short time we are passing through 25.000 feet and the Vulcan rumbles as we pick up the turbulence of the jet stream.

'As we continue on our way up to 40,000 feet I clamber up to the flight deck to watch the pilots at work. The instrument panel is bathed in a gentle orange glow. Every figure stands out crystal clear but there is no suspicion of glare. At our height the weather is fine and clear but, as we look ahead towards Ostend. There are thunderstorms flashing miles below us. The jet stream dies out sooner than expected and Squadron Leader Lewis, the navigator, is soon asking the captain for an increase in Mach number. On an exercise such as this, with more than three hundred other attacking aircraft in the same piece of sky, he does not want to be a second out in his timing.

'At one quarter of an hour before midnight. Smailes reports a green light about a thousand feet below us. A night-fighter?

'I don't think it's going to attack,' says Smailes, 'but we'd better log it.'

'Pilot Officer Knight, the AEO, picks up his rear-view periscope and searches the sky behind us. He sees a light falling off to the rear, but cannot identify it. The light remains a mystery, but we are not attacked.

'By now we are almost thirty seconds late. Lewis is concerned and calls for yet more speed. By the time we are nearing the exercise 'base line' over Denmark from which we will turn into England, we are on schedule again.

'In front of Lewis is a Doppler Navigator, an instrument also used by civil airlines. It shows him his actual speed over the ground and the amount of drift. A 'mileometer' shows the number of miles flown on any one trip. The incessant 'click-click-click' as one-tenth of a mile clicks up faster than once a second is one of the background noises to the

A Vulcan crew on 617 'Dam Busters' Squadron prepare to board at Scampton.

An Avro Vulcan B.2A on 617 Squadron being refuelled at night at RAF Scampton, Lincolnshire is prepared for a sortie with a Blue Steel nuclear stand-off weapon.

Vulcan. It is instruments such as this which help Lewis to know where he is - virtually within a few yards. From a height of over nine miles, this is no mean achievement.

'As we leave the Danish west coast Huggett, the navigator/bomb aimer, reports some 'scatter' on his screen.

'Could be someone else's night-fighter,' suggests Smailes. But Huggett doesn't think so. 'This is fairly common interference when flying over the sea,' he explains.

'But by this time we are well on our way to England and can expect an attack at any time. We fly on in silence broken only by the half hourly oxygen check called by the co-pilot. We all check the doll's eye indicators on our oxygen equipment. They blink as we breathe and we report 'OK.'

'Outside, the temperature is 52 degrees centigrade but our air conditioning system keeps us perfectly comfortable. Occasionally earphones are filled with a rasping noise as someone accidentally leaves his intercom switch on and treats the rest of the crew to his breathing noise. There is a warning, 'Microphone!' from the captain and we all check our switches. The guilty one switches off.

'From the flight deck I watch England approach. Co-pilot 'Harry' Hopkins is busy in the right-hand seat with a slide-rule as he works out our fuel state. Smailes keeps a watchful eye on the instruments and a sharp lookout for night-fighters. The auto-pilot is flying the Vulcan. Not until we are virtually over the coast does the warning flash from the night-fighter tell us that we haven't quite made it...'

Derek Jolley meanwhile, was with the defending squadrons at Horsham St. Faith near Norwich:

'It is anything but 'Sunbeam' as I sit here in the control tower at Horsham St. Faith, looking out on to a windswept, rain-soaked airfield. It has been raining most of the day but, unlike the late war, rain and high winds do not ground modern bombers and so the fighters, too, must be able to cope with all conditions. Out on the aircraft service park the Javelins of 23 Squadron are waiting, the rain dripping incessantly from them, for the night operations. So far the Javelins have marked up 39 kills on only 25 sorties. Their crews are now sleeping in readiness for tonight's operations, if the enemy comes again. Two Hunter 6s of 65 Squadron were telescrambled about five minutes ago and their return is now awaited to see if they have added to the squadron's total of 25 kills on fourteen missions. Unlike the Javelins the Hunters are being scrambled in pairs and have generally been vectored on to the target together. Although the number of kills compares favourably with the night fighters' results, the Hunter pilots have had to be content with sharing the kill with one of their colleagues.

'While we are waiting for the two Hunters to return the Commanding Officer of the station, genial looking, rangy, Group Captain Barry Sutton, compares the operation with the Battle of Britain. He does not hanker for the old days. 'After flying the Hunter you realise just how inefficient the Spitfire was,' he says.

Three Vulcans in anti-flash white overall scheme in formation.

'There is little similarity between this exercise and the battles of the last war. No lengthy briefing. No mad scramble when the Tannoy crackles out its ominous warning. Methodical planning has taken over from slap-happy, but nevertheless effective, casualness. The briefing is short. Crews are told all necessary met details; reminded of their range in these conditions; given details of diversion airfields. Then with little more ado they are sent off to join their aircraft. Out there on dispersal some of the pilots have already been sitting in their cockpits for over an hour waiting for a telescramble over their headphones. The enemy are being constantly watched by radar and fighters are only scrambled as they are needed. Not in whole squadrons but in pairs. After the take off they are vectored on to their target by the radar station.

'I hear muffled instructions from the next room and within seconds two more Hunters are flashing down the runway. They climb into the cloud and are lost to sight. But within seconds one of them is flashing back across the airfield towards the control tower. 'Chap's in a spot of trouble,' murmurs the Groupie, looking up as the Hunter roars past a few feet from the control tower. The unfortunate pilot has a jammed undercarriage. His plight is noted but the battle must go on. Over the telescramble goes the alert to another Hunter which roars off to take the place of his unlucky comrade. Meanwhile instructions go out to the disabled Hunter. 'Yes, you're OK now,' he is told, 'but get rid of some of that fuel before you come in.' While he is circuiting, the two planes which were first off come in and land. The pilots are immediately debriefed. Yes they contacted the target and destroyed it. The score moves up to 26.

'As soon as the pilots leave their aircraft the machines are pounced upon by the ground crews. Quickly they refuel the Hunters, change the gun packs and turn the planes round ready for another scramble.

The crippled Hunter comes in; a splash goes up as the wheels touch-down and the undercarriage holds. One more incident in the exercise; and the battle goes on...'

In 1959 Geoffrey Norris, writing in RAF *Flying Review* after a visit to the Victors on

The Avro Blue Steel air-launched, rocket-propelled nuclear armed standoff missile of 17,000lbs, built to arm the V bomber force (seen here being unloaded for loading on a Victor) finally entered service in February 1963, by which point improved surface-to-air missiles with longer range had greatly eroded the advantages of the design. 'Blue Steel' required up to seven hours of launch preparation and was highly unreliable; the RAF estimated in 1963 that half the missiles would fail to fire and would have to be dropped over their targets, contradicting their purpose of serving as standoff weapons while still outside the range of SAMs. The missile proceeded to the target at high speeds up to Mach 3 and would trigger within 100 metres of the pre-defined target point.

A 15 Squadron Victor QRA demonstration 'Scramble' at RAF Cottesmore in June 1959.

15 Squadron at RAF Cottesmore, asked 'Is the Force Ready?'

'Sleek, impressive - and terribly expensive - Britain's V-bomber force is slowly taking its final streamlined shape as more and more squadrons of Vulcans and Victors come into being. These aircraft together with the men who fly and service them, represent one of the most efficient bombing forces in the world today. But can the V-bombers match up to the task set them in this missile age? Can they be quick enough off the mark? These are questions which many people must be asking. In a recent exercise, three Victors were scrambled in just under four minutes - at a special 'show' put on for the benefit of the Prime Minister [Harold MacMillan]. At the time, there were some who dubbed this exercise ' unrealistic,' whilst others thought that the exercise meant that our entire bomber force could be scrambled off the ground at the rate of three every four minutes at any time in an emergency. Both these views are wrong, as I found out for myself when I visited 15 Squadron at Cottesmore recently to see another simulated Victor scramble. There was a very evident air of realism in the way these highly-efficient crews swung into their aircraft in the shortest possible time and were ready to go. All of them were anxious to show me that their display for Mr. Macmillan was no mere flash in the pan. Ground crews, under the direction of the Crew Chiefs, had been in action much earlier. Every aircraft, as it became available, had been fuelled, serviced and bombed up. In an emergency like this, aircrew would be confined to their stations and, as soon as their respective Crew Chiefs announce that the aircraft are ready, pre take-off checks are made. These checks are carried out right up to engine starting sequence. The bomber is then shut down. It is ready for the crew to scramble whenever the word is given. All that is necessary is for the engines to be started and take-off made. The full pre take-off checks are gone through once in every twenty-four hours.

'During this brief stage of the alert the crews are briefed. Met information is, of course, brought up to date. The scramble signal can be given at any time and then the crews literally run for it and take off as soon as ready. The number of aircraft taking off naturally vary according to the nature of the exercise, but the aim is gradually to improve techniques until the whole of the V-Force can be made ready to go in the shortest possible

B-52s on Ground Alert getting airborne.

time. Scrambling a complex piece of mechanism like a V-bomber requires split second timing and excellent team-work. If the warning goes while the crew are still in the Operations Block then the precision work begins as soon as the crew are in the bus which is waiting to take them to their aircraft. They line up at the door with the Air Electronics Officer in front, followed by the two pilots. The AEO is first out at dispersal. His seat in the aircraft is immediately to the right of the entrance and, as he flings himself into it he throws the switches which bring in the external power supply needed to start the engines. His warning lights tell him whether this is functioning and, as soon as he knows that it is, he yells, 'Externals on!' to the Captain who has followed him up the ladder.

'The cry 'externals on' usually comes as the Captain is sliding into his seat. He immediately reaches up for the engine starter switch on the roof panel and begins to start the first engine. Now the co-pilot who follows the Captain is in his seat and ready to play his part in the starting procedure as the first engine begins turning. Fourth man in is the navigator/radar who goes straight to his seat on the far side from the entrance hatch while the last man, the navigator, closes the door. The two busiest men at this time are the pilots. They are strapping themselves into their ejection seats, putting on helmets and connecting intercom and oxygen leads, as they start the engines.

'Outside the aircraft the Crew Chief stands by the exterior intercom, in touch with the Captain, ready to help with external checks. Ground-crew members stand by chocks and the external power cable ready to whip them away when the Crew Chief gives the word. It takes thirty seconds to start each engine and to this time must be added the few seconds needed for getting into the aircraft and taxiing during which any final checks are made. A Victor has been off within two minutes 45 seconds from the word 'go.' This is the sort of scramble practised regularly by crews in the V-Force. It ensures that they are always on their toes and will be ready whenever their services are needed.

'What of the quality of the aircraft themselves? Precise performance figures are, of course secret; but what is known is that the Victor and Vulcan are among the finest bombers in the world today. They are comparable to the Boeing B-52 which is at present the backbone of the United States Strategic Air Command. And for the day after tomorrow there will be the Mark 2 versions of the Victor and Vulcan with their possibilities of higher speeds and altitudes. True enough, there is no case here for

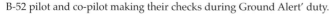

B-52 pilot and co-pilot making their checks during Ground Alert' duty.

complacency and as techniques improve, so Britain will have to keep up with them. At the moment, however, Bomber Command has the tools for the job. And, by strict attention to bombing accuracies, meticulous application of the operational role to all training flights, quick reaction to warnings and long range overseas flights, Bomber Command is making sure that the tools can be used to the greatest effect.'

In America by the end of 1960 428 B-47s, B-52s and B-58s were on alert duty. In March 1961 President John F. Kennedy directed that half of the B-47/B-52 force be placed on alert duty. By late 1961 SAC had forty-one B-52 squadrons, thirty-eight of which were combat ready. Of these, twenty-eight were dispersed. Nineteen of these squadrons with fifteen B-52s each were assigned to strategic wings and the other nine were assigned to bomb wings. SAC's eleven wings were capable of launching twelve sorties per day.

As a B-52 crewdog (having started his Air Force career as an air traffic controller and later a B-52 navigator) about a third of Charlie Hough's life was spent on Alert. 'That meant we worked, played, ate and slept right next to our heavily loaded, heavily armed 'Buffs' (acronym for Big Ugly Fat F**ker the standard crewdog name for a B-52). And because we were working for SAC we knew that there would be very little time during our seven days of alert that we weren't being trained, tested and prodded. In other words they had us prisoner; why not screw with us! For instance we knew that at least once during each tour we would be subject to the rude sound of the klaxon. When the horn blew we were supposed to get to our airplane as quickly as possible, start the engines, decode a message from headquarters and do exactly what it said. And we were timed to

B-52Ds of SAC on 'Ground Alert' duty in the US.

A 4136th Bomb Wing B-52H crew at Torrejón AFB on 11 January 1962 during Exercise 'Persian Rug'.

make sure we were ready to go to war immediately. So one bright and sunny day on alert at a base on the west coast (that doesn't exist anymore) we heard the call of the klaxon, jumped into our truck and blasted out to the ramp to our own special bomber. As the pilot popped the cartridges that fired the engines, the Nav and I copied down the coded message from command post. It usually decoded to a message that told us to just start engines and equipment and report ready to go or do all that and taxi to the runway to show how fast we could lean that much farther forward. We decoded, agreed and told the pilot it was a taxi exercise. We moved out of our parking stub heading for the runway when the whole crew heard me and the Nav say, 'Oh, shit!' We had both discovered our error. It wasn't a taxi exercise. We were supposed to stay put. The pilot just about lost it. Results from each exercise were reported to the head of SAC almost the minute they happened. We were about to become famous. The only thing we could do was get back to our parking place as soon as possible. But moving a big-assed bomber full of fuel and weapons is no easy thing. Finally the pilot team decided that going down the runway and back the taxiway would get us home in the shortest amount of time. We got clearance on the runway and hit the power for a high speed taxi. But we forgot to tell command post what we were doing. Two full colonels, a major and three captains almost had heart attacks when they thought a bomber loaded with major crowd-pleasers was about to launch. Once again we had blown it. We belatedly told everyone what we were doing, hopefully preventing any further heart attacks and silently headed back to the alert pad.

'Man, are we going to be deep in the barrel when we get back,' the pilot said.

'Yeah,' said the gunner. 'But I don't think we're going to be on the bottom.'

'Why's that, guns? Who's going to be in deeper shit than us?'

'Oh, probably those guys behind us.' The pilot and co-pilot almost wrenched their necks to check and confirm that someone else had followed our mistaken lead. Yep. There they were. The good old number one elite Standardization and Evaluation crew. They hadn't even bothered to copy and decode the message. They just followed us out. And when everyone in charge was through yelling at them they barely had breath enough left for us. I guess two wrongs don't make a right...but it sure worked for us!

'We used to fly a lot of low level in the B-52. It was thought to be the only way to avoid the radar sites protecting the USSR so we practiced it a lot.'

In July 1961 Geoffrey Norris wrote an article entitled *'The Independent Deterrent'* for *RAF Flying Review:*

Needle up ... ten miles to go.' The voice of the pilot of the Victor Mark la came quietly over the intercom. 43,000 feet below was Norway. We were approaching Stavanger, a target we had been briefed to 'bomb.' Our ground speed was 525 knots - Mach 0.93 - yet the 'V' bomber seemed to be just humming quietly through the stratosphere. The lack of noise heightened the air of concentration as the crew prepared to carry out a simulated bombing attack. Some minutes previously a check list had been called out between pilot and the Nav/Radar to ensure that the complex bombing equipment was in order. It was and we were all set for the attack.

'The aircraft was on auto-pilot and in the starboard of the three rearward facing seats behind me the Nav/Radar was studying the picture in his radar tube, eyes glued on the pin-point of his target. Every few seconds he fed corrections into the auto-pilot to keep us exactly on course. Up in front the pilot watched a special indicator and called off the miles to the target. 'Eight ... six ... four ... two ...'

'Now!' The Nav/Radar's voice chipped in and the bomb was away. Bomb doors were closed and the Nav/Plotter called out a new course. We heeled over in a turn to starboard. If this had been war we would have been assured that within the next few seconds our target would have ceased to exist.

'But the big question was: did this simulated attack with no worry about fighters or enemy missiles bear any relation to what Bomber Command could do in war? In other words, could Bomber Command effectively carry out its commitments if a global war should develop? It was to find the answers to these questions that I flew with the men of Bomber Command in their latest aircraft, met high-ranking staff officers and visited bomber stations in many parts of the country. From it all emerged the story of RAF Bomber Command - an often misunderstood section of Britain's armed forces. Despite the criticisms which have been levelled at the 'V' force, it is an encouraging story. Bomber Command philosophy has been developed steadily ever since the end of World War Two. It has now crystallized into four main parts. Britain must have - and be known to have - a deterrent force. This must he an independent force with no international tie-ups. It must not be thought capable of being knocked out on the ground. In wartime, Bomber Command must be capable of destroying the enemy's will to fight. The first two points are easily answered. The 'V' force is very much in being, and frequent overseas training flights to all parts of the world ensure that the four-engined, white painted jets are well known. Independence, too, is very real. The 'V' force is Britain's to deploy as she will. In time of war the British Prime Minister is the man who will, eventually, decide when and where the bombers should be used. He will not have to consult any foreign power. It is, perhaps, the defensive aspect of Bomber Command which has been receiving the closest attention in recent years. A lot of planning has gone to ensure that the 'V' force is not caught napping. Much publicity has been given to the ability of the Command to 'scramble' within the space of a few minutes but the actual 'scrambling' is only a small part of a vast readiness plan. A close intelligence watch is kept on any potential enemy and this might be said to be Bomber Command's first line of defence.

Line up of Avro Vulcan and Victor bombers in white anti-flash scheme at Scampton in Linconshire.

RAF Handley Page Victor and Avro Vulcan V-bombers at Richmond, NSW, Australia in 1964. (Alec Crisdale)

As international tension increases so does the readiness of the bombers. States of readiness range from 'Blue Alert,' which is thirty minutes warning, to the cockpit readiness of 'Amber Alert' which means that the bombers could be away well within four minutes. As a double safety measure Bomber Command is giving close attention to the policy of dispersal. Just how effective this was I was able to see for myself during the recent 'Mayflight Matador' exercise of Bomber and Fighter Command.

'For the purpose of the exercise it was assumed that international tension was greatly increased. It reached a stage where war seemed inevitable and then at Bomber Command headquarters at High Wycombe, Bucks, it was decided that the 'V' force should be dispersed. Aircraft concentrated at their bases in Squadrons were quickly on their way to pre-arranged dispersal fields covering all the United Kingdom. In a 600-miles flight covering East, Central and Western England I flew over many airfields where four 'V' bombers were parked ready for takeoff but away from the main part of the establishment. At that time there were no more than four 'V' bombers at any one airfield in the United Kingdom.

'At a secret west of England dispersal I dropped in on the crews of four Victors. They had been there for two days waiting and wondering if the alert would go any further. They were at fifteen minutes readiness. It was a stiff test of stamina and nerves. While I was there chatting to the crews, busy playing cards, sunbathing (as far as full flying kit would allow) or otherwise passing away the time, loudspeakers blared out the fact that the alert had changed to 'Amber' - four minutes readiness. Immediately cards were dropped and the crews raced for their aircraft. The four Victors were already at 'scramble ready.' Another long wait. Then scramble link from Bomber HQ which was connected to each aircraft came the order 'Scramble! Scramble! Scramble!' Sixteen Sapphire engines were started simultaneously and well within four minutes the Victors had swung round a length of specially laid taxi-track, on to the runway and were off. So much importance is attached to this scramble and dispersal techniques that all 'V' bombers have been specially modified so that all four engines can be started at once instead of the normal practice of starting one engine at a time. In this way valuable seconds are saved. At the dispersal airfields special bays have been equipped with caravans for the crews and a temporary command post.

'Normally planning for a training flight involving simulated attacks takes up more than one working day of the navigator's time, but this fact is not allowed to slow up 'scramble' procedure. Each Bomber Command crew is allotted its own target to be attacked if the Cold War should become 'hot.' All navigation work in connection with this is already worked out and only last minute meteorological and timing details need to be inserted When the order 'scramble 'is given it does not merely get the bombers off the ground. It sets in motion the whole master plan of Bomber Command. Each aircraft will fly off towards its allotted target - but it will not go beyond a certain line unless further coded orders tell it to proceed Thus the use of manned bombers allows for a certain amount of 'brinkmanship' to be used in the early stages of any global outbreak if politicians should decide that this is necessary - a point difficult to achieve with missiles. A last link in the Bomber Command intelligence system will be the Fylingdales early warning radar on the Yorkshire Moors. This will provide adequate warning of any missile attack.

'But it is in the last part of the Bomber Command 'creed' that most interest must lie. Is it capable of destroying the enemy's will to fight? This is simply a question of men and machines. Much publicity has recently been given to the fact that, at the age of 23 and straight from training, a young pilot can become the captain of a 'V' Bomber. This may have taken away some of the mystery attached to flying these aircraft but it does not mean any drop in the standards of the crews. They continue to be the most carefully chosen members of any of the armed services. It is the machines of Bomber Command, however which have received the main brunt of any criticism in recent years. Can the manned bombers which comprise the bulk of Britain's attacking force, really function satisfactorily in this missile age? A few years ago Britain was on the verge of becoming entirely dependent on inter-Continental missiles for her deterrent. This policy was finally reversed - and for very good reasons. An all missile force would be inflexible. It could only be used in an all-out atomic war and it could not be effectively paraded around in front of other countries - an important point in this age when many nations are hovering between East and West and international prestige is vital.

'Therefore to be fully equipped to deal with both global and local wars Britain would

'Blue Steel' being hoisted into position aboard a Vulcan. Forty-eight live operational rounds were deployed on 48 Vulcan and Victor bombers and a further five live rounds were produced as operational spares. Blue Steel remained the primary British nuclear deterrent weapon until 1969 when the Royal Navy began operating Polaris missile armed Resolution-class submarines.

need both missiles and manned aircraft. She could not afford a complete arsenal of long-range missiles and a manned bomber force. Because it was felt that the 'V' Bombers could be as effective as missiles the wise decision was taken to build up a limited force of American Thor intermediate range ballistic missiles and pin the main deterrent task on the manned bombers. The result is a fully equipped nuclear deterrent force which, at the drop of a hat is able to double as a task force for use in non-nuclear local wars, for the 'V' bombers can operate just as well with high explosive bombs as well as nuclear bombs. But the vital question is 'Will the 'V' bombers be able to get through to their targets?' Obviously security bars a direct and detailed answer to this but what can be said is that morale in Bomber Command is extremely high.

'What we do know is that the Mark 1 versions of the Victor and Vulcan fly at high sub-sonic speeds and that their ceiling is above 50,000 feet. The difficulties of intercepting a target at this speed and altitude must not be underestimated. The Mark II versions are well on the way and the first Vulcan IIs are already in Squadron service. These will have significantly better performance both in speed and altitude. But speed and altitude are not the only criteria by which the bombers' ability to get through can be judged. Electronics play a vital part in aerial strategy today. Electronic Counter Measures is a phrase which is much bandied around. Its importance should not be under-estimated. It can be said that many Valiants are flying around packed with gear designed to disorganise enemy radar. Such is the importance of this operation that Victors are being used for it as well. On top of this the individual 'V' bombers each carry equipment to help protect them from the spying radars of enemy ground installations, missiles and fighters. How effective this equipment is has not been revealed but it is well-known that British electronic equipment is among the finest in the world.

'Given the ability to penetrate enemy defences, can Bomber Command go far enough to attack worthwhile targets. Again the picture is an encouraging one. The Mark I versions of the Vulcan and Victor, judging by their performances in long-distance training flights, should be able to reach as far East in Russia as a little beyond Magnitogorsk without re-fuelling. Inside this area is the majority of the populated parts of Russia, the missiles bases around Sverdlovsk, the Aral Sea and Archangel and large towns such as Moscow, Stalingrad, Leningrad and Odessa. All these places and many more could be reached by a Mark I 'V' bomber carrying a free-falling nuclear bomb. But in the future the picture improves even more. To the added range of the Mark II versions must be added again the range of Blue Steel, the British stand-off bomb and then, in 1964, the Douglas Skybolt. Development of Blue Steel appears to be progressing well and, there have been no postponements of delivery dates. Skybolt, on the other hand, has been surrounded by a sea of rumour ever since it was projected. The facts on Skybolt are these: there has been no cut-down in the cost allotted, to this missile in the USA and development has continued steadily. Britain is to get Skybolt concurrently with the USAF and will not be kept waiting until the Americans have had their fill. Skybolt has been designed not with a lot of technical breakthroughs in mind but to be a thoroughly reliable missile. Therefore no difficult new problems are expected to cause long hold ups in the development programme. This missile will add 1,000 miles to the effective range of the aircraft which carries it. It is expected that Britain's deterrent will be based mainly on the 'V' bombers for the next ten years - ten years during which the effectiveness of the force should steadily improve. But after that time a replacement weapon will have to be found. Current thinking is still veering away from missiles although by 1970 the world picture may well be a little different. At the moment, however, the most likely successor to the Victor and Vulcan seems to be an aircraft similar in concept to the TSR-2 - a low level, supersonic long-range attack aircraft capable of sneaking below enemy radar coverage.

A Strategic Air Command Alert Crew runs to man RB-52B-15-BO 52-8711 of the 22nd Bombardment Wing (Heavy) at March AFB, California. This aircraft, which has the unit insignia *'Ducemus'* ('we shall lead, we shall guide') on the side of the nose, was the first Stratofortress to be delivered to SAC, arriving at Castle AFB, California on 29 June 1955 and was assigned to the 93rd Bombardment Wing (Heavy). 52-8711 is now in a protected environment at the Strategic Air and Space Museum, Ashland, Nebraska. (USAF)

'But at the present it cannot be denied that Bomber Command is a force with a great potential. Strict attention to training ensures that the crews are able to make the most of their aircraft's capabilities. Regular overseas 'Lone Ranger' flights ensure that they are used to flying and navigating in a wide variety of climates.

'Recently I accompanied the crew of a Victor la of 55 Squadron on a four-hour training flight. During it we, with many other bombers, acted as 'Stooges' for RAF Fighter Command. But we also carried out simulated attacks on targets in Norway and on others in the United Kingdom. Each one of our attacks was carefully logged and assessed by markers on the ground. The results were forwarded to Bomber Command so that a strict check could be kept on the accuracy of the crews.

'Like all 'V' bombers the Victor la was comfortable, quiet, smooth and had a high level of pressurisation. It was, at times, difficult to imagine that we were engaged in a war-like operation. Only the seriousness and efficiency of the crew pointed to the fact that this was no pleasure trip. For one point above all others must be stressed: Bomber Command means business.'

SAC came closest to launching a retaliatory nuclear attack during the Cuban Missile Crisis in mid-October 1962 following Russia's decision to base Il-28 'Beagle' medium bombers and SS-4 'Sandal' medium range and SS-5 'Skean' intermediate-range ballistic missiles (IRBMs) on Cuba, just one hundred miles from the USA. On Monday evening, 22 October, as President Kennedy went on national television to announce the presence of missiles on Cuba SAC cancelled all leaves and put battle staffs on twenty-four hour operations. Fifty-four B-52s carrying hydrogen bombs took off to join twelve already on airborne alert. One of them circled Thule AFB in Greenland to report on any Soviet strike on the early-warning system. US forces in the crisis went to Defense Condition 3. All SAC's 1,519 attack aircraft were loaded with nuclear weapons and as the crisis deepened SAC's 136 ICBMs were brought to a higher state of alert and fifty-seven B-52s and sixty-one tankers went to Defcon 2 or continuous airborne alert. No B-52 could land before its replacement aircraft was airborne. The next stage - Defcon 1 - would mean nuclear war. President Kennedy's 'Big Stick' had the desired effect. On 24 October shipping carrying the missiles to Cuba came to a stop in mid-Atlantic and on 28 October Soviet Premier, Nikita Khrushchev agreed to remove the aircraft from Cuba. But SAC did not stand down the alert until 21 November when a B-52H of the 379th Bomb Wing returned to its home base at Wurtsmith AFB, Michigan. [54]

In the US 'Steeltrap' and 'Chrome Dome' airborne alert operations involving B-52s carrying live nuclear bombs ceased in 1968 after a fifth and final incident involving B-52s carrying nuclear bombs, on 21 January when a B-52G plunged into the sea ice of North Star Bay seven miles south-west of the Thule base at 560 mph. On impact the primaries of all four MK28 nuclear weapons detonated, blasting plutonium and uranium over a wide area. A fire fed by 35,000 gallons of jet fuel subsequently destroyed most bomb fragments. The fire burned for twenty minutes with a 2,200 feet long smoke plume, which covered an area 2,000 feet wide. A complete MK28 secondary assembly melted through the ice and settled on the sea floor. It has never been retrieved. About 237,000 cubic feet of contaminated ice, snow and water and crash debris were removed from a three square mile, twenty-six acre area during a near eight-month clean-up operation by an American recovery team, in cooperation with the Danish Government to a storage facility in the United States. This accident and an earlier one in Spain hastened the demise of the airborne alert programme whose costs were by now becoming prohibitive. In any event a large part of the more sophisticated and survivable ICBM force was proving a more cost-effective deterrent. [55]

Endnotes for Chapter 6

54 'Used effectively to stem the Cuban Crisis, the 'Chrome Dome' tactic challenged the B-52 combat crew force to reach new heights. Take off fully loaded with fuel and nuclear weapons (a gross weight of almost 300,000lbs), fly a pre-designated route and refuel twice in the air (taking on 120,000lbs of fuel during each refuelling) and remain airborne until relieved approximately twenty-five hours later by the next Chrome Dome' aircraft. The key element of the 'Chrome Dome' mission was to position the bombers in such standoff orbiting patterns that they could respond in a relatively short time to pre-designated targets in the Soviet Union if directed by the NCA.' Adams, Chris, *Inside the Cold War: A Cold Warrior's Reflections*. Air University Press, Maxwell AFB, Alabama, September 1999.

55 Vulcans and Victors continued to provide a British nuclear deterrent until 1969 when the Polaris fleet became operational. In the US thirty-four years of Ground Alert duty finally ended on 18 September 1991 although it was made abundantly clear that America remained prepared for nuclear war with ICBMs and a proportion of its bomber fleet could be returned to alert status if needed.

Chapter Seven

Yom Kippur (Ramadan) War

In 1973 the Sinai was once again the arena of conflict between the Israelis and the Egyptians, the fifth such occasion. The Yom Kippur or Ramadan War, also known as the Arab-Israeli War, was a war fought by the coalition of Arab states led by Egypt and Syria against Israel from 6 to 25 October. The war began when the Arab coalition launched a joint surprise attack on Israeli positions in the Israeli-occupied territories on Yom Kippur, the holiest day in Judaism, which occurred that year during the Muslim holy month of Ramadan. Egyptian and Syrian forces crossed ceasefire lines to enter the Sinai Peninsula and Golan Heights respectively, which had been captured by Israel in the 1967 Six-Day War. Both the United States and the Soviet Union initiated massive resupply efforts to their respective allies during the war and this led to a near-confrontation between the two nuclear superpowers.

The 1967 Arab-Israeli War laid the foundation for future discord in the Middle East. Massive re-re-equipment of the Tsvah Haganah le Israel - Heyl ha'Avir (Israel Defence Force - Air Force) followed and late that same year Israel ordered forty-eight Douglas A-4H Skyhawks and TA-4H trainers. On 1 July 1968 Israel and the US signed the 'Peace Echo' agreement for the supply of fifty F-4Es and six RF-4Es to the Heyl ha'Avir. These entered service with three squadrons in 1969.[52] On 10 March 1969 McDonnell Douglas and Israel Aircraft Industries concluded a licensing and technical assistance agreement and deliveries began in September

Tail of an Egyptian MiG-17 at Ofira after the dogfight over Sharm el-Sheikh on the southern tip of the Sinai Peninsula, one of the first air battles of the Yom Kippur War, on 6 October 1973 when over 200 Egyptian aircraft took part in a massive surprise attack on Israel. Two IAF Phantoms reportedly engaged 20 MiG-17s and their eight MiG-21 escorts and in a brief six-minute battle, seven MiGs were confirmed destroyed.

Right: An IAF attack on Nazaria air base in Northern Syria.

Below: Syrian antiaircraft missile site twenty-five miles southeast of Damascus under heavy attack by IAF fighter-bombers.

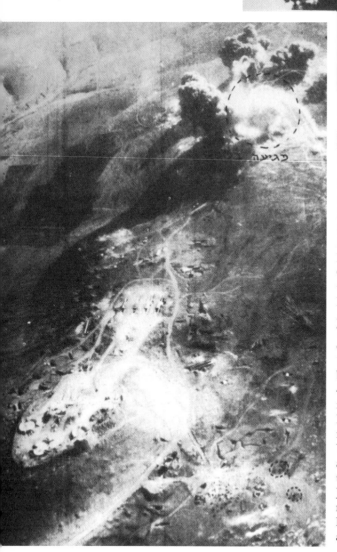

1969. (In total the Heyl ha'Avir received 240 F-4Es, including 86 Phantoms ordered under FMS contracts and F-4Es transferred from the USAF inventory). Following increased tension, on 22 October 1969, just six weeks after the Phantoms entered service, the F-4Es went into action with strikes against SAM missile sites in Egypt. The first Phantom victory occurred on 11 November. In early January 1970 the first deep penetration bombing raids took place. While A-4s attacked artillery and fortifications the F-4s flew far into Egypt attacking camps and military installations in the Nile Valley near Cairo. A few days later a massive attack was carried out on targets in Cairo itself and on 13 January the IAF raided SAM sites near Cairo International Airport. MiG-21J interceptors made their appearance in the spring and many battles ensued. Finally, an American- sponsored ceasefire came into effect on 7 August 1970.

From the end of 1972, Egypt began a concentrated effort to build up its forces, receiving MiG-21 jet fighters, anti-aircraft missiles, T-55 and T-62 tanks, RPG-7 anti-tank weapons and the AT-3 'Sagger' anti-tank guided missile from the Soviet Union and improving its military tactics, based on Soviet battlefield doctrines. Political generals, who had in large part been responsible for the rout in 1967, were replaced with competent ones. President Gamal Abdel Nasser of Egypt died in September 1970 and was succeeded by President Anwar Sadat. In a 24 October 1972 meeting with his Supreme Council of the Armed Forces, Sadat declared his intention to go to war with Israel even without proper Soviet support. Planning had begun in 1971 and was conducted in absolute secrecy - even the upper-echelon commanders were not told of war plans until less than a week prior to the attack and the soldiers were not told until a few hours beforehand. The plan to attack Israel in concert with Syria was code-named Operation 'Badr' (Arabic for 'full moon') after the Battle of Badr in which Muslims under Muhammad defeated the Quraish tribe of Mecca.

By 1973 Israel was faced by Arab air forces largely equipped with Soviet-supplied aircraft and hundreds of SA-2 'Guideline', -3 'Goa' and -6 'Gainful' SAM missiles, SA-7 'Grail' infrared directed, shoulder launched AA missiles and ZSU-23-4 Shika radar-directed mobile AA guns. The interlocking air defence system was superior even to the belt protecting Hànôi in the Viêtnam War. The Hey! ha'Avir had 432 aircraft in its inventory, of which Phantoms were the second most numerous aircraft, against 600 aircraft operated by Egypt and 210 by Syria.

Several times during 1973, Arab forces conducted large-scale exercises that put the Israeli military on the highest level of alert, only to be recalled a few days later. The Israeli leadership already believed that if an attack took place, the Heyl ha'Avir could repel it. By mid-1973 however, Israeli Intelligence knew that the Egyptian Second and Third Armies would attempt to cross the Suez Canal and advance ten kilometres into the Sinai, followed by armoured divisions that would advance towards the Mitla and Gidi passes and that naval units and paratroopers would then attempt to capture Sharm-el-Sheikh. The Israelis were also aware of many details of the Syrian war plan. In April and May 1973 they began picking up clear signals of Egypt's intentions for war, recognizing that it had the necessary divisions and bridging equipment to cross the Suez Canal and a missile umbrella to protect any crossing operation from air attack. In May and August the Egyptian Army conducted military exercises near the border and the Israeli Army was mobilized at considerable cost. These exercises were to ensure that the Israelis would dismiss the actual war preparations right before the attack was

launched as another exercise. For the week leading up to Yom Kippur, the Egyptian army staged a week-long training exercise adjacent to the Suez Canal. Movements of Syrian troops towards the border were also detected, as were cancellation of leaves and a call-up of reserves in the Syrian army. These activities were not considered a threat

MiG-21 kill by Major Moshe Meinick in a IAF F4E Phantom.

IAF Phantom over a Israeli armoured column.

because Israel believed that Syria would not attack without Egypt and Egypt would not attack until they were supplied MiG-23 fighter-bombers to neutralize the IAF and Scud missiles for use against Israeli cities as a deterrent against Israeli attacks on Egyptian infrastructure. No MiG-23s had been received and Scud missiles only arrived in Egypt from Bulgaria in late August and it would take four months to train the Egyptian ground crews. Even so, Israel sent reinforcements to the Golan Heights, which were to prove critical during the early days of the war.

Anticipating that Israel might not be prepared, Egypt and Syria invaded Israel on 6 October 1973 - Yom Kippur, the Jewish fast day. According to General El-Gamasy, 'On the initiative of the operations staff, we reviewed the situation on the ground and developed a framework for the planned offensive operation. We studied the technical characteristics of the Suez Canal, the ebb and the flow of the tides, the speed of the currents and their direction, hours of darkness and of moonlight, weather conditions and related conditions in the

Mediterranean and Red Sea.' He explained further by saying: 'Saturday 6 October 1973 was the day chosen for the September-October option. Conditions for a crossing were good, it was a feast day in Israel and the moon on that day, 10 Ramadan, shone from sunset until midnight.' The war coincided that year with the Muslim month of Ramadan, when many Arab Muslim soldiers also fast. Ironically, the attack being launched on Yom Kippur may have helped Israel to more easily marshal reserves from their homes and synagogues, because roads and communication lines were largely open and this eased mobilizing and transporting the military.

Upon learning of the impending attack, Prime Minister of Israel Golda Meir made the controversial decision not to launch a pre-emptive strike for fear of being accused of starting the war. 'If we strike first, we won't get help from anybody', she said. Early on 6 October, Golda Meir agreed to the mobilization of the entire Air Force and four armoured divisions, a total of 100,000 to 120,000 troops. Operation 'Badr' began at 2:00pm on 6 October under cover of an artillery barrage and the Egyptian assault force of 32,000 infantry began crossing the Suez Canal in twelve waves at five separate crossing areas. Facing them were 450 soldiers of the Jerusalem Brigade, spread out in sixteen forts along the length of the Canal. There were 290 Israeli tanks in all of Sinai divided into three armoured brigades and only one of these was deployed near the Canal when hostilities commenced. The Heyl ha'Avir conducted air interdiction operations to try to prevent bridges from being erected, but took losses from Egyptian SAM batteries. The air attacks were ineffective overall, as the sectional design of the bridges enabled quick repair when hit. A concentrated air attack by 250 Egyptian aircraft well-coordinated between the Egyptian and Syrian fronts and other services of the Arab armed forces conducted simultaneous strikes against the Meleez, Thamad and Ras Nasrani air bases, ten Hawk surface-to-air missile batteries, three command centres, two long-range artillery positions and three radar positions and direction and warning stations; two interference and

Strike camera of an IAF Phantom pilot who took this picture of his wingman chasing an Egyptian MiG-17 low over the Sinai before destroying it moments later.

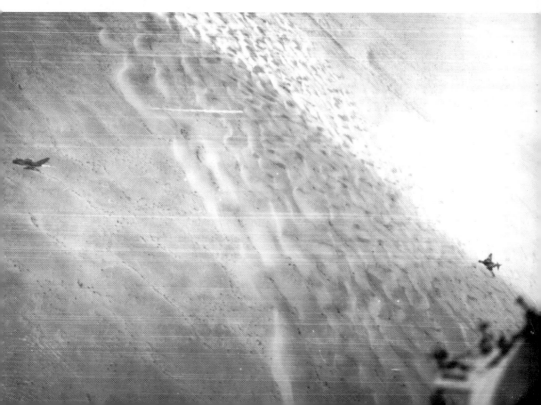

jamming stations in the Sinai (Om Khushaib and Om Margam); three logistics areas; and the strongpoint east of Port Fuad. Airfields at Refidim and Bir Tamada were temporarily put out of operation and damage was inflicted on a Hawk battery at Ophir.

Egypt acknowledged the loss of five aircraft during the attack (eighteen Egyptian aircraft were shot down and these losses prompted the cancellation of the second planned wave). In one notable engagement during this period, a pair of Israeli F-4E Phantoms challenged 28 Egyptian MiGs over Sharm-el-Sheikh and within half an hour, shot down between seven and eight MiGs without loss. One of the Egyptian pilots killed was Captain Atif Sadat, President Sadat's half-brother. Simultaneously, fourteen Egyptian Tupolev Tu-16 bombers attacked Israeli targets in the Sinai with 'Kelt' missiles, while another two Egyptian Tupolevs fired two 'Kelt' missiles at a radar station in central Israel. One missile was shot down by a patrolling Israeli Mirage fighter and the second fell into the sea. The attack was an attempt to warn Israel that Egypt could retaliate if it bombed targets deep in Egyptian territory.

Large bridgeheads were established on the east bank on 6 October and Egyptian forces advanced approximately four to five kilometres into the Sinai Desert with two armies. By the following morning, 850 tanks had crossed the canal. For the next several days, the Heyl ha'Avir played a minimal role in the fighting largely because it was needed to deal with the simultaneous and ultimately more threatening, Syrian invasion of the Golan Heights.

Israeli armoured forces launched counter-attacks on the Egyptian forces from 6 to 8 October, but they were often piecemeal and inadequately supported and were beaten back principally by Egyptians using portable anti-tank missiles. The scale and effectiveness of the Egyptian strategy of deploying anti-tank weapons coupled with the Israelis' inability to disrupt their use with close air support (due to the SAM shield) greatly contributed to Israeli setbacks early in the war. Israel, which had invested much of its defence budget building the region's strongest air force, would see the effectiveness of its air force curtailed in the initial phases of the conflict by the SAM presence.

Egypt (and Syria) had heavily fortified their side of the ceasefire lines with SAM batteries provided by the Soviet Union, against which the Israeli Air Force had no time to execute a Suppression of Enemy Air Defences (SEAD) operation due to the element of surprise. As a result, the IAF was obliged to mount long-range strike missions against enemy ground forces in Egypt and the Suez Canal zone before tackling the SAMs. On 7 October the Israelis planned a cautious counter-attack for the following day. The same day, the IAF carried out Operation 'Tagar', aiming to neutralize Egyptian Air Force bases and its missile defence shield. Seven

Propaganda picture of Israeli pilots and F-4 Phantoms taking off.

Camera-gun footage of a MiG-21 kill by Major Moshe Meinick in a IAF F4E Phantom.

Egyptian airbases were damaged with the loss of two A-4 Skyhawks and their pilots. Two more planned attacks were called off due to the increasing need for airpower on the Syrian front. The Heyl ha'Avir carried out additional air attacks against Egyptian forces on the east bank of the canal, reportedly inflicting heavy losses. Israeli jets had carried out hundreds of sorties against Egyptian targets by the following day, but the Egyptian SAM shield had taken a toll and losses had mounted to three aircraft for every 200 sorties, an unsustainable rate. The Heyl ha'Avir lost thirty-three of its 140 F-4Es, mainly to SAMs. Israel admitted to total losses of 115 aircraft (US estimates were nearer 200) sixty of them in the first week of the Yom Kippur War. To evade the SA-2 the F-4E pilots found that they had to enter the zone of the SA-6 and there the only effective counter action was to dive inside and below the missile before it had time to gain high altitude and speed. Then they ran headlong into the range of the SA-7 and SA-9 and the massed array of ZSU-23-4s. Israel was supplied with AGM-54A 'Shrike' anti-radiation missiles but these were largely unsuccessful against the continuous wave-guidance SA-6, which the Phantoms had great difficulty in outmaneuvering once they had been launched. Eventually the IAF gained the upper hand on the Sinai Front by making massed attacks using squadrons of attacking aircraft rather than in groups of four and ground targets were bombed accurately by American-supplied 'smart' bombs and the F-4Es were fitted with decoy flares to counter the heat-seeking SAMs.

The Syrians co-ordinated their attack on the Golan Heights to coincide with the Egyptian offensive and initially made threatening gains into Israeli-held territory. Within three days, however, Israeli forces had managed to push the Syrians back to the pre-war ceasefire lines. They then launched a four-day counter-offensive deep into Syria. Within a week, Israeli artillery began to shell the outskirts of Damascus. As Egyptian president Anwar Sadat began to worry about the integrity of his major ally, he believed that capturing two strategic passes located deeper in the Sinai would make his position stronger during the negotiations. He therefore ordered the Egyptians to go back on the offensive, but the attack was quickly repulsed. The Israelis then counterattacked at the seam between the two Egyptian armies, crossed the Suez Canal into Egypt and began slowly advancing southward and westward towards Cairo in over a week of heavy fighting that inflicted heavy casualties on both sides.

The Heyl ha'Avir initially lost forty aircraft to Syrian anti-aircraft batteries, but Israeli pilots soon adopted a different tactic; flying in low over Jordan and diving in over the Golan Heights, catching the Syrians in the flank and avoiding many of their batteries. Israeli aircraft dropped conventional bombs and napalm, devastating Syrian armoured columns. However, the Syrian Air Force repeatedly struck Israeli positions during this period. On the second day of the war, the Heyl ha'Avir attempted to take out the Syrian anti-aircraft batteries. Codenamed 'Doogman 5', the attempt was a costly failure. The Israelis destroyed one Syrian missile battery and lost six aircraft. On 9 October, Syrian FROG-7 surface-to-surface missiles struck the IAF base of Ramat David, killing a pilot and injuring several soldiers. Additional missiles struck civilian settlements. In retaliation, seven Israeli F-4 Phantoms flew into Syria and struck the Syrian General Staff Headquarters in Damascus. The jets attacked from Lebanese airspace to avoid the heavily defended regions around the Golan Heights, attacking a Lebanese radar station along the way. The upper floors of the Syrian GHQ and the Air Force Command were badly damaged. A Soviet cultural centre, a television station and other nearby structures were also mistakenly hit. One Israeli Phantom was shot down. The strike prompted the Syrians to transfer air defence units from the Golan Heights to the home front, allowing the Heyl ha'Avir greater freedom of action. The Syrian Air Force attacked Israeli columns, but its operations were highly limited due to Israeli air superiority and it suffered heavy losses in dogfights with Israeli jets.[53]

By 8 October, Israel had encountered military difficulties on both fronts. In the Sinai, Israeli efforts to break through Egyptian lines with armour had been thwarted and while Israel had contained and begun to turn back the Syrian advance, Syrian forces were still overlooking the Jordan River and their air defence systems were inflicting a high toll on Israeli aircraft. It became clear by 9 October that no quick reversal in Israel's favour would occur and that IDF losses were unexpectedly high. During the night of 8/9 October, an alarmed Dayan told Golda Meir that 'this is the end of the third temple.' He was warning of Israel's impending total

Since 1966, Israel purchased 217 A-4s, plus another forty-six transferred from US forces to compensate for large losses during the Yom Kippur War when A-4s flew 4,695 sorties, losing fifty-three aircraft. The primary ground attack aircraft in the War of Attrition and the Yom Kippur War, they bore the brunt of losses to SA-6 Gainful missile batteries and AAA, partially because of their relatively low penetration speed. At least nine A-4 Skyhawks were downed by MiG-21s and MiG-17s. The A-4E (re-designated A-4H for Hebrew) had a larger-area square-tipped fin, a 'camel hump' avionics fairing and twin 30mm DEFA cannon in place of the USN 20mm weapons.

defeat, but 'Temple' was also the code word for nuclear weapons. In a cabinet meeting Dayan warned that Israel was approaching a point of 'last resort'. That night Meir authorized the assembly of thirteen 20-kiloton-of-TNT (84 TJ) tactical atomic weapons for 'Jericho' missiles at Sdot Micha Airbase and F-4 Phantoms at Tel Nof Airbase, for use against Syrian and Egyptian targets. They would be used if absolutely necessary to prevent total defeat, but the preparations were carried out overtly and the United States learned of the nuclear alert on the morning of 9 October. President Nixon ordered the commencement of Operation 'Nickel Grass', an American airlift to replace all of Israel's material losses. Israel began receiving supplies via US Air Force cargo planes on 14 October, although some equipment had arrived on aircraft from Israel's national airline El Al before this date. By that time, the IDF had advanced deep into Syria and was mounting a largely successful invasion of the Egyptian mainland from the Sinai, but had taken severe material losses. By the end of 'Nickel Grass', the United States had shipped 22,395 tons of matériel to Israel.[54]

By 9 October when the IDF chose to concentrate its reserves and build up its supplies while the Egyptians remained on the strategic defensive, the Egyptians were unable to advance further. The Egyptian units generally would not advance beyond a shallow strip for fear of losing the protection of their surface-to-air missile (SAM) batteries, which were situated on the west bank of the canal. Between 10 and 13 October, both sides refrained from any large-scale actions and the situation was relatively stable. It was decided to counter-attack once Egyptian armour attempted to expand the bridgehead beyond the protective SAM umbrella and Operation 'Gazelle' was launched on 15 October. IDF forces spearheaded by Ariel Sharon's division broke through the Tasa corridor and crossed the Suez Canal to the north of the Great Bitter Lake. After intense fighting, the IDF progressed towards Cairo and advanced southwards on the east bank of the Great Bitter Lake and in the southern extent of the canal right up to Port Suez.

On 13 and 15 October, Egyptian air defence radars detected an aircraft at an altitude of 82,000 feet and a speed of Mach 3, making it impossible to intercept either by fighter or SAM missiles. The aircraft proceeded to cross the whole of the Canal Zone, the naval ports of the Red Sea (Hurghada and Safaga), flew over the airbases and air defences in the Nile delta and finally disappeared from radar screens over the Mediterranean Sea. The speed and altitude were those of the SR-71A 'Blackbird' long-range strategic-reconnaissance aircraft. According to Egyptian commanders, the intelligence provided by the reconnaissance flights helped the Israelis prepare for the Egyptian attack on 14 October and assisted it in conducting Operation 'Stouthearted Men'.

On the night of 15 October, 750 Israeli paratroopers crossed the canal in rubber dinghies. They were soon joined by tanks ferried on motorized rafts and additional infantry. The force encountered no resistance initially and fanned out in raiding parties, attacking supply convoys, SAM sites, logistic centres and anything of military value, with priority given to the SAMs. Attacks on SAM sites punched a hole in the Egyptian anti-aircraft screen and enabled the Heyl ha'Avir to more aggressively strike Egyptian ground targets. The combination of a weakened Egyptian SAM umbrella and a greater concentration of Israeli fighter-bombers meant that the Heyl ha'Avir was capable of greatly increasing sorties against Egyptian military targets, including convoys, armour and airfields. The Egyptian bridges across the canal were damaged in Israeli air and artillery attacks. Israeli jets began attacking Egyptian SAM sites and radars, prompting General Ismail to withdraw much of the Egyptians' air defence equipment. This in turn gave the Heyl ha'Avir greater freedom to operate in Egyptian airspace. Israeli jets also attacked and destroyed underground communication cables at Banha in the Nile Delta, forcing the Egyptians to transmit selective messages by radio, which could be intercepted. Aside from the cables at Banha, Israel refrained from attacking economic and strategic infrastructure following an Egyptian threat to retaliate against Israeli cities with Scud missiles. Israeli aircraft bombed Egyptian Scud batteries at Port Said several times. The

About 220 F-4Es and RF-4Es were delivered to the Tsvah Haganah le Israel/Heyl Ha'Avir between 1969 and 1976 under US aid programmes. In Israeli service the F-4E was known as Kurnass ('Heavy Hammer') and the RF-4E Orev ('Raven').

Egyptian Air Force attempted to interdict IAF sorties and attack Israeli ground forces, but suffered heavy losses in dogfights and from Israeli air defences, while inflicting light aircraft losses on the Israelis. The heaviest air battles took place over the northern Nile Delta, where the Israelis repeatedly attempted to destroy Egyptian airbases.

On 16 October IDF forces attacked entrenched Egyptian forces overlooking the roads to the canal. After three days of bitter and close-quarters fighting, the Israelis succeeded in dislodging the numerically superior Egyptian forces and Israeli forces began pouring across the canal on two bridges and motorized rafts. On 21 October Israeli troops occupied Ismailia city's outskirts. The Israelis continued to expand their hold on the east bank and claimed that the IDF bridgehead was twenty-five miles wide and twenty miles deep by the end of the day. The Israelis slowly advanced, bypassing Egyptian positions whenever possible. Israeli forces shelled and destroyed the SAMs, allowing the IAF to provide close air support. When a ceasefire came into effect on 22 October, Israel had lost territory on the east side of the Suez Canal to Egypt but gained territory west of the canal and in the Golan Heights but the ceasefire broke down and fighting was renewed. On 23 October, a large air battle took place near Damascus during which the Israelis shot down ten Syrian aircraft. The Syrians claimed a similar toll against Israel. The IDF also destroyed the Syrian missile defence system. The Heyl ha'Avir utilized its air superiority to attack strategic targets throughout Syria, including important power plants, petrol supplies, bridges and main roads. The strikes damaged the Syrian war effort, disrupted Soviet efforts to airlift military equipment into Syria and disrupted normal life inside the country.

By 24 October, the Israelis had improved their positions considerably and completed their encirclement of Egypt's Third Army and the city of Suez. This development led to tensions between the United States and the Soviet Union. As a result, a second ceasefire was imposed co-operatively on 25 October to end the war. Though most heavy fighting ended on 28 October, the fighting never stopped until 18 January 1974. Israeli Defence Minister Moshe Dayan stated that 'The cease-fire existed on paper, but the continued firing along the front was not the only characteristic of the situation between 24 October 1973 and 18 January 1974. This intermediate period also held the ever-present possibility of a renewal of full-scale war. There were three variations on how it might break out, two Egyptian and one Israeli. One Egyptian plan was to attack our units west of the canal from the direction of Cairo. The other

During the Yom Kippur War the Skyhawk order of battle was reinforced with TA-4F and TA-4J models for operations as well as advanced training and retraining. The IAF at one time operated 278 A-4s (46 A-4E, 90 A-4H, 117 A-4N and 25 TA-4H). In 1968 the A4H/TA-4H aircraft were immediately pressed into service in the ongoing War of Attrition. In May 1970 the type scored its sole aerial kills with the IAF when Ezra Dotan shot down a pair of Syrian MiG-17s, one using unguided air-to-ground rockets.

was to cut-off our canal bridgehead by a link-up of the Second and Third Armies on the east bank. Both plans were based on massive artillery pounding of our forces, who were not well fortified and who would suffer heavy casualties. It was therefore thought that Israel would withdraw from the west bank, since she was most sensitive on the subject of soldier's lives. Egypt, at the time, had a total of 1,700 first-line tanks on both sides of the canal front, 700 on the east bank and 1,000 on the west bank. Also on the west bank, in the second line, were an additional 600 tanks for the defence of Cairo. She had some 2,000 artillery pieces, about 500 operational aircraft and at least 130 SAM missile batteries positioned around our forces so as to deny us air support.'

Israel devoted approximately half its fighters to fly cover over Sinai. Of the total 10,322 combat sorties that the Israelis flew on the Egyptian front from the 6 to the 22 October, 4,098 were flown as air cover. The Heyl ha'Avir lost 102 aircraft: thirty-two F-4s, fifty-three A-4s, eleven Mirages and six Super Mystères.[55] Two helicopters, a Bell 205 and a CH-53, were also lost. According to Defence Minister Moshe Dayan, nearly half of these were shot down during the first three days of the war. IAF losses per combat sortie were less than in the Six Day War of 1967. Between 341 and 514 Arab aircraft were shot down; 334 of these aircraft were shot down by the Israeli Air Force in air-to-air combat for the loss of only five Israeli aircraft. The last aerial engagement on the Egyptian front, which took place on 6 December, saw Israeli F-4s engage North Korean-piloted MiG-21s. The Israelis shot down one MiG and another was mistakenly shot down by Egyptian air defences. Egyptian sources said that the North Koreans suffered no losses but claimed no aerial victories in their engagements.

On 11 April 1974, Golda Meir resigned. Her cabinet followed suit, including Dayan, who had previously offered to resign twice and was turned down both times by Meir. A new government was seated in June and Yitzhak Rabin became Prime Minister. On 9 November 1977 Sadat stunned the world when he told parliament that he would be willing to visit Israel and address the Knesset. Sadat was assassinated on 6 October 1981 while attending a parade marking the eighth anniversary of the start of the war, by Islamist army members who were outraged at his negotiations with Israel.

Endnotes for Chapter 7

52   Israel obtained the loan of two RF-4Cs August 1970-March 1971 pending delivery of the RF-4Es which were increased to twelve with the delivery of a second batch.

53   Besides Egypt, Syria, Jordan and Iraq, several other Arab states were also involved in this war, providing additional weapons and financing. Algeria sent a squadron each of MiG-21s and Su-7s to Egypt, which arrived at the front between 9 and 11 October. Libya, which had forces stationed in Egypt before the outbreak of the war, provided two squadrons of Mirage V fighters, of which one squadron was to be piloted by the Egyptian Air Force and the other by Libyan pilots. In addition to its forces in Syria, Iraq sent a single Hawker Hunter squadron to Egypt. The squadron quickly gained a reputation amongst Egyptian field commanders for its skill in air support, particularly in anti-armour strikes. North Korea sent twenty pilots and 19 non-combat personnel to Egypt. The unit had four to six encounters with the Israelis from August until the end of the war. Pakistan Air Force pilots flew combat missions in Syrian aircraft and shot down one Israeli fighter.

54   C-141 Starlifter and C-5 Galaxy aircraft flew 567 missions throughout the airlift. El Al planes flew in an additional 5,500 tons of matériel in 170 flights. The airlift continued after the war until 14 November. The US also delivered approximately 90,000 tons of matériel to Israel by sealift until the beginning of December, using 16 ships. By the beginning of December, Israel had received between 34 to 40 F-4 fighter-bombers, 46 A-4 attack aircraft, twelve C-130 cargo planes, 8 CH-53 helicopters, 40 unmanned aerial vehicles, 200 M-60/M-48A3 tanks, 250 armoured personnel carriers, 226 utility vehicles, twelve MIM-72 Chaparral surface-to-air missile systems, three MIM-23 Hawk surface-to-air missile systems, 36 155mm artillery pieces, seven 175 mm artillery pieces, large quantities of 105 mm, 155 mm and 175 mm ammunition, state of the art equipment, such as the AGM-65 Maverick missile and the BGM-71 TOW; weapons that had only entered production one or more years prior, as well as highly advanced electronic jamming equipment. Most of the combat aircraft arrived during the war and many were taken directly from USAF units. Most of the large equipment arrived after the ceasefire. The total cost of the equipment was approximately US$800 million. Starting on 9 October, the Soviet Union began supplying Egypt and Syria by air and by sea. The Soviets airlifted 12,500-15,000 tons of supplies, of which 6,000 tons went to Egypt, 3,750 tons went to Syria and 575 tons went to Iraq. Arab losses were so high and the attrition rate so great that equipment was taken directly from Soviet and Warsaw Pact stores to supply the airlift. Antonov An-12 and AN-22 aircraft flew over 900 missions during the airlift. Israeli military intelligence reported that Soviet-piloted MiG-25 Foxbat interceptor/reconnaissance aircraft conducted flyovers over the Canal Zone.

55   Operation 'Nickle Grass' ensured that Israeli losses in the war were made good with the urgent delivery of 36 F-4Es from USAFE and TAC units. Many modifications were made to the F-4Es throughout their service life. A non-retractable refuelling probe canted upward and outboard to place the nozzle within easy sight of the pilot was attached to the starboard fuselage and connected to the dorsal fuel receptacle. Provision was also made for carrying indigenous 'Shafrir' and 'Python' air-to-air missiles and 'Gabriel' air-to-surface missiles, Elta EL/M-2021 radar and a forward-looking infrared (FLIR) sensor. The 20mm M-61A1 rotary gun was replaced by two 30mm DEFA cannon. On 3/4 July 1976 Israeli Phantoms escorted Lockheed C-130s and Boeing 707s over the Red Sea en route to Uganda during the daring rescue of hostages in Entebbe. By 1978 204 F-4Es had been delivered to the Heyl ha'Avir, of which about 65 had been lost in combat and operational accidents. In June 1982 when Israeli forces invaded Lebanon and fought against Syrian forces, F-4Es armed with anti-radiation missiles and bombs attacked and destroyed Syrian SAM batteries in the Bekaa Valley. By now Israel had F-15s and F-16s and Kfir (lion cub') C-2 air superiority fighters, which nullified the Syrian fighters. The Israeli Aircraft Industries' Kfir was an improved version of the Mirage IIICJ which was built following General de Gaulle's refusal to sanction delivery of fifty Mirage VJs which had been developed for Israel after the IAF asked Dassault in 1966 to build a simplified version of the Mirage IIIE optimised for the daytime VFR ground-attack mission. By the end of the decade 110 F-4Es still equipped five squadrons of the *Heyl ha'Avir*. Israel planned to replace the J79 engines with 20,600lb thrust Pratt & Whitney PW1120 engines, fit canard surfaces, install more modern systems and equipment and strengthen the airframes to extend service life, but budgetary considerations forced most improvements to be cancelled. By now most of the Phantoms were high-time aircraft and it would not be very cost effective to modernize them.

Chapter Eight

Carrier-borne Combat Viêtnam 1964-1973

Air-to-air warfare in Southeast Asia began on 3 April 1965 when a US Navy strike force of four F-8Es bombing the Thanh Hóa Bridge was attacked by MiG-17s. One Navy aircraft was damaged during the engagement. Until 17 June, on which day a US flight of F-4Bs downed two MiG-17s with Sparrow missiles, aerial engagements had been infrequent. By mid-1965 the air-to-air contest was well inderway. The aerial battles in Viêtnam bore little resemblance to the dogfights of World War II or even Korea. The equipment had become so sophisticated and the speed of aircraft so significantly increased that it took coordination and teamwork to kill a MiG. Every air-to-air encounter involved the ability and training of many people - support personnel, ground crews, strike and protective flight air crews and the airborne and ground-radar operators. Unlike the air-to-air engagements of previous wars, in which a single pilot pitted his aircraft against a single opponent, some modern aircraft required two-man crews, working as an integrated and well-disciplined team.

RF-8G Crusader of VFP-63 'Eyes of the Fleet' is catapulted off the flight deck of the USS *Kitty Hawk*, which was deployed to SE Asia in September 1963. The RF-8A of Lieutenant Charles 'Chuck' F. Klusmann of VFP-63 (PoW-escaped) was the first jet shot down and ejection of the air war in SE Asia, on 6 June 1964. F-8Es of VF-211 'Fighting Checkmates' from the USS *Hancock* were the first to tangle with NVAF MiG-17s, on 3 April 1965, when eight MiG-17PFs of the 921st 'Sao Đỏ' (Red Star) Fighter Regiment from Nội Bài northwest of Hànôi attacked a USN strike force attacking bridges at Hàm Rồng. The gun camera in the lead MiG, piloted by 31-year old Captain (later General) Phạm Ngọc Lan, revealed that his cannons had set an F-8 ablaze, but Lieutenant Commander Spence Thomas landed his damaged Crusader at Đà Nẵng; the remaining F-8Es returning safely to their carrier. Lan had to break off low on fuel and he crash landed on the banks of the Đuống River.

F-4B-19-MC Phantom BuNo 151485 of VF-21 'Free Lancers' dropping Mk 82 Snakeye bombs over Viêtnam. VF-21 was assigned to Carrier Air Wing 2 (CVW-2) aboard the aircraft carrier USS *Midway* (CVA-41) for a deployment to Viêtnam from 6 March to 23 November 1965. During a combat air patrol on 7 May 1968 this aircraft, now with VF-92 on the *Enterprise,* was part of a section of five F-4Bs led by Lieutenant Commander Ejnar S. Christensen that became engaged in a running fight with several MiGs of the VPAF 921st Regiment north of Vinh. BuNo 151485 was shot down by Nguyen Van Coc for his seventh aerial victory after he fired two R-3S Atoll missiles from an altitude of 4,900 feet. The F-4B burst into flames and crashed into the sea. Christenson and his Radar Intercept Officer, Lieutenant (jg) Worth A. Kramer ejected safely from their aircraft before impact and were recovered a short time later.

The Korean War had shaken the military might of America and it led to far-reaching changes in the equipment it would need to fight any similar war anywhere in the world. The Navy replaced its F9F Panther and F2H Banshee straight-winged jets with the F-4 Phantom and the Vought F-8 Crusader became the standard carrier-based fighter, although propeller-driven aircraft, like the Douglas A-1 Skyraider[56] still had a role to play. Ed Heinmann's Douglas A-4 Skyhawk was designed to replace the Skyraider and fulfill a multiplicity of roles for the Navy, including interceptor and nuclear weapons carrier, but for a while both aircraft served alongside each other when war broke out in South-East Asia. The Republic of South Viêtnam was created in July 1954 using the 17th Parallel to separate it from the Communist North. However, Hô Chi Minh's Viêt Minh forces, led by General Võ Nguyên Giáp, planned to take over control of the South using a new Communist guerrilla force called the Viêt Công (VC) or National Liberation Front (NLF). The VC campaign increased in intensity in 1957 and finally, in 1960, Premier Ngo Dinh Diem appealed to the United States for help. In 1961 'special advisers' were sent in and later President Lyndon B. Johnson began the first moves, which would lead to total American involvement in Viêtnam.

When, in 1964, two Crusaders were brought down during a reconnaissance mission over Laos, the USAF flew a retaliatory strike on 9 June against AAA sites. On 2 August, against the background of open warfare in Laos, and increasing infiltration across the North/South Viêtnamese border, North Viêtnamese torpedo boats attacked the destroyer USS *Maddox* in international waters in the Gulf of Tonkin. The destroyer was cruising along a patrol line in the northern region of the Gulf in order to gather intelligence as part of Operation 'Plan 34A'. This was a covert campaign that started in February 1964 and it was intended to deter the North Viêtnamese from infiltrating the South. One of the torpedo boats that attacked the *Maddox* was sunk by a flight of four F-8E Crusaders led by 40-year old Commander James Bond Stockdale of VF-53 from the *Ticonderoga*, who made several strafing runs on the boats, firing their 20mm cannon and Zuni unguided rockets.[57]

During the night of 4/5 August *Maddox*, now reinforced by USS *Turner Joy*, returned to its station off the North Viêtnamese coast to listen for radio traffic and monitor communist naval activity. Shortly after a covert South Viêtnamese attack on a coastal radar station near Cua Rim, the two destroyers tracked on radar what they took to be enemy torpedo boats. Debate still rages whether there really was any North Viêtnamese boats in the vicinity of the two destroyers. Apparently no attack developed and no boats were seen by the pilots of the aircraft launched to provide air cover. However, the incident was enough to force President Johnson into ordering Operation 'Pierce Arrow', a limited retaliatory raid on military facilities in North Viêtnam. On 10 August the US Congress passed what came to be known as the Gulf of Tonkin Resolution which was as close as the US ever came to declaring war on North Viêtnam but which actually fell far short of that. The Gulf of Tonkin Incident also resulted in a major increase in US air strength in the Southeast Asia theatre and saw US involvement change from an advisory role to a more operational role, even though US aircraft and airmen had been participating in operations

A-4C 149574 of VA-153 'The Blue Tailed Flies' is launched from the deck of the USS *Coral Sea* off Viêtnam in 1965. On 25 June this Skyhawk and Commander Peter Mongilardi, CAG, Carrier Air Wing 15 was leading two other Skyhawks on an armed reconnaissance mission when he spotted a small bridge over the Sông Cho River about 10 miles northwest of Thanh Hóa. As the formation rolled into the attack, Mongilardi's aircraft was struck by 37mm flak. The first CAG to be lost in the war, he had been lucky to survive damage to his Skyhawk during the 29 March raid on Bạch Long Vĩ when he had to be 'towed' back to the carrier by a tanker as his aircraft was leaking fuel almost as fast as it was receiving it.

On 17 June 1965 two VF-21 'Freelancers' F-4Bs from the USS *Midway* (CVA-41) scored the first MiG kills of the war when they attacked four MiG-17s south of Hànôi and brought down two with AIM-7 Sparrow missiles. L-R: Commander Louis C. Page; Lieutenant John C. Smith; Lieutenant Jack E. D. Batson, Page's Radar Intercept Officer; and Lieutenant Commander Robert B. Doremus, Smith's RIO.

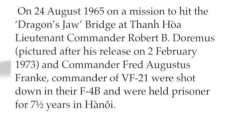

On 24 August 1965 on a mission to hit the 'Dragon's Jaw' Bridge at Thanh Hòa Lieutenant Commander Robert B. Doremus (pictured after his release on 2 February 1973) and Commander Fred Augustus Franke, commander of VF-21 were shot down in their F-4B and were held prisoner for 7½ years in Hànôi.

ever since they first arrived in the region.

The political and physical restrictions on the basing of us aircraft in South Viêtnam was to some extent solved by the permanent stationing of aircraft carriers in the South China Sea. By the end of August four aircraft carriers, the *Bon Homme Richard* (CVA-31), *Constellation*, *Kearsarge* and *Ticonderoga* had arrived in position in the Gulf and started a pattern of line duty that continued until August 1973. The carriers and their protecting forces constituted the US 7th Fleet's Task Force 77, which in March 1965 developed a pattern of positioning carriers at Yankee Station in the South China Sea off Đà Nẵng from which to launch attacks against North Viêtnam. On 20 May TF 77 established Dixie Station 100 miles southeast of Cam Ranh Bay from where close air support missions could be mounted against South Viêtnam. The carriers developed a system that normally kept each ship on line duty for a period of between twenty-five and thirty-five days after which the carrier would visit a port in the Philippines, Japan or Hong Kong for rest and replenishment of supplies. Each carrier would normally complete four spells of duty on the line before returning to its homeport for refitting and re-equipping. However, the period spent on line duty could vary considerably and some ships spent well over the average number of days on duty. The establishment of Dixie Station required the assignment of a fifth carrier to the Western Pacific to maintain the constant presence of at least two carriers at Yankee Station and one at Dixie Station. By the summer of 1966 there were enough aircraft based in South Viêtnam to provide the required airpower and Dixie Station was discontinued from 4 August.

Operation 'Pierce Arrow' began in the early afternoon of 5 August with twenty aircraft from *Constellation* (ten A-1H Skyraiders, eight Skyhawks and two F-4 Phantoms) attacking the torpedo boat base near the coal-mining town of Hon Gai northeast of Hànôi while twelve more (five Skyhawks, four Skyraiders and three Phantoms) from the same carrier struck the Loc Chao base. Simultaneously, the *Ticonderoga* dispatched six F-8E Crusaders to the torpedo boat bases at Quảng Khê and Bến Thuỷ and 26 other aircraft to bomb an oil storage depot at Vinh. Unfortunately, President Johnson's premature television announcement that the raids were to take place may have warned the North Viêtnamese who put up a fierce barrage of anti-aircraft fire at all the targets resulting in the loss of two aircraft. Lieutenant (jg) Richard Christian Sather's Skyraider from VA-145 was hit by AAA while on its third dive bomb attack and crashed just off shore from Thanh Hóa. No parachute was seen or radio emergency beeper heard and it was assumed that Sather died in the crash, the first naval airman to be killed in the war.[58] Skyhawk pilot, 26-year-old Lieutenant (jg) Everett Alvarez Jr of San Jose, California, stationed aboard the *Constellation* in VA-144, who was on his first tour since graduating as a pilot in 1961 also took part in the 'Pierce Arrow' attack on torpedo boats at Hon Gay. During the night he had taken part in the abortive hunt for North Viêtnamese torpedo boats. Alvarez, who had been assigned his objective in advance, recalled years later: 'I was among the first to launch off the carrier. Our squadron, ten airplanes, headed toward the target about 400 miles away - a good two hours there and two hours back. It was sort of like a dream. We were actually going to war, into combat. I never thought it would happen, but all of a sudden here we were and I was in it. I felt a little nervous. We made an identification pass, then came around and made an actual pass, firing. I was very low, just skimming the trees at about 500 knots. Then I had the weirdest feeling. My airplane was hit and started to fall apart, rolling and burning. I knew I wouldn't live if I stayed with the airplane, so I ejected and luckily I cleared a cliff.'

Alvarez landed in shallow water, fracturing his back in the drop. Local North Viêtnamese militia soon arrived and took him to a nearby jail, where he was briefly visited by Prime Minister Pham Van Dong, who had been coincidentally touring the region at the time. Alvarez became something of a celebrity - the first of nearly 600 American airmen to be captured by the Communists during the Viêtnam War. Transferred to Hỏa Lò the notorious prison built in Hànôi by the French in 1896 which American PoWs held there until 29 March 1973 would nickname the 'Hànôi Hilton' he was held until the signing of the cease-fire agreement more than eight years later. Unable to get Alvarez to volunteer anything more than his name, rank and serial number, the North Viêtnamese isolated him in a squalid cell where huge rats darted about at night. Meanwhile he was kept on a starvation diet - including feathered blackbirds - which gave him chronic dysentery. 'Suddenly I was thrown into this medieval environment and kept thinking, 'God, why me?' Alvarez recalled. 'I fully expected the door to open and someone to say he was here to take me home. But as the days went by, I didn't know how much longer it would be.' Held in solitary confinement for fifteen months, Alvarez struggled to maintain his sanity by keeping the past alive in his mind. 'Everyone, all the PoWs, looked up to Ev,' says Paul Galanti who was captured two years after Alvarez. 'He was one of those optimists who always thought we would get out the next day.' Alvarez's spirit was nearly broken in his seventh year of captivity, when the North Viêtnamese handed over correspondence announcing that his wife had divorced him, remarried and given birth to a child with her new husband. Everett Alvarez was released in Operation 'Homecoming' on 12 February 1973. He was known to other PoWs as the 'Old Man of the North' due to his longevity in the PoW camps.

Following the establishment of TF 77 aircraft carriers in the South China Sea in August 1964 it was six months before the US Navy was again in action although thirteen naval aircraft had been lost in accidents over Southeast Asian waters during this time. Although air strikes against North Viêtnam were part of President Johnson's 2 December plan they were not immediately instigated. However, VC attacks on US facilities at Sàigòn on 24 December and Pleiku and Camp Holloway on 7 February caused President Johnson to order the first air strike against North Viêtnam since 'Pierce Arrow' in August 1964. In retaliation, the order was given for a strike from carriers in the Gulf of Tonkin. On 7 February 'Flaming Dart I', as the strike was code-named, saw 49 aircraft launched from the decks of the *Hancock* and *Coral Sea* against Viêt Công

F-4B-21-MC Phantom BuNo 152218 of VF-21 'Free Lancers' armed with two AIM-9B Sidewinder missiles and an AIM-7 Sparrow over Viêtnam in 1965. VF-21 was assigned to Carrier Air Wing 2 (CVW-2) aboard the aircraft carrier USS *Midway* (CVA-41) for a deployment to Viêtnam from 6 March to 23 November 1965. BuNo152218 was lost with VMFA-323, MAG-11 based at Đà Nẵng on 10 January 1966 after one of its bombs exploded prematurely. 1st Lieutenant R. T. Morrisey and the pilot, 1st Lieutenant G. E. Perry ejected, the latter sustaining major injuries.

installations at Đông Hới, while the *Ranger* sent thirty-four aircraft to bomb Vit Thu Lu. The new strike, code named 'Flaming Dart I', was due to be flown by the US Navy from the carriers *Coral Sea*, *Hancock* and *Ranger*. The targets were at Đông Hới and Vit Thu Lu while other targets were hit by VNAF A-1s. The raid was led by Commander Warren H. Sells, Commander of *Hancock's* Air Wing 21. In the event, monsoon weather forced the thirty-four aircraft of *Ranger's* strike force to abort their mission against Vit Thu Lu but Đông Hới's barracks and port facilities were attacked by twenty aircraft from the *Coral Sea* and twenty-nine from the *Hancock*. The strike was carried out at low level under a 700 feet cloud base in rain and poor visibility. An A-4E Skyhawk from the *Coral Sea*, flown by Lieutenant Edward Andrew Dickson, a section leader of a flight of four aircraft of VA -155 was lost. (Dickson had had a miraculous escape from death just one year earlier when he was forced to eject from his Skyhawk over the Sierra Nevada Mountains in California during a training exercise. His parachute failed to deploy properly but he landed in a deep snowdrift that broke his fall causing only minor injuries.) About five miles south of the target, Dickson reported that he had been hit by AAA and requested his wingman to check his aircraft over as they commenced their run in to the target. Just as the flight was about to release its bombs, Dickson's A-4E was seen to burst into flames, but despite a warning from his wingman, he continued with his bomb run and released his Snakeye bombs on target. Dickson headed out towards the sea but his aircraft became engulfed in flames and, although he was seen to eject, his parachute was not seen to deploy, and the aircraft crashed into the sea about half a mile offshore. There was no sign of Lieutenant Dickson in the water despite a SAR effort that continued for two days.

The 'Flaming Dart I' mission of 7 February did not appear to have the effect on the North Viêtnamese that Washington had hoped for. On 10 February the Viêt Công struck at an American camp at Quy Nhơn causing serious casualties. The immediate response to this was 'Flaming Dart 2', flown the following day[59] when a total of ninety-nine naval aircraft from the *Coral Sea*, *Hancock* and *Ranger* were sent against NVA barracks at Chánh Hóa near Đông Hới. The target was attacked in poor visibility with low cloud and the *Coral Sea* suffered two aircraft and one pilot lost on this raid. The first to be brought down was Lieutenant Commander Robert Harper

Shumaker's F-8D Crusader of VF-154, which was hit in the tail (possibly by debris from his own rockets) when he was pulling out from an attack on an anti-aircraft gun position. The aircraft's afterburner blew out and the hydraulic system must have been damaged as the F-8D soon became uncontrollable forcing Shumaker to eject over land although his aircraft crashed a few miles off shore from Đồng Hới. Shumaker's parachute opened about thirty feet above the ground and he broke his back on landing for which he received no medical treatment. A few minutes after Shumaker's Crusader was shot down another wave of aircraft hit the Chánh Hóa barracks and another aircraft was lost. Lieutenant W. T. Majors of VA-153 from the *Coral Sea* in an A-4C was also attacking enemy AAA, using CBU-24 cluster bombs. After delivering his bombs he climbed the Skyhawk to 4,000 feet and set course for the carrier. However, his engine suddenly seized and could not be relit. Faced with no alternative, Majors ejected over the sea but was picked up almost immediately by a USAF rescue helicopter. Bomb damage assessments at Chánh Hóa showed that twenty-three of the seventy-six buildings in the camp were either damaged or destroyed during the raid.

In March, Operation 'Rolling Thunder', an air offensive against North Việtnam, was launched and the Navy's first strike took place on 18 March when aircraft from the *Coral Sea* and *Hancock* bombed supply dumps at Phu Văn and Vinh Sơn. The US Navy's second 'Rolling Thunder' mission, on 26 March, resulted in the loss of three aircraft out of seventy dispatched. The ability of the North Việtnamese air defence system to monitor US raids was a concern even in the early days of the war and the targets for this mission were radar sites at Bạch Long Vi, Cap Mùi Rắn, Hà Tĩnh and Vinh Sın. Lieutenant (jg) C. E. Gudmunson's A-1H Skyraider of VA-215 from the *Hancock* was hit on his sixth pass over the target at Hà Tinh but he managed to fly to Đà Nẵng where he crash-landed about five miles west of the airfield. Commander Kenneth L. Shugart's A-4E Skyhawk of VA-212 from the *Hancock* was hit on his second run as he dropped his Snakeye bombs on the radar site at Vinh Sơn. Shugart headed out to sea as the aircraft caught fire but the electrical system failed, forcing him to eject about ten miles off shore. He was picked

A-6s BuNos 151789 and 151798 of VA-85 from the USS *Kitty Hawk*. On 21 April 1966 BuNo151798, flown by Commander Jack Elmer Keller and Lieutenant Commander Ellis Ernest Austin, and another Intruder took off just before dusk for a night attack on the heavily defended Tan Loc barracks and supply area on the coast ten miles north of Vinh. On the run in to the coast, Keller's wingman had a problem and broke away to dump his bombs on Hon Mat Island, after which he waited for his leader to return. It was Keller's intention to fly past the target then turn over high ground and bomb the target before heading straight out to sea. The wingman saw a bright flash, which he initially thought might have been a bomb explosion, but at the same time the Intruder disappeared from an E-2 Hawkeye's radar screen. It was thought that the Intruder was either shot down or flew into high ground during the run in to the target.

up by a USAF helicopter. Lieutenant C. E. Wangeman, an F-8D pilot in VF-154 on the *Coral Sea*, did not realise that his Crusader, actually the *Coral Sea* Air Wing Commander's aircraft, had been hit as he was attacking an AAA site at Bạch Long Vi. However, after leaving the target area his aircraft began to lose oil pressure and his wingman observed an oil leak. Wangeman climbed to high altitude and he managed to fly the aircraft for over 200 miles before the engine seized and he was forced to eject twenty miles north of Đà Nẵng. He was rescued by a USAF rescue helicopter.

On 29 March the *Coral Sea's* air wing returned to Bạch Long Vi Island, which it had visited three days earlier. Again, seventy aircraft were despatched on the mission including six A-3B bombers from VAH-2. Three aircraft were lost in the first wave as they were attacking AAA sites around the target. Commander Jack H. Harris' A-4E Skyhawk in VA-155 was hit during his low level bomb run causing his engine to wind down. Despite attempts to restart the engine the Commander had to eject over the sea close to the target but was picked up by a Navy ship. VA-154 pilot, Commander William N. Donnelly's F-8D Crusader was hit during his first attack and his controls froze as he was making his second pass. He ejected at 450 knots at about 1,000 feet with the aircraft in an inverted dive and was extremely lucky to survive the ejection with only a fractured neck vertebra and dislocated shoulder. He came down in the shark-infested waters four miles north of Bạch Long Vi and for 45 hours he drifted in his life-raft, which sprang a leak and needed blowing up every twenty minutes. Twice during the first night he had to slip into the water to evade North Viêtnamese patrol boats that were searching for him. Fortunately he was spotted by an F-8 pilot on 31 March and was picked up by a USAF HU-16 Albatross amphibian. Another squadron commander, Commander Pete Mongilardi of VA-153, was almost

A USMC F-8 streaks past the explosion of another F-8's bomb at Đà Nẵng in early 1966 before dropping his own munitions.

On Sunday 12 June 1966, 40-year old Commander Harold 'Hal' Marr, CO of VF-211 'Flying Checkmates' equipped with F-8Es aboard the *Hancock*, became the first Crusader pilot to shoot down a MiG when he destroyed a MiG-17 51 miles northwest of Hảiphòng with his second Sidewinder missile at an altitude of only fifty feet.

lost when his A-4E was hit and had to be 'towed' back to a safe landing on the *Coral Sea* by a tanker as the Skyhawk leaked fuel as fast as it was being pumped in. Lieutenant Commander Kenneth Edward Hume's F-8D in VF-154 was hit by ground fire as he was firing his Zuni unguided rockets at an AAA site on the island. A small fire was seen coming from the engine and Hume attempted to make for Đà Nẵng but after a few minutes the aircraft suddenly dived into the sea and although the canopy was seen to separate there was no sign of an ejection.

The battle against the North Viêtnamese radar system continued on 31 March with further raids on the Vinh Sơn and Cap Mui Ron radar sites involving sixty aircraft from the *Hancock* and *Coral Sea*. Lieutenant (jg) Gerald Wayne McKinley's A-1H in VA-215 from the *Hancock* was hit by ground fire during its second low-level bomb run and the aircraft crashed immediately. By this time both the USN and the USAF were flying regular missions over the Hô Chi Minh Trail in Laos in an attempt to staunch the flow of arms and other supplies from North Viêtnam to the Viêt Công in the South. On 2 April Lieutenant Commander James Joseph Evans of VA-215 from the *Hancock* flying an A-1H was shot down by AAA north of Ban Mương Sen during an armed reconnaissance mission while in the process of attacking another AAA site.

In March 1965 the decision to interdict the North Viêtnamese rail system south of the 20th parallel led immediately to the 3 April strike against the giant 540 feet by 56 feet Chinese-engineered Thanh Hóa road and rail Bridge which stands fifty feet above the Song Ma River. The bridge, three miles north of Thanh Hóa, the capital of Annam Province, in North Viêtnam's bloody 'Iron Triangle' (Hảiphòng, Hànôi and Thanh Hóa) was a replacement for the original French-built Bridge destroyed by the Viêt Minh in 1945, blown up by simply loading two locomotives with explosives and running them together in the middle of the structure. Now a major line of communication from Hànôi seventy miles to the north and Hảiphòng to the southern provinces of North Viêtnam and from there to the DMZ and South Viêtnam, it was heavily defended by a ring of 37mm AAA sites that were supplemented by several 57mm sites following these initial raids.

Shortly after noon on 3 April USAF and USN aircraft of 'Rolling Thunder', 'Mission 9-Alpha', climbed into South-East Asian skies for the bridge, known to the Viêtnamese as the 'Hàm Rông' (Dragon's Jaw). Lieutenant Colonel Robinson Risner, a Korean War ace, was designated overall mission coordinator for the attack. He assembled a force consisting of seventy-nine aircraft - forty-six F-105s, twenty-one F-100s, two RF-101C's tasked with pre and post-strike photographic reconnaissance runs over the target and ten KC-135 tankers to refuel the aircraft before they crossed the Thai border. The F-100s came from bases in South Viêtnam, while the rest of the aircraft were from squadrons TDY at various Thailand bases. Sixteen of the forty-six 'Thuds' were loaded with pairs of Bullpup missiles and each of the remaining thirty carried eight 750lb GP bombs. The aircraft that carried the missiles and half of the bombers were scheduled to strike the bridge; the remaining fifteen (and seven F-100s) would provide flak suppression. The plan called for individual flights of four F-105s from Koran and Takhli which would be air refuelled over the Mekong River before tracking across Laos to an initial point (IP) three minutes south of the bridge. After weapon release, the plan called for all aircraft to continue east until over the Gulf of Tonkin where rejoin would take place and a Navy destroyer would

On 2 December 1966 during a night armed reconnaissance mission A-4Cs 145143 piloted by Commander Bruce August Nystrom (left) and 145116 (below) flown by Ensign Paul Laurance Worrell from the USS *Franklin D Roosevelt* disappeared near Phúc Nhạc, 50 miles down the coast from Hảiphòng. Worrell had been heard by another flight to warn his leader that he had a SAM warning. Commander Nystrom told the wingman to commence evasive action and then announced a SAM launch. A pilot some distance away saw two flashes on the ground about a minute apart, which were probably SAM launches, followed by two explosions in the air. It was assumed that the two Skyhawks were either hit by the SA-2s or flew into the ground trying to evade the missiles. The SAMs downed four American aircraft that day. Nystrom had been flying with the Navy since 1948 and had flown the F4U Corsair during the Korean War as well as the F8F Bearcat and the F2H Banshee. He joined VA-172 as executive officer in December 1964 and assumed command of the Squadron on 23 December 1965. In July 1985 the Viêtnamese returned the remains of Paul Worrell.

be available to recover anyone who had to eject due to battle damage or other causes. After rejoin, all aircraft would return to their bases, hopefully to the tune of *The Hàm Rồng Bridge is falling down.*

The sun glinting through the haze made the target somewhat difficult to acquire, but Risner led the way 'down the chute' and 250lb missiles were soon exploding on the target. Since only one Bullpup missile could be fired at a time, each pilot had to make two firing passes. On his second pass Risner's aircraft took a hit just as the Bullpup hit the bridge. Fighting a serious fuel leak and a smoke-filled cockpit in addition to anti-aircraft fire from the enemy, he nursed his crippled aircraft to Đà Nẵng and to safety. The 'Dragon' would not be so kind on another day. The first two flights had already left the target when Captain Bill Meyerholt, number three man in the third flight, rolled his Thunderchief into a dive and squeezed off a Bullpup. The missile streaked toward the bridge and as smoke cleared from the previous attacks, Meyerholt was shocked to see no visible damage to the bridge. The Bullpups were merely charring the heavy steel and concrete structure. The remaining missile attacks confirmed that firing Bullpups at the 'Dragon' was about as effective as shooting BB pellets at a Sherman tank. The bombers, undaunted, came in for their attack, only to see their payload drift to the far bank because of a very strong southwest wind. 1st Lieutenant George C. Smith's F-100D was shot down near the target point as he suppressed flak. The anti-aircraft resistance was much stronger than anticipated. No radio contact could be made with Smith, nor could other aircraft locate him. Smith was listed MIA and no further word has been heard of him.

The last flight of the day, led by Captain Carlyle S. 'Smitty' Harris, adjusted their aiming points and scored several good hits on the roadway and super structure. 'Smitty' tried to assess bomb damage, but could not because of the smoke coming from the 'Dragon's Jaw'. The smoke would prove to be an ominous warning of things to come.

The USN mounted two raids against bridges near Thanh Hóa on the 3rd. A total of 35 A-4s, sixteen F-8s and four F-4s were launched from the *Hancock* and *Coral Sea*. Lieutenant Commander Raymond Arthur Vohden of VA-216 from the *Hancock* who was flying an A-4C

Commander Richard M. Bellinger describes his victory on 9 October 1966 when he destroyed a MiG-21.

RF-8G 144624 of Detachment 42, VFP-62 on the USS *Franklin D. Roosevelt*. This aircraft was lost on 6 September 1966 during a photographic reconnaissance mission when it was last seen to be manoeuvering close to the water about 10 miles off shore from Thanh Hóa before it crashed killing the pilot, Lieutenant (jg) Norman Lee Bundy. The crash was thought to have been a misjudgement of altitude above the sea.

Skyhawk was hit by small arms fire during his first bombing run during an attack on a bridge at Đồng Phổ Thông about ten miles north of the 'Dragon'. His wing-man saw the aircraft streaming fluid and the arrester hook drop down. Soon afterwards, Vohden ejected and was captured to become the Navy's third PoW in North Viêtnam. The raids were the first occasion when the Viêtnamese People's Air Force employed its MiG-17 fighters, thus marking a significant escalation of the air war in Southeast Asia. During this raid three MiG-17s attacked and damaged a Crusader when four of the F-8Es tried to bomb the bridge. The F-8E pilot was forced to divert to Đà Nẵng. This was the first time a MiG had attacked a US aircraft during the war in Southeast Asia. Captain Herschel S. Morgan's RF-101 was hit and went down seventy-five miles southwest of the target area, seriously injuring the pilot. Captain Morgan was captured and held in and around Hànôi until his release in February 1973.

When the smoke cleared, observer aircraft found that the bridge still spanned the river. Thirty-two Bullpups and ten dozen 750lb bombs had been aimed at the bridge and numerous hits had charred every part of the structure, yet it showed no sign of going down. A re-strike was ordered for the next day.

The following day, flights with call signs 'Steel', 'Iron', 'Copper', 'Moon', 'Carbon', 'Zinc', 'Argon', 'Graphite', 'Esso', 'Mobil', 'Shell', 'Petrol' and the 'Cadillac' BDA (bomb damage assessment) flight, assembled at IP to try once again to knock out the 'Dragon'. On this day, Captain Carlyle 'Smitty' Harris was flying as call sign 'Steel 3'. 'Steel 3' took the lead and oriented himself for his run on a 300 degree heading. He reported that his bombs had impacted on the target on the eastern end of the bridge. 'Steel 3' was on fire as soon as he left the target. Radio contact was garbled and 'Steel Lead', 'Steel 2' and 'Steel 4' watched helplessly as 'Smitty's aircraft, emitting flame for twenty feet behind, headed due west of the target. All flight members had him in sight until the fire died out, but observed no parachute, nor did they see the aircraft

BuNo149993 A-4E of VA-163 'Saints' from the USS *Oriskany* taking on fuel from KA-3B tanker 138974 of VAH-4 from the same carrier in the summer of 1967. On 26 May 1970, now with VA-152 on the USS *Shangri-La* this Skyhawk was abandoned during a tanker mission when the engine suddenly lost power. It was suspected that the A-4E had ingested fuel into the engine air intakes as the aircraft was taking on fuel from another tanker. The pilot survived and was picked up safe and sound.

impact the ground. 'Smitty's aircraft had been hit by a MiG whose pilot later recounted the incident in '*Viêtnam Courier*' on 15 April 1965. It was not until much later that it would be learned that 'Smitty' had been captured by the North Viêtnamese. 'Smitty' was held prisoner for eight years and released in 1973. Fellow PoWs credit Smitty with introducing the 'tap code' which enabled them to communicate with each other.

MiGs had been seen on previous missions, but for the first time in the war, the Russian-made MiGs attacked American aircraft. 'Zinc 2', an F-105D flown by Captain James A. Magnusson, had its flight bounced by MiG 17s. As Zinc Lead was breaking to shake a MiG on his tail, 'Zinc 2' was hit and radioed that he was heading for the Gulf if he could maintain control of his aircraft. The other aircraft were busy evading the MiGs and Magnusson radioed several times before 'Steel Lead' responded and instructed him to tune his radio to rescue frequency. Magnusson's aircraft finally ditched over the Gulf of Tonkin near the island of Hòn Mê and he was not seen or heard from again. He was listed MIA. Captain Walter F. Draeger's A-1H (probably an escort for rescue teams) was shot down over the Gulf of Tonkin just northeast of the 'Dragon' that day. Draeger's aircraft was seen to crash in flames, but no parachute was observed. Draeger was listed MIA. The remaining aircraft returned to their bases, discouraged. Although over 300 bombs scored hits on this second strike, the bridge still stood. From April to September 1965, nineteen more pilots were shot down in the general vicinity of the 'Dragon'.

The threat of MiG activity over Southeast Asia resulted in increased efforts to provide combat air patrols and airborne early warning and the F-4 Phantom and F-8 Crusader were tasked with air defence of the fleet and protection of strike forces. On 9 April two Phantoms of VF-96 on the *Ranger* were launched to relieve two other aircraft flying a BARCAP (Barrier Combat Air Patrol) racetrack pattern in the northern Gulf of Tonkin. However, the first aircraft to launch crashed as it was being catapulted from the carrier. The aircraft's starboard engine failed during the catapult shot and the aircraft ditched into the sea but both Lieutenant Commander William E. Greer and Lieutenant (jg) R. Bruning ejected just as the aircraft impacted the water and were rescued. Lieutenant (jg) Terence Meredith Murphy and Ensign Ronald James Fegan were then launched and took over as section leader with a replacement aircraft flown by Lieutenant Watkins and Lieutenant (jg) Mueller as their wingman. As the two Phantoms flew north they were intercepted by four MiG-17s that were identified as belonging to the air force of the Chinese People's Liberation Army. The two Phantoms that were waiting to be relieved on BARCAP heard

Murphy's radio calls and flew south to engage the MiGs. The air battle took place at high altitude near the Chinese island of Hainan and Murphy's Phantom was not seen after the MiGs disengaged. The aircraft was thought to have been shot down by the MiGs but a Chinese newspaper claimed that Murphy had been shot down in error by an AIM-7 Sparrow missile fired by another Phantom. One of the MiG-17s was seen to explode and was thought to have been shot down by Murphy during the dogfight but it was never officially credited due to the sensitivity of US aircraft engaging Chinese aircraft. Murphy's last radio call was to the effect that he was out of missiles and was returning to base. Despite an extensive two-day SAR effort no sign of the Phantom or its crew was ever found.

On 8 May the US Navy mounted its first raid against a North Viêtnamese airfield when Vinh air base was attacked by a strike force from the *Midway*. Commander James David La Haye, the CO of VF-111, was attacking the airfield's AAA defences with Zuni unguided rockets and 20mm cannon fire when his aircraft was hit by ground fire. The Crusader was seen to turn towards the coast with its wings level but streaming fuel until it crashed into the sea a few miles offshore near the island of Hon Nieu. No attempt at ejection was seen although the pilot had radioed that his aircraft had been hit. About six hours after the strike on Vinh airfield Detachment A, VFP-63, *Midway's* photographic reconnaissance detachment flew a BDA mission to assess the damage done to the target. During the run over the airfield Lieutenant (jg) W. B. Wilson's RF-8A Crusader was hit by ground fire and sustained damage to the fuel tanks, hydraulic system and tail fin. Despite the damage and loss of fuel, Wilson managed to make for the coast and fly south towards a tanker where he took on enough fuel to reach the carrier or Đà Nẵng. Unfortunately, soon after taking on fuel, two explosions were heard from the rear of the aircraft as either fuel or hydraulic fluid ignited. The aircraft's controls froze and Lieutenant Wilson ejected over the sea about thirty miles off Đông Hới from where he was rescued by a USAF Albatross.

Midway's run of bad luck continued. On 27 May the US Navy flew a strike against the railway yards at Vinh, one of the most frequently hit targets in the southern part of North Viêtnam. Commander Doyle Wilmer Lynn, CO of VF-111 was attacking an AAA site near the target when his F-8D Crusader was hit by ground fire. Lynn, who had been one of the first Navy

On 29 July 1967 an electrical anomaly discharged a Mk.32 Zuni rocket on the flight deck of the USS *Forrestal* in the Gulf of Tonkin killing 134 men, injuring 161 and writing off 21 aircraft.

A-4 Skyhawks of VA-146, F-4Js of VF-143, A-6 Intruders, an A-3B, RA-5C Vigilante and a RA-3B Skywarrior of VAP-61 painted glossy-black for night sorties over the Hó Chi Minh Trail in Laos on the crowded flight deck of the USS *Constellation* (CVA-64) in 1967. A few RA-3Bs operating with VAP-61 (and to a lesser extent, VAP-62) were usually based at Đà Nẵng but occasionally deployed to carriers at Yankee Station in the South China Sea off Đà Nẵng.

pilots to be shot down in South East Asia when his Crusader was shot down on 7 June 1964 over the Plain of Jars, radioed that the aircraft had been hit and the F-8 was seen to go out of control and hit the ground before an ejection could take place. On 1 June in preparation for further attacks on the railway yards at Vinh, the *Midway* sent Lieutenant (jg) M. R. Fields, one of its Detachment A, VFP-63, photographic reconnaissance RF-8A Crusader pilots, to check the state of damage and to see which areas needed to be attacked again. At 500 feet over the target the aircraft was hit by ground fire which damaged its hydraulic system. Fields felt the controls gradually stiffening as he raced for the sea. He was fortunate to be able to get over thirty miles from the coastline before the controls eventually froze solid and he was forced to eject. He was soon rescued by a USAF Albatross amphibian.

Next day two more *Midway* aircraft were lost. During a raid on a radar site a few miles south of Thanh Hóa, an A-4E flown by Lieutenant (jg) David Marion Christian of VA-23 was hit by AAA when pulling up from its second attack with Zuni rockets. The aircraft caught fire immediately and Christian radioed that his engine had flamed out. It could not be confirmed if Christian ejected from the stricken Skyhawk before it hit the ground. Thirty minutes after the aircraft was lost, an EA-1F Skyraider of Detachment A, VAW-13 arrived from the *Midway* to co-ordinate a SAR effort for Lieutenant Christian. As the Skyraider was about to cross the coast at low level near Sam Son, east of Thanh Hóa, it was hit by ground fire and crashed. The *Midway* lost its fifth aircraft in three days on 3 June during an armed reconnaissance mission in the 'Barrel Roll' area of Laos. Lieutenant Raymond P. Ilg's A-4C

On 20 October 1967 with both legs shattered by North Việtnamese anti-aircraft fire, Lieutenant (jg) Denny Earl successfully lands his VA-163 Saints A-4E Skyhawk BuNo 149959, AH-300, aboard the USS *Oriskany.* Six days later this same Skyhawk was shot down over Hànôi. The pilot, John S McCain, spent 5½ years as a PoW. (USN)

Skyhawk of VA-22 was hit by AAA over Route 65 near Ban Nakay Neua, ten miles east of Sam Neua. The aircraft caught fire and Ilg ejected immediately. He evaded for two days until he was picked up by an Air America helicopter.

On 17 June two VF-21 'Freelancers' F-4Bs from the USS *Midway* (CVA-41) scored the first MiG kills of the war when they attacked four MiG-17s south of Hànôi and brought down two with radar-guided AIM-7 Sparrow missiles. One of the F-4Bs was flown by Commander Louis C. Page and his radar intercept officer, Lieutenant Jack E. D. Batson. The other was flown by Lieutenant John C. Smith and 33-year old Montclair, New Jersey-born Lieutenant Commander Robert B. Doremus his Naval Flight Officer (NFO) also serving as Radar Intercept Officer (RIO). They were each awarded the Silver Star. Lieutenant Commander Doremus citation for first of two Silver Star's reads: '...Engaging at least four and possibly six FRESCO aircraft, Commander (then Lieutenant Commander) Doremus accounted for one confirmed kill and contributed to a second confirmed kill by the other F-4B aircraft in the flight by diverting the remaining enemy planes from their threat to the US striking forces. With heavy antiaircraft fire bursting throughout the patrol area, his crew relentlessly maintained their vigil and pressed forward their attack, seeking out and destroying the enemy aircraft and thereby preventing damage to friendly strike aircraft in the area.'

On 24 August on a mission to hit the 'Dragon's Jaw' Bridge at Than Hòa, Doremus was flying with thirty-eight-year old Brooklyn, New York born Commander Fred Augustus Franke, commander of VF-21 in F-4B call sign 'Sundown' when they were hit by a SAM SA-2 at about 11,000 feet near the village of Phù Banh, north of Than Hòa. They both successfully ejected and were captured in the rice fields almost immediately but his wingman had reported seeing no

Catapult bridle cables are hooked up to an A-7A Corsair of VA-147 'Argonauts' and F-4B Phantom 153014 of VF-21 'Freelancers' on the flight deck of the USS *Ranger* in the Gulf of Tonkin on 14 December 1967. On 28 April 1968 153014 was pulling up from its attack on storage caves at Ben Thuy, just to the south of Vinh when AAA set the port wing on fire and the port engine had to be shut down. Lieutenant Commander Duke E. Hernandez headed out to sea but within a few minutes the starboard engine also caught fire, the hydraulic system failed and the aircraft went out of control so he and Lieutenant (jg) David J. Lortscher ejected close to a SAR destroyer about fifteen miles offshore. They were quickly rescued by a Navy helicopter. Lortscher ejected from another F-4 near San Diego on 14 September 1970 and again on 22 September 1971 when the canopy of his F-4 separated. On 15 October 1973, during an exchange posting with the Royal Navy he ejected from a Phantom for the fourth time. Hernandez had ejected from a Phantom during a raid on Hảiphòng on 16 December 1967.

chutes, so they were declared killed in action (KIA).[60]

On Sunday 12 June 1966 forty-year old Commander Harold 'Hal' Marr, CO of VF-211 'Flying Checkmates' equipped with F-8Es aboard the *Hancock* became the first Crusader pilot to shoot down a MiG when he destroyed a MiG-17 fifty-one miles northwest of Hảiphòng with his second Sidewinder missile at an altitude of only fifty feet. 'I've waited eighteen years to do that,' Marr, of Roseburg, Oregon, said. He was also credited with a probable after blasting more MiGs with his 20mm cannon. He was one of a flight of Crusader pilots flying Combat Air Patrol for a flight of A-4 Skyhawks that were attacking the Đại Tấn military area, twenty-four miles northwest of Hảiphòng. Marr and his wingman, Lieutenant (jg) Philip V. Vampatella, aged twenty-six of Islip Terrace, New York were flying at 2,000 feet when the MiGs appeared from the east. 'We were flying in the missile envelope around the Hảiphòng-Hànôi area,' Marr said. 'We wouldn't be flying very high and take the chance of getting a telephone pole (missile) shoved into us.' When Vampatella spotted the MiGs, he flew his plane into them and overshot them. For the next four minutes, at speeds between 350-550 mph and as low as fifty feet, Marr and the pilot of the communist jet banked and turned to get into position to shoot. Marr maneuvered his Crusader behind the MiG and fired a heat-seeking Sidewinder missile, which missed the MiG and streaked to earth. Marr was alone in the fight. Vampatella and a third pilot ran out of 20mm cannon ammunition and were low on fuel and returned to the ship. Marr manoeuvred his aircraft around and fired again at the MiG. 'The missile clipped the tail off and it went right into the ground,' Marr said. Marr sighted another flight of MiGs and the chase began again. Having used both of his Sidewinders on one MiG, Marr only had 20mm cannon fire, which he began firing at a second MiG. He hit it and saw parts of the plane's wing fly off. Low on fuel and short on ammunition himself, Marr returned to his ship. The F-8 enjoyed the highest kill ratio of any fighter engaged in the Việtnam air war.

Nine days later, on 21 June, Lieutenant Vampatella shot down another MiG-17 while covering a rescue attempt to bring home an RF-8 pilot shot down earlier. On 9 October an F-8E pilot, Commander Dick Bellinger, CO of VF-162 from the *Oriskany* became the first Navy pilot to destroy a MiG-21 when he obliterated one of the enemy fighters with heat-seeking missiles during an escort mission for A-4s from the *Intrepid*.

At 1525 hours on 27 July 1965 Archie Taylor, commander, Det 4, Pacific Air Rescue Center (PARC) was notified that there was a downed pilot, southwest of Hànôi and not far from Hànôi. He was said to be in the river. Then at 1530 the word came in a second aircraft was down. A HH-43 'Pedro' launched from LS-98 at 1532. They were next notified there was a mid-air collision about ten miles southeast of Udorn in Thailand at 1540. One chute was spotted. The accident was between two F-105Ds returning from their mission in the North. Then at 1549 Udorn reported that 'Cedar 2' was down just west of Hànôi. Two B-57 Canberra bombers were launched from Đà Nẵng. At 1610 the SAR force informed all hands that men were down 'in the ring' (in the middle of enemy forces) and that ground defences were southeast of the downed

On 10 January 1968, F-4B 151506 (pictured) and F-4B 151499 of VF-154 on the USS *Ranger*, flew a radar-directed bombing mission over low cloud in Laos. As the aircraft set course for the return trip to the *Ranger* the leader inadvertently homed onto the TACAN of the northern SAR destroyer instead of that of the carrier. When the Phantoms broke out from the cloud they were over 100 miles from the *Ranger* and the aircraft had to be abandoned over the South China Sea when they ran out of fuel. All four crewmen were rescued.

F-4B BuNo150466 'Old Nick 204' of VF-111 'Sundowners' dropping Mk.82 500lb 'buddy bombs' using navigation fixes, over North Viêtnam with BuNo149457, 'Screaming Eagle 113' from VF-51 'Screaming Eagles', both on the USS Coral Sea. BuNo150466 was lost on 2 September 1970 with VMFA-115, MAG-13 USMC at Chu Lai in a ground accident when taxiing to fuel pits. Three ground crew were killed.

Two heavily armed A-6A Intruder attack aircraft of VA-156 in the Gulf of Tonkin in July 1968 during a combat mission flown off the USS *Constellation* (CVA-64). On 18 December 1968 154150 now with VA-196 was shot down by ground fire 70 miles West of Đà Nẵng during a daylight 'Steel Tiger' strike. Lieutenant (jg) John Richards Babcock and Lieutenant Gary Jon Mayer were killed.

crew members. At 1620 Archie noted that another F-105D call sign 'Dogwood' was down, also up near Hànôi. 'Dogwood' was working with SAR forces on the radio, operating as a kind of controller, which meant he was on the ground and in pretty good shape. At 1650 the HC-54s controlling the SAR mission were told to stay out of the ring. A call also went out at this time to see if a HU-16 Albatross was on its way.

At 1710, a CH-3C Jolly Green 'call sign Shed 85' fired up his engines and was aloft by 1714. At 1743 another HH-43 was launched. At 1845 a report came in that 'Canister Flight' had a good location on 'Dogwood' and that he was okay. 'Canister' also reported that a CH-3C was about to go in after him. At 1905 'Healy 1' who was flight lead said 'Healy 2' went in to the river and 'Healy 1' saw a dingy but never saw the pilot. 'Healy 1' was running out of fuel and had to leave and on his way out he reported seeing boats within 300 yards of the dingy. After getting refuelled and returning to the scene, 'Healy 1' saw nothing in the area. Also at 1905 a CH-3C was hovering over 'Dogwood' who was hiding in the woods but could not get at him with the hoist. So he looked for a place to land. At 1915 the SAR force reported picking up 'Dogwood' and all the SAR forces were on their way out. Dogwood was picked up and rescued.

This entire sequence of events was part of Operation 'Spring High', which was the first strike against Soviet SA-2 surface-to-air missile (SAM) sites. The NVN introduced SAM missiles in the summer of 1965. Up to this point, the NVN felt it could get by with its anti-aircraft artillery (AAA), fighter aircraft and radar network. After all, many of the US air attacks were largely symbolic, so as not to cause undue concern in the USSR and China. Slowly but surely the US ramped up to hit the radar networks and other more important targets.

Captain William J. Barthelmas, Jr. flying F-105D 'Pepper 02' in the 357th TFS out of Korat

RTAFB was KIA, hit by a SAM thirty miles from Hànôi. Major Jack G. Farr, flying F-105D 'Pepper 01' crashed in Thailand, obviously trying to make it home and was also killed. They were on their way out after hitting a SAM site thirty miles west of Hànôi. Barthelmas was apparently hit by a SAM but he was able to make his way back to Thailand. 'Pepper 01' of course stuck with him. On their way back to Thailand, 'Pepper 01' inspected 'Pepper 02' and said, 'I can see daylight right through you.' The battle damage was severe. The conjecture is Barthelmas' hydraulics gave out and his aircraft unexpectedly pitched up. 'Pepper 02's tail slammed into 'Pepper 01's cockpit. Bathelmus ejected but his parachute did not fully open. He is said to have landed in a rice paddy alive, but with multiple injuries. Tragically, he drowned in the paddy. Also tragically 'Pepper 01' was sufficiently damaged that he crashed about ten miles south of Ubon RTAFB. Farr did not eject and was killed.

Captain Walter Kosko, flying F-105D 624257 'Healy 02' in the 563rd TFS out of Takhli targeted a SAM site thirty miles west of Hànôi and reportedly was hit by AAA. He landed in a river and drowned. Kosko was part of a flight of four F-105Ds out of Takhli on a bombing mission over Phú Thọ Province. AAA fire was said to be intense. There was an explosion near Kosko's aircraft and he reported he was hit and had smoke in his cockpit. He later ejected and flight members saw a fully deployed chute in the water and survival gear, but there was no voice contact and no beeper after ejection. His colleagues on the mission tried to find him even through heavy hostile fire, but to no avail. Later attempts to find his remains revealed that he was down in the Black River. US forces searched the river but could not find him. He was later declared dead - body not recovered.

Captain Kile Dag Berg flying F-105D 610113, call sign 'Hudson 2' in the 563rd TFS at Takhli and Captain Robert B. 'Percy' Purcell flying F-105D 6224252, call sign 'Ceader 2' in the 12th TFS out of Korat were both shot down about forty miles northwest of Hànôi and taken prisoner. Both men's target was the barracks at Can Doi and they both were reportedly hit by AAA.[61] Right after he dropped his napalm Berg's aircraft was seen on fire from in front of the inlets past the afterburner. It slowly pulled up, rolled right and then crashed. Berg ejected at fifty feet and 540 knots which blew some panels in his chute and without a doubt gave him 'one helluva jolt' as well.

Captain Frank J. Tullo, flying F-105D 624407 call sign 'Dogwood 02' in the 12th TFS out of Korat, was rescued. Tullo's group had entered the fray after most of the beating took place. Their

Viêtnam People's Air Force (NVNAF) Soviet- and Chinese-built MiG-17Fs and their pilots in North Viêtnam.

job was 'to clean up' Tullo said when he arrived over the target area. 'To a good Catholic boy, this was a description of hell.' The enemy fire was the worst he had seen and the burning fires and smoke below was a cauldron. Tullo said they approached at about 200 feet and 700 knots. Right away he was hit, his fire warning lights blazing. 'Dogwood 01', Major Bill Hosmer, came over to take a look. Hosmer told him to get rid of his tanks and rocket pods to lighten the aircraft. Flames were now trailing about 200 feet behind him. He was still flying and had control. They were still over Hànôi. Hosmer told him to bail out, but Tullo refused, saying he could still fly. He wanted to make it to the hills of 'Thud Ridge' - a north-south mountain range between US bases in Thailand and Hànôi - where a bail out might result in a rescue. But the aircraft then lost control and he had to bail out, but again, at the speed he was travelling, he really got whipped around on the way out. From his parachute Tullo could see Hànôi about twenty-five miles away. Once on the ground, he hid his chute and called on the radio and made contact. But his partners were running out of fuel and had to leave. After some time on the ground and attempting to climb up a hill, which was what they were taught to do - make the enemy climb the hill and if they do, then you are close to the top and can go over the top of the hill and try to hide - he heard an A-1H Spad, call sign 'Canasta' who had a good indication that 'Dogwood 02' was okay and that a CH-3C Jolly Green was closing in. 'Canasta' Flight consisted of two Navy A-1Hs. Then two F-105s came by and Tullo contacted them. They asked him to pop smoke so they could get his location. Tullo refused, fearing he would give away his location to the enemy, as he knew the enemy was coming to his area. Some enemy started climbing the hill; Tullo dug in to hide and the enemy troops moved away and down the hill. The hill strategy seemed to work.

The CH-3C flown by Captain George Martin USAF was at NKP and was flying to LS-36 to pull SAR alert, call sign 'Shed 85'. His USAF crew consisted of his co-pilot, Lieutenant Orville Keese, 'hoist mechanic' Sergeant Curtis Pert and pararescueman Sergeant George Thayer. Martin was told to divert to get 'Dogwood 02' but he had to land at LS-36 to drop off supplies and passengers and could not hover the way he needed to for a rescue with such a heavy load. After landing at LS-36, his number two engine warning lights indicated they had overheated; a condition which would normally mean he was grounded. But he was Tullo's only chance at that moment. He was worried he would not be able to restart his engines, informed the crew he felt they should go get Tullo; the crew agreed, the engine started without a hitch and off he went. He had little idea of where he was going other than to head for Hànôi. About fifty miles from Hànôi he was met by 'Canasta' flight, flown by Lieutenant Commander Ed Greathouse and Holt Livesay from VA-25 embarked aboard the USS *Midway*. It was getting late, dusk was

The notorious Thanh Hòa (Dragon's Jaw') bridge.

Napalm attack on a suspected Việt Công position.

coming. 'Canasta' reported to Tullo he had a chopper and flew directly over Tullo's position, with 'Shed 85' right behind him. Tullo expected something like a HH-43 Pedro and had never seen one this big. It turns out this would be the CH-3C Jolly Green's first rescue. The Jolly crew had a very hard time pulling Tullo up the hoist, which was not yet designed for this kind of work. And, of course, the CH-3C's engine started to overheat again but he lifted up, dragging Tullo through bushes etc into the air and finally found a spot where he could let him down on the ground. Tullo got out of his harness and the Jolly landed about fifty feet away. Incredibly, now they started receiving hostile fire from the ground. The 'Jolly' had all kinds of problems, an overheated engine, coming darkness, and clouds at altitude. Plus the crew had no maps of the area. The 'Jolly' crew hollered at Tullo to board. He did, diving through the door and off they went. Martin pointed the Jolly in the direction of LS-36 which was surrounded by enemy. LS-36 lit up landing lights by igniting flares in fifty-five gallon drums and Martin landed the CH-3C with all hands in one piece.

This was the farthest north a successful rescue had been made. Just a few weeks earlier, Captain Martin and his crews were flying support missions with the CH-3 in Florida! So here they are, now in the Việtnam War, flying a beat-up old CH-3 on a SAR mission, no previous SAR experience, a rigged up winch to pull up the downed aircrew member and they were penetrating deeply into the NVN and conducting the first CH-3 rescue mission in the war.

'Spring High' involved more than a hundred Air Force, Marine and Navy aircraft. A pair of EC-121 radar planes monitored VPAF (NVNAF) activity, directing the combat air patrol. Ten electronic warfare craft jammed the enemy radars. A dozen Phantoms and eight more F-104 Starfighters flew air cover. There were fifteen KC-135s for aerial refuelling and a search and rescue flight to recover downed aircrews. On the cutting edge, forty-six F-105s hit SAM sites and nearby barracks presumed to house the defenders with napalm and cluster bombs. Four RF-101s then streaked past to photograph the targets for bomb-damage assessment. 'Spring High' cost four F-105s over the targets, plus one more damaged so badly the aircraft lost control making an emergency landing at Udorn, colliding with its escort and destroying both warplanes. All the losses were inflicted by flak, not SAMs. One pilot was rescued. Damage assessment showed that one of the target-SAM sites had been a dummy and another was unoccupied. The Soviet Union did not respond openly, but Moscow secretly accelerated its shipment of SAMs to North Việtnam. These engagements in the summer of 1965 marked the beginning of a whole new facet of 'Rolling Thunder'. Henceforth the air campaign featured extensive efforts to neutralize VPAF surface-to-air-missile installations. In fact, SAM site attacks were a major element in the next bimonthly plan for the air effort.'[62]

On 29 August Lieutenant Henry S. McWhorter of VFP-63, USS *Oriskany* flying RF-8A call-sign 'Corktip 919' on a photo reconnaissance in Nghe An Province, North Việtnam when he was hit by enemy fire about twenty-five miles northwest of Vinh. Both he and his wingman had encountered heavy AAA at 8,000 feet. They took evasive action. McWhorter's wingman reported him flying straight and level, but with no canopy or ejection seat. The wingman concluded the AAA hit in a location that fired off the ejection seat and probably killed McWhorter. The wingman reported McWhorter's landing gear coming down as a result of the damage to the hydraulic systems. The aircraft entered a gentle glide until it hit the ground. Two A-1s were on the scene five minutes after the crash and said they saw a chute leaving the aircraft. However, other reports said no chute was sighted. A HU-16 Flying Albatross also responded, but had to abort due to an engine loss. Another one came to the scene, but again, no contact. There was no beeper heard. He was listed as killed/body not recovered as the assessment was that there was a slim hope of survival.[63]

Lieutenant Allan Russell Carpenter, born 14 March 1938 in Portland, Maine got his navy wings in November 1963 and flew A-4 Skyhawks in VA-72 in Việtnam in 1965 on the USS *Independence*. 'We operated as most ships did in air wings for three or four days or a week in South Việtnam getting the ship exercised and pilots and equipment all ready to go and then we moved north and started flying missions. North Việtnam in 1965 was exciting because we were putting our skills to use in the environment that we had been trained for. We were, after all, combat pilots and now it was our first exposure to combat. However, the ground and air defences were not what they later became. We flew road reconnaissance flights and we bombed bridges and some army barracks and things like that. Eventually my squadron was involved in

An F-8D of VF-111 'Sundowners' about to be launched from the No.2 catapult. During the Vietnam War, VF-111 were based at NAS Miramar, California with the squadron making seven deployments to Southeast Asia, flying 12,500 combat sorties. In 1967-68, VF-111 deployed a less-than-full-strength detachment from USS *Intrepid* (CVS-11).

the first attack on a mobile SAM site in North Viêtnam. My commanding officer led that flight and we destroyed the site. We developed tactics as a result. We lost a significant number of people on that cruise, many of whom I would see later in prison in North Viêtnam. On 13 September 1965 my roommate [Lieutenant (jg) Joe Russell Mossman] was shot down and killed in the southern part of North Viêtnam. We got home in early December.

'We enjoyed a few weeks off before the Navy had decided to move all the A-4s to Cecil Field in Florida. It took a while to get the squadron set up in its new digs and learn our way around. Then we started training because our squadron had been picked in Washington to turn right around and make another WestPac cruise from the east coast, on the USS *Franklin D. Roosevelt*, leaving in June. We stopped in Rio de Janeiro on the way, which was a nice break and then crossed the equator a time or two again. We got on the line in August 1966 and things were different this time around. Again, we spent a few days down in South Viêtnam getting ready. And I had been promoted at that time to lieutenant in the Navy. I was a flight leader; a combat veteran. I was also experienced in the 'Iron Hand' SAM suppression mission, which were kind of risky. In the air force it was called 'Wild Weasel'.

'The defences had improved considerably from 1965. There was a lot of flak. There were more MiGs in the air and a lot more surface-to-air missiles. Over the course of time the aircraft that I was flying in was hit on seven different occasions, one of which on 21 August 1966 resulted in very serious damage to the aircraft. I was able to make it back to the ship but could not wait around until they could clear the deck and get me back on board and I was forced to eject from my aircraft which was fully engulfed in flame. I was in the vicinity of the ship and at low altitude and relatively low airspeed and so it was a somewhat uneventful ejection. I was picked up by the ship's helicopter and brought aboard, given a shot of whiskey and told to get some rest. Then the next morning I was the first aircraft launched off the ship, the old theory being that you get back on that horse that threw you before you get scared. And it seemed to work. I continued flying missions and in the interim we went back and forth to various ports. We went into Japan twice and got to see a little foreign culture and do some shopping, sending things back to my wife Carolyn.

'We were back on the line on 1 November 1966. My mission on that day was to lead a flight of three A-4s, providing SAM suppression for a flight of photo F-8 Crusaders taking pictures of Hảiphòng Harbour, shipping and docks. After that portion of the mission I was to lead my flight on up the coast toward the border with China looking at coastal installations and seeing if we could find any patrol boats or vehicular traffic or trained traffic that we could attack in North Viêtnam. Unfortunately, that didn't come to pass. The SAMs came on line. I was monitoring their radars and could tell that they were on line searching and when they launched the missiles I could hear them tracking. I looked down. It was a pretty dark, very rainy, miserable day everywhere except right where we were. For the first time in North Viêtnam I saw a light on the surface. These people were being pretty foolish to allow a light to be shown in a combat

MiG-17Fs of the Viêtnam People's Air Force (NVNAF) taxi out.

Sparrow and Sidewinder-armed F-4B-27-MC 153045 of VF-114 'Aardvarks' from the USS *Kitty Hawk* (CVA-63) over the Gulf of Tonkin in March 1968. This aircraft was the US Navy's final MiG killer when a Việtnam Peoples Air Force MiG-17 flown by Senior Lieutenant Luu Kim Ng was shot down by Lieutenant Victor Kovaleski and Lieutenant James R. Wise of VF-161 'Chargers' from the USS *Midway,* near Hải Phòng, using an AIM 9 Sidewinder heat-seeking air-to-air missile. This was the last air combat victory by a US aircraft during the Việtnam War.

environment. The light got bigger and brighter and suddenly I realized that it was a SAM. I launched a Shrike anti-SAM radar missile at the site. It tracked properly and destroyed the radar trails. I followed up by leading my flight of three in an attack on a site. I was armed with four- or five-inch rockets from my first run. My wingers just had 500lb bombs. The flak was intense and it was big stuff; 85mm for the most part, some 57mm but not the little 37's and 57's that we normally encountered. Right in the pull-out over the target the place was in a shambles which gave me a lot of satisfaction. But about that time as I was pulling out I heard a very loud explosion. The airplane shook and my fire warning light came on. I knew that I'd been hit and I'd been hit hard. I told my wingmen that I had been hit and that we were headed inland. It only made sense to turn around and come back out and I just might as well drop my bombs on the way. So I said, 'let's put the bombs on them on the way out' but the airplane was progressively either coming apart or failing to work the way it was supposed to. A lot of the systems fell off the line. Eventually, in the turn coming back around, I decided to just clean everything off on the bottom of the airplane and just drop it inert. All the bombs, drop tanks; everything that was on the bottom of the airplane came off, which made me go a lot faster than my wingmen because I was at a hundred percent power.

'I headed back towards Hảiphòng harbour. My intent was to climb to altitude. By this time I had heard from my wingman that I was on fire and I was burning bad and he was advising me to get out. I didn't want to get out of an airplane which seemed to be taking me where I wanted to go, so I just stuck with it. (Later he told me that all he could see was a fire ball with two wing tips sticking out of it). I got up to about 5,000 feet with the intention of going to 9,000 feet but at 5,500 feet the stick and the right rudder pedal went all the way in the right-hand corner and the airplane started a non-commanded rudder roll. By the time I could take stock I was almost inverted. Pilots just don't really want to jump out of an airplane inverted. I had plenty of altitude so I let it go. I didn't pull the power back because I didn't want to be hanging forward in the straps. That's not a good way to eject. By the time I came around to full upright the nose was forty-five to sixty degrees nose down. I was at full power and a clean airplane. I was accelerating pretty rapidly. I looked down at my air speed indicator and the needle was moving quite rapidly. It was passing 550 knots at that time when I pulled the face curtain to

F-4B-28-MC BuNo153065 of VF-114 'Aardvarks' is recovered on the deck of the aircraft carrier USS *Kitty Hawk* (CVA-63) in the Gulf of Tonkin after a combat mission over North Viêtnam on 21 April 1968. VF-114 was assigned to Carrier Air Wing 11 (CVW-11) aboard the *Kitty Hawk* for a deployment to Viêtnam from 18 November 1967 to 28 June 1968.

eject from the aircraft because there was no control anymore. I had already stowed my kneeboard and my flashlight and other things that might be in the way and could hurt me. I had two options for getting out. One was a handle between the legs which you would pull. I had used that first time and thought that was pretty neat. But the second time I was going so fast. The face curtain was designed to protect your face from damage from a high speed ejection and I decided to use it. I kept my knees together, my back up against the seat and my elbows in at my side and grabbed the face curtain with both hands and pulled. I heard the canopy go off, felt the rush of air and the noise level increased incredibly. It felt very much to me as though I might be lying on the ground between the railroad tracks as a freight train or passenger train rushed over. It was very loud. I continued to pull and felt the seat fire. Once the rocket stopped firing I was immediately separated from the seat and it started trailing behind me. I was still holding on to the face curtain. I lost a grip with one arm. The other arm caught the wind stream and my shoulder dislocated. The humeral head broke several pieces off the top of the arm and it started flailing around out in the wind. I felt the curtain cutter fire and it released and the elbow popped out. My right shoulder was already dislocated and the left was now dislocated and it broke, too, so, for a little while I was holding the curtain in my left hand and both arms and legs were flailing around and I was corkscrewing through the air at around 600 mph. The A-4 seat was not designed to protect you at those speeds. The pain was incredible. I didn't see how anybody could survive that kind of pain. You think of it abstractly. You're not screaming or yelling or anything like that. I guess this is what it's like to die. Never having died before I wasn't sure, but it seemed reasonable that that's what it was like. It was quite conceivable that my arms could have been torn from my body. And then I could feel the chute pack snap open and suddenly I was just hanging in the chute. When the seat fires the force of gravity was supposed to be about 19 Gs. So you would very briefly weigh nineteen times more than you would normally weigh. The opening shock of the chute had to be almost twice that.

'I opened my eyes because I had them closed. And now I had a new problem to face because I was totally blind. But you react as you had been trained to do. I reached up with both hands to release my oxygen mask but it was not in its normal position. I kept reaching but I had no glove on this hand because it had been torn off in the ejection. I finally came right up against something hard and smooth and it seemed like it was wet. And I thought 'that's my skull'. I snapped the oxygen mask off and threw it away and reached up. The front of the helmet was around my right ear. So I grabbed the side of the helmet with my right hand and pulled around and suddenly I could see. It was one of the best feelings I've ever had. I was just in time to see where my aircraft had impacted the water. It had gone in almost vertically close to a mile below me. There was a big cloud of water and steam and smoke coming up. My right shoulder hurt like the devil but it was somewhat functional. The left arm didn't work. There was no shoulder there.

'I got my personal survival radio out with one hand and called up and said, 'I'm okay, but don't pick me up.' I couldn't get it back in the place where it was supposed to go and I could only get half of my flotation equipment inflated and I was getting close to the water. I hit going pretty fast and went down fairly deep. I was in Hảiphòng harbour. The canopy immediately started to pull me through the water. Just before I ran out of air the tugging on the chute suddenly stopped and I popped to the surface.

'I still wasn't out of the woods. I only had partial inflation of my flotation equipment. I was

A-7A Corsair '602' of VA-27 'Royal Maces' attached to CVW-14 preparing to launch from the USS *Constellation* in 1968.

F-4B 3011 of VF-213 after trapping on the USS *Kitty Hawk* in the Gulf of Tonkin on 28 January 1968. F-4B-28-MC BuNo 153068 (behind with '115' on the nose) was flown on 18 May 1972 by Lieutenants Henry A. 'Bart' Bartholmay and Oran R. Brown, on their first combat mission over North Viêtnam when they shot down a MiG-19 with an AIM-9 Sidewinder near Kep Air Base, northeast of Hànôi. On14 January 1973 when BuNo153068 was flown by Lieutenant Victor T. Kovaleski and Ensign D. H. Plautz of VF-161 'Chargers' from the USS *Midway* (CVA-41) this aircraft was hit by 85mm AAA about 10 miles south of Thanh Hóa and began leaking fuel. After flying offshore the crew ejected and were rescued. This was the very last US aircraft lost to enemy action during the Viêtnam War.

riding quite low in the water and it didn't take long before I could feel something tugging at my legs. The risers on the chute had wrapped around my boots and with the waves moving me up and down I was gradually sinking and being pulled down by the chute. I couldn't get the other part of my floatation inflated and I was within five or ten minutes at the most from drowning. I had to tip my head back to be able to get a breath of air occasionally but I could see two or three sailing vessels coming toward me. As they got closer I could see that they all had guns. My wingmen were flying cover for me trying to keep the boats away but I found out later that the guns jammed in both of my wingmen's' airplanes. You don't really want to drop a bomb to try to save your buddy because you're liable to kill him so they dropped their drop tanks trying to scare the boats away and keep them from picking me up, but they weren't dissuaded at all. And the flak was awfully heavy. I found out later that a helicopter was on its way to get me but he got shot up pretty badly and had to turn around and go back. The next thing I knew there was a boat pulling up alongside me and a guy pointing a rifle at me and screaming very excitedly in Viêtnamese. He kept motioning up as though he wanted me to lift my arms up. I would have been happy to lift them up to show them that I was no threat but I couldn't. I think the handle of my pistol could be seen by my chin and he was probably looking at that and figuring when I had an opportunity I was liable to try to shoot him. So I decided that he was more than likely going to shoot me before they could get me on board. I wondered what that was going to feel like. And if it hurts, how long will it hurt? But he didn't shoot. One of the men

A heavily armed A-6A of VA-35 'Black Panthers' heads for a target over North Viêtnam on 15 March 1968 while operating from the nuclear powered carrier USS *Enterprise* (CVAN-65) at 'Yankee Station'. Combined USN and USMC A-6/KA-6D losses during the war in SE Asia totalled 67 aircraft.

on board reached down and grabbed my left hand to try to pull me up onto the boat. I screamed in pain. He let go, reached around and grabbed my other arm. That shoulder was dislocated too and I screamed again in pain. They just kept pulling and found the chute was pulling me down. Somehow they got that loose. I think they just cut it with a machete. And the next thing I knew I was on the deck of the boat. I had become increasingly aware that there was an awful lot of noise. A guy with a .30 calibre machine gun on a bi-pod with another guy directing him was trying to get good shots at my wingmen. I could see one of the guys coming in really low making a high speed pass and I wanted him to get out of there because he's just going to get shot down. Just as he got in to where this guy with the machine gun started to fire, the boom came around. It probably weighed three or four hundred pounds and it caught him right in the back and pushed him over. Whew, the gun just started firing down in the water. Each time he started shooting at my wingmen, the boom would catch him in the back and down he'd go. And one time the other boat was in the way and he strafed right across the deck. It was a moment of slight humour and every little bit helps. Then things got quiet. The airplanes went away. I could hear some in the distance. The triple-A stopped firing.

'The people on the boat took off my helmet and then my torso harness, my G suit, my boots and my flight suit and left me in just my underwear. I still hurt pretty badly and they tied a rope around my right arm, the good arm. Then they opened up a hatch in the deck and pitched me into it head first. My feet caught by the edge of the hatch - they put the hatch cover back down, holding my feet outside and the rope outside. But I was head first down into the hold which was probably about three feet to the bottom. The hold was about a third full of water but there was also oil. It was pretty yucky. And it was over my head. It was another opportunity for me to drown and I wondered just what that would be like, drowning in fuel and water and fish guts. But I decided 'do the best you can to live'. So every time the boat rocked in my direction

Top Left: Lieutenant Allan Russell Carpenter, an A-4 Skyhawk pilot in VA-72 who was shot down and taken prisoner on 1 November 1966. Top (Centre) Captain Carlyle S. 'Smitty' Harris who was shot down on the raid on the bridges near Thanh Hóa on 3 April 1965 and taken prisoner. He was held prisoner for eight years and released in 1973. (Top Right) Commander Doyle Wilmer Lynn, CO of VF-111 who was shot down and killed by ground fire in his F-8D Crusader on 27 May 1965 during an attack an AAA site. Lynn had been one of the first Navy pilots to be shot down in South East Asia when his Crusader was shot down on 7 June 1964. Right (centre) Lieutenant Commander Richard Danner Hartman, pilot of one of three A-4Es of VA-164 lost on 18 July 1967. Hartman ejected about twenty-five miles south of Hànôi and evaded the North Viêtnamese for three days until he was eventually captured and was either killed at the time of capture or died soon after in a PoW camp. Bottom (left) In 1973 Americans welcomed home their returning Viêtnam prisoners of war, among them Lieutenant Colonel Robinson 'Robbie' Risner. During 33 years of service, he fought in three wars and on two separate occasions received the Air Force's highest award, the Air Force Cross. Bottom, Centre; Skyhawk pilot, 26-year-old Lieutenant (jg) Everett Alvarez Jr. in hospital in 1973 after his release. Bottom (right) Commander Frederick H. Whittemore, the executive officer of VA-212 on the *Bon Homme Richard* who was shot down on 20 July 1967 and was rescued by a Navy helicopter. Commander Whittemore was lost at sea while serving with VA-93 on 11 April 1968 on a ferry flight in a A-4F.

and I got one side of my face above water, I'd take a big breath of air and hang on until I got a chance to do it again. And that's how I breathed until they were able to get the boat into shore. It was low tide apparently and we stopped probably 2- or 300 feet from shore. They opened the hatch cover, pulled me out. I was a real mess by then. They got me to the side of the boat and tossed me overboard and there were several civilians in the mud out there with bamboo poles. They laced me up somehow and wrapped my shoulders around the other pole and tied me on to it and four of them started carrying me across this mud flat into this village. They had tried to get me to walk but I also had a broken leg and I couldn't walk. I didn't know about the broken leg until they wanted me to walk on it.

'Eventually they got me to military people who took me to pier side in Hàiphòng. It was after dark by then and they transferred me to an army vehicle. They had at least one English speaker who could communicate with me. And they took me a ways blindfolded and in the back of a covered truck. It was very noisy outside. It seemed like there were millions of people around. And they kept getting closer and closer to a centre of activity. And even through the blindfold I could see some light. Eventually they took the blindfold off and I found that I was probably in the central square in Hàiphòng. There were lights all around and wall-to-wall people, just packed as tightly as they could get and there was a roped-off area that was probably 50 feet on one side by a hundred feet on the long side. It was kind of like a boxing ring. Remember, I was wearing my underwear and had a rope tied to me. They took me to the edge of this roped-off area and as soon as the crowd saw me they quieted down. They took me to the edge of the area and pushed me out into it and they had taken the rope off my arm. I didn't know what they wanted. I looked back at the guy who was in charge and he made some sort of a motion which I didn't understand. Then he got angry and he indicated he wanted me to walk around that roped-off area. I took maybe five steps and the crowd started screaming at the top of their lungs. The ropes came down and I was surrounded. I was at least fifteen or twenty feet

USS *Ranger* (CV-61) launching a bomb-laden A-7 Corsair from her waist catapult, during operations in the Gulf of Tonkin in January 1968.

F-4B BuNo153006 of VF-154 flown by Lieutenant (jg) J. Quaintance of Honolulu, Hawaii, attached to Carrier Air Wing 2 aboard the USS *Ranger* (CVA-61) dropping bombs on an artillery site north of the DMZ to provide air support for the 3rd US Marine Division in February 1968. This aircraft served later with VMFA-314 at Chu Lai.

away from the army guys. It was a pretty scary situation. I was on my feet with a broken leg, two broken and dislocated shoulders and broken arms. Not feeling too spiffy at all. And here I was now suddenly surrounded by people. Most of them were shorter than I was and they hit me. As badly hurt as I was it was really no big deal. I said, 'let them hit away. You're not going to hurt me much more than I've been hurt.'

'The 'Voice of Viêtnam' that night announced that they had captured an American pilot and I was the only one who'd been shot down. They said they had captured several American pilots, one of them alive, which was their way of exaggerating. They took me to a hospital and the next night they took me to Hànôi in the back of a truck covered up with a tarp and drove through the front gate of Walo Prison. I didn't know it at that time, but I assumed that I was in Hànôi. I was in prison a total of six years and four months.'[64]

Phantoms and MiGs met each other in the sky over Viêtnam on many occasions throughout the first half of 1967 and American crews also continued to run the gauntlet of SAM missiles and ground fire. On 24 March Lieutenant Commander John Cooley 'Buzz' Ellison, pilot of an A-6A Intruder in VA-85 'Black Falcons' on board *Kitty Hawk* was lost along with his bombardier/navigator Lieutenant (jg) James Edwin Plowman during a four-aircraft night strike force SAM suppression mission against Bắc Giang Thermal Power Plant near Kep in North Viêtnam. SAM sites, light, medium and heavy AA batteries, automatic weapons and small arms defended the target. (John Ellison had been forced to abandon an A-6A on 15 May 1966 when the aircraft was unable to take on fuel as it was returning from a mission). After the crew radioed that they had released their bombs the Intruder was tracked by radar (probably by an E-2 Hawkeye) to be about ten miles north of their planned course. The radar plot disappeared in Hà bắc Province when the aircraft probably fell victim to AAA. One source claims that Ellison made voice contact with a SAR force but neither crewman was rescued or ever heard from again although rumours persist that at least one of the men was held captive in China. However, after the end of the war when China released the US airmen who had been shot down over Chinese

F-4s of VF-84 'Jolly Rogers' on the USS *Independence* (CVA-43) off Viêtnam in September 1965. VF-84 ended its association with the *Independence* on 27 January 1969. Their new home would be the USS *Franklin D. Roosevelt*. BuNo151478 was shot down near Đại Lãnh/An Hoa, South Viêtnam serving with VMFA-122 at Chu Lai on 7 June 1970. 1st Lieutenant Kurt Michael Wilbrecht died in the crash. 1st Lieutenant W. T. Pepper ejected and was rescued by helicopter.

Vought F-8 Crusader of VF-162 'The Hunters' about to be launched from the port cat of the USS *Ticonderoga* (CVA-14) in the Gulf of Tonkin in July 1969. (via Bob Gaines)

territory, neither Ellison nor Plowman was amongst them.

On 18 May 1967 Lieutenant Robert John Naughton of VA-113 from the *Enterprise*, who was on his second tour in Southeast Asia and flying his 194th mission, led another pilot on an armed reconnaissance mission during which they attacked the Đông Thương railway bridge, ten miles northeast of Thanh Hóa. As the aircraft started a 30-degree dive to fire a pod of unguided rockets it was hit by ground fire. The aircraft burst into flames, probably having taken a hit in a fuel line or tank and within seconds Naughton lost control of the aircraft and ejected. He was captured and spent the rest of the war as a PoW until released on 4 March 1973. Commander Kenneth Robbins Cameron, the executive officer of VA-76 on the *Bon Homme Richard* led an attack on the trans-shipment point ten miles north of Vinh. This was an important facility where supplies could be transferred from the railway, which terminated at Vinh, to the main coastal road that fed other roads heading south. Cameron rolled in to attack the target from about 10,000 feet but during the dive his aircraft was hit by AAA and Cameron ejected. He was captured but, according to the Viêtnamese, he died on 4 October 1970.[65]

The 19th of May - Hô Chi Minh's birthday - proved to be one of the worst days of the war when the first Navy raids on targets in Hànôi itself resulted in the loss of six aircraft and ten aircrew over North Viêtnam. The three participating carriers, the *Enterprise, Bon Homme Richard* and the *Kitty Hawk* each lost two aircraft. The first Alpha strike of the day was on the Văn Điễn military vehicle and SAM support depot near Hànôi, which had already been bombed on 14 December 1966 when two aircraft were shot down. Among the first aircraft into the target area was the CAP flight of F-4s from VF-96 led by Commander Richard Rich, the Squadron's executive officer. Volleys of SAMs were fired at the formation forcing the aircraft down to a lower altitude, which was dangerous due to the intense AAA and small arms fire. Commander Rich's aircraft was damaged by an SA-2 that detonated close to the F-4. Two minutes later, with the Phantom even lower, a second SAM was seen to explode close to the aircraft at which point a command ejection sequence was initiated by the NFO. Rich's back-seater, Lieutenant Commander William Robert Stark was knocked unconscious by the ejection and suffered compound fractures of the lower vertebrae, a broken arm and a broken knee. He landed about twenty miles southwest of Hànôi but there was no sign of Commander Rich, who is presumed to have been killed in the crash.

The *Kitty Hawk's* CAP flight fared no better when it took over about an hour later and it also lost one of its F-4s. The SAMs were still being fired in great numbers and despite violent evasive manoeuvres, Lieutenant (jg) Joseph Charles Plumb's aircraft in VF-114 was hit in the belly by an SA-2. The aircraft became a mass of flames and the engines wound down rapidly. As the tail section began to disintegrate, Plumb and his back-seater, Lieutenant (jg) Gareth Laverne Anderson decided that it was time to leave and ejected near Xan La, twelve miles southwest of Hànôi. Plumb recalls being captured by peasants and thrown into a pen where a bull buffalo was goaded by the villages into charging the pilot. Luckily, the animal was less than enthusiastic about the whole affair. The two fliers were incarcerated in the 'Hànôi Hilton'.

One of the waves of bombers that attacked the Văn Điển depot consisted of six Intruders from the *Enterprise*. When the formation was thirty miles southwest of Hànôi they began to receive warnings on their APR-27s of Fan Song radar signals, which meant that they were being tracked by a SAM site. 'Fan Song' got its name from its horizontal and vertical fan scanning

F-4Js 155870 of VF-143 'Pukin Dogs' and 155838 to VF-142 'Ghostriders' are prepared for launching from the USS *Constellation* (CVA-64) in 1969, when in August the carrier returned to Viêtnam for a fifth combat deployment. Following an initial 20-day period of supporting strikes in South Viêtnam as well as Laos, *Constellation* sailed to Defender Station in the Sea of Japan, which had been created as a result of increased tensions on the Korean Peninsula. On return to Yankee Station on 1 November the 'Connie' conducted her 100,000th arrested landing. During a mission on 28 March 1970 the VF-142 crew of Lieutenant Jerome E. Beaulier and Lieutenant Steven J. Barkley downed a North Viêtnamese MiG-21.

An F-4 Phantom of VF-142 Ghostriders is launched from the flight deck of the Attack Aircraft Carrier USS *Constellation* (CVA-64) in the Gulf of Tonkin on 24 February 1970. This squadron was assigned to Carrier Air Wing 14 aboard the *Constellation* from 11 August 1969 to 8 May 1970.

Launching a A-6A of VMA(AW)-224 from the USS *Coral Sea* on 9 May 1972.

antennas and its distinctive sounding emissions, which could be picked up by the B-52's warning equipment. 'Fan Song' performed two functions: target acquisition and missile guidance. It acquired as many as four targets before firing. After launch, it guided up to three SA-2s against one target. (The North Viêtnamese sometimes placed the radars away from the missiles to make the site harder to destroy.) The SA-2 missile had a solid fuel booster rocket that launched and accelerated it and then dropped off after about six seconds. While in boost stage, the missile did not guide. During the second stage, the SA-2 guided and a liquid-fuel rocket propelled it to the target. The success of the system depended almost entirely on the skill of its seven-man missile crew; the battalion commander, a fire control officer, three guidance officers, a plotter and a missile technical officer in their un-air-conditioned command van. Flying at 12,000 feet, Lieutenant Eugene Baker 'Red' McDaniel of VA-35 saw an SA-2 coming towards his aircraft so he rapidly jettisoned his bombs and made a hard right turn, but the missile exploded directly in the path of the A-6. The hydraulics must have been hit as the aircraft became uncontrollable after a few seconds and the crew ejected about twenty miles south of Hànôi. His NFO, Lieutenant James Kelly Patterson, broke his leg on landing but hid for four days as enemy forces searched for him. A Fulton extraction kit was dropped to him on the morning of the 21st but it was recovered by North Viêtnamese troops before he could reach it.[66] One of his last radio messages was to say that he was moving further up a hill to avoid enemy forces. Jim Patterson was not seen in any of the PoW camps in North Viêtnam but information suggests that he had been captured. 'Red' McDaniel was captured almost as soon as he touched down and suffered very badly at the hands of his captors.

A special raid on the North was targeted at Hànôi's thermal power plant. The attack was made by just two A-4s, equipped with Walleye TV-guided bombs and escorted by four A-4 'Iron Hand' aircraft and twelve F-8s, six for flak suppression and six for fighter escort. During the raid on the power plant both of the 'Bonnie Dick's Crusader squadrons provided aircraft for the CAP over this 'hot' target. However, the SAM sites that had wrought such havoc in the morning were still active. Lieutenant Commander Kay Russell of VF-211 was the leader of a six-plane escort flight that engaged a number of MiG-17s just to the west of Hànôi. As the Crusaders were chasing the MiGs away from the target area, Lieutenant Commander Russell's aircraft was hit first by ground fire and then by an SA-2, which caused the aircraft to burst into flames and the pilot to lose control. Kay Russell ejected and was quickly captured. A total of four MiGs were shot down by the F-8s during the engagement. Six F-8s of VF-24 were assigned the flak suppression mission during the Hànôi raid. This flight also had to contend with MiGs and SAMs but it was the intense anti-aircraft fire that brought Lieutenant (jg) William John Metzger down. He had chased MiG-17 away from the target but as the Crusader was climbing through 1,500 feet it was hit twice in the fuselage by AAA. One of the anti-aircraft shells tore a hole in the cockpit and wounded the pilot in the left arm and leg and broke his right leg. Metzger ejected about ten miles west of Hànôi and was soon captured. He was eventually released along with Lieutenant Commander Russell on 4 March 1973. The Walleye attack on the power plant failed as the bombs were released at too low an altitude to guide to the target. However, two days

An A-7E bombing the Hải Dương road and railway bridge in North Viêtnam in 1972. Note the bombed remains of a second bridge further up river.

Guerrilla soldiers search the wreckage of A-7C 156798, flown by 26-year old Lieutenant (jg) Stephen Owen Musselman of VA-82 'Marauders' which was shot down on 10 September 1972 when an 'Iron Hand' flight of Corsairs from the USS *America* was attacking SAM sites during a Linebacker raid in the Hànôi area. As the aircraft approached Hànôi from the south, a large number of SAMs were fired and Musselman and the other members of the flight started to take evasive action. A missile was seen to hit Musselman's aircraft forcing him to eject about five miles south of the city. The Viêtnamese returned his remains to the USA on 8 July 1981. (Doàn Công Tinh).

later another Walleye attack scored a direct hit on this important target.

The final loss on what came to be known in Navy circles as 'Black Friday' was an RA-5C reconnaissance aircraft of RVAH-13 from the *Kitty Hawk*. Lieutenant Commander James Lloyd Griffin and Lieutenant Jack Walters were tasked with obtaining BDA photographs of the Văn Điền depot, which had been attacked about four hours earlier. As the aircraft made its initial turn over Hànôi for its photo run it was at about 3,500 feet and doing around 700 knots. The aircraft was next seen to be engulfed in flames and flying in a north-westerly direction. About ten miles from the city the Vigilante suddenly pitched up and the forward fuselage started to break up. Both crew ejected from the flaming, disintegrating wreck and apparently both men were taken to the 'Hànôi Hilton' but survived only a few days, whether as a result of their injuries or from torture is not known.

Despite the heavy losses of the previous day, the Navy was out in force again on the 20th. An Alpha strike on the Bac Giang thermal power plant near Phù Lạng Thương , about twenty-five miles northeast of Hànôi, resulted in the loss of the A-4 flown by Commander Homer Leroy Smith, the CO of VA-212[67] who was leading seventeen aircraft from the *Bon Homme Richard*. He had just pulled up, having launched his Walleye bomb when his Skyhawk was hit by AAA and burst into flames. Accompanied by his wingman, he headed for the coast but was forced to eject about twenty miles north of Hàiphòng. Like Griffin and Walters, Commander Smith was apparently taken to the 'Hànôi Hilton' but survived only a few days and was reported to have been tortured to death.[68] On 21 May the Navy again raided the Hànôi thermal power plant and the Văn Điền depot. The raid on the thermal power plant was accompanied by several sections of Crusaders dedicated to flak suppression but one of these aircraft fell victim to the intense anti-aircraft fire around the target. Lieutenant Commander R. G. Hubbard of VF-211 on the *Bon*

Homme Richard was jinking to avoid the flak when his aircraft took a hit in the afterburner section. The afterburner nozzle was stuck in the open position and fuel was leaking from the aircraft but fortunately did not ignite. Hubbard was escorted out to sea where he refuelled from a tanker before flying to the 'Bonnie Dick'. However, when the gear was lowered, the hydraulic system must have ruptured and the aircraft burst into flames. Hubbard ejected and he was picked up by one of the carrier's Seasprite helicopters.

A strike on the Văn Điển SAM and vehicle support depot also resulted in the loss of a single aircraft and the rescue of its crew. The TARCAP flight was once more provided by the F-4Bs of VF-114 on the *Kitty Hawk*. One of the Squadron's Phantoms was flown by Lieutenant H. Dennis Wisely, who had shot down an An-2 Colt biplane on 20 December 1966 and a MiG-17 on 24 April 1967. His back-seater was Ensign James 'Jim' H. Laing. Their F-4B was hit as it was retiring from the target at low level. The TARCAP flight had evaded three SAMs but came down low and ran into intense flak. The aircraft was peppered with automatic weapons fire and suffered failures of the hydraulic and pneumatic systems. The pilot decided to make for Thailand rather than risk the gauntlet of the intense air defences between Hànôi and the coast. The decision was a wise one as the aircraft crossed the Laotian border before becoming uncontrollable, forcing the crew to eject near Sai Koun, eighty-five miles southwest of Hànôi. Jim Laing's parachute started to open the instant his ejection seat fired with the result that he broke an arm and sprained his other limbs. Both men were picked up safely by a USAF HH-3 after a Navy SH-3A had to be abandoned in Laos after running out of fuel during the first rescue attempt. This was the second ejection and rescue for Ensign Laing who had been shot down with Lieutenant Commander Southwick on 24 April.

On 24 May Lieutenant (jg) M. Alsop of VA-93 from the *Hancock* was taking part in an attack on a target ten miles southwest of Ninh Binh when he felt his A-4E hit by an anti-aircraft shell. He headed due south for the coast with the engine making ominous rumbling and grinding noises. Once out to sea the engine flamed out and Alsop ejected about fifteen miles off Thanh Hóa, from where he was picked up by a Navy helicopter. Two days later the MiG base at Kep was a target for the *Hancock's* A-4Es. Twenty-five year old Lieutenant (jg) Read Blaine Mecleary

Viêtnam People's Air Force (NVNAF) MiG-21 pilots.

of VA-93 was flying in the flak suppression section, on his 56th mission of the war and had just reached the target area at 13,000 feet when his aircraft was hit by AAA. With the aircraft performing a series of rolls to the right, Mecleary managed to fly about twelve miles to the east before having to give up the unequal struggle and eject. 'When I ejected I was badly injured due to the 600+ mph winds blasts and was unable to walk for about two months. I was held prisoner in seven different prison camps in and around Hànôi and one about ten kilometres south of the Chinese border. Like most other American PoWs I was tortured with ropes for military and political information. On 4 March 1973 after sixty-nine months and five days I was released.

On 30 May the SAMs claimed their tenth and final victim of the month during a raid on the Do Xa trans-shipment point fifteen miles south of Hànôi. Commander James Patrick Mehl, the executive officer of VA-93 aboard the *Hancock*, who was piloting an A-4E, was leading an 'Iron Hand' section in support of the raid and started to receive warnings of SAM activity near the target. The section evaded one missile but as Mehl started to climb through 16,000 feet to fire a Shrike, his aircraft was hit by another SA-2. He tried to make for the sea but was forced to eject near Hung Yên and was immediately captured. On 31 May a series of raids by the Air Force and the Navy was flown against targets at Kep on the final day of the month. Four Skyhawks of VA-212 from the *Bon Homme Richard* were on their way to Kep airfield when they encountered intense anti-aircraft fire about twenty miles northeast of Kep. Lieutenant Commander Arvin Roy Chauncey's aircraft was hit in the engine and caught fire. He turned towards high ground and jettisoned his stores but the aircraft lost power and he was forced to eject. He was captured and joined the rest of his shipmates in the 'Hànôi Hilton'. Like most of the others, he was released on 4 March 1973. When Lieutenant Commander Chauncey's aircraft was hit, his flight called for SAR assistance and stayed in the area to protect their leader and the SAR forces when they arrived. However, Lieutenant (jg) M. T Daniels almost suffered the same fate as the Lieutenant Commander when his aircraft was hit by AAA about eight miles northeast of Kep. He headed out to sea in search of a tanker but with his radio inoperative he was unable to rendezvous and take on fuel. Unable to refuel he found a SAR destroyer and ejected close by when the Skyhawk's engine flamed out. He was picked up by the destroyer's Seasprite SAR helicopter.

On 22 June the Hài Dương railway bridge was attacked by a flight of A-4Es from the Hancock. Like all bridges in North Viêtnam, it was well defended with numerous AAA sites of various calibres. Lieutenant Commander James Glenn Pirie of VA-93 was pulling up from his attack and jinking violently when his aircraft was struck twice by anti-aircraft fire. With the aircraft on fire and the engine winding down, James Pirie ejected near the bridge and was quickly captured. Six days later Commander William 'Bill' Porter Lawrence, the CO of VF-143, led a flak suppression section of F-4Bs during a raid on an important trans-shipment point ten miles northwest of Nam Định, a city in the Red River Delta about forty-five miles southeast of Hànôi. His back-seater was Lieutenant (jg) James William Bailey, a veteran of 183 combat missions over Southeast Asia, having flown with VF-143 on board the *Ranger* in 1966. The Phantoms were at 12,000 feet and were preparing to roll in on the target when Commander Lawrence's aircraft was hit by 85mm flak. With the aircraft's hydraulics failing, Lawrence released his CBUs on the target and had difficulty in pulling out of his dive before part of the tail section separated from the Phantom. The crew ejected and were captured and suffered the usual torture and beatings.

On 30 June four A-4C Skyhawks were launched from the Intrepid to hit the Bến Thuỷ thermal power plant on the Song Ca River just south of Vinh. One of the pilots was Lieutenant LeGrande Ogden Cole, who was on his second tour on board the Intrepid having flown 100 missions from the ship in 1966. In the face of intense flak the Skyhawks rolled in one after the other to bomb the target but Lieutenant Cole's aircraft was not seen after the attack started. However, Cole's wingman did report seeing a large explosion and fire to the south of the target which at first he thought was a stray bomb. When Lieutenant Cole failed to rendezvous with

Launching an A-6A of VMA(AW)-224 the "Fighting Bengals' from the USS *Coral Sea* (CV-43) on 9 May 1972. On 29 September 1956 the squadron became the first Marine unit to operate the A-4D Skyhawk. In 1965 the Bengals deployed to South Viêtnam and for almost a year operated their 'Scooters' from Chu Lai. On 1 November 1966 the squadron acquired the A-6 Intruder and was re-designated VMA(AW)-224. As part of Carrier Air Wing 15, the squadron completed six line periods on Yankee Station and participated in numerous operations including the historic Operation 'Pocket Money' mining of Haiphong Harbour.

the rest of the flight it was surmised that he had been shot down. Photographs of the target area taken by an RF-8 showed no sign of the Skyhawk's wreckage and no SAR beeper or radio transmissions were ever heard.

The last Navy aircraft lost during the month of June was a VA-146 A-4C Skyhawk from the USS *Constellation* which was on an armed reconnaissance sortie over North Viêtnam. A metal bridge was seen near Thiệu Ăng, thirty miles southwest of Nam Định and the aircraft rolled in to drop their bombs. As Lieutenant John Michael McGrath was pulling up from the target his aircraft was hit in the wing by AAA causing sudden and total loss of control. McGrath ejected immediately but his parachute only just opened as he fell through some tall trees. During the ejection and subsequent landing he broke and dislocated his arm and fractured a vertebra and a knee. Further injuries suffered during the torture sessions soon after arrival at the Hànôi Hilton.

During a raid on the railway yard at Hải Dương on 2 July, Lieutenant (jg) Frederick Morrison Kasch, an A-4B pilot of VSF-3 from the *Intrepid* was just pulling up from his bombing run when his aircraft was hit by AAA, causing partial engine failure. He trimmed the aircraft in the hope of reaching the coast and was accompanied by his wingman as he flew thirty-five miles to the south. However, as they approached the coast near Lục Linh, Kasch was down to 500 feet and he was advised to eject. His wingman lost sight of him as Kasch was flying so slowly and when he came round again all he saw was the wreckage of Kasch's aircraft among some houses. There was no sign that Kasch had survived. On 4 July an Independence Day raid on the railway at Hải Dương resulted in the loss of an A-4C and its pilot, Lieutenant Phillip Charles 'PC' Craig of VA-15 aboard the *Intrepid*. Craig had flown 100 missions on a previous tour. The raid itself was successful and the aircraft headed back to the coast. However, despite radio calls from Lieutenant Craig indicating that he had reached the coast, he did not rendezvous with the rest of the formation and could not be contacted on the radio. A SAR mission was quickly mounted but found no trace of the pilot or his aircraft. North Viêtnamese radio later reported that two aircraft had been shot down during the raid. Although this was inaccurate, as only one Skyhawk was missing, it was assumed that Craig had indeed been shot down near the coast to the south of Hảiphòng.

On 9 July the USS *Constellation* mounted a strike on the main Hảiphòng POL (Petrol-Oil-Lubricants) storage site. A formation of A-4Cs of VA-146 was approaching the target at 12,500 feet and was just about to roll in when a volley of SAMs was launched against them. One of the SA-2s hit Lieutenant Charles Richard Lee's Skyhawk and blew its tail off. The aircraft entered a slow inverted spin until it hit the ground about ten miles southwest of Hảiphòng. Lee was not seen to escape and was probably incapacitated by the SAM detonation. At almost the exact same moment that Lieutenant Lee was being shot down, a SAM battery scored another hit a few miles away to the northwest. The *Intrepid's* aircraft were targeted at the Army barracks at Ban Yên but before they arrived at the target they also encountered SAMs. Lieutenant Commander Edward Holmes Martin, the executive officer of VA-34, who was on his 19th mission over North Viêtnam, was leading the formation at about 10,000 feet and was taking evasive action but an SA-2 exploded close to his aircraft and peppered the Skyhawk with shrapnel. The aircraft caught fire and quickly became uncontrollable forcing Martin to eject about ten miles south of Hải Dương. He was quickly captured and spent the rest of the war in various PoW camps until his release on 4 March 1973.

On 12 July, two days before the *Oriskany* officially took its place back on the line on its third tour of duty off Southeast Asia; it lost its first aircraft. A VA-163, A-4E Skyhawk was launched for a training flight as part of the pre-combat training programme but the aircraft left the deck with insufficient airspeed and crashed in the sea after the pilot ejected. The Navy lost a Skyhawk of VA-212 from the *Bon Homme Richard* on its way to a strike on the railway at Mai Truong in North Viêtnam. Lieutenant Commander J. H. Kirkpatrick was five miles south of Hải Dương when his aircraft was hit in the port wing and fuselage by ground fire. The aircraft suffered hydraulic failure, fuel pump failure, an unsafe undercarriage indication and a loss of engine power. Soon after crossing the coast about fifteen miles south of Hảiphòng, with the aircraft barely able to stay airborne, Lieutenant Commander Kirkpatrick ejected. He was rescued by a Navy SAR helicopter.

On 14 July, on its first day on the line, the *Oriskany* suffered its first combat loss. Lieutenant (jg) L. J. Cunningham's A-4E in VA-164 was hit by AAA as it attacked barges on an inland waterway near Gia La, fifteen miles southeast of Vinh. The aircraft was hit in the nose and the engine must have then ingested debris as it started running rough on the way back to the carrier. By the time Cunningham reached the 'Mighty O', flames were coming from the engine exhaust and the aircraft was obviously in no shape for a carrier landing. He ejected at very low level close to the carrier and was rescued by a Seasprite from the *Oriskany's* HC-1 detachment. A flight of VA-76's A-4Cs from the *Bon Homme Richard* was sent on an armed reconnaissance mission in search of PT boats when the aircraft came under fire just off the coast near Van Ly, twenty-five miles south of Nam Định. The 'Spirits of VA-76', assigned to Air Wing 21, reached the coastal waters of Viêtnam in January 1967. One of the aircraft was hit in the port wing by an anti-aircraft shell, which caused a fire in a rocket pod carried under the wing. The rockets exploded and the debris caused the engine to fail. Lieutenant J. N. Donis ejected about fifteen miles off the coast and was picked up thirty minutes later by a Navy helicopter. Commander Robert Byron Fuller, the CO of VA-76, born 23 November 1927 in Quitman, Mississippi, who had started his flying career in 1952 in the F9F-5 Panther and had flown 110 missions in Southeast Asia, led a strike against the Co Trái railway and road bridge near Hung Yên on the Red River in Hai Hung Province, twenty miles southeast of Hànôi. Just as the aircraft commenced its attack it was rocked by the explosion of an SA-2 missile but Commander Fuller delivered his bombs before he encountered any control problems with his aircraft. The Skyhawk's tail was seen to be on fire and fuel was streaming from a leaking tank. As the aircraft started rolling uncontrollably, the pilot ejected and was soon captured. Fuller was the second CO that VA-76 had lost within

A-7E BuNo156831 of VA-146 'Blue Diamonds' ready for launching from the flight deck of the USS *Constellation* (CVA-64) in the South China Sea for a strike on a target in South Viêtnam on 25 April 1972.

eight months. He had taken command of the Squadron on 6 December 1966 when Commander A. D. McFall was accidentally killed during a night launch in the Pacific. During captivity Fuller was subjected to torture by ropes, leg irons and twenty-five months in solitary confinement. He spent sixty-eight months in captivity and was finally released on 4 March 1973 during Operation 'Homecoming'.[69]

On 16 July the *Oriskany's* Air Wing was having a rough return to combat, losing its third aircraft in as many days. Before the month was over, the 'Mighty O' would lose a total of ten aircraft in combat and three in accidents. Lieutenant Commander Demetrio A. 'Butch' Verich of VF-162 flying an F-8E Crusader who had been shot down on 18 August 1966 during the *Oriskany's* second war cruise and was leading the flak suppression element of three F-8s during a raid by A-4s on the Phù Lý railway yard, thirty miles south of Hànôi. As the formation approached the target it came under attack from a SAM site. Verich started a split-S manoeuvre to evade two of the missiles but his aircraft was hit by a third SA-2 as the Crusader was diving through 5,000 feet. The aircraft began to disintegrate and Verich ejected immediately. His position was only about sixteen miles south of Hànôi when he landed so he was most fortunate to be rescued by a Navy SH-3 of HS-2 from the Hornet at first light on the 17th after fifteen hours on the ground close to an AAA position. The helicopter pilot, Lieutenant Neil Sparks, was awarded the Navy Cross for his courage and skill in rescuing the pilot. The helicopter had spent a total of two hours and twenty-three minutes over North Viêtnam during the rescue, much of that time under fire.

The 18th turned out to be another bad day for the *Oriskany* with the loss of three A-4Es and one pilot. VA-I64 mounted a raid on the Co Trai railway and road bridge, which had been the target just five days earlier. Lieutenant Commander Richard Danner Hartman had successfully bombed the target and was leaving the area when his aircraft was hit by AAA. The Skyhawk caught fire and Hartman ejected about twenty-five miles south of Hànôi. Encouraged by the success in recovering Lieutenant Commander 'Butch' Verich on the 16th, a SAR mission was quickly organised and aircraft from VA-164 orbited over Hartman's position to provide protection. However, this was an extremely 'hot' location and after about twelve minutes another A-4 was hit by anti-aircraft fire. Lieutenant Larrie J. Duthie was jinking to avoid being hit but there was so much flak in the sky that there was very little chance of avoiding it for long. His flight controls began to fail and his oxygen supply failed, probably as a result of the oxygen tank being hit and burning its way through the aircraft's structure. Duthie came down near Nam Định. Worse was to follow a little while later as a rescue attempt was made by an SH-3 but was beaten back by strong anti-aircraft fire. One of the escorting A-4Es from Duthie's section was hit as it pulled out of a forty-five-degree dive to launch Zuni rockets against gun positions. Lieutenant Barry T. Wood noticed his fuel gauge was rapidly unwinding, indicating a fuel leak so he jettisoned his ordnance and made for the coast. He ejected about eight miles out to sea and was picked up by a boat from a SAR destroyer, the USS *Richard B. Anderson*. Meanwhile both Navy and USAF rescue forces were attempting to reach Lieutenant Duthie. In the face of intense ground fire that damaged several helicopters and escorting aircraft, an HH-3E piloted by Major Glen York made a successful pick up. York was awarded the AFC for this daring rescue. The next day a SH-3A from the Hornet's HS-2, piloted by Lieutenant D. W. Peterson, attempted to reach Hartman once again. The helicopter was hit by ground fire and crashed, killing all on board including the pilot and Ensign D. P. Frye, AX2 W. B. Jackson and AX2 D. P. McGrane. Following this tragedy the SAR mission to rescue Lieutenant Commander Hartman was reluctantly called off. It had cost the Navy two A-4s and a helicopter with the lives of four men. Meanwhile, through all the activity overhead, Lieutenant Commander Hartman was in hiding on a karst hill and in radio contact with his flight. He evaded the North Viêtnamese for three days and was resupplied by air during this time. However, he was eventually captured and was either killed at the time of capture or died soon after in a PoW camp. His remains were returned by the Viêtnamese on 6 March 1974.

Douglas EKA-3B Skywarrior BuNo 142661 from Tactical Electronic Contermeasures Squadron VAQ-135 Det.5 'Black Ravens' refuels Vought F-8J Crusader BuNo 150660 from VF-211 'Checkmates' off Viêtnam. Both squadrons were assigned to Carrier Air Wing 21 (CVW-21) aboard the aircraft carrier USS *Hancock* (CVA-19) for a deployment to Viêtnam from 7 January to 3 October 1972.

On 19 July the Go Trai railway and road bridge, which had been the scene of the losses on the 18th was hit again. Once more the raid resulted in tragedy and for VF-162 this raid was exactly a year from a raid on the same target with similar tragic results. Commander Herbert 'Herb' Perry Hunter, the executive officer of VF-162, who had previously flown as a member of the Blue Angels aerobatic team, was leading the flak suppression element during the raid when his Crusader was hit in the port wing by 57mm anti-aircraft fire. The fuel tanks in the wing were ruptured and the aircraft's hydraulics partially disabled. Commander Hunter and his wingman, Lieutenant Lee Fernandez, crossed the coast and headed towards the *Bon Homme Richard*, thinking it was the *Oriskany*. The damage to the aircraft meant that two bombs could not be jettisoned nor could the Crusader take on fuel. The Crusader's wing was unusual in that the entire wing was raised at the leading edge to give more lift during the approach and landing. However, Commander Hunter could not raise the wing and attempted a landing with the wing in the normal flight position. The aircraft hit the deck hard and fast, missed the arrester wires, wiped off its landing gear and plunged over the side into the water. Commander Hunter may have been stunned as he hit the deck as he was found floating under water with a partially deployed parachute. This traumatic incident, together with his moral opposition to the war and an eyesight problem, badly affected Lieutenant Fernandez who later turned in his wings and then retired from the Navy.

On 20 July a series of strikes on the My Xa POL storage facility, fifteen miles northwest of Hảiphòng, resulted in the loss of two Navy A-4E Skyhawks on the 20th. The first aircraft was hit in the tail by AAA as it climbed to commence its attack on the target. Commander Frederick H. Whittemore, the executive officer of VA-212 on the *Bon Homme Richard*, disconnected the flight controls after experiencing complete hydraulic failure. He was only able to control the aircraft by using the horizontal stabilizer and rudder but nevertheless flew out to sea before ejecting sixty miles east of Hon Gai. As the aircraft meandered thirty degrees either side of the desired heading and its altitude varied involuntarily between 2,000 feet and 6,000 feet, it is a miracle that Whittemore managed to position himself over the water where he could be rescued by a Navy helicopter.[70]

Another raid on the My Xa POL storage site later in the day resulted in the loss of a VA-163 Skyhawk from the Oriskany. Approaching the coast about twelve miles east of Hon Gay, Lieutenant R. W. Kuhl encountered light flak and felt his aircraft hit and his engine start to vibrate. Kuhl lost his radio and the cockpit began to fill with smoke, forcing him to turn back. He continued out to sea but as he approached the northern SAR destroyer, which was positioned about 45 miles south of Hon Gay, the aircraft became uncontrollable and he ejected safely.

On 25 July a truck convoy was spotted near Hà Tinh, twenty miles south of Vinh by a section of two VA-163 A-4Es from the *Oriskany* during a night armed reconnaissance mission. Under the light of flares dropped by one of the Skyhawks, Lieutenant Commander Donald Vance Davis started his strafing run but was either shot down or flew into the ground by accident. It was apparent that the pilot had not survived the crash. On 29 July a KA-3B of Detachment G, VAH-4 on board the *Oriskany* suffered a double engine failure while on a tanker mission over the Gulf of Tonkin about 150 miles northeast of Đà Nẵng. Unable to rectify the problem, all three crew abandoned the aircraft but only the pilot was found and rescued.[71]

On 29 July one of the greatest tragedies of the war in Southeast Asia occurred as the result of a Simple electrical malfunction. The Atlantic Fleet carrier *Forrestal* (which in 1955 had been the first carrier built to handle jet aircraft) had left Norfolk, Virginia on 6 June after a major refit and was assigned to TF 77 on 8 July. After working up in the South China Sea, the *Forrestal* took up her position at Yankee Station on 25 July for her combat debut off Viêtnam. Four days later, after flying just 150 combat sorties; she was limping away from Viêtnam towards Subic Bay in the Philippines for temporary repairs before returning to Norfolk, Virginia on 14 September for a major refurbishment. On the morning of 29 July as a launch was under way, a stray voltage ignited a Zuni rocket pod suspended under F-4B 153061 of VF-11. One of the rockets fired and

A-6A Intruder BuNo155668 of VA-85 'Black Falcons' attached to CVW-14 on the USS *Constellation* (CVA-64) dropping Mk.81/82 'Snakeye' 250lb General purpose bombs with Mk.14 TRD (Tail Retarding Device) attached over Viêtnam.

zoomed across the deck to hit a VA-46 A-4E fuel tank, causing a chain reaction of explosions and fire on the flight deck. The Skyhawk pilot, Commander Fred D. White, was incredibly fortunate to escape and be rescued by his plane captain. The aircraft on the deck were soon well ablaze, the fire fed by over 40,000 gallons of aviation fuel together with bombs and other ordnance. Bombs detonated, blowing holes in the armoured deck through which fell burning fuel and ordnance that set fire to six lower decks. After the inferno was eventually brought under control the next day, a total of 134 men were dead, sixty-two more injured and twenty-one aircraft destroyed with another thirty-four damaged.

On 31 July the *Oriskany* had had an extremely tough re-introduction to combat in Southeast Asia with the loss of twelve aircraft and seven airmen since the ship started combat operations on 14 July. An SA-2 claimed the last victim of the month. Lieutenant (jg) Charles Peter Zuhoski of VF-111 was flying as escort to an 'Iron Hand' operation to the east of Hànôi. The aircraft found what they were looking for and started manoeuvring to avoid a volley of missiles. Lieutenant Zuhoski was climbing through 11,000 feet when his aircraft was hit in the rear fuselage by a SAM. The engine seized and, with the rear of the aircraft a mass of flames,the pilot ejected and landed near the village of Ngû nghi, ten miles east of Hànôi. Like many pilots now coming into Southeast Asia, Charles Zuhoski was on his first operational tour of duty after completion of flying and combat training. He joined VF-111 in March 1967, got married on 3 June, departed Alameda on the *Oriskany* on 16 June and became a PoW on his 14th mission on 31 July. He was released by the North Viêtnamese on 14 March 1973.

During April-July 1967 the Navy accounted for another dozen enemy aircraft but one of its worst days occurred on 21 August when three A-6A Intruders in a four-plane strike force of Milestone flight from VA-196 'Main Battery' aboard the *Constellation* were shot down during a raid on the Duc Noi rail yards five miles north of Hànôi. The naval strike was unleashed at exactly the same time as the USAF strike was going in at Yên Vinh nearby. The Intruders were led by Commander Leo Twyman Profilet, the CO of VA-196 and a veteran of the Korean War where he had flown ninety-eight combat missions in the Skyraider. The Intruders' route from the coast-in point had been uneventful with the exception that the cloud base was between 3,000 feet and 5,000 feet and storm clouds were building up. Further along their route they received indications of launched SAM missiles and observed bursting 85mm AA fire. Lieutenant (jg) Forrest G. Trembley in the Intruder flown by Lieutenant (jg) Dain V. Scott reported that they had been hit and were advised to reverse course and return to the coast. Trembley transmitted that they were experiencing no difficulty and that they would proceed to the target rather than egress alone. Several SAMs had been launched at this time and a transmission was made, 'Heads up for the Air Force strike' which was being conducted in the vicinity of the Intruders' target. Commander Profilet and Lieutenant Commander William M. Hardman were hit in the target area. As Profilet's aircraft rolled into a thirty degree dive from 7,500 feet, an SA-2 exploded close by, which badly damaged the aircraft's starboard wing. A few moments later the wing came off and the aircraft cart-wheeled towards the ground. The crew ejected and landed close to Hànôi and were quickly captured and taken to the 'Hànôi Hilton'. Profilet and Hardman were on their 59th mission together when they were shot down. A total of fifty-one SAMs were fired at the *Constellation's* aircraft during a series of strikes on this day.

Of the three remaining Intruders of 'Milestone' flight, two of them, flown by Lieutenant Commander Jimmy Lee Buckley and his bombardier-navigator Lieutenant Robert J. Flynn and his bombardier-navigator Lieutenant (jg) Dain V. Scott and Lieutenant (jg) Forrest G. Trembley became separated from the deputy leader in the other aircraft but were tracked on his radar screen and those of an orbiting E-2 Hawkeye and on the *Constellation* itself. Flynn was well-

A-4F Skyhawks of VA-55 'Warhorses' of Attack Carrier Air Wing 21 (CVW-21) on the flight deck of the attack aircraft carrier USS *Hancock* (CVA-19), armed for a mission over Viêtnam on 25 May 1972. Skyhawks NP-501, -505, and -510 belong to VA-55; NP-316 to VA-212 'Rampant Raiders', NP-412 and NP-416 to VA-164 'Ghost Riders'. The aircraft are armed with Mk 82 (500 lb and Mk 83 1,000lb bombs.

known throughout his Air Wing for carrying his cornet with him on combat missions with which to sound the US Cavalry charge into a keyed microphone just before roll-in. The two Intruders flew northeast away from the target but instead of turning out to sea they continued heading northeast until they crossed into China, almost 110 miles from Hànôi. It was possible that low cloud and thunderstorms forced them to head further north than had been planned and they apparently missed their pre-planned turning points. Whatever the cause, when the aircraft crossed into Chinese airspace they were attacked and shot down by Chinese MiG-19s and the event was loudly proclaimed on Peking Radio.

On 31 August on the last day of the month the *Oriskany* dispatched ten A-4E Skyhawks from VA-163 'Saints' and VA-164 'Ghost Riders' against a railway bridge at near Hàiphòng. A concerted campaign had started the previous day to isolate Hàiphòng through which about 85% of the North's imports arrived. As the ships bringing in the supplies could not be attacked or the harbour mined, the only alternative was to try to cut all routes out of the city. About thirteen miles southwest of Hàiphòng on the approach to the target the formation encountered a volley of SAMs. One of the missiles exploded directly in the path of Lieutenant Commander Hugh Allen Stafford and his wingman, Lieutenant (jg) David Jay Carey. Stafford was flying at about 16,000 feet and the force of the explosion blew him out of the cockpit of his aircraft still strapped to his ejection seat. Fortunately, his seat separated and his parachute deployed automatically and, although badly injured, he was lucky to survive at all. Lieutenant Carey, who was on his first mission over North Viêtnam, was also in trouble. His engine wound down and the rear end of his aircraft was on fire. He ejected from the aircraft and, like his leader, was quickly captured. A few minutes after the first two aircraft went down, the aircraft of Lieutenant Commander Richard Clark Perry, the leader of the VA-164 element, was hit by another SA-2. Streaming fuel, Lieutenant Commander Perry turned out to sea escorted by two other VA-164 aircraft. About two miles off the coast, the aircraft became uncontrollable and Perry ejected. A SAR helicopter was already on the scene and a helicopter crewman saw Lieutenant Commander Perry hanging limp in his parachute. When he entered the water he failed to surface and when the para-rescue man reached him he was found to be dead, probably from a chest wound. As the parachute lines were twisted around the pilot's body and the North Viêtnamese were firing mortars at the helicopter from the shore, Lieutenant Commander Perry's body had to be left in the water.

On 24 October 1967 seven hours after Kep airfield was bombed, the Navy and Air Force made a coordinated attack on Phuc Yên, the first time this major air base had been attacked. The raid was accompanied by several flights of Phantoms that flew CAPs over various points in North Viêtnam. Radio Hànôi announced that, in the afternoon, eight US warplanes had been shot down and that a number of pilots had been captured. Two of the losses were F-4B Phantoms of VF-151 'Vigilantes' from the *Coral Sea*. One was crewed by pilot Commander Charles R. Gillespie the CO of VF-151 who led one of the Phantom sections and his NFO (Naval Flight Officer or navigator), Lieutenant (jg) Richard C. Clark, the other, by Lieutenant (jg)'s Robert F. Frishmann and Earl G. Lewis, which were brought down by SAM missiles during a strike on the Hànôi, Hàiphòng and Vinh Phuc region of North Viêtnam.

As the raid was flying down Thud Ridge, still thirteen miles north of the target, it was engaged by a SAM battery. Commander Gillespie saw one of the SA-2s and dived to 14,000 feet to avoid it but moments later the aircraft was hit by another missile that the crew had not spotted. The aircraft burst into flames and the hydraulics failed, leading to loss of control. The cockpit filled with smoke, the intercom went dead and Gillespie had to use hand signals to order abandonment. He ejected safely but was not able to tell if his NFO escaped from the aircraft although other members of the section reported seeing two parachutes. It seems that Lieutenant Clark did not appear in any of the PoW camps. The other members of Gillespie's flight remained overhead near Thud Ridge to provide cover for any possible rescue attempt. About fifteen minutes later another Phantom was hit by a SAM. Lieutenant Robert F. Frishmann was flying straight and level at 10,000 feet when it was damaged by a missile that exploded behind the Phantom. One of the engines failed and caught fire but before the crew could take any action another SA-2 exploded just in front of the aircraft. The Phantom immediately rolled out of control and both crew ejected. Frishmann thought his NFO had been killed but the pair met up after more than four hours on the ground. However, both men were found and captured by the Viêtnamese. Frishmann's arm was badly injured when the SAM exploded but a North Viêtnamese doctor operated on the arm removing the elbow joint and shortening the arm by eight inches.

On 26 October the Navy lost two A-4Es and an F-8E Crusader to North Viêtnamese SAM batteries. The first aircraft was lost during another raid on Phuc Yên. Commander Verlyne Wayne Daniels, a Korean War veteran having flown Skyraiders with VA-155 in 1953, had returned to his old squadron in 1967 as executive officer of VA-155 operating from the Coral Sea. On 26 October he was leading the second division of Skyhawks towards the target area at about 9,000 feet when a barrage of SAMs was fired at the aircraft. Daniels started evasive manoeuvres but his aircraft received a direct hit from an SA-2 that hit the rear fuselage. The aircraft was engulfed in flames and went out of control when the hydraulics failed. Commander Daniels ejected about fifteen miles northwest of Thai Nguyen and was soon captured. A little later in the morning the *Oriskany* launched an A-4E strike on a thermal power plant at Hànôi. Again the target was well protected by SAM batteries and two aircraft were shot down. Lieutenant Commander John Sidney McCain of VA-163, who was flying his 23rd mission, was in the leading division of the raid but as he started his dive on the target his aircraft was hit by an SA-2, which blew most of the starboard wing off. Unable to control the remnants of his aircraft, McCain ejected over Hànôi itself and landed in Truc Bach Lake, a small lake in the city. During the high-speed ejection he broke both arms and his right leg and was barely able to save himself from drowning. Lieutenant Commander McCain was captured and spent the next five years as a prisoner until released on 14 March 1973. About an hour after McCain had been shot down, another raid of twenty-five aircraft from *Oriskany* attacked the thermal power plant at Hànôi. A flight of four F-8Es of VF-162 was assigned to flak suppression but one of the aircraft had to return to the carrier with a malfunction. As the three remaining aircraft approached the target the flight received SAM warnings and the Crusaders took immediate evasive action. Two SAMs were fired and Lieutenant (jg) Charles Donald Rice's aircraft was hit by a missile at 15,000 feet as the F-8 was inverted during a split-S manoeuvre. The aircraft's port wing was blown off and Rice ejected to land three miles northwest of Hànôi. He was quickly captured and imprisoned in the 'Hànôi Hilton'.

On 19 November two more VF-151 F-4Bs were lost. Switchbox flight from VF-151 was providing TARCAP coverage in the vicinity of Hảiphòng during strikes by aircraft from the *Intrepid* on airfields and bridges near the city. The two Phantoms were stalking a flight of MiGs when they were themselves engaged by other MiGs just south of Hảiphòng. The MiGs were from Gia Lam but were operating undetected from a forward airfield at Kiên Ân. Lieutenant Commander Claude D. Clower's aircraft was hit by an air-to-air missile and its starboard wing was blown off. Clower ejected and was captured but Lieutenant (jg) Walter O. Estes may have been injured as he was not seen to escape. Moments later Lieutenant (jg) James F. Teague's aircraft was also hit and damaged. The NFO, Lieutenant (jg) Theodore G. Stier, thought that the aircraft was hit by cannon fire from a MiG but it is also possible that the aircraft was damaged by debris from Clower's aircraft, which had just exploded close by. Stier, a veteran of 155 missions, ejected but his pilot was not seen to escape from the aircraft.

On the night of 30 October 1967 a lone A-6 Intruder jet aircraft was launched from a Seventh Fleet carrier in the Gulf of Tonkin. Its target was in Hànôi - the most heavily defended city in the world and perhaps in the history of air warfare. For this single-plane strike, the pilot, Lieutenant Commander Charles Hunter and the bombardier-navigator, Lieutenant Lyle Bull were awarded the Navy Cross for 'extraordinary heroism' and performance 'above and beyond the call of duty'. This is their story.[72]

The previous afternoon was like many others. The two had coffee in the stateroom Bull shared with another bombardier-navigator from their unit, VA-196. Bull had just finished the planning for a routine night hop in which they would be going after trucks in North Viêtnam. Finding and hitting moving targets in complete darkness was no trick for the crew or the highly sophisticated electronic black boxes in the A-6 Intruder. 'Piece of cake,' they called it. They discussed the mission thoroughly, but Bull did the actual planning. The pilot looked over his navigator's work very carefully, but, as was usually the case, made no changes.

The final weather briefing was scheduled for 1800. There was time to relax. It was only 1630 - until a phone call from the squadron duty officer changed their plans. 'Better get down to IOIC[73] Lyle,' said the duty officer, 'you're going to Hànôi tonight.'

In IOIC Lieutenant (jg) Pete Barrick, the squadron air intelligence officer, was ready for them. Charts were spread out on a long table. While Barrick left to get the target folder, Hunter and Bull glanced at the air defence charts of the Hànôi area, noting fresh red markings which indicated new surface-to-air missile (SAM) sites. In addition, hundreds of black dots showed anti-aircraft gun positions and in the vicinity of their target - the Hànôi railroad ferry slip - it was almost solid. Hunter said one approach looked as bad as another. This was to be a single-plane strike. The success of the mission depended entirely upon one A-6 and its crew. Barrick, Hunter and Bull studied the target carefully. The photography of the area was good. Exact measurements were made to provide precise inputs for the computers in the aircraft. The Hànôi air defences were evaluated. Hunter's initial impression was right; there was no 'best' way to get in or out. It was going to be rough because Hànôi was loaded. Leaving IOIC, the two of them went up to the forward wardroom for a quick dinner. The meal was served cafeteria style. There was a short waiting line made up mostly of their squadron mates. 'Stand back, you guys,

F-4J 155799 of VF-92 with F-4J-35-MC 155800 of VF-96 (behind) on the USS *Constellation* (CVA-64) in early 1972. 155800 was flown by Lieutenant Randy H. 'Duke' Cunningham and Lieutenant (jg) William P. Driscoll on 10 May on a flak suppression flight on a raid on Hải Dương when they destroyed three MiG-17s. Their third kill made Cunningham and Driscoll the first aces of the Viêtnam War as they had previously shot down two MiGs on 19 January and 8 May. They had little time to celebrate their new 'ace' status. They headed out towards the coast passing several more MiGs but as they approached Nam Định, climbing through 16,000 feet, their aircraft was damaged by an explosion from an SA-2 missile. Shrapnel peppered the rear underside of the fuselage and the starboard wing tip was blown off. Soon afterwards the hydraulics started to fail. They reached the coast but the aircraft was on fire and started to spin so Cunningham and Driscoll ejected about five miles out to sea. They were soon rescued by SH-3 Sea King helicopters from HC-7 and were taken to the USS *Okinawa*.

On 10 May 1972 Lieutenant Randy 'Duke' Cunningham, pilot of a VF-96 F-4J Phantom operating from the *Constellation* and Lieutenant (jg) William P. 'Irish' Driscoll his RIO became the first American aircrew to qualify as aces solely as a result of action in Viêtnam when they downed their third, fourth and fifth MiGs.

here come Charlie and Lyle. They go first. This may be their last meal,' said one of the young officers. The two aviators laughed self-consciously and moved to the head of the line. There was more joking, but pervading it all was the uncomfortable feeling that perhaps the well-intended humour was getting too close to the truth.

The whole squadron knew Hànôi for what it was - a closely knit web of anti-aircraft guns and SAM sites. There were at least 560 known anti-aircraft guns of various calibres in the area Hunter and Bull were to flyover. Thirty MiG aircraft were based within a few seconds' flying time from their target. They knew full well that the flight would be opposed by fifteen 'hot' SAM sites; sites that had been firing with devastating accuracy in previous days. During intelligence briefings, they were told that the North Viêtnamese were transferring additional defence firepower to protect their capital city. Hunter and Bull did not discuss the fact that they might not make it back. After all, six other crews from their squadron had gone through the heart of Hànôi three nights before. They took missiles and flak, but they all came home without a scratch. But that strike was different. It was one of the first strikes to hit in the area of the railroad ferry slip and it obviously took the North Viêtnamese defenders by surprise. The planes shot through with ten-minute separations, but each successive aircraft encountered steadily increasing defensive fire. Six SAMs were fired at the last plane.

Commander Robert Blackwood, the squadron's executive officer, returned from the raid convinced that the luxury of surprise would not be available to any more multi-plane strikes going into Hànôi, but a single plane might make it. He discussed the alternatives available with the task force commander, as well as the odds of success and survival. They both knew that shore-based as well as carrier-based aircraft had taken a terrible 'hosing down' in the Hànôi area. The Admiral was convinced that there was no single best way of accomplishing this mission, but he also believed in making frequent variations in tactics. If they were to achieve surprise the strike would have to go in low and at-night. Could the A-6 do it? Hunter and Bull would be the first to know.

The launch, when it came, was much the same as the many that had preceded it. The catapult hurled the twenty-seven-ton aircraft down the deck with the always impressive acceleration force that, in a space of 230 feet, propelled the aircraft to an air speed of 150 knots. The A-6 was airborne from its home, the attack carrier *Constellation*. The lone Intruder swept over the beach at the coast-in point they called the 'armpit,' an inlet north of Thanh Hóa and south of Nam Định. The planned approach to the target used the rocky hills to the southwest of Hànôi in order to take advantage of the radar 'masking' which they provided. Absolute minimum altitude would be the only way the A-6 would be able to stay below the lethal envelope of a radar-guided SAM. The jet, moving at 350 knots, was now at an altitude of 500 feet.

As the jet flew to within eighteen miles of the target, a signal flashed in the cockpit, indicating that a SAM radar was locked on the A-6. Immediately Hunter snapped, 'Take me down.' With precision accuracy, Bull guided the pilot by search radar down to 300 feet, with the jagged hills rising on either side. At the lower altitude, their instruments indicated they had lost the SAM lock-on. In the radarscope, Bull could see only the ridges of the hills on both sides above them and the reflection of the valley floor below. Four miles straight ahead was the Initial Point (IP), a small island in the Red River. The IP would be the final navigational aid en route to the target. From this spot, distance and bearing had been precisely measured to the railroad ferry slip. Both the pilot and navigator had to work as one if the mission was to be a success.

With his eyes fixed on the radarscope, Bull placed the crossed hairs on the IP in his radar screen. At the proper instant, Hunter was ready to turn on the final in-bound leg to the target. And again the warning flashed that another SAM radar had locked-on the A-6. Hunter eased the craft down to less than 200 feet and he moved the stick to the left as the A-6 passed just short of the island in the Red River. The target was now ten miles ahead. The SAM warning signal did not break off with the drop in altitude. As the Intruder flew at near treetop level, Hunter and Bull could see a missile lift off from its pad. The SAM was locked-on and guiding perfectly toward the cockpit of the Intruder. Hunter waited until the last second and then he yanked back on the stick, pulling the aircraft into a steep climb. With the nose of the A-6 pointed almost straight up, the SAM exploded underneath it. The laden bomber shook violently, but continued into a modified barrel roll, topping out at 2,500 feet. At the peak of the high-G roll, the A-6 was on its back. Bull raised his head and could see the ground beneath him lit up by flak. The Intruder rolled out close to the target heading. Bull fixed his attention on the radarscope, noting that the radar cursors had stayed on the target through the roll. 'I'm stepping the system into attack,' he told Hunter.

Something caught his eye and he looked up. 'I have two missiles at two o'clock, Charlie,' Bull announced. 'And I have three missiles at ten o'clock,' was Hunter's cool reply. Evasion was virtually impossible with five missiles guiding in on the A-6 from two different directions. Hunter quickly manoeuvred the plane, dropping the A-6 to 50 feet. The terrain, illuminated by

F-4J BuNo 153787 of VF-74 'Be-Devilers' of Carrier Air Wing (CVW) 8, recovers aboard USS *America* (CVA-66) off Viêtnam 1972.

flak, appeared to be level with the wing tips. Bull could clearly see trucks and people on the road below. They were now only seconds from the target. The five missiles guided perfectly in azimuth, but could not reach down to the A-6. Bull sensed that the missiles exploded above the canopy, but he didn't look up. His attention was momentarily fixed on the ground where multiple rows of anti-aircraft guns were firing at the aircraft. He watched the muzzle blasts as the jet shot past each row. They were like mileage markers along the road to the ferry slip. Then came the searchlights, scanning the sky as if celebrating the opening of a giant new supermarket. Some illuminated the Intruder momentarily, but could not stay with the speeding aircraft. Now they were on the target. On signal, Hunter eased back on the stick and the bomber moved up to 200 feet. The next three-and-a-half seconds would be critical to the accuracy of the bomb drop. Hunter must hold the wings level and the course steady, so that Bull and the computers could do the job they had come so far to accomplish. The weapons, eighteen 500lb bombs, fell toward the ferry slip. Feeling the loss of nearly 10,000lbs of dead weight, Hunter pulled the A-6 into a hard right turn. The aircraft was turned into an outbound, southeast heading and Hunter, giving the Communist gunners a run for their money, began manoeuvring the A-6 up and down, back and forth. Again the SAM warning was given - four more missiles were locked on the Intruder. They followed, but could not track the Intruder through its evasive manoeuvres and they exploded above and behind.

They passed over another flak site without incident and then they were safely on their way back to the *Constellation*. For the first time Charlie Hunter and Lyle Bull had time to realize what they had been through. Only a limited number of military airmen have challenged the main battery of guns in the Hànôi area of North Viêtnam. Fewer yet can claim membership in the elite group who have successfully flown unescorted, at night, over North Viêtnam's capital city. For those of the latter group, certainly, any subsequent, new experience promised to be anticlimactic.

Early in 1968 President Johnson forbade all strikes further than the 19th Parallel and on 1 November he ordered a halt to all bombing of North Viêtnam. The next incoming President, Richard F. Nixon, confirmed this policy in January 1969 and the ban on bombing of the North remained in force until May 1972 when the North Viêtnamese offensive prompted Nixon to authorize a resumption. 'Linebacker I' as it was called began with raids against road and rail systems, to prevent supplies reaching the Communists operating in South Viêtnam. On 8 May A-6 Intruders sowed minefields in Hàiphòng, Hon Gai and Câm Phà in the North and in five ports in the South. At this time the North Viêtnamese had one of the best air defence systems in the world, with excellent radar integration of SA-2 SAMs, MiGs and AAA. Losses, though, were kept to within acceptable limits.

The period 10 May to 15 October 1972 produced all four American aces (three USAF and one USN) of the Viêtnam War.[74] On the 10 May strike (the second that day) two Navy fliers - Lieutenant Randy 'Duke' Cunningham, pilot of a VF-96 F-4J Phantom and Lieutenant (jg) William Driscoll, his RIO - operating from the *Constellation* became the first American aircrew to qualify as aces solely as a result of action in Viêtnam when they downed their third, fourth and fifth MiGs before their F-4J was hit by a SAM and went down off the coast. Two MiG-17s latched onto Cunningham and Driscoll's wingman 1,000 feet behind. Just as Cunningham turned the F-4 around the enemy pilot made the fatal mistake of momentarily exposing his underside in a vertical climb. Cunningham fired off a Sidewinder and the MiG-17 exploded. Cunningham turned away and tried to lure another MiG into his wingman's line of sight, but the F-4 pilot had his hands full with other MiGs and Cunningham was forced to disengage. Scanning the sky Cunningham and Driscoll spotted another F-4 with two MiGs on its tail and another off to the right. Cunningham picked out the nearest MiG-17 and let him have it with another Sidewinder. The enemy jet exploded and the pilot ejected. This action brought four MiG-21s down onto the double MiG killers and the outnumbered Phantom crew knew it was time to head for the open sea and home. Nearing the coast Cunningham spotted a MiG-17 and,

Lieutenant Commander John Sidney McCain III, an A-4E Skyhawk pilot, after being released from captivity in Hànôi in 1973. Almost killed in the 29 July 1967 USS *Forrestal* fire, on 26 October 1967 he was shot down, seriously injured and captured by the North Viêtnamese flying his 23rd bombing mission over North Viêtnam when his was shot down by a missile over Hànôi. McCain fractured both arms and a leg ejecting from his Skyhawk and nearly drowned when he parachuted into Trúc Bạch Lake. Some North Viêtnamese pulled him ashore and then others crushed his shoulder with a rifle butt and bayoneted him. McCain was then transported to Hòa Lò Prison, nicknamed the 'Hànôi Hilton'. Although McCain was badly wounded, his captors refused to treat his injuries, beating and interrogating him to get information; he was given medical care only when the North Viêtnamese discovered that his father was a top admiral.

needing just one more for ace status, he decided to try to shoot it down. The two Americans tacked onto the MiG and a vicious, twisting dogfight ensued. Cunningham realised that this was no ordinary MiG pilot. Neither side could gain the initiative and finally Toon broke off, probably low on fuel and headed for home. The Phantom crew gained their first advantage. Now above and behind him they seized the opportunity to fire their one remaining Sidewinder at the retreating MiG. The heat-seeking missile locked on to the enemy's tailpipe and blew the jet to pieces. Cunningham had always said a SAM would never hit him. But now, as he turned for home near Hảiphòng, his F-4 was hit by one of the long telegraph pole-shaped missiles. It failed, however, to bring down the jet. Cunningham managed to fly the badly damaged Phantom back to the *Constellation*, where at 10,000 feet the two men ejected into the sea. They were picked up by a CH-46 helicopter from the *Okinawa* and returned safely to a hero's welcome aboard their own carrier where the two fliers, who had scored their two previous victories on 19 January and 8 May when they destroyed a MiG-21 and a MiG-17 respectively, shared their victories with their colleagues.[75]

Cunningham and Driscoll - Call sign 'Showtime 100' - had begun their mission as part of flak support for a strike group attacking Hải Dương railroad yard. After delivering their ordnance they were attacked from 7 o'clock by two MiG-17s firing cannon. 'Showtime 100's wingman called 'break' and the MiGs overshot. The F-4J crew fired a Sidewinder, which hit the MiG and it burst into flames before impacting on the ground. Eight MiG-17s were then seen in an anti-clockwise orbit around the target area at 10-15,000 feet and four more dived in column from the Northeast. Just south of Hải Dương 'Showtime 100' fired their second Sidewinder which knocked the tail off a MiG-17 whose pilot ejected. 'Showtime 100' met their third victim head-on. Cunningham pulled up into a vertical scissors manoeuvre with the MiG-17, which was firing its cannons. After about three minutes the MiG pilot tried to disengage but Cunningham manoeuvred into the enemy's 6 o'clock position and fired another Sidewinder. The MiG-17 pitched over and impacted the ground with a resulting explosion and fireball. Cunningham and Driscoll attempted to exit the target area but were jumped by a fourth MiG-17 and the F-4J crew attempted to engage but broke off when another F-4J crew called four more MiG-17s at 'Showtime 100's 6 o'clock position. Cunningham broke away and accelerated toward the Gulf of Tonkin but at 16,000 feet his F-4J was hit by a SA-2 fired from the vicinity of Nam Định. No RHAW was observed by the crew although Cunningham spotted the SAM just before impact and Driscoll observed an orange cloud after the burst. The Phantom's hydraulic systems progressively failed and both crew were forced to eject about five NM from the mouth of the Red River. Cunningham and Driscoll were rescued by a helicopter from the *Okinawa* and returned uninjured to the *Constellation*.

Unrestricted use of air warfare finally forced the North's hand. During 18-26 December 1972 'Linebacker II' operations - all-out, intensive aerial bombardment of industry, communications, ports, supply depots and airfields in the Hànôi and Hảiphòng areas by the USAF, USN and USMC - were among the most effective of the war. Pilots who flew the missions claimed that the North Viêtnamese had 'nothing left to shoot at us as we flew over. It was like flying over New York City.' When the Communists indicated their desire for a peace settlement on 30 December, the bombing above the 20th Parallel was halted, although missions below the 20th Parallel continued for the first half of January 1973. A peace agreement was signed in Paris on 23 January 1973 and all air operations ceased four days later.

Viêtnam cost the Americans 58,022 dead and brought the USA worldwide condemnation for its role in South-East Asia. The USAF and USN could at least draw some solace from the fact that their final intensive campaign had persuaded Hànôi to seek an end to the war and conclude a peace treaty. Although all US ground forces were withdrawn from South Viêtnam, air raids into neighbouring Cambodia and Laos continued until August 1973. Both countries then fell to the Communists and the North turned its attentions to the final take-over of South Viêtnam. Inevitably, the South, now without US military support, collapsed under the full might of the Communists' spring offensive. On 12 April 1975 the American Embassy in Sàigòn was evacuated and 287 staff were flown to carriers offshore. On 29 April 900 Americans were airlifted by the Navy to five carriers. Next day Sàigòn was in Communist hands and the South was under the control of North Viêtnam.

Endnotes for Chapter 8

56   The AD Skyraider (re-designated A-1 in 1962) remained in combat until 1968.

57   On his next deployment, while Commander of Carrier Air Wing 16 aboard the carrier USS *Oriskany* (CV-34), he was shot down over enemy territory on 9 September 1965. Stockdale ejected from his A-4E, which had been struck by enemy fire and completely disabled. He parachuted into a small village, where he was severely beaten and taken prisoner. Stockdale was held prisoner in the notorious Hỏa Lò prison (The Hànôi Hilton') for the next seven and a half years. As the senior Naval officer (Stockdale was the highest-ranking naval officer held as a PoW in Viêtnam), he was one of the primary organizers of prisoner resistance. Tortured routinely and denied medical attention for the severely damaged leg he suffered during capture, Stockdale created and enforced a code of conduct for all prisoners which governed torture, secret communications and behavior. In the summer of 1969, he was locked in leg irons in a bath stall and routinely tortured and beaten. When told by his captors that he was to be paraded in public, Stockdale slit his scalp with a razor to purposely disfigure himself so that his captors could not use him as propaganda. When they covered his head with a hat, he beat himself with a stool until his face was swollen beyond recognition. When Stockdale was discovered with information that

could implicate his friends' 'black activities' he slit his wrists so they could not torture him into confession. Stockdale was released on 12 February 1973. His shoulders had been wrenched from their sockets, his leg shattered by angry villagers and a torturer and his back broken. He was awarded 26 personal combat decorations, including the Medal of Honor (in 1976) and four Silver Stars. During the late 1970s, he served as President of the Naval War College. He died aged 81 on 5 July 2005.

58 The North Viêtnamese eventually repatriated his body in August 1985. Results claimed for Operation 'Pierce Arrow' included the destruction of 90 per cent of the petroleum storage facility at Vinh together with the destruction or damage of an estimated 25 torpedo boats, representing two-thirds of the North Viêtnamese force. In an incident unrelated to Operation 'Pierce Arrow', an F-8E Crusader of VF-191 on *Bon Homme Richard* was lost through engine failure during a training flight in the South China Sea. Lieutenant W. D. Storey survived. *Viêtnam Air Losses*, Chris Hobson (Midland Publishing 2001).

59 A more far-reaching response was a plan agreed by President Johnson to send four tactical squadrons to Southeast Asia and thirty B-52 strategic bombers to Anderson AFB, Guam. On 13 February the President authorised the start of operation 'Rolling Thunder', a sustained bombing campaign against military targets in North Viêtnam, the first mission being flown on 2 March. *Vietnam Air Losses*, Chris Hobson (Midland Publishing 2001)

60 Franke and Doremus were held prisoner for 7½ years in Hànôi. They were released on 2 February 1973.

61 Berg and Purcell were released with the other PoWs in February 1973.

62 *Talking Proud Archives - Military HH-43 SAR pilot's diary, 1964-1965, Vietnam: from diary entries by Archie Taylor, commander, Det 4, Pacific Air Rescue Center (PARC), October 1964-May 1965* edited by Ed Marek.

63 Remains were found in 1987 and identified as those of Lieutenant McWhorter. These remains were returned to his family in February 1987. *Talking Proud Archives - Military HH-43 SAR pilot's diary, 1964-1965, Vietnam: from diary entries by Archie Taylor, commander, Det 4, Pacific Air Rescue Center (PARC), October 1964-May 1965.*

64 Adapted from an interview by Reed Graham of the Library of Congress.

65 Several PoWs reported that Commander Cameron was with them until that month but was in poor physical and mental health, by then having spent most of his time in solitary. When other prisoners were about to be moved from one part of the 'Hànôi Hilton' to another, guards told the PoWs that Cameron was in the camp hospital. He was never seen again until his remains were repatriated on 6 March 1974. *Viêtnam Air Losses*, Chris Hobson (Midland Publishing 2001).

66 The Fulton system consisted of an inflatable balloon and harness that enabled the airborne recovery of a person from the ground. It was used primarily by Special Forces and intelligence agents.

67 Commander Smith had been awarded the Silver Star for leading an attack on the Bac Giang POL (Petrol-Oil-Lubricants) depot on 30 June 1966 and had dropped the Navy's first Walleye bomb during an attack on the Sam Son Army barracks on 11 March 1967. *Viêtnam Air Losses*, Chris Hobson (Midland Publishing 2001).

68 He was posthumously awarded the Navy Cross for his part in the attack on the Bac Giang thermal power plant. Homer Smith's remains were handed over by the Viêtnamese on 16 March 1974. *Viêtnam Air Losses*, Chris Hobson (Midland Publishing 2001).

69 Robert Fuller retired from the United States Navy as a Rear Admiral in 1982.

70 Commander Whittemore was lost at sea while serving with VA-93 on 11 April 1968. *Viêtnam Air Losses*, Chris Hobson (Midland Publishing 2001).

71 Ensign Bruce Merle Patterson and AE2 Charles David Hardie were KIA. This aircraft had only just been converted in June to KA-3B tanker standard at the Naval Air Rework Facility at Alameda, California. *Viêtnam Air Losses*, Chris Hobson (Midland Publishing 2001).

72 *Hanoi Tonight* by Lieutenant Commander William S. Graves, Public Affairs Officer, US Seventh Fleet Attack Carrier Striking Force. (US Naval Institute Proceedings July 1969).

73 Integrated Operational Intelligence Center.

74 Remarkably, between January-June 1967 USAF jets shot down 46 MiGs, including seven MiG-17s by two Phantoms and five F-l05s on one day, 13 May. From April-July 1967 the USN accounted for a dozen MiGs.

75 Cunningham and Driscoll had shot down their first MiG on 19 January when the second of two Sidewinders fired blew the tail off a MiG-21. It was the 112th MiG brought down in the war and the tenth to fall to a Navy fighter. Cunningham and Driscoll scored their second kill on 8 May when they downed a MiG-17 with another Sidewinder.